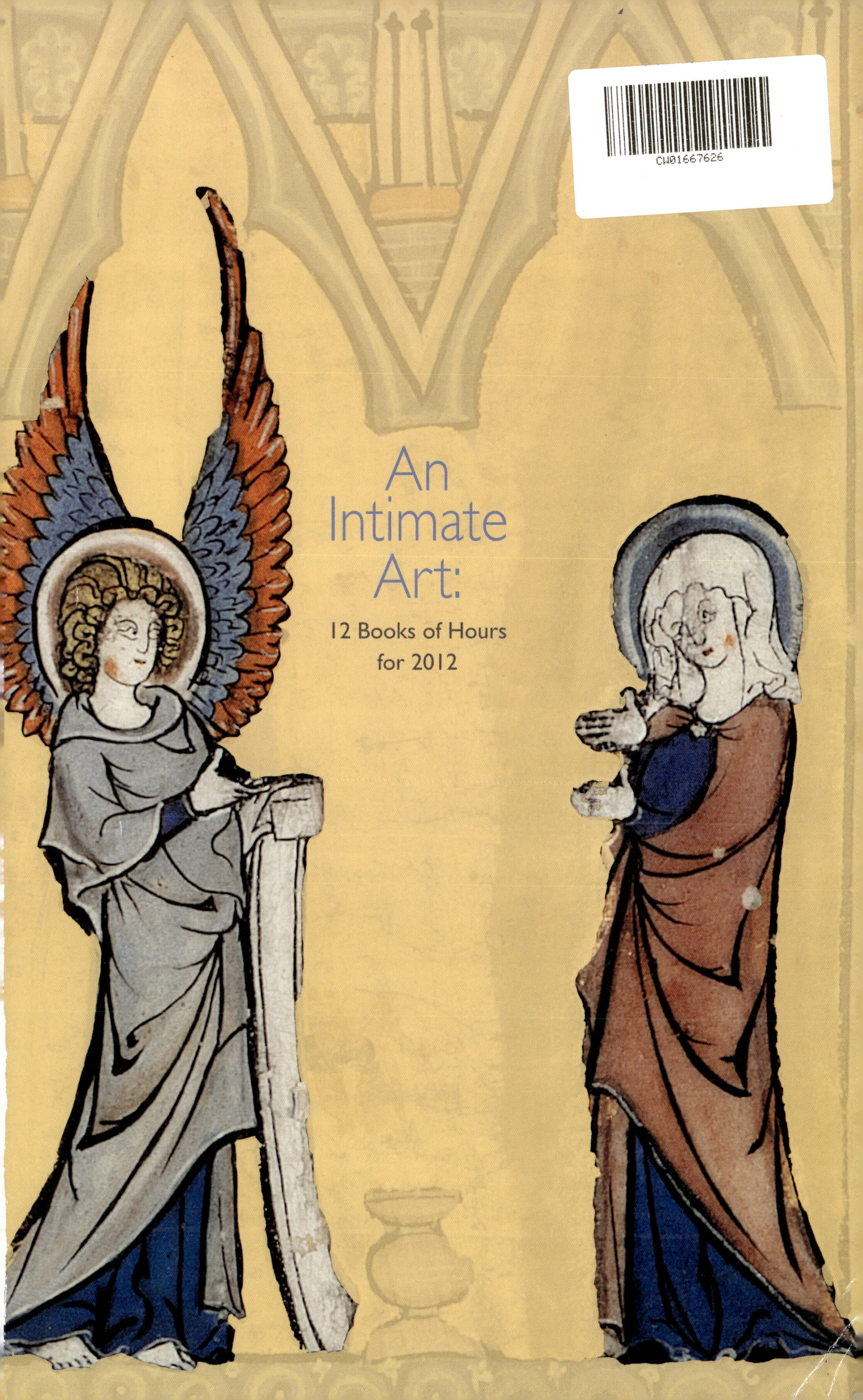

An Intimate Art:

12 Books of Hours for 2012

EXHIBITION:
MAY 2 TO MAY 25, 2012

Les Enluminures
23 East 73rd Street
7th Floor
New York, NY 100221
Tel: (212) 717 7273
Fax: (212) 717 7278
newyork@lesenluminures.com

Les Enluminures Ltd.
2970 North Lake Shore Drive
Chicago, Illinois 60657
Tel: (773) 929 5986
Fax: (773) 528 3976
chicago@lesenluminures.com

Les Enluminures
Le Louvre des Antiquaires
2 place du Palais-Royal
75001 Paris
Tel: (33) 01 42 60 15 58
Fax: (33) 01 40 15 00 25
info@lesenluminures.com

www.lesenluminures.com
www.medievalbooksofhours.com

FULL DESCRIPTIONS AVAILABLE UPON REQUEST

ISBN 978-0-9838546-3-0

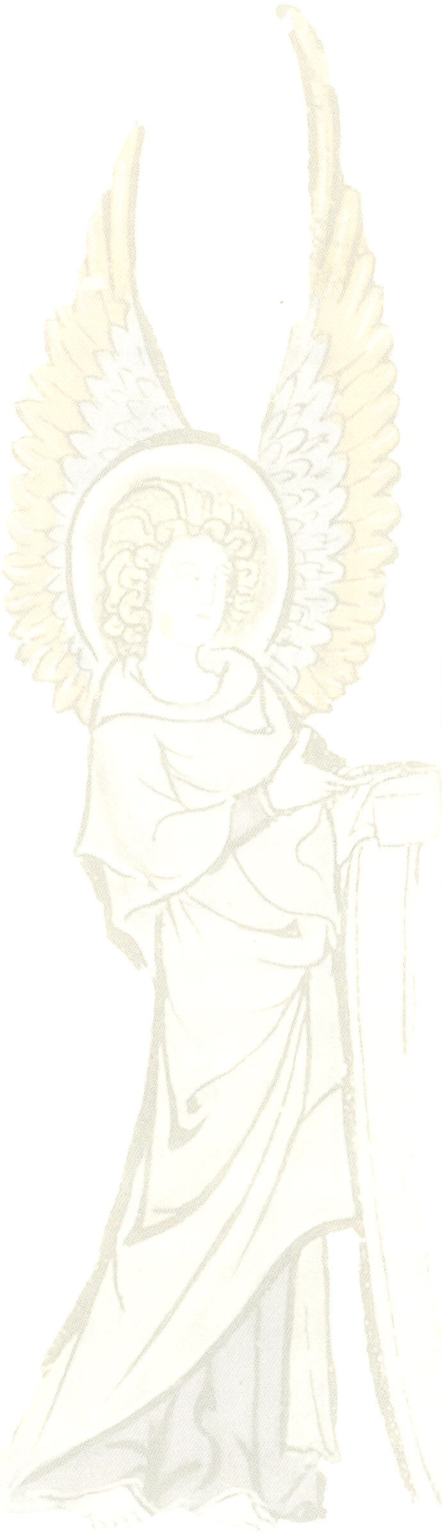

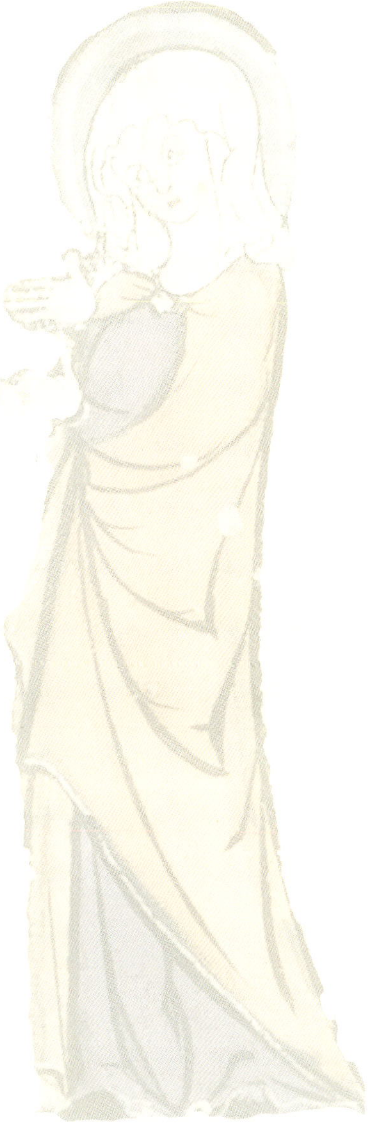

An Intimate Art:

12 Books of Hours for 2012

Catalogue 17

SANDRA HINDMAN

ARIANE BERGERON-FOOTE

INTRODUCTION
CHRISTOPHER DE HAMEL

PAUL HOLBERTON PUBLISHING, 89 BOROUGH HIGH STREET, LONDON SE1 1NL

WWW.PAUL-HOLBERTON.NET

FOR LES ENLUMINURES • PARIS • CHICAGO • NEW YORK

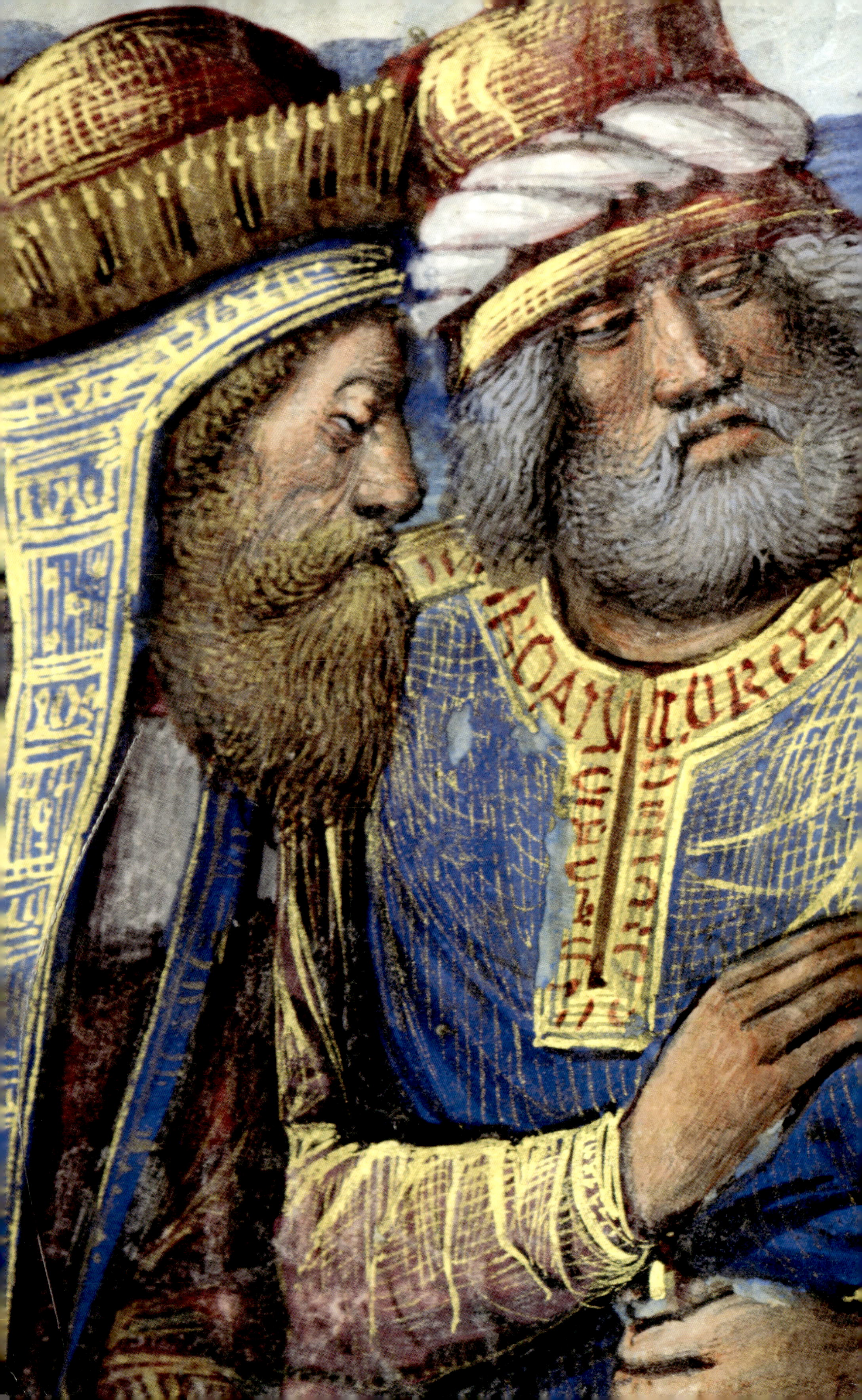

Preface

This catalogue presents twelve Books of Hours to celebrate the opening of our New York gallery on 23 East 73rd Street in May 2012. We have carefully selected a diverse group of Books of Hours that date from the origins of the genre in the thirteenth century to its imminent eclipse in the sixteenth century. Our goal was not to choose the most lavish examples, but rather representative examples from different centers, made for different types of owners, and with different texts and illustrations. Examples come from France, Italy, and the Southern and Northern Netherlands. Some are richly illuminated; others are more modest. Each manuscript is wholly unique, offering a captivating glimpse into the lives and preoccupations of their owners, the concerns and contributions of their illuminators.

One Book of Hours, perhaps one of the earliest of the genre and illustrated with historiated initials that anticipate the fixed program for later Boooks of Hours, belonged to a Spanish textile merchant (no. 1). It conveys a vivid image of the tradesman traveling through Europe carrying with him his Book of Hours like a vade mecum; our merchant wrote on its flyleaves, adding the quantities of textiles in his inventory as well as a list of the Champagne Fairs where he went to buy and sell. An early Spanish binding completes the ensemble. Another early Book of Hours, previously entirely unknown, boasts a beautiful full-page Psalter cycle with striking historiated initials; evidently considered precious by a later owner, the manuscript was transformed, adding an Hours of the Virgin with miscellaneous prayers between the Calendar and the Psalter, to turn it into an "up-to-date" Book of Hours (no. 2).

Many notable artists contributed to our Books of Hours: Pietro da Pavia, Belbello da Pavia, the Masters of Zweder van Culemburg, the Masters of the Gold Scrolls, Willem Vrelant, Guillaume II le Roy, and Jean Poyer, among others, are represented here. Some patrons left emphatic evidence of their ownership, such as Giangaleazzo Visconti and Francesco Sforza (no. 3). Traces of others materialize in pictures: for example, a male member of the Third Order of St. Francis appears twice in one Bruges manuscript, accompanied by his wife (no. 6); and a woman and her daughter worship at the Pietà in a manuscript of Norman origin. In other instances, we are left to imagine the readers: a pious adherent of the Devotio Moderna contemplating the angels holding Instruments of the Passion while reading the weekday Hours in his or her native tongue (no. 5), or a member of the clergy or priesthood reading the Thursday Hours of the Sacrament in Latin next to the unusual image of the Gathering of Manna (no. 7). The uncommon texts of both these Horae confirm they were special commissions for still-unidentified patrons.

Certain major centers of production emerge with greater clarity. One example represents Paris during its "golden age" at the beginning of the fifteenth century; it is by the Luçon Master, a collaborator of the great Boucicaut Master (no. 4). As a center of production, Norman Rouen was second only to Paris in the fifteenth century (nos. 9 and 10). Surely the production of Bruges equaled or surpassed that of Paris during the period, and the city supplied books for buyers throughout Europe; three Books of Hours afford an in-depth look at manuscript painting in Bruges in the third quarter of the fifteenth century (nos. 6, 7, 8). South of Paris, Tours and Lyons both come into focus as locales with distinctive styles, heralding the French Renaissance (nos. 11 and 12).

The introduction by the incomparable Christopher de Hamel underscores the "intimacy" of Books of Hours as a genre. A team of distinguished scholars contributed to the essays, bringing up-to-date research to the project that helps situate each manuscript in the most recent scholarship. Comparative photographs of manuscripts in institutions throughout the world further place these twelve Horae in their artistic and cultural contexts. The team at Les Enlumi-nures, including my co-author, worked from dawn to dusk – or from Matins to Compline! – to realize this project on time. We are grateful to everyone.

Sandra Hindman

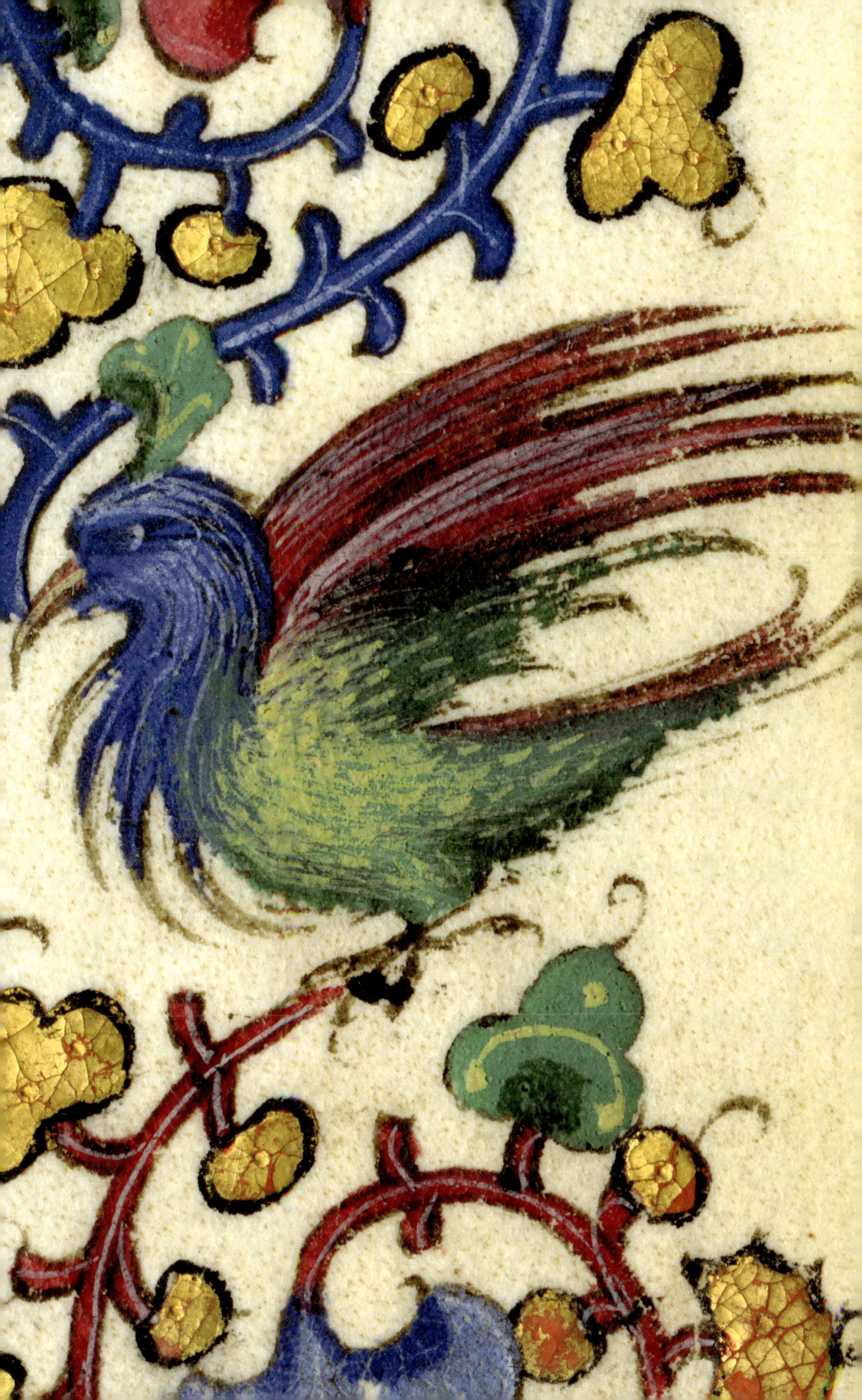

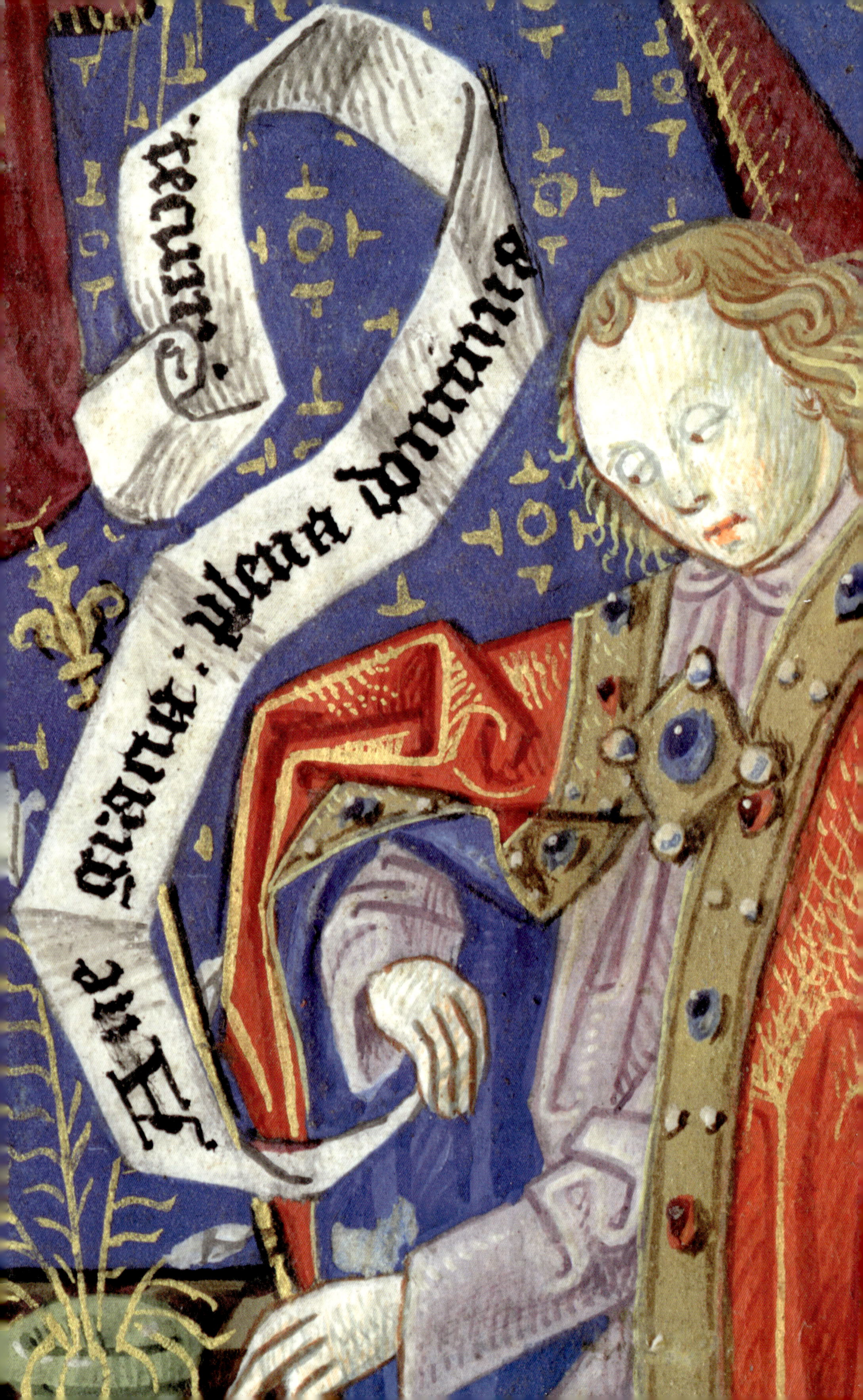
Ave gratia : plena dominus
tecum

Introduction: An Intimate Art

Books of Hours are probably the most famous of all medieval illuminated manuscripts, but they are quite unlike other kinds of book, for all sorts of reasons. First of all, there is no real text in a Book of Hours, at least not as we would know it: there is no story, no narrative, no specific written information, not even one sentence necessarily following sequentially from the last, and, in any case, many of the first owners of Books of Hours could probably scarcely read anyway. It was a book which could evidently be used without the necessity of reading it. In the Middle Ages, Books of Hours were often known as *Heures de Notre-Dame*, or "Hours of Our Lady," but the Virgin Mary hardly appears in the text at all and is not usually the subject of the prayers. Almost all Books of Hours have pictures – including some of the finest and most famous in all of medieval art – but these do not illustrate the text. They seem to bear almost no obvious relation to the contents of the book at all. Finally, these are not books ever destined for libraries. They were at best intended to be kept wrapped up and stored in boxes or in cupboards with jewelry and precious relics. Even now, Books of Hours sit uneasily with more conventional manuscripts in modern rare-book libraries, and many are, and perhaps should be, still in private possession. Let us take each of these in turn.

Books of Hours have no narrative text

Books of Hours are commonly described as lay people's prayer-books, which is true, but they are not service-books in the modern sense. They are artifacts which encapsulate the spiritual life. Much of the text is assembled around a consistent selection of Old Testament psalms and other biblical quotations in Latin, such as multiple pieces from the book of Job used in the Office of the Dead, which go back ultimately to liturgical practice in the ancient Jewish world. Already in apostolic times the early Christians were meeting together to recite passages of Old Testament Scripture. Regular recitation of the psalms became a central part of early medieval monastic life. It is impossible to exaggerate the importance of Saint Benedict (c. 480-c. 550) and the eventual establishment of enclosed Benedictine monasteries all across Christian Europe in the Middle Ages, where monks (and nuns) chanted endless and unvarying cycles of psalms and prayers at the daily monastic hours of Matins,

Lauds, Prime, Terce, Sext, None, Vespers, and Compline. In the twelfth century, the monasteries of Christendom were multiplying prodigiously, together with new Cistercian, Carthusian, Augustinian and other houses, all participating in similar unending recitations eight times a day. From the early thirteenth century they were joined by convents of friars and nuns, Franciscans and Dominicans. Monasteries were a ubiquitous and very prominent part of the landscape of medieval Europe.

Now imagine the general public living outside but in the neighborhood of such establishments. People must have sensed that something rather special, spiritually efficacious and exclusive was going on every day within the fortress-like walls of monastic communities. They were dimly aware, or were assured (perhaps even by self-justifying monks), that regular daily recitation of psalms was an effective passport to eternal salvation. It was noticed that monks seemed to have a monopoly, sometimes profitable, in commemorating the dead and interceding with saints. People in secular life began to wish that they too were part of this spiritually advantageous world. By the late twelfth century, they had begun to commission personal Psalters, for reading psalms at home. Thirteenth-century Psalters, made for the laity, are relatively common, and they are among the earliest privately-owned books. Around 1250, these Psalters started to be supplemented with miniaturized versions of the monastic offices, intended now for lay use, and gradually these additional texts expanded and incorporated the required psalms into each "hour" of a typical devotional day. As a result, the full Psalter fell away, and what remained was a Book of Hours.

In a strange way, rather like the survival of some living fossil, a Book of Hours preserves elements of monastic practice, centuries after the texts had emigrated into the secular world. The eight "hours" of the day, from Matins to Compline, preserve the prescribed times when monks or nuns would gather in the chapel, from well before dawn until shortly before retiring to bed in the dormitory. Miniatures of the Office of the Dead in a Book of Hours sometimes depict the setting, with hooded figures huddled by candlelight in stalls on either side of the choir. Monks there would chant antiphons and responses, back and forth, from one side of the choir across to the other. These same liturgical exchanges, often abbreviated to *ant.* and *resp.*, still occur in Books of Hours, even though they are not being used in a choir, or by more than one person at once. The Calendars at the beginning of Books of Hours descend directly from monastic use, when members of religious orders needed to know the current saint's day. For most lay people in everyday life, knowledge of minor liturgical festivals was hardly relevant except as a reflection of what was going on out of sight in a church or monastery.

People clearly sensed a spiritual benefit in having a monastery in the local village or neighborhood, praying for humanity around them. So too they probably came to feel reassured and engaged by the possession of a Book of Hours with its monastic liturgy in miniature, domesticated into a household setting. Did owners actually read them aloud at fixed hours eight times a day? Most people had no clocks or even knew the precise time of day, unlike monks regulated by bells. A word like "Prime" or "Terce" had little practical meaning in the ordinary civilian world. Some owners undoubtedly did read their Books of Hours daily, but many probably looked at them only from time to time, struggled with a few familiar words, and still felt a shared participation, even for a moment, in the parallel monastic life. This is not to doubt a very genuine piety, but possession of the manuscript was the important part. It touched hands with more than a thousand years of prayer and it made communal religion personal. A Book of Hours, in short, was a facility for the armchair monk.

They hardly mention the Virgin Mary at all

The popular cult of the Virgin, the Mother of God and the Queen of Heaven, increased rapidly from the twelfth century onwards. This is reflected in countless aspects of medieval art, literature, and ecclesiastical architecture. What did people actually know about the historical Mary in her earthly life? She was a laywoman: that was important. She lived in the time of the Romans, in the reigns of Augustus and Tiberius, according to Luke 2:1 and 3:1, and therefore, it must have been tacitly supposed, she spoke Latin. She would have been familiar with the psalms, since these are part of the Old Testament. While she was at her devotions one day, shown in all medieval art as kneeling in front of a book, the Archangel Gabriel appeared to her, and told her that she, of all people in the entirety of creation, had been singled out for having found favor with God. That supreme moment, at the absolute instant of the Incarnation, represented the utter and unparalleled union between God and mankind in the person of a devout handmaid of the Lord.

Men in the Middle Ages were often encouraged to imagine undergoing the harrowing experience of the Passion of Christ. Devout women, however, were taught to imagine themselves as participants in the Annunciation, submitting to the will of God, as took place during the ultimate spiritual experience in the Virgin's lifetime. What was she doing, at that moment? Mary was at home, alone, reading her early morning devotions, from the Old Testament (of course), in Latin (as none would doubt), or, in other words, Matins. The reason for owning a Book of Hours was to help recreate the Annunciation. That is one reason why most Books of Hours are in Latin, even though throughout much of Europe vernacular translations were entirely legal and better understood by the laity: in Latin, one might be gazing at the actual words of the very psalm which had been read at that moment by Mary. Pictures of the Virgin Mary, kneeling in prayer before an ancient exemplar of a Latin Book of Hours, thus open most manuscripts.

The pictures do not illustrate the text

The pictures in the Hours of the Virgin illustrate events in the experience of the Virgin Mary herself, which took place at the same time of day as that particular monastic hour. There is no biblical evidence of the time of the original Annunciation in Nazareth, but it was assumed to have taken place before dawn. In some Books of Hours the scene is set in the Virgin's bedroom. Pictures of the Annunciation almost always preface Matins in a Book of Hours. Lauds, which follows soon afterwards, was generally illustrated by a scene of the Visitation, when Mary went "with haste" to stay with her cousin Elizabeth (Luke 1:39). She was presumed to have arrived there just before dawn. Prime, at daybreak, is represented by the Birth of Christ in the stable in Bethlehem. It is appropriate that the Light of the World should have first opened his eyes at dawn. Terce, at the third hour of the morning, usually has the shepherds watching their sheep in the hills above the town. The Gospels, and indeed popular imagination today, sets the scene at night (Luke 2:8) but doubtless it was mid-morning before they arrived at the stable. Sext, around midday, is when the three kings, or Magi, are supposed to have arrived to offer their treasures before Mary and her child (Matthew 2:11). The word "None" survives into modern English as "noon," meaning 12 o'clock, but, rather like the day's main meal in the Middle Ages, it probably took place in the mid-afternoon (and indeed the modern word "luncheon" probably also reflects "None"). In a Book of Hours the hour of None is commonly represented by the presentation in the Temple, when Jesus's parents brought him to be blessed by the high priest Simeon (Luke 2:27). Vespers was the evening office. It generally shows Joseph leading a donkey with the Mary and Jesus towards exile in Egypt, fleeing from the manic wrath of Herod (Matthew 2:14), sometimes painted against a scene of the setting sun. The image varies for Compline, the night office, but it frequently shows the Virgin Mary having ascended into Heaven and being crowned by God, against a starry night sky.

The images for each "hour" in the Hours of the Virgin thus accompany words which the Virgin Mary might conceivably have been reading or thinking about when the events depicted happened for the first time. Beyond that, these are not at all illustrations of the texts. The words of the psalms and prayers chosen for each hour have no specific allusion to those events. On the contrary, the New Testament canticle of the *Magnificat* (Luke 1:46-55) is part of Vespers, although in the New Testament it happened following the Visitation (Lauds), and the *Nunc dimittis* (Luke 2:29-32) is read at Compline, although it was actually spoken by Simeon during the Presentation in the Temple (None). That is because these elements were carried over from the earlier monastic offices, before the grafting on of Marian overtones.

Calendars in Books of Hours are sometimes illustrated with scenes of activities associated with the month or season, most famously in the *Très Riches Heures* of the Duc de Berry. Again, these are not precisely illustrations of the manuscript text (at that point merely lists of sacred names) but representations of things that happened at parallel times of year. The pictures in a Book of Hours chosen to illustrate the openings of the seven Penitential Psalms and the Office of the Dead vary enormously. The former may show the Last Judgment; or (very often) King David, as author of all the Psalms including these seven, a reinvention of the old "author portraits" which go back to manuscripts of classical antiquity; or (sometimes) unexpectedly graphic portrayals of Bathsheba bathing naked (II Samuel 11:2-4), or other sins which David had committed, for which these particular psalms were suitably remorseful. The Office of the Dead may be marked by a wide range of pictorial subjects. They include scenes of funeral services and examples of the imminence and suddenness of death. All these are appropriate to the relevant section of the Book of Hours, but they do not in any normal way show anything actually mentioned in the words of the text.

What, then, are the pictures for? The answer is three-fold (that is a characteristically medieval phrase, for it opens many scholastic sermons). First of all, in our cynical post-Marxist age, let us not dismiss a fundamental human desire to honor a religious text with beautiful and fashionable art. The more patrons pay for the finest available illumination, the more they feel that they are expressing devotion to the subject. Genuinely pious people probably simply bought the best they could afford. Without question, the illuminations in Books of Hours include some of the finest and most accomplished in all of medieval art, and artists and patrons doubtless consciously competed to outdo each other. It is a striking characteristic of Books of Hours, more than any other text, that they were often upgraded and improved with new illumination from one generation to the next. To commission or buy a Book of Hours, with wonderful decoration, was a pious act akin to endowing the building of a cathedral, on a smaller scale.

Secondly, the pictures help the reader find his or her way around the text. Books of Hours, unlike medieval Bibles, have no running-titles along the tops of the pages. Surprisingly, when one comes to think about it, they have no page numbers or tables of contents. Reading a few words at random will often not at all help locate a place in the text. Flip quickly through to the pictures, however, and one will immediately identify particular texts. Look for knocking down acorns by Pigs, and you will have the Calendar page for saints in November; look for the Magi, and there is Sext; look for Bathsheba, and one has the Penitential Psalms. Medieval owners of the manuscripts undoubtedly did this, and so do modern people admiring and cataloguing Books of Hours.

Finally, the pictures helped the owners to memorize the text. In an age more visual than ours, when memory was more finely tuned, a picture is easier to impress on the mind than a page of script. Illuminated initials and fanciful borders make every leaf different. One remembers a text by recalling the page where it occurs. In a time when literacy was not as widespread as now, or necessarily as deep, gazing at a picture could be as religious an experience as reading words of Latin text. A user of devotional texts was encouraged to fix the page in the mind and then, even after the book itself had been closed up and put away, he or she could still recall the picture; and that process of recollection was itself an act of piety. One could, in theory, continue to gain on-going spiritual benefit from a Book of Hours even when the manuscript itself was closed up and put away. That makes it a very special type of text.

These are not library books

Books of Hours were mostly owned by people who probably had no other book in the household. Their special status in people's lives is underlined by their frequent use as family record books, for recording births, marriages and deaths. No other medieval manuscripts are used so frequently for this purpose. They were scrupulously bequeathed within families, often through the female line. They are often mentioned in wills and inventories. If there was only one book in the house, it was likely to be precious. Untouched original bindings of Books of Hours are not very common, but they are often depicted in medieval paintings. The volumes were stitched onto thongs threaded into boards, usually of wood (these do survive), and then the whole was usually sewn into what is called a "chemise," a dangling textile wrapper which covers the sides and extends far beyond the edges of the volume. When the book was closed, this covering was wrapped several times around it, like colorful parcel in silk or damask, tied up with a projecting ribbon. When the book was opened, however, the chemise became a kind of attached tablecloth on which the manuscript was laid out safely for reading. Knotted corners of the wrapping enclosed weights to keep the cloth spread open.

This wrapping and unwrapping was undoubtedly part of the experience of handling a Book of Hours in the Middle Ages. It must have been almost as ritualistic as a Japanese tea ceremony. The manuscript was untied, unfolded, unwrapped, unclasped, and opened to reveal what was inside. Sometimes, especially in England and the Netherlands, there were even tiny hanging curtains stitched over the miniatures, so that the process of revelation was extended to the very page. Each unveiling creates a feeling of engagement and discovery. Then the manuscript was closed again, and folded back into its cloak, and wrapped and tied, becoming invisible once more. Books of Hours were probably mostly kept on bedside tables, or in little cupboards in the sides of medieval prayer-stools, or in chests with precious family possessions and jewels, or maybe occasionally in private chapels, but, if so, they were not for communal worship but for contemplation alone and in silence.

Probably the three largest public collections today of Books of Hours are in the Bibliothèque nationale de France, the Fitzwilliam Museum in Cambridge, and the Walters Art Museum in Baltimore. Other libraries and museums possess Books of Hours in the hundreds. Such manuscripts are studied by historians (Sandra Hindman in her earlier life was just such a scholar in countless public collections), and Books of Hours are quite rightly now very famous manuscripts indeed. But there is something out of context about seeing such manuscripts in the captivity of great modern libraries and on the public tables of rare-book reading rooms. They are private books, very personal, very intimate, very tactile. They are books made to cradle in the hand, at home, late at night, or early in the morning. No one can claim understanding of the late Middle Ages who has not read a Book of Hours in bed. They are books to open up and to reveal a lost age, ancient and religious, and they are books to wrap up and carry into the street, or to bring out during times of childbirth or death or family reunions, or to squirrel away upstairs, where their special powers seem to remain efficacious even when they are out of sight. I hope that all medieval manuscripts will eventually end up in public collections, for everyone to enjoy, but let us hope too that, for a few more generations, some Books of Hours remain, as they always were, in private possession. As long as that continues, the Middle Ages are not entirely finished.

Dr. Christopher de Hamel

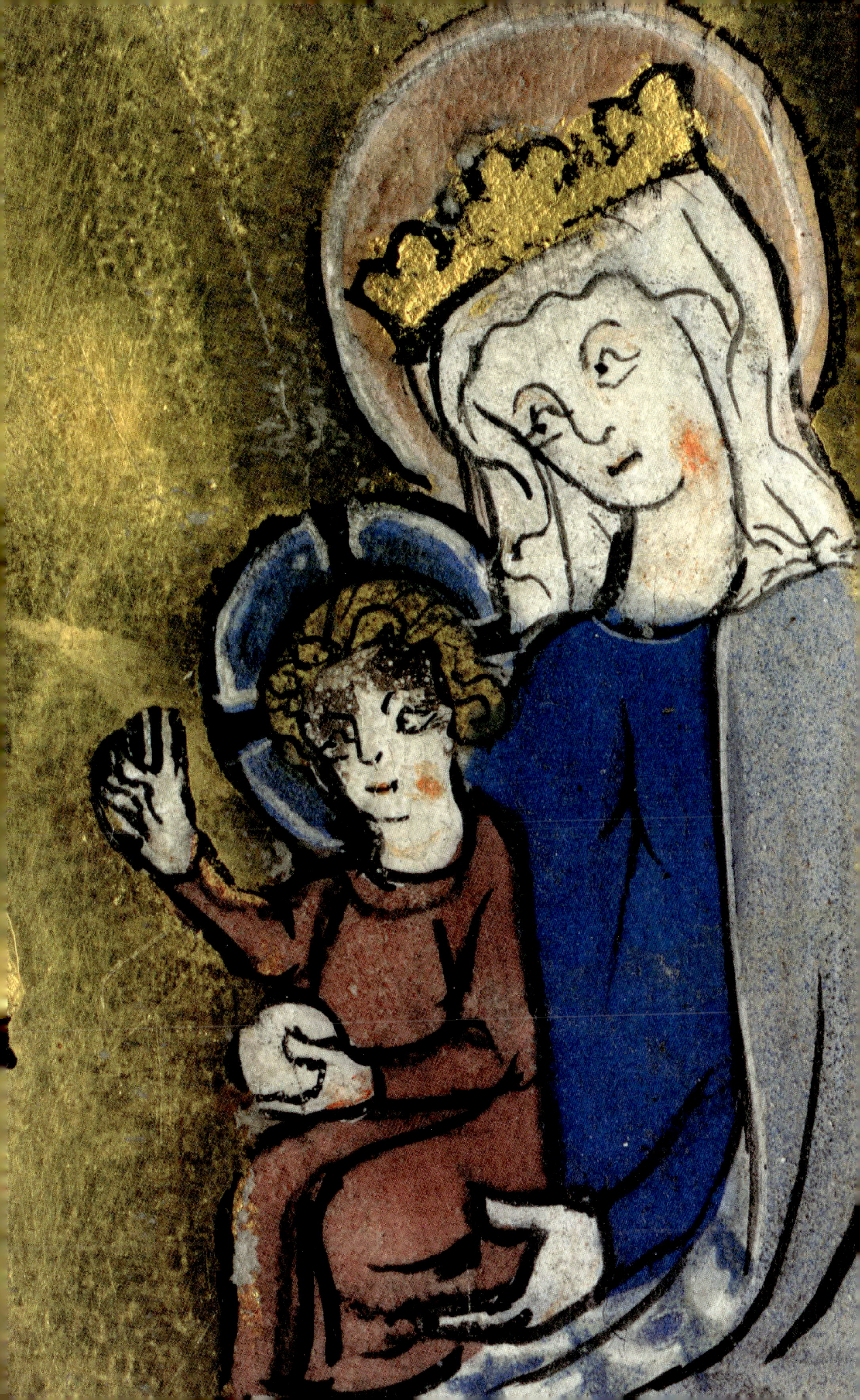

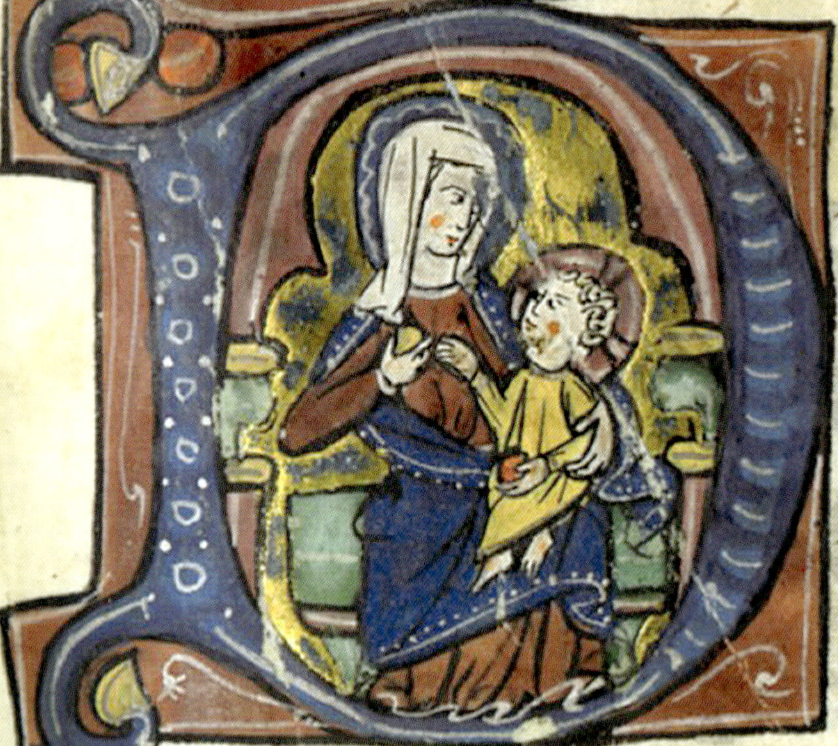

Domine
labia me
a. aperies
et os me
um an
nunciabit laudē tuā.
Deus in adiutoriū
meum intende
Domine ad adiuuan
dum me festina.
Gloria pr̄i et filio.
et spiritui sancto.

1

Book of Hours
(Unidentified use, apparently of Troyes)

In Latin with additions in Catalan, illuminated manuscript on parchment
France, perhaps Champagne, possibly Troyes, c. 1260-1270
9 historiated initials by an unidentified hand (stylistic unicum?)

Books of Hours – especially the early thirteenth-century extant examples – can well be referred to as "domesticated liturgical books" (as coined by M. Clanchy, 1993). They rapidly superseded Psalters and even Psalter-Hours as the preferred prayer book of the laity. Books of Hours became important for the lay in the thirteenth century especially in connection with the edicts of the Fourth Lateran Council of 1215, which adopted a decree imposing on the laity a confession at least once a year to a priest. A Book of Hours was a visual and textual support for individual devotions through daily prayer, satisfying a new form of personal piety, especially amongst the laity. To date, some seventy Books of Hours, or Psalter-Hours, that date before 1300 and were made in France have been identified. But, the discovery of any new example merits close attention, because there is much research still to be done on the origins of Book of Hours, their patronage, production, and use.

The present manuscript is one of the earlier surviving independent French Books of Hours, similar in size and page-layout to the de Brailes Hours (London, BL, Add. MS 49999), considered the earliest surviving English example. A census of the extant north French examples of thirteenth-century Books of Hours is underway (undertaken by A. Bennett), and this survey reveals that each one appears singular in make-up and sequence of texts and in choice of illustrations, probably because each was made at the behest of a particular individual (Bennett, 1996, p. 21). Bennett studied this personalization of Books of Hours in the particular case of a French Book of Hours made for a laywoman named Marie in the 1270s, now on loan to the Cloisters (New York, Metropolitan Museum of Art, MS L. 1990.38). The Hours for Marie offer a "rich yield of textual and pictorial information on the devotional practices of a woman and her family early in the reign of Philip III" (Bennett, 1996, p. 21).

Like the Hours of Marie, our exceptionally early and important Book of Hours is of French origin but it was once owned by a Catalan textile merchant

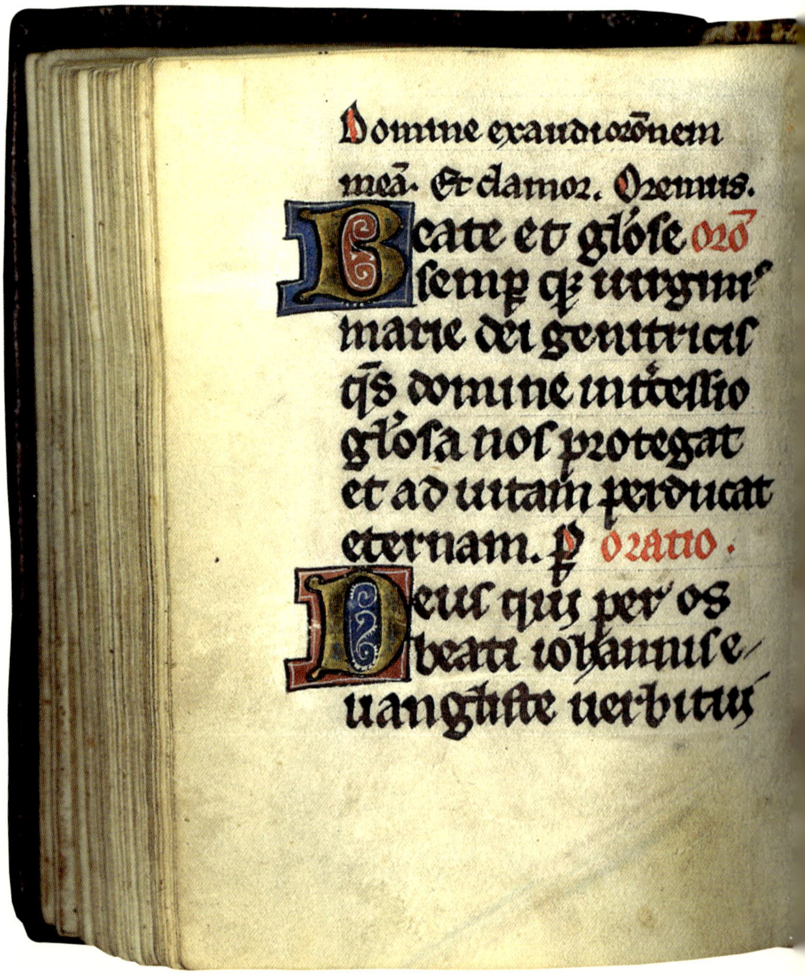

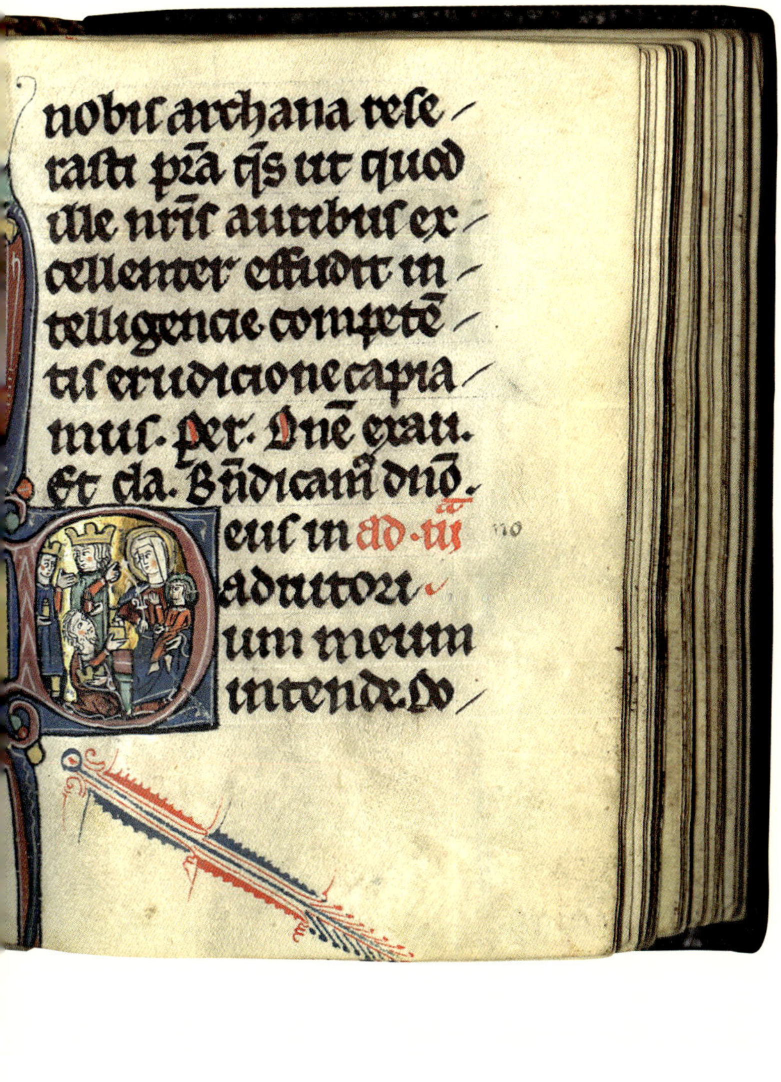

ff. 64v-65, Initial D, Adoration of the Magi

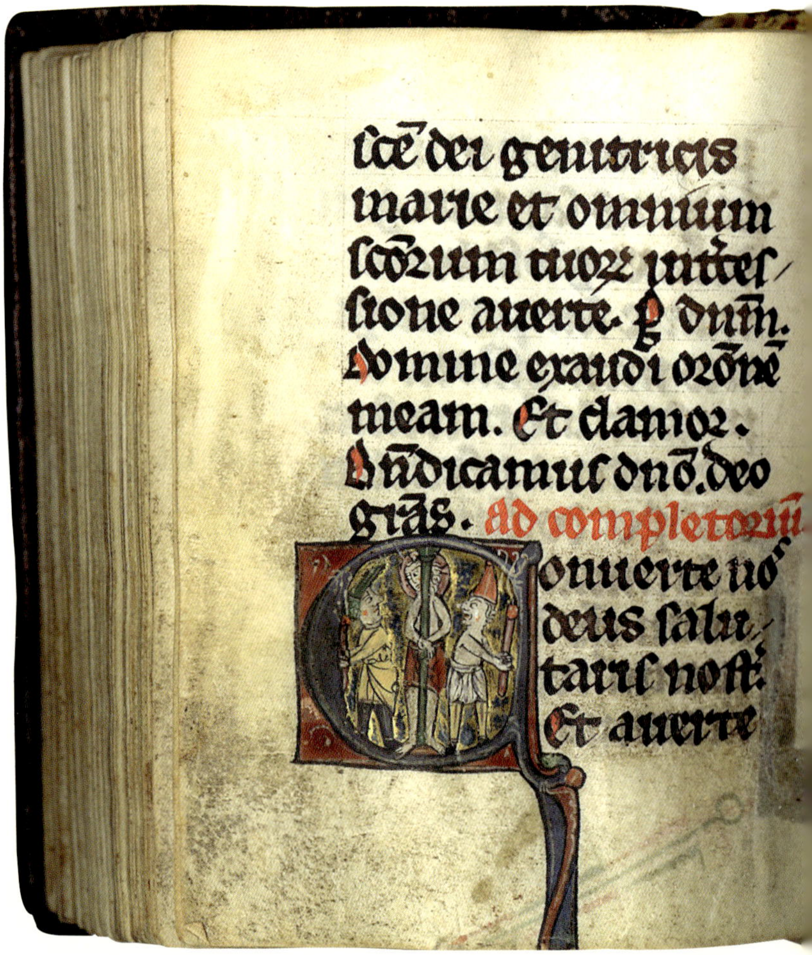

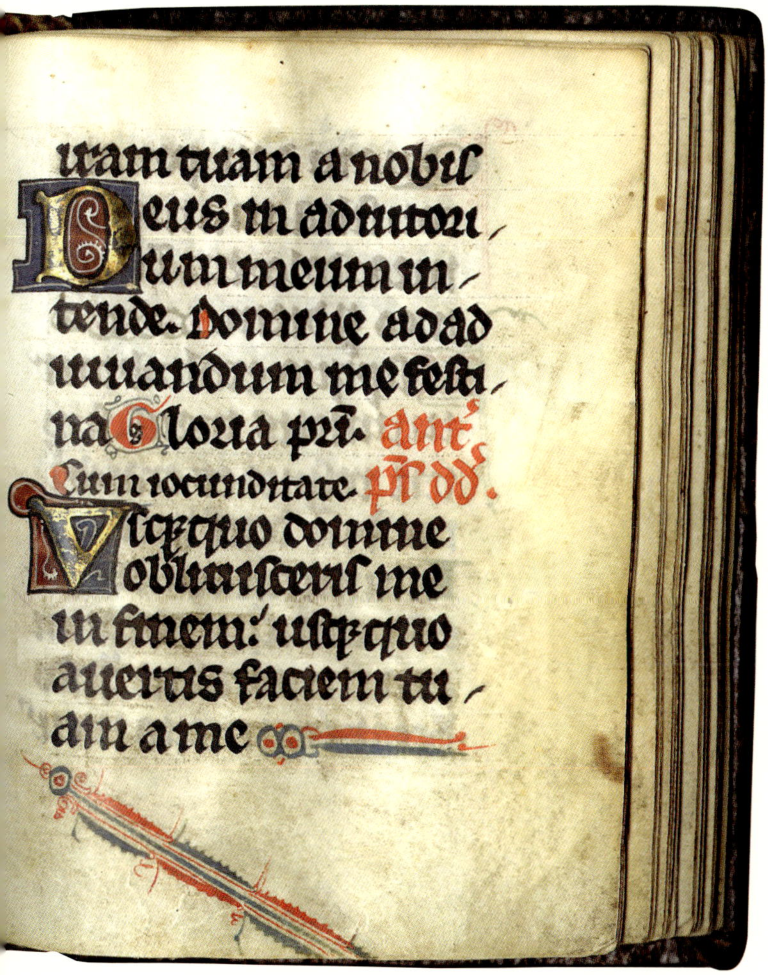

ff. 80v-81, Initial D, Flagellation

in the late thirteenth or early fourteenth century. It is preserved in a fine early Mudejar binding, probably added by a subsequent Spanish owner. The upper pastedown and facing page are inscribed, in Catalan, with a list of quantities of textiles, beginning: "Dra]p [d]arras — xlvi al Pelos darras — xl al Drap engles...." The place-names include Arras, England, Chillons, Ypres, Ghent, Lille, Douai, Cambrai, Valenciennes, St. Quentin, Bonneville, St. Omer, Beauvais, Provins, Huy, Saintes, Venice, Trieste, Reims, Vitry, and St. Fergera. On the following page is inscribed, by another hand but also in Catalan, a list of the so-called Champagne Fairs and their dates, beginning: "The Lagny fair begins on the day after New Year; The Bar-sur-Aube fair begins on the Tuesday before mid-Lent; The Provins May fair begins on the Tuesday before the Ascension; The Troyes fair of St John begins on the first Tuesday after the fortnight of St. John's Day..." (on the Champagne Fairs, see J.L Abu-Lughod, 1989, chapter 2). The Champagne Fairs were of great importance economically and culturally. Abu-Lughod describes the installation, the lodgings, the storage halls, with traders and bankers flocking from all parts of Europe and even from further afield. The heyday of the Champagne Fairs was the mid-thirteenth to the mid-fourteenth century. The decline arguably started in 1284 when Philip the Fair, the future king of France, married Joan I of Navarre, Countess of Champagne, and thus the County of Champagne became part of the royal domain: the incentives for traders that the Counts of Champagne had previously offered were removed.

Textually this manuscript is quite simple, with only the most essential contents of a Book of Hours (Hours of the Virgin, Seven Penitential Psalms, Litany with Petitions and Collects), without additional texts such as the Hours of the Cross and Holy Spirit, or Office of the Dead. There are no personal prayers. Although of unknown use, liturgical evidence points tentatively to the region of Troyes and Sens as the origin of these Horae (with the Little Hours from Prime to None, and the last hour of Compline, following Troyes use). The original Calendar points to southeast Ile-de-France, that is Champagne and Burgundy. The litany ends with Romana of Beauvais, who was a follower of Lucian of Beauvais, and both are included in the litany, and Lucian is mentioned in the Calendar. These Horae are quite endearing as a portable model of simple contents with pictured initials that would satisfy the basic needs of a user. The gender is not specific enough, except one very small clue in the *preces*: "Sacerdotes tui induantur iusticiam" found in two Brabant Psalter-Hours, perhaps for beguines, and one French Book of Hours for an abbess (Paris, BnF,

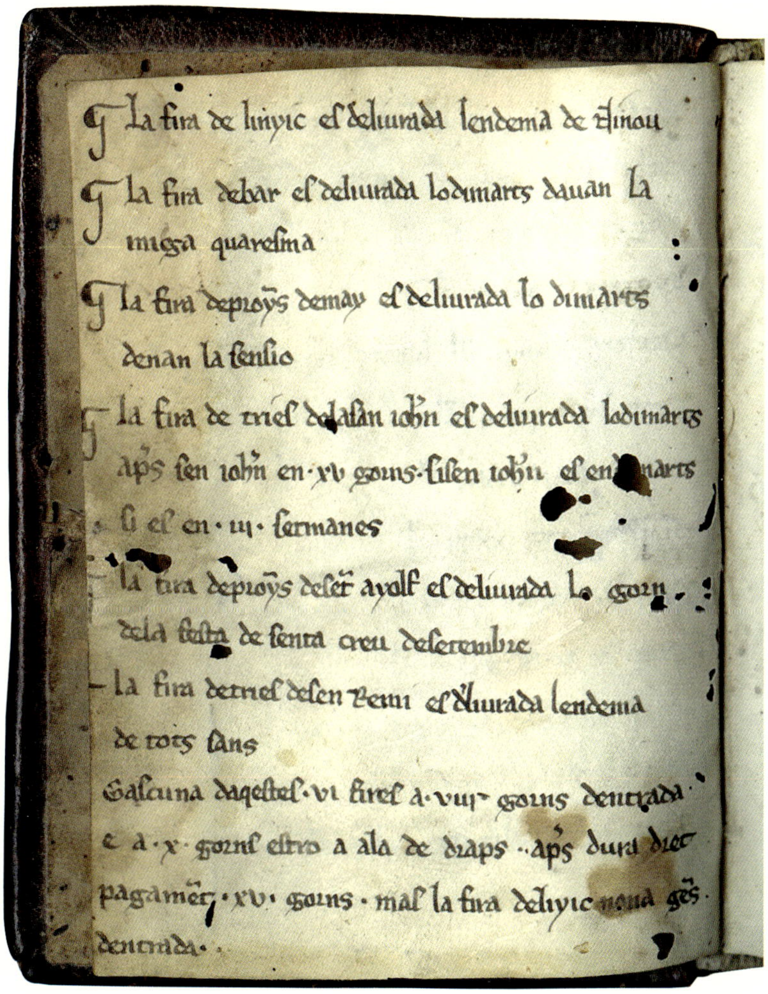

La fira de linyic es deliurada lendema de Tinou
La fira debar es deliurada lo dimarts dauan la
miga quaresma
La fira de proys de may es deliurada lo dimarts
denan la sensio
La fira de tries de la sant iohn es deliurada lo dimarts
apres sent iohn en ·xv· gorns · si sent iohn es en dimarts
si es en ·iii· semanes
La fira de proys de sent ayolf es deliurada lo gorn
de la festa de senta creu de setembre
La fira de tries de sen Remi es deliurada lendema
de tots sans
Cascuna daquestes ·vi· fires a ·viii· gorns dentrada
e a ·x· gorns estro a ala de draps ·· apres dura dret
pagament ·xv· gorns · mas la fira de liyic nona gens
dentrada ·

Front flyleaf, verso, Notes in Catalan, Date of Fairs

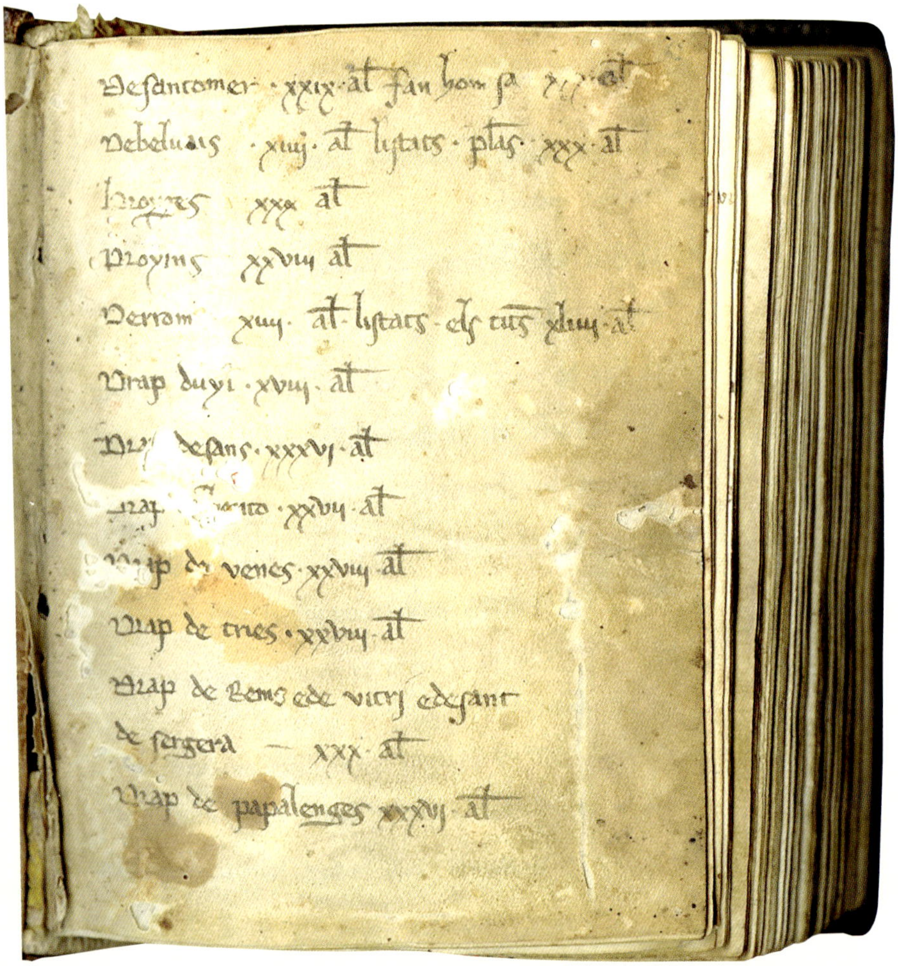

Front flyleaf, recto, Notes in Catalan, List of Quantities of Textiles

MS n.a.l. 560, f. 148v: [Here for the Priest]." Sacerdotes tui induantur iusticiam. Et sancti tui exultent" [from Psalm 131:9]; see Leroquais, 1927, vol. II, pp. 256-258, no. 283).

It appears that the historiated initials in the present Horae ought to be considered something of stylistic unicum, with charming but nevertheless simple short figures composed of angular contours; vivid colors of blue, maroon, green and golden yellow; simple, black contours and facial details; and plain foliage-spatulate leaves. A distinctive feature of female and male figures is the charming rouge used for their cheeks. Amongst the interesting decorative features, one should note the diagonal penwork shafts (or pen-flourished diagonal sprays) in lower margins on nearly every page, comparable to those found in other Horae of the same era such as Baltimore, Walters MS 40, Walters MS 97 and the Hours of Marie (New York, Metropolitan Museum of Art, MS L. 1990.38). These were popular in thirteenth-century manuscripts in Paris or the Ile-de-France region from the 1220s to the 1270s (see Bennett, 1996, note 28: "Penwork sprays, diagonal or horizontal, in lower margins warrant further investigation").

With regards to the pictorial program of the historiated initials, which serve as visual cues to each particular text, so far no close parallels are known for the style of the artist of this book. The initials (with the exception of the Scene of Flagellation at Compline) adopt a cycle for the Infancy of Christ (in six initials, from Lauds to Vespers). The Matins initial (height higher than the others) continues the iconographic subject of the Virgin and Child since c. 1220 (Vienna Hours ÖNB, Cod. 1904; Rouen, BM, MS Leber 6; New York, PML MS M. 92; Baltimore, MSS Walters 40, Walters 97; New York, Metropolitan Museum of Art, MS L. 1990.38 "Hours of Marie"). To quote Bennett: "In French books of hours for the most of the thirteenth-century, representations of the Virgin and Child were customary for Matins of the Virgin..." (Bennett, 1996, p. 25). Of interest in the present Horae is the very early occurrence of the Infancy cycle in the historiated initials that illustrate the Hours of the Virgin. Indeed, prior to these Horae, one finds full-page miniatures of the Christological cycle prefacing the Psalter-Hours (e.g., Rouen, BM, MS Leber 6), or Hours (New York, PML MS M.92). In the present "Troyes" Horae, the narrative illustrations are, so to speak, transferred to and integrated with the initials of the canonical hours of the Virgin (except Matins and Compline).

The historiated initials found in these Horae apparently constitute one of the earliest examples to picture a Christological cycle directly in the initials of all the canonical hours. Painted towards the end of the reign of King Louis IX (1216-1270) and the beginning of the reign of Philippe III le Hardi (1270-1285), this book is situated in the interesting period that paved the way for the renewal of illumination that started to take place under the reign of Philippe IV le Bel onwards. A book such as the present one testifies to the slow but sure resurgence of provincial ateliers — such as here Troyes or Champagne — in place of the domination of Paris and the region of Ile-de-France region, effectively ending the "monopoly" of Paris. Our codex was painted locally in Champagne (Troyes) but destined to travel and be used across Europe, going beyond local liturgical use and particularities to suit a very early Catalan and Iberic owner.

PHYSICAL DESCRIPTION: [1] + 118 ff., missing a calendar leaf and 2 leaves likely blank (collation: i^6 [of 8, lacking iii (excised leaf), and vi; i is the pastedown], ii-xi^8, xii^4, xiii-xv^8, xvi^7 [of 8, lacking vii, probably blank; viii the pastedown]), occasional catchwords, single column of 12 lines, ruling of single verticals bounding 13 horizontals, two top and bottom projected across, in black (justification 85 x 57 mm.), rubrics for each hour of the Virgin and textual components of the Hours of the Virgin, such as Hymnus, A(ntiphona), Ps(almus), Capitula, Oratio, written in a Gothic textura semi-quadrata in black, with red dabs for capitals, calendar entries and antiphons written in a gothic textura rotunda; some scribal errors suggesting unfamiliarity with the text, 2-line champide initials for hymns, psalms, lessons, chapters, canticles, and Kyrieleyson of Litany, penwork with prominent display of diagonal pen-flourished shafts (or "daggers") in blue and red in the lower margin of each recto, blue and red line-endings of abstract ornament, including wavy and zigzag lines, and short shafts, the color red at top and blue at bottom of each line-ending, blue and red versals with red and blue flourishes in alternation, one historiated initial of 5-line high for Matins of Hours of the Virgin and 8 historiated initials of 4-line high for Lauds-Compline of the Hours of the Virgin and Psalm 6, the first of Penitential Psalms, all with gold backgrounds, colored in blue with rose spandrels or pink with blue spandrels, all with foliate extensions, usually of spatulate leaves. Bound in a 14th-15th century Spanish Mudejar binding of brown goatskin tooled with intertwined ropework, on wooden boards (clasp lacking), codex placed in a red morocco case gilt (Parchment leaves trimmed in the 15th century (?) for rebinding; wanting one calendar leaf and two blanks, some thumbing and darkening of leaves, some rubbing and flaking of pigment, pastedowns somewhat wormed). Dimensions 122 x 93 mm.

TEXT: ff. 1v-12, Calendar, graded in red and black (lacking second half of February and first half of March), with the following noteworthy saints: Lucian of Beauvais (1.8), William of Bourges (1.10), Vincent of Saragossa, in red (1.22), Urbanus of Langres (1.23), 6th bishop (430-450), buried in Dijon (Holweck, 997), Policarp of Smyrna (1.26), Alexander the

Bishop, possibly Alexander I, Pope (Holweck, 45), Venantius of Dalmatia (4.1, Holweck, 1007), Peter the Martyr (4.29 +, canonized in 1253), Gengulphi the Martyr (5.13, Holweck, 413 = Gangulf, 5.11 venerated in Burgundy, Langres), Germanus of Paris (5.28) (Holweck, 430, abbot of S. Symphorien near Autun, bishop of Paris), Medard of Soissons (6.8), Apostle Barnabas, written as Bernabe (6.11), Eligius of Noyon (6.25), Theobald of Provins, Champagne (7.1, Holweck, 955, sometimes called Theobald of Sens), Arnulphus of Metz (7.18, Holweck, 106), Dominic of Bologna (8.5, canonized 1234, probably an addition), Philibert of Tournus (8.20, inscribed Filibert, cf. Philibert in Holweck, 810), Lupus of Sens (9.1, Holweck, 628, not Lupus of Troyes (7.29)), Marcellus of Châlons-sur-Saône, (9.4, Holweck, 650, venerated at Lyons and Autun, mispelled Sancti Macelli), Remigius of Reims (in red, 10.1), Francis of Assisi (10.4), Dionysius of Paris (10.9), Valancius (10.20, not in Holweck), Martin of Tours (11.11), Brictus of Tours (11.13), Columbanus of Luxeuil and Bobbio (11.21, Holweck, 227), Conception of the Virgin (12.8), Nichasius of Reims (12.14), Lazarus (12.17, Holweck, 596-67, venerated at Autun), Thomas of Canterbury (12.29, rubbed); on f. 4, note the addition of Peter Martyr (4.9), canonized 1253; Added to the Calendar are the following Spanish, Catalan, South French and other saints or feasts: Paula the Widow (1.27, Holweck, 784, 1.16, friend of Jerome), Valerius the Bishop of Saragossa (1.29, Holweck, 1005), Deposicio sancti Sabini (2.9, Holweck, 878, celebrated at Bari), Eulalia of Barcelona (2.12), her translation to Barcelona (12.23), Baudelius the Martyr of Nimes (5.20), "Pax hinc domui" (5.21), Quiteria of Galicia (5.22, Holweck, 844, venerated in Gascony and Northern Spain), Ferreolus of Besançon (6.16, Holweck, 378), Raymond of Roda (6.21, Holweck, 848), Martialis of Limoges (6.30, Holweck, 666), Cucufas of Barcelona (7.25, Holweck, 246), Licerius of Conserans, diocese of Pamiers, France (8.27, Holweck, 611), Nunilo and Alodia, both of Huesca (10.22, here 10.21, Holweck, 750), Translation of Eulalia of Barcelona (10.23, Holweck, 337), Ermengaud / Ermengol of Urgel (11.3, Holweck, 828), Acisclus of Cordova and Victoria (11.17, Holweck, 11), Leocadia (12.9), Eulalia of Merida (12.10), Paul of Narbonne (12.11, not in Holweck), Eugenia the Virgin (12.29, Holweck, 12.30); f. 12v, blank; ff. 13-88v, Hours of the Virgin, for use of Troyes (?), with Matins (ff. 13-29); Lauds (29v-46v); Prime (46v-54v) ; Terce (ff. 55-60); Sext (ff. 60-65); None (ff. 65-70v); Vespers (ff. 70v-80v); Compline (ff. 80v-88v); ff. 88v-110, Penitential Psalms; ff. 110-115v, Litany and Petitions; amongst the Litany, one should signal Romana (f. 113); ff. 115v-117v, Prayers; 117v-118v, Collects, 1) *Oratio. Deus cui proprium est misereri semper et parcere suscipe deprecationem nostram...* [Corpus Orationum 2: no. 1143. Appropriate after litany, for citation of sins committed and for daily recitation on p. 135, according to rubrics in manuscripts]. 2) *Oratio. Deus qui nos a seculi uanitate conuersos ad superne uocationis amoris...* [Corpus Orationum 3: no. 1835]. The two collects on ff. 117v-118v also appear as the first two of ten collects in Paris, BnF, MS n.a.l. 915, ff. 59v-60.

ILLUSTRATION: The Adoration of the Magi is out of its normal biblical sequence, which is perhaps related to the fact that the adjacent rubric mistakenly identifies the hour of None as Terce. The subjects of the historiated initials are: f. 13, Initial D, Virgin and Child enthroned; f. 29v, Initial D, Annunciation; f. 46v, Initial D, Visitation; f. 55, Initial D, Nativity, with the ox, ass, and Christ above, Mary and Joseph below; f. 60, Initial D, Flight into Egypt; f. 65, Initial D, Adoration of the Magi; f. 70v, Initial D, Presentation in the Temple; f. 80v, Initial D, Flagellation; f. 89, Initial D, David enthroned.

OWNERSHIP: 1. Apparently written for use, and perhaps at, Troyes. The Hours of the Virgin is not entirely consistent with the Troyes text of the later Middle Ages, but where it deviates it usually corresponds with the readings of Sens, about 35 miles to the west. The original calendar points to southeast of Ile-de-France, most likely Champagne and Burgundy. The litany ends with Romana, who was a follower of Lucian of Beauvais, and both are included in the litany; Lucian of Beauvais is also mentioned in the calendar (8 Jan.). - 2. Late-13th or early 14th -century Catalan owners, surely itinerant textile merchants, used the blank flyleaves for memoranda concerning their stock and the Champagne Fairs, two of which were held in Troyes. There are lists of quantities of textiles found on the upper pastedown and first flyleaf: similar lists are printed in B. Oliver y Esteller, *Historia del derecho en Catalunia, Mallorca y Valencia...*, 1876, p. 413, and in B. Alart, *Documents sur la langue catalane des anciens comtes de Roussillon et de Cerdagne*, 1881, pp. 78, 110. There are also a number of southern French and Spanish entries which have been added to the calendar, including 'Eulalia barch'. (i.e. of Barcelona, 12 February), her translation (24 October), Ermengardus bishop of Urgell (3 November), and the dedication of Barcelona cathedral (18 November). Another Spanish owner made further alterations to the Calendar and had the volume rebound. - 3. Laurence Witten, New Haven, Catalogue 4 (1957) no 53, with his (?) pencil annotations on a front flyleaf.- 4. Sotheby's, New York, 21 May 1974, lot 220, use of Sens, not sold; Christie's, 27 Nov. 1992, lot 10 p. 19; color pls. ff. 29v, 55, p. 18; Quaritch, Catalogue no. 4882, lot 10, for 27,500 Pounds.

LITERATURE: Published in Bennett, 1996, p. 28 and note 72; Bennett, 2004, p. 220, note 48. - Abu-Lughod, J.L. *Before European Hegemony: The World System A.D. 1250-1350*, New York and Oxford, 1989. - Bennett, A. "A Thirteenth-Century French Book of Hours for Marie," *Journal of the Walters Art Gallery [Essays in Honor of Lilian M. C. Randall]* 54 (1996), pp. 21-37. - Bennett, A. "The Transformation of the Gothic Psalter in Thirteenth-Century France," in *The Illuminated Psalter: Studies in the Content, Purpose and Placement of its Images*, ed. F. O. Büttner, Turnhout, Brepols, 2004, pp. 211-221. - Clanchy, M. *From Memory to Written Record: England 1066-1307*, Oxford and Cambridge, 1993. - Donovan, C. "The Mise-en-Page of Early Books of Hours in England," in *Medieval Book Production: Assessing the Evidence*, ed. L.L. Brownrigg, Los Altos Hills, 1990, pp. 147-161. - Holweck, F.G. *Calendarium liturgicum festorum Dei et Dei Matris Mariae, collectum et memoriis historicis...*, Philadelphia, 1925. - Leroquais, V. *Les livres d'heures manuscrits de la Bibliothèque nationale*, Mâcon, 1927, 3 vol.

ONLINE RESOURCES:

For comparison for only the Little Hours of the Virgin from Prime to None, and the last Hour of Compline: http://chd.dk/use/

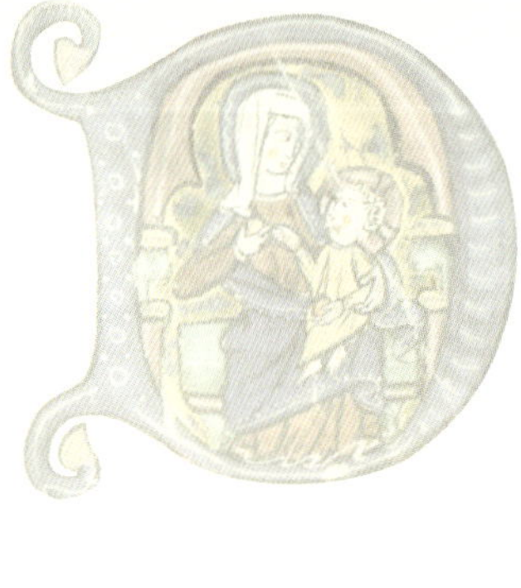

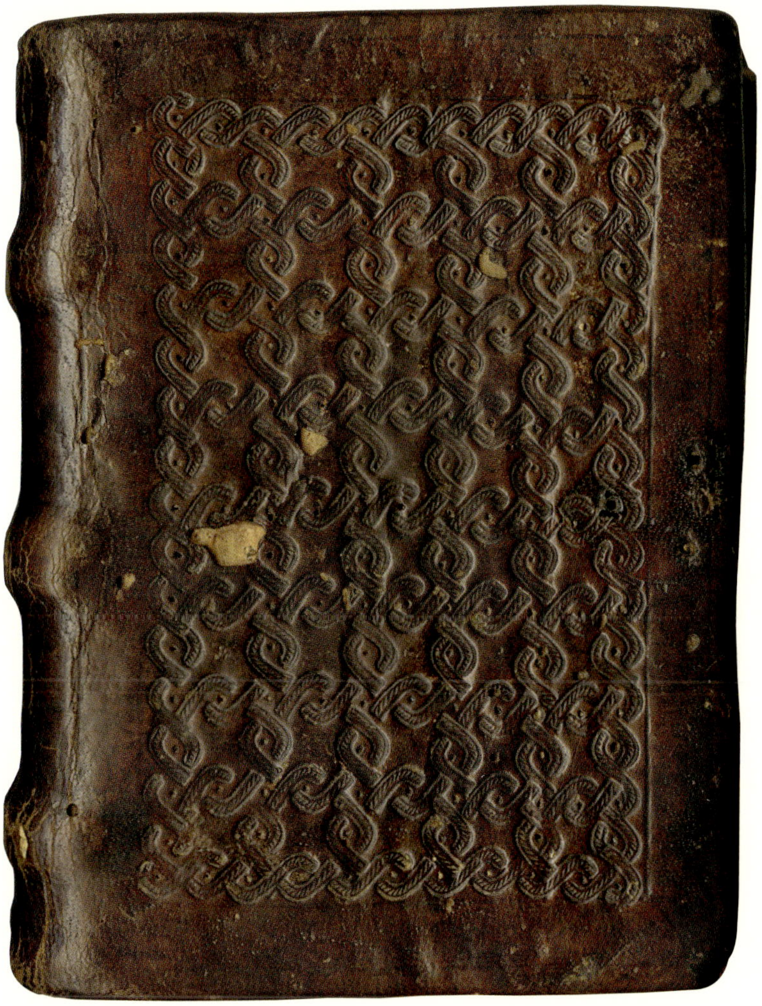

Binding, Upper Cover

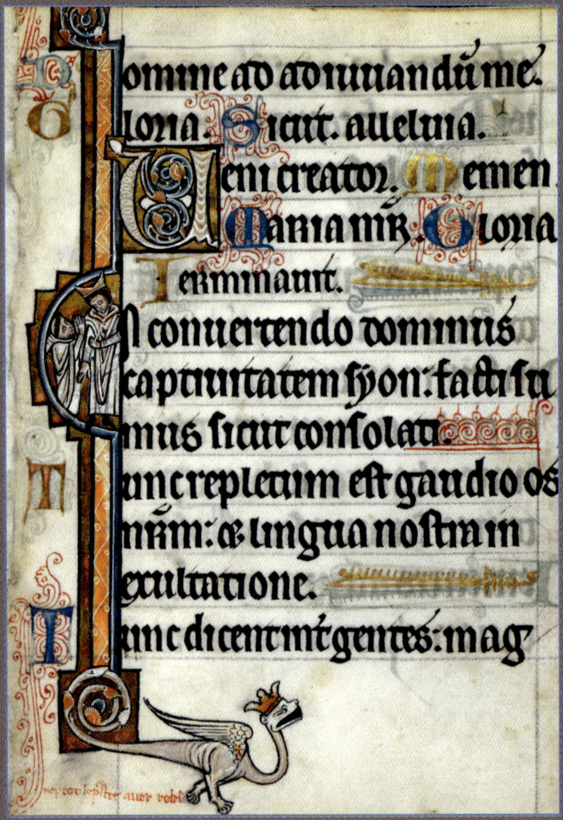

London, BL, Add. MS 49999, f. 48, Monk Kneeling before Bishop

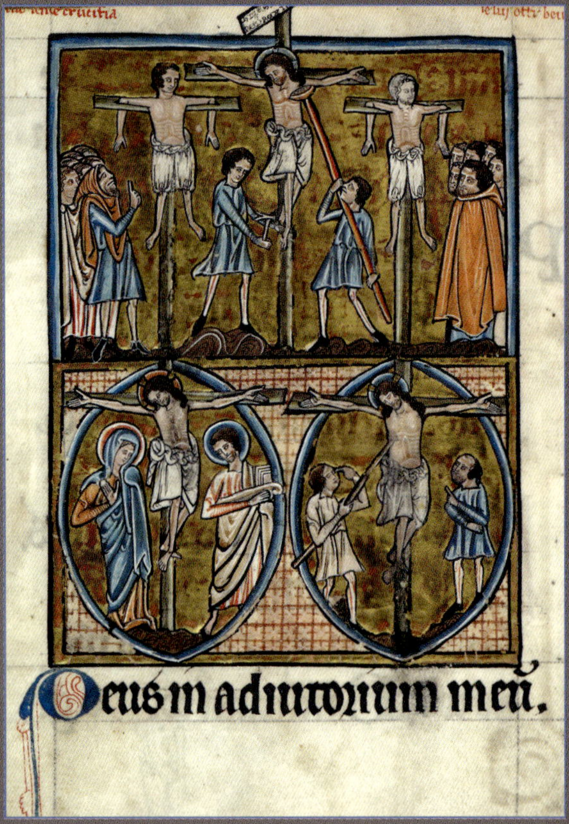

London, BL, Add. MS 49999, f. 47v, Crucifixion Scenes

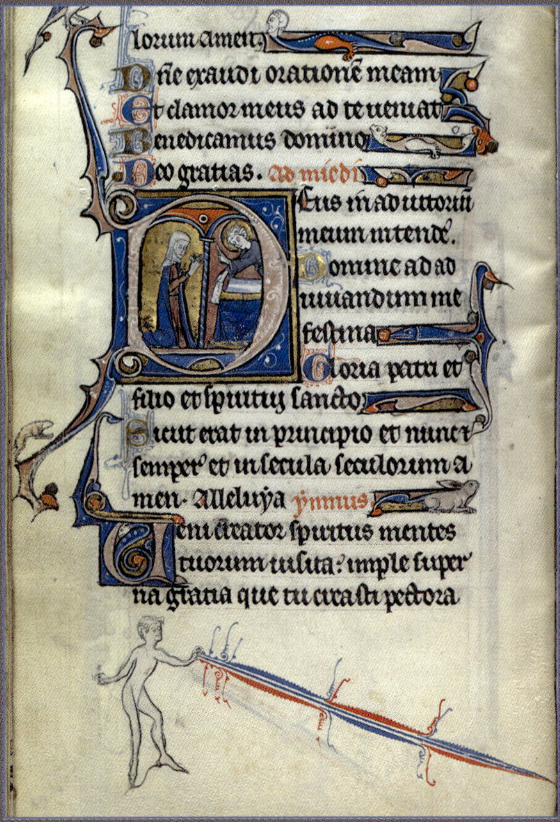

New York, Metropolitan Museum of Art, MS L. 1990.38,
Book of Hours, f. 50v,
Veiled Woman Praying before an Altar with Sainted Figure

Facing page, f. 55, Initial D, Nativity

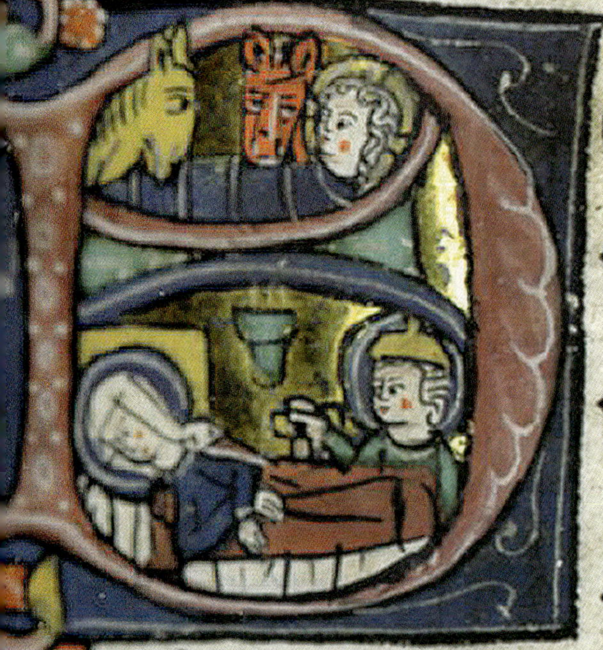

Deus in adiu-
torium me-
um intende
Domine ad
adiuuandum me
festina.
Gloria patri. Hymnus.
Veni creator spiritus.
Memento salutis.
Gloria tibi domine. a' Tota pulchra
Ad dominum es
cum tribularer

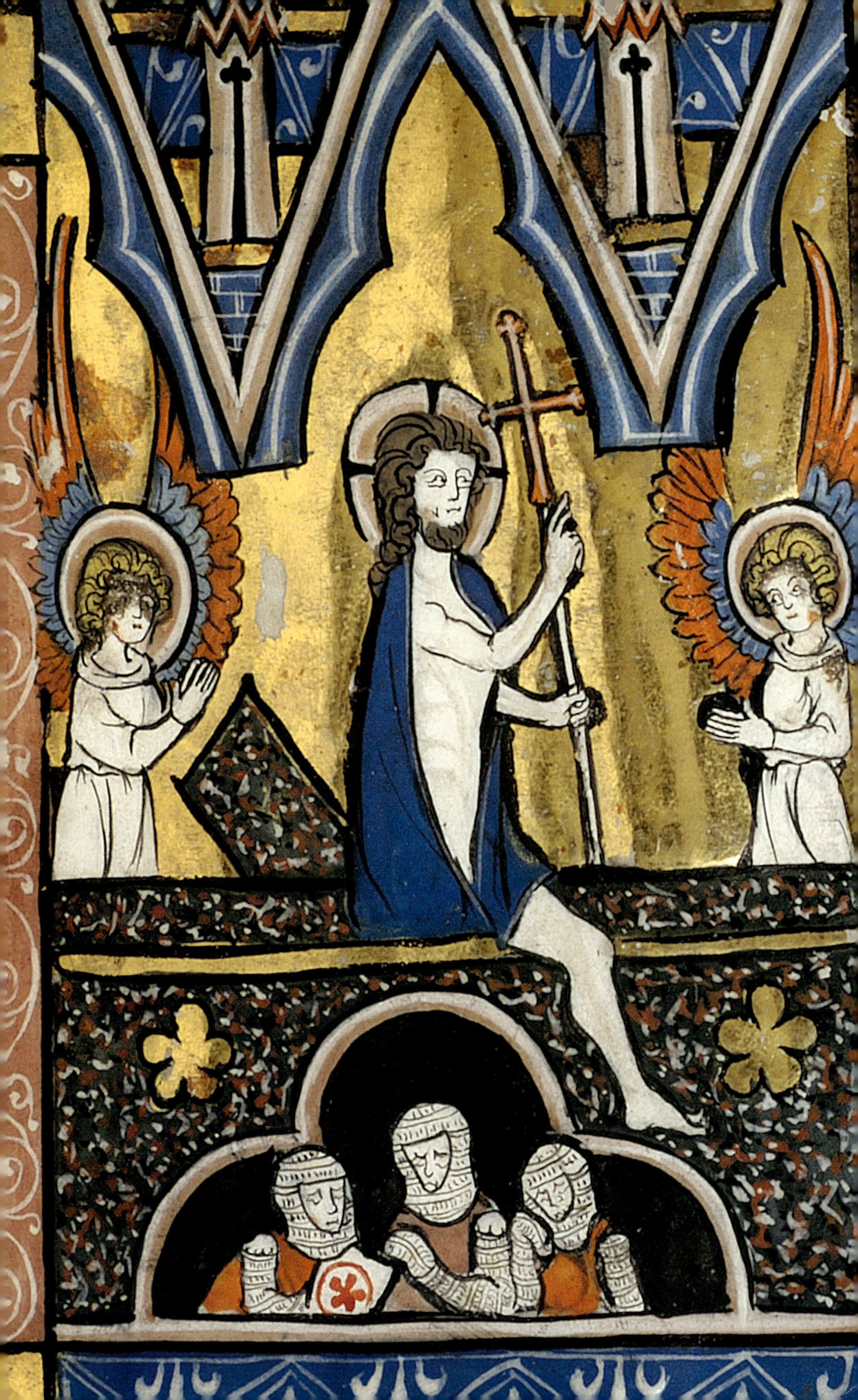

2

Psalter-Hours
(Use of St. Omer, diocese of Thérouanne)

In Latin, Flemish, and French, illuminated manuscript on parchment
Northern France, Thérouanne?, c. 1285, with additions c. 1425-1450 and c. 1450-1475
4 full-page illuminations and 9 historiated initials by the illuminator of Cambrai 87 and workshop.

This beautiful and previously unrecorded Psalter-Hours is a composite manuscript that reflects well, in its thirteenth-century portion, the renewed aesthetic tied to manuscript illumination in the age of Philippe le Bel (1285-1314), considered something of "transitional" period (see Avril, 1998, pp. 256-257). The Psalter portion with its full-page prefatory miniatures and its historiated initials witnesses the growing importance of provincial ateliers, especially in the north of the realm, in urban settings such as Amiens, Arras, Cambrai, St. Omer, Thérouanne and perhaps also St. Quentin and Soissons. The geographic position of these centers of illumination allowed for varied influences, coming from Flanders and England, but also of course Paris. Avril coined this trend as the "end of the monopoly of Paris" (Avril, 1998, p. 256).

When exploring the development of Books of Hours, one of the main questions scholars and liturgists address is the way in which the Book of Hours evolved out of the Psalter and the status of the type of book labeled "Psalter-Hours." This manuscript offers interesting insights into this trend. The codex began life as a thirteenth-century Psalter. A century later, the Hours of the Virgin with miscellaneous prayers were added between the Calendar and the Psalter to turn the manuscript into an "up-to-date" Book of Hours. Then, later again in the fifteenth century, the Hours of the Holy Spirit, the Hours of the Cross and various prayers were added at the end. The result of this amplification is a composite book, a Psalter-Hours that, thus expanded, better suited the spiritual needs and preferences of its fifteenth-century lay owner. These Psalter-Hours are a good example of how the laity adapted an existing book to new needs.

In France, the choice of illuminated Gothic Psalters for use as a private devotional book underwent changes in the thirteenth century, when progressively

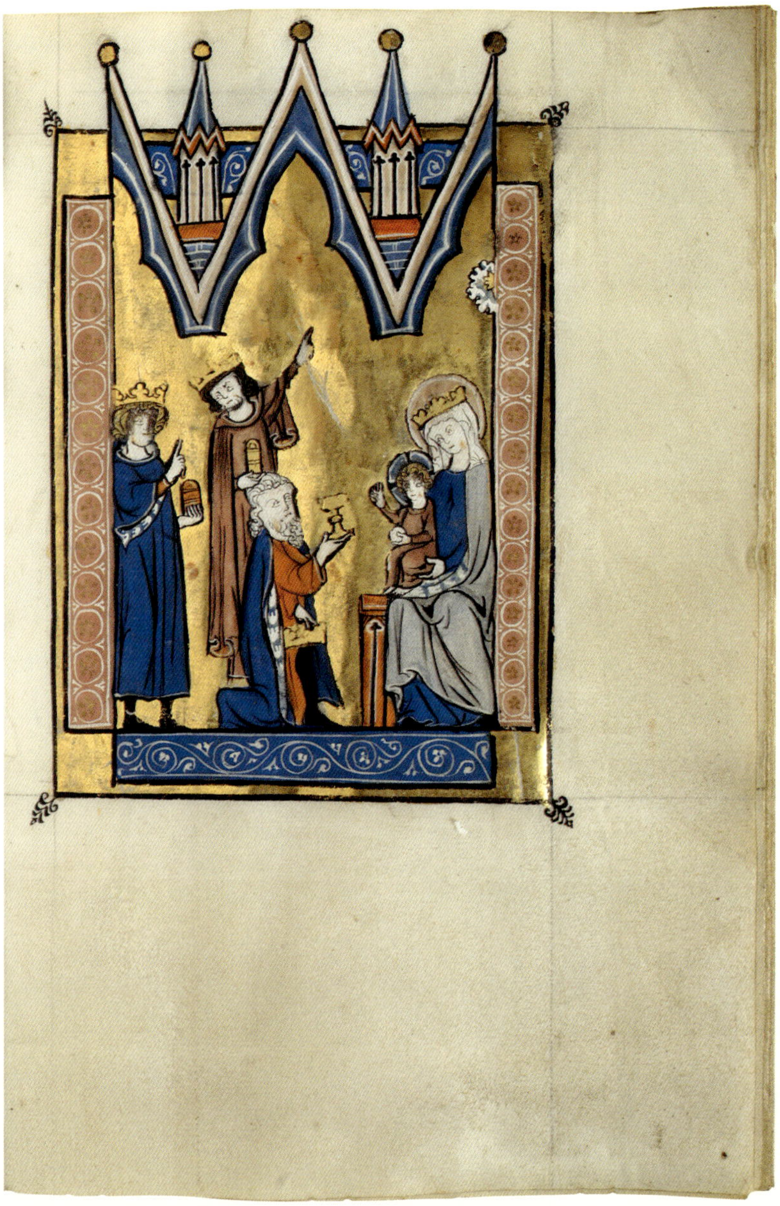

f. 8, Adoration of the Magi

Books of Hours would supplant Psalters as aids for private devotion amongst the laity. Illustrated French Psalters of Parisian and northeast regions reached their peak by the middle third of the century, after which the demand decreased. By the end of the century, they were supplanted by Books of Hours, which began to emerge as a more desirable prayerbook already in the third quarter of the thirteenth century.

The Psalter portion of this manuscript was illuminated during the last quarter of the thirteenth century, a period during which one notes a phenomenal surge of manuscript production in north France. A remarkable feature of this book, although not uncommon in Psalters, is the cycle of prefatory miniatures grouped together at the beginning, here a pictorial cycle dedicated to the Infancy and Passion of Christ. These fine full-page prefatory miniatures and the nine historiated initials introducing the Psalter with a nine-fold division of the Psalms (common in northeast French or Franco-Flemish Psalters) are stylistically related to a group of manuscripts tied to a Book of Hours in Cambrai, BM, MS 87 made for Gauthier de Châtillon d'Autresche and his wife. The workshop of Cambrai 87 produced deluxe Psalters and Horae for noblemen and women in northeastern France (discussed by A. Stones, in Collet and Foehr-Janssens, 2010, pp. 244-246; see also Stones, 2012, forthcoming, cat. III-90).

The primary artist of Cambrai 87 illuminated a coherent group of codices, including a Book of Hours, Los Angeles, J.P. Getty Museum, Ludwig IX.3 (see von Euw and Plotzek, 1982, p. 80); Chantilly, Musée Condé MS 62, also a Book of Hours (use of St.Omer); a Psalter in Oxford, Bodleian Library, MS Laud. Lat. 84; a Cistercian Missal in Krakow, Czartoriski Lib. 3204, datable between 1295 and 1302, as well as several literary manuscripts in Brussels, BR, MS 9433, *Laurin*; Vienna, ÖNB, Cod. 2621, Literary Miscellany of Treatises on Love (with another artist); and Paris, BnF, MS lat. 10286, a Chess Treatise (with some heraldry related to Jean de Dampierre or his son Guillaume). To quote A. Stones: "The artist of Cambrai 87's frontispiece can also be identified in a large number of liturgical, devotional and literary manuscripts datable between 1286 and 1297, and locatable in Cambrai, St.Omer and Thérouanne...; a hitherto unknown psalter-hours with full-page Life of Christ miniatures which I attribute to the Cambrai 87 painter has just come to light at Les Enluminures ...." (Stones, in Krause and Stones, 2006, p. 381). Cambrai 87 is a Book of Hours for mixed use (Calendar for Paris; Hours of the Virgin, use of Reims) apparently datable before 1297 as the Feast of Saint Louis is included in the Calendar as a later addition (dated later c. 1310-1315 in [Exhibition], Avril, 1998, cat. 210, p. 310). The thirteenth-century portion of the present Psalter-Hours appears to be an early product of this workshop, closer to circa 1285 (the Feast of Saint Louis is not included in the Calendar for August). There are no other recorded manuscripts from this group remaining in private hands, and the present manuscript may be the earliest of the group.

Although Cambrai 87 constitutes something of a "linchpin" within the group of stylistically related codices studied by A. Stones (2006, 2010, 2012), other stylistic origins are perceptible. For instance, the architectural frames found in the full-page Infancy cycle miniatures are similar to those found in a Psalter of Gui de Dampierre (Brussels, BR, MS 10607), and parallels are to be noted between the figures with tight curly hair. Stones notes however that the female faces are closer to the work of Maître Henri in Paris, BnF, MS fr. 412 (Hainaut) dated 1285 (see Stones, 2012 (forthcoming), cat. III-56; see also [Exhibition], Avril, 1998, no. 200, pp. 296-297). The full-page prefatory cycle of miniatures placed at the beginning of the Psalter is of interest. Close in style (the same artist as Cambrai 87 according to A. Stones) and composition are the miniatures found in a Psalter, Oxford, Bodeleian Library, MS Laud. 84, datable to the beginning of the fourteenth century. The full-page miniatures clearly show stylistic comparisons and it is interesting to find the same lay-out with prefatory miniatures that are followed after by historiated initials. In addition, one should note the presence of some ornamental elements characteristic of northeastern illumination of this period, such as the large dragons with colored wings (in our manuscript, see ff. 189, 208v, 229) that are found in numerous Cambrai and northeastern manuscripts.

Patrons of the group of manuscripts related to Cambrai 87 include members of the nobility in northeastern France, with personalities such as Gautier de Châtillon d'Autrêche and his wife (owners of Cambrai 87) and perhaps Guy de Dampierre (Psalter, Brussels, BR, MS 10607). In addition, noble women constitute a core group of these early owners, and it is precisely in this region that the earliest Books of Hours originate. The later fifteenth-century amplifications were copied in a northeastern French environment, with a number of clues including French rubrics with northeastern linguistic features such as "tierche," "douche dame," "je vous cri merchi," "rechepvoir" and others. Another

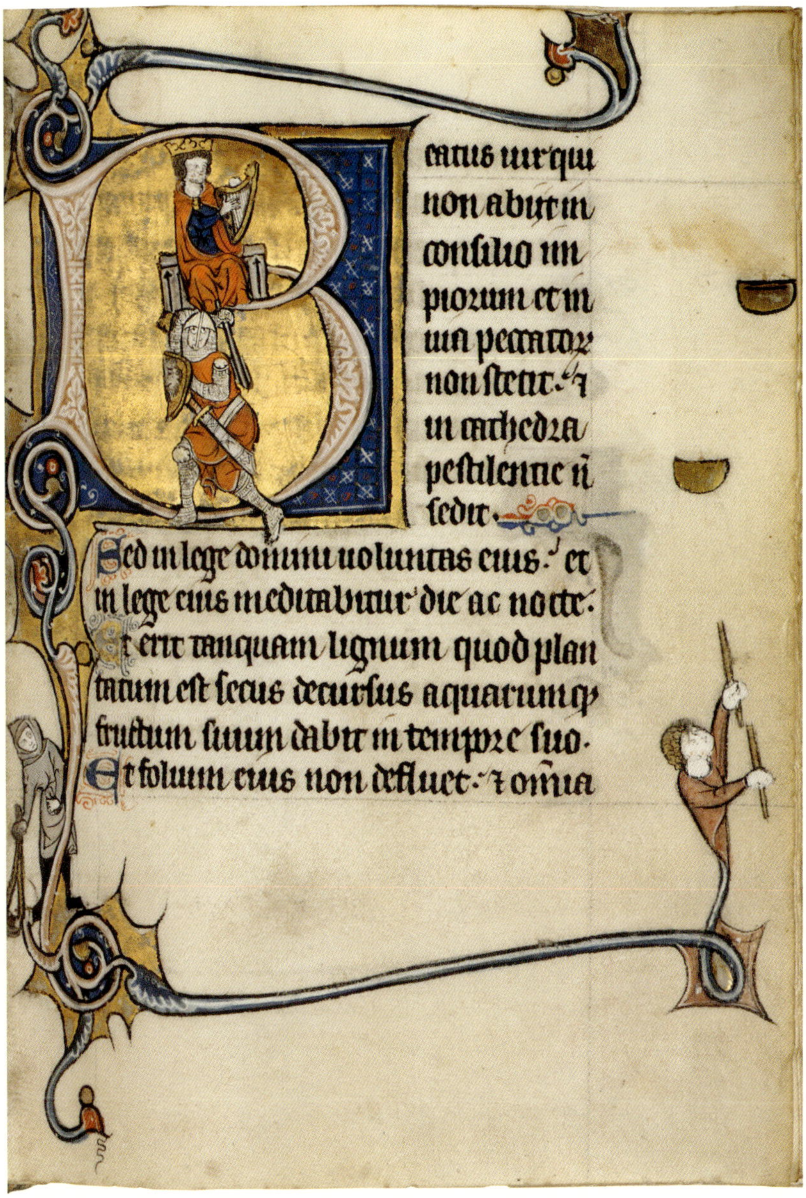

f. 87, David Playing his Harp (above); David (in the decender) and Goliath (in the initial)

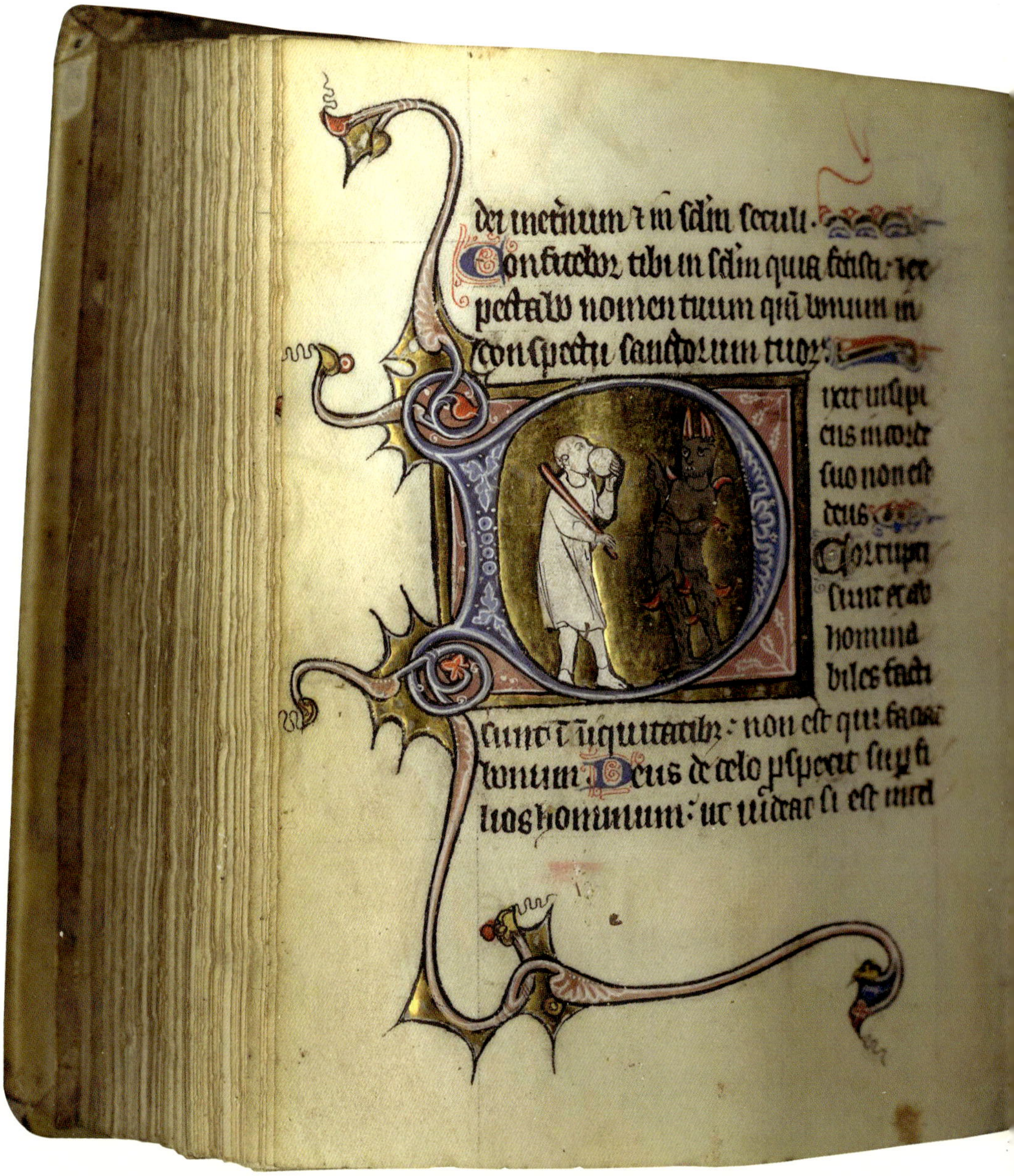

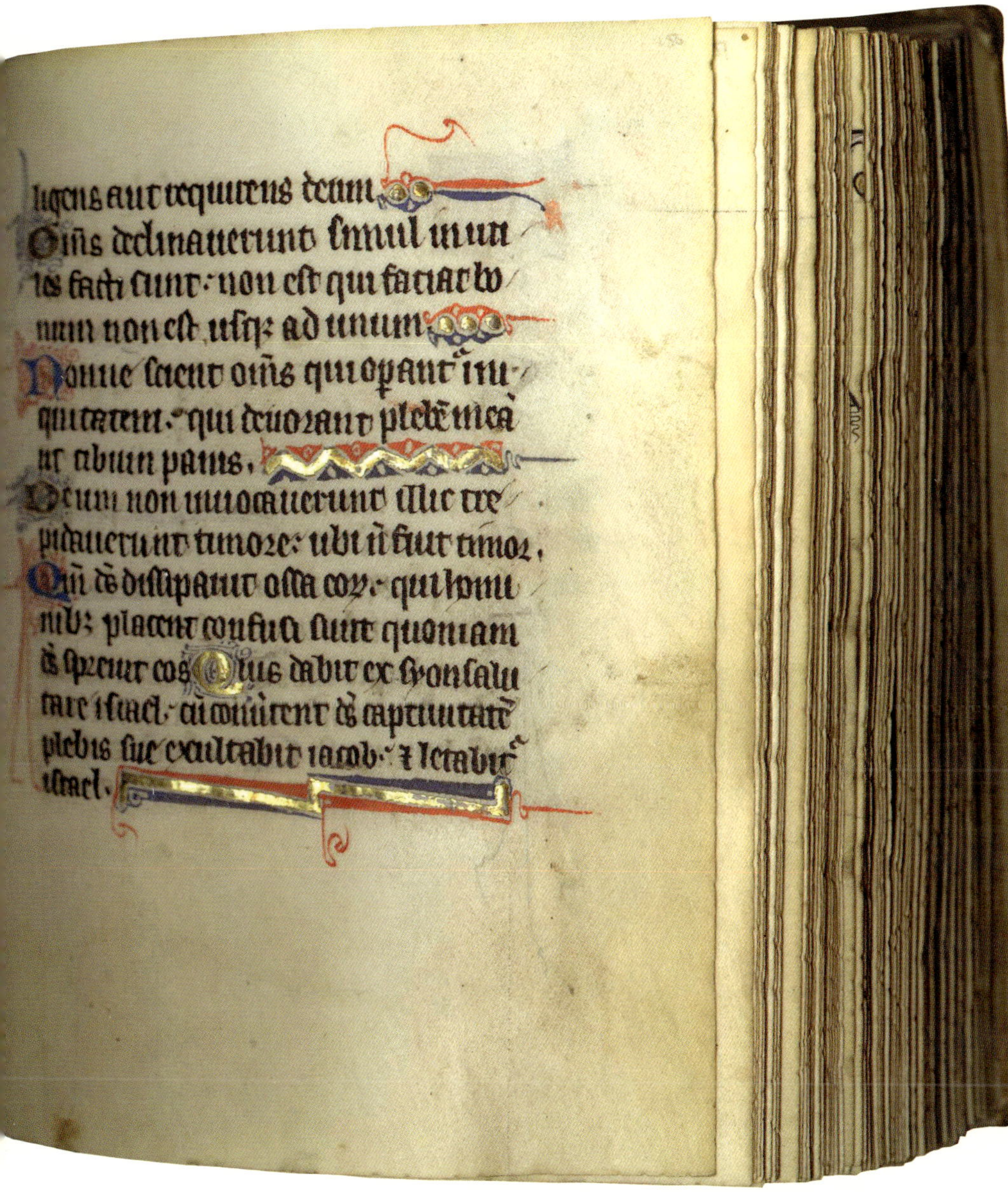

ff. 149v-150, The Fool Eating a Loaf of Bread, a Devil Pointing to Him

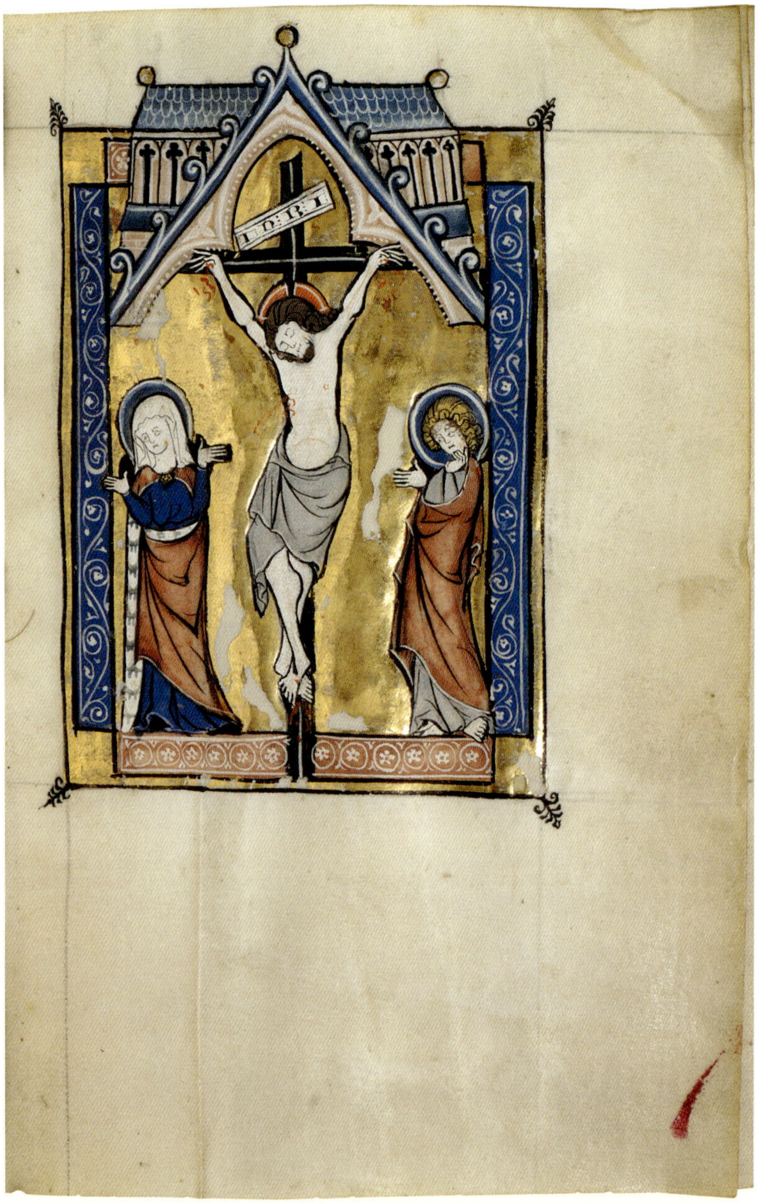

f. 9, Crucifixion

interesting feature is the attempt to reach some sort of homogeneity between the original thirteenth-century portion of this codex and the fifteenth-century additions: the scribe and decorator attempted (quite well at that) to render uniform the line-fillers, the decorated versals and the small filigree initials (compare f. 26v [15th c.] and f. 143 [13th c.]). The result is a Psalter-Hours that fooled no one but preserved a certain homogeneity to the reader's eye.

The distinguished and unusual provenance in the collection of the Count Waldstein, whose librarian was none other than the famous Jacques Casanova de Seingalt, adds interest. The manuscript was once in the library of the Count in the Castle of Dux, whose important collection was dispersed after the First World War. Since Casanova died in 1798, and there is an inscription indicating that the codex was "bought in 1809," it is probable the present codex was acquired after Casanova had left his functions as librarian upon his death. Unless of course the inscription "bought in 1809" dates after the Dux bookplate, and was sold by Count Waldstein. Casanova might thus have held these Psalter-Hours in his hands and pondered on his past "turbulent" existence. These Psalter-Hours have been handed down to us and still dazzle our modern eye.

PHYSICAL DESCRIPTION: 333 ff, composite manuscript with 13th c. sections (ff. 1-10; 87-297) intermixed with 15th c. additions (ff. 11-86; 298-333), collation difficult but nonetheless ([15th c. portion] i6, ii^{4}, iii-vii^{8}, viii^{4}, ix-x^{8}, xi^{6}, xii^{8}, xiii^{7}; [13th c. portion] xiv-xxxix^{8}, xl^{4}; [15th c. portion] xli-xliv^{8}, xlv^{3} [4-1, with iii a canceled blank]), catchwords - [13th c. portion] written in an early Gothic liturgical bookhand in black ink, on 15 lines, no rubrics, parchment ruled in plummet (justification 65 x 80 mm), line-endings in red, blue, and gold leaf, versals in alternating burnished gold leaf and lapis with alternating blue and red calligraphic penwork, 2-line initials in burnished gold leaf on alternating red and blue grounds with alternating infill, 4 prefatory full-page miniatures on inserted leaves (ff. 7-10) and 9 historiated initials, with illuminated marginalia (ff. 87, 115, 132v, 148v, 149v, 166v, 189, 208v, 229) - [15th century additions], written in a Gothic liturgical hand, in dark brown to black ink, on up to 15 lines, parchment ruled in plummet (justification 70 x 90 mm.), rubrics in red, line-fillers in red, blue and burnished gold, versals in burnised gold or blue with opposing dark blue or red penwork, 2-line high initials in burnished gold on pink and blue grounds highlighted in white tracery, major textual breaks with larger 3-line high initials in burnished gold on pink and blue grounds with white tracery (the first initial at Matins has an infill of four fleur-de-lis), burnished gold baguette with full floral and ivyleaf borders with green foliage, to be note that the later additions contain 15th century ornamentation that sought to place itself in the continuity of the earlier portion of the psalter, in order to maintain some homogeneity [line-fillers and versals clearly imitate earlier 13th century equivalents on ff. 87-297]; later additions (c. 1450-1475) on ff. 298-332 (Hours of the Holy Spirit, Hours of the Cross and prayers) with parti-colored initials in red and blue, more elaborate than the first 15th c. portion (ff. 11-86), with filigree penwork extending well into the margins; a few 15th c. inscriptions pepper the codex (e.g. f. 12v, 332v). Bound in a late sixteenth-century binding of vellum over pasteboards, upper and lower covers with central gilt "IHS" and "MAR[IA]" monograms in an oval cartouche lined with gilt rays [Jesuit?], single gilt filet border composing the frame on boards, smooth spine with gilt filets and fleurons, title in red ink on spine (later 18th or 19th c.): "Manuscrit du XIII siecle contenant les p[rieres] [de] plusieurs offices...," edges gilt and gaufered, a date inscribed on recto of first flyleaf in brown ink (24 januari 1580) (Binding in good condition, a few internal stains, some leaves trimmed short; two miniatures suffering very slight loss of gold leaf, some smudging and a few faces rubbed (e.g. ff. 208v, 229)). Dimensions 155 x 115 mm.

TEXT: ff. 1-6, Calendar, in Latin and Flemish, with noteworthy saints: *Pouwels* (Paul, in red, 25 Jan.; Amant (6 Feb.); *De dach van sancti victorini* (25 Feb.); in red, *Onservrauwen* (25 March); Bezelis (14 June); Bertin (5 Sept.); *Onser vrauwe* (8 Sept.); *Omaer* (in red, 9 Sept.); *Loys* [Eloi] (1 Dec); *Niclaus* (in red, 6 Dec.); [15th c.] ff. 11-53v, Hours of the Virgin, use of St-Omer; ff. 53v-54, *Memoire de saint Nicholay*; f. 54v, blank; ff. 55-68v, Office of the Dead (use of Saint Omer), rubric, *Ci commencent vespres de mors*; ff. 69-73v, Fifteen Joys of the Virgin (northern French spellings), rubric, *Les .xv. goyes nostre dame*; ff. 73v-76, Seven Requests of Our Lord; ff. 76-76v, Prayer to the Holy Cross; ff. 77-83v, Prayers and Gospel readings, including *Salve sancta parens*; ff. 83v-86, Prayer on the Passion, rubric, *Chi s'ensieut une orison de le ramenbrance de le passion de nostre signeur ihesucrist et des .vii. Paroles que il dist de sa precieuse bouche en pendant en le crois...*; f.86v, blank; [13th c.] ff. 87-287, Psalter, nine-fold division, with ff. 87-115, Ps. 1: Beatus Vir, "Blessed is the man who hath not walked in the counsel of the ungodly"; ff. 115-132v, Ps. 26: Dominus illuminatio mea, "The Lord is my Light"; ff. 132v-148v, Ps. 38: Dixi custodiam, "I will take heed to my ways that I not sin with my tongue"; ff. 148v-149v, Ps. 51: Quid gloriaris in malicia, "Why would you be glorified in malice"; ff. 149v-166v, Ps. 52: Dixit insipiens in corde, "The fool said in his heart: There is no God"; ff. 166v-188v, Ps. 68: Salvum me fac deus, "Save me, O God: for the waters are come in even unto my soul"; ff. 188v-208v, Ps. 81: Exultate deo, "Rejoice to God our helper"; ff. 208v-228v, Ps. 97: Cantate domino canticum, "Sing to the Lord ..."; ff. 228v-289, Ps. 109, Dixit dominus domino, "The Lord said to my Lord: Sit thou at my right hand"; ff. 289-91, Kyrieleyson and Litany (including Amand, Rémi, Bertin (*Bertinc*), Bavon; also present are the Franciscan saints Francis, Dominic and Clare); [15th c.] ff. 298-322v, Hours of the Holy Spirit, with rubrics in French, *Les heures du saint esprit*, note linguistic forms such as "tierche" (f. 313); ff. 322v-325v, Hours of the Cross, rubric, *Ci commencent les heures de la crois*, again "tierche" (f. 324); ff. 326-330, O intemerata; ff. 330-332v, Obsecro te (masculine form); f. 333, blank and ruled.

ILLUSTRATION: Full-page prefatory cycle consists of an abbreviated Infancy and Passion narrative: f. 7, Annunciation; f. 8, Adoration of the Magi; f. 9, Crucifixion; f. 10, Resurrection. - Nine-part division of the Psalter is illustrated by large and lavish historiated initials in colors on gold grounds: f. 87, David playing his Harp; David and Goliath (David in the descender; Goliath in the initial), with marginalia showing a figure growing out of the vegetation and playing with gold balls that he bats with two sticks or batons; f. 115, David pointing to his Eyes; f. 132v, David pointing to his Mouth; f. 148v, Man wielding a Sword and holding a Child by the Hair, with a horned devil blowing a trumpet and slightly defaced in the upper margin; the unusual theme of Christian persecution is illustrated here, taking inspiration from the opening lines of the Psalm "Why would you be glorified in malice, you who are powerful in iniquity?"; f. 149v, The Fool eating a Loaf of Bread, a Devil pointing to him; f. 166v, David naked in the Water, God above; f. 189, David Playing the Carillon; f. 208v, Monks Singing before an open book on a Lectern, with figures playing music in the margin; f. 229, Christ and God the Father Enthroned.

OWNERSHIP: 1. Written and illuminated in the diocese of Thérouanne, for the liturgical use of St. Omer, the use of the Office of the Dead also for St. Omer; the calendar includes in red St. Omer, the seventh-century bishop of Thérouanne. - 2. Inscription in French, in a 17th or 18th c. hand: "Ce manuscript paroit etre du treizieme siecle comme les caracteres et les expressions en vieux gaulois l'insinuent. L'autheur etoit sans doute un allemant d'origine...," follwed by a "table de ce qu'il renferme" (Table of Contents). - 3. Count Waldstein of Bohemia, "Bibliothèque du Chateau de Dux" (armorial bookplate pasted on upper pastedown). The Castle of Dux (Bohemia) housed the library made famous by Giacomo Casanova (1725-1798), who was librarian at Dux from 1784 until his death in 1798. To quote Childs, 1956 (p. 106): "What has happened to the manuscripts once in the possession of Count Waldstein at Dux is not known. When the Dux Municipality acquired the castle at Dux after the First World War Count Waldstein removed the library and manuscripts to Hirschberg in Czechoslovakia. Their subsequent fate is a mystery. Guzlitz has suggested to me that they may be in the National Museum at Prague." - 4. In France in the nineteenth century, when the new owner in 1809 wrote "Acheté de Francois Lenfumé a Vellefry le 9 novembre 1809." Vellefrey is a town in modern-day France, Franche-Comté, near the Swiss border. - 5. Private Collection, Switzerland.

LITERATURE: Published in Stones, in Collet and Foehr-Janssens, 2006, pp. 244-246; Stones, in Krause and Stones, 2010, note 13, p. 381; also to be discussed in A. Stones, 2012 (forthcoming), p. 579 and entry cat. no. III-90, pp. 564-581 dedicated to Cambrai, BM, MS. 87. - Bennett, A. "Devotional Literacy of a Noblewoman in a Book of Hours of ca. 1300 in Cambrai," in *Manuscripts in Transition: Recycling Manuscripts, Text and Images* (Proceedings of the International Congress held in Brussels 5-9 November 2002), ed. by Brigitte Dekeyzer and Jan Van der Stock, Louvain, 2005, pp. 149-205. - Bennett, A. "The Transformation of the Gothic Psalter in Thirteenth-Century France," in *The Illuminated Psalter: Studies in the Content, Purpose and Placement of its Images*, ed. F. O. Büttner, Turnhout, Brepols, 2004, pp. 211-221. - Childs, J. Rives. *Casanoviana: An Annotated World Bibliography of Jacques Casanova de Seingalt and of Works Concerning Him*, Vienna, 1956. - Euw, Anton von and J. M. Plotzek. *Handschriften der Sammlung Ludwig*, 4 vols., Cologne, 1979-85. - [Exhibition] Paris, Grand Palais, *L'art au temps des rois maudits. Philippe le Bel et ses fils*, Paris, 1998. - Krause, K and A. Stones. *Gautier de Coinci: Miracles, Music, and Manuscripts*, Turnhout, Brepols, 2006. - Stones, A. "Les prières de Gautier de Coinci, leur distribution et leur réception d'après la tradition manuscrite," in *Le recueil au Moyen âge: le Moyen âge central*, Yasmina Foehr-Janssens and Olivier Collet (dir.), Turnhout, Brepols, 2010, pp. 237-268. - Stones, A., *Illuminated Manuscripts Made in France, Gothic Manuscripts 1260-1320*, London, Harvey Miller, 2012 (forthcoming).

ONLINE RESOURCES:
Paris, BnF, MS lat. 10286, related to the group of Cambrai, MM, MS 87:
http://images.bnf.fr/

Paris, BnF, MS fr. 412, attributed to Maître Henri:
http://images.bnf.fr/

Oxford, Bodleian Library, MS Laud. 84, Psalter with prefatory miniatures:
http://digital.bodleian.ox.ac.uk/

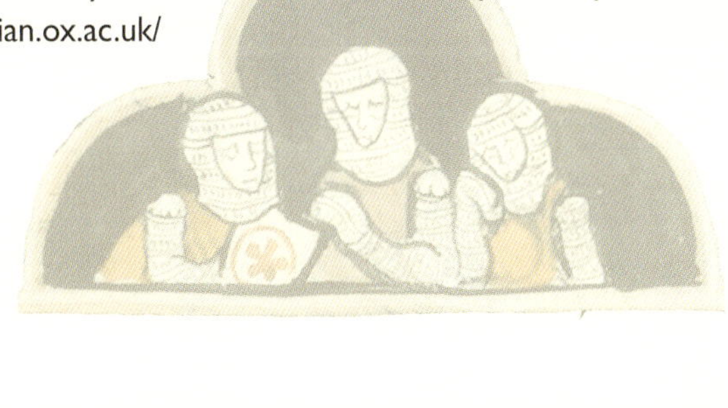

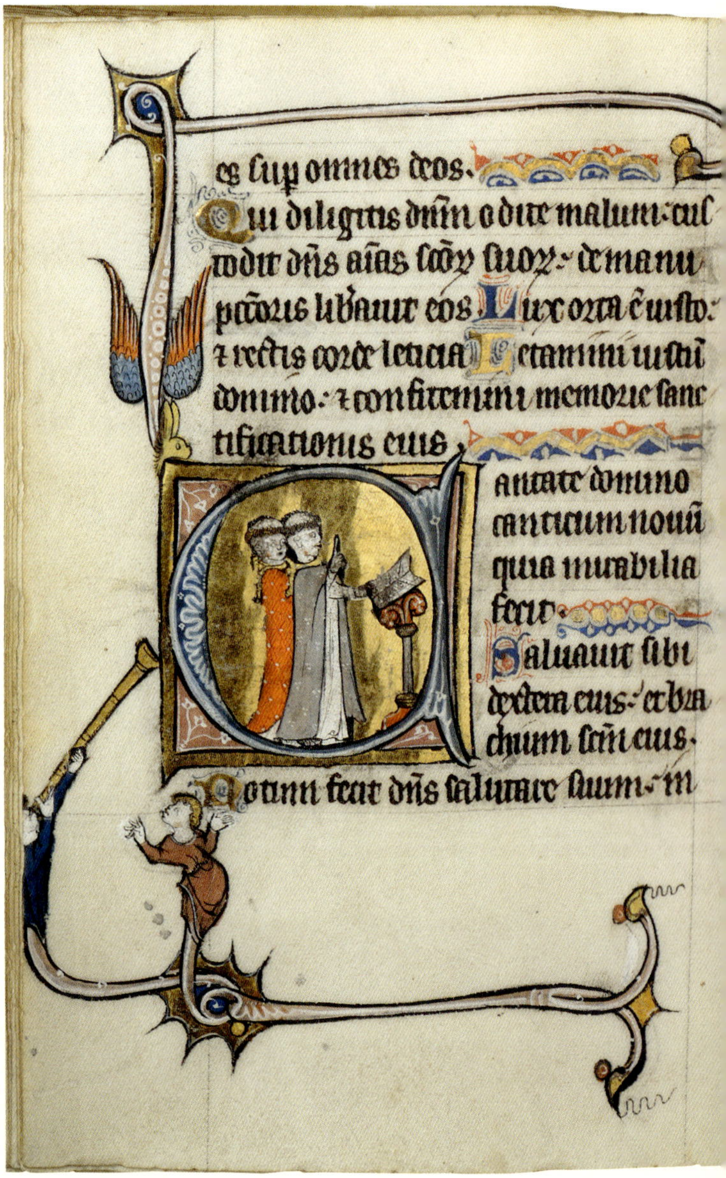

f. 208v, Monks Singing before an Open Book on a Lectern, Figures Playing Music in the Margin

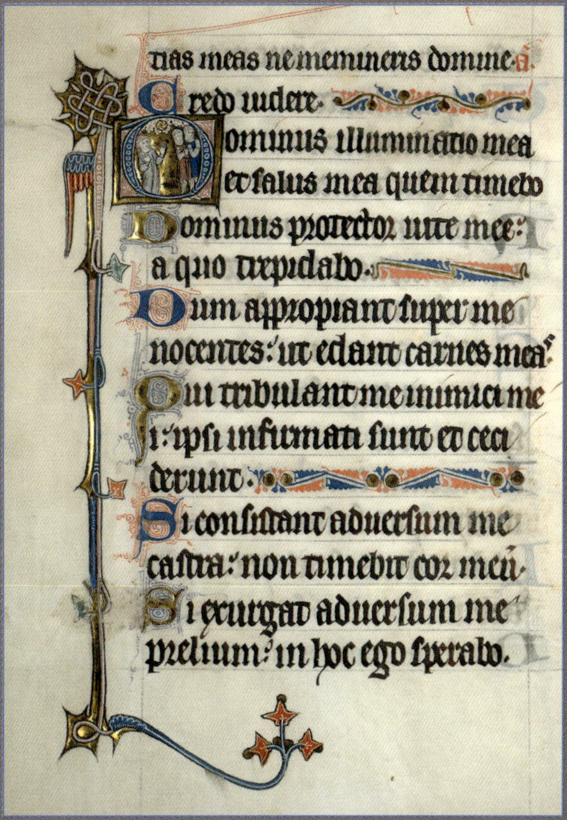

Cambrai, MM, MS. 87,
Book of Hours, f. 128v, Veiled Woman before Two Soldiers

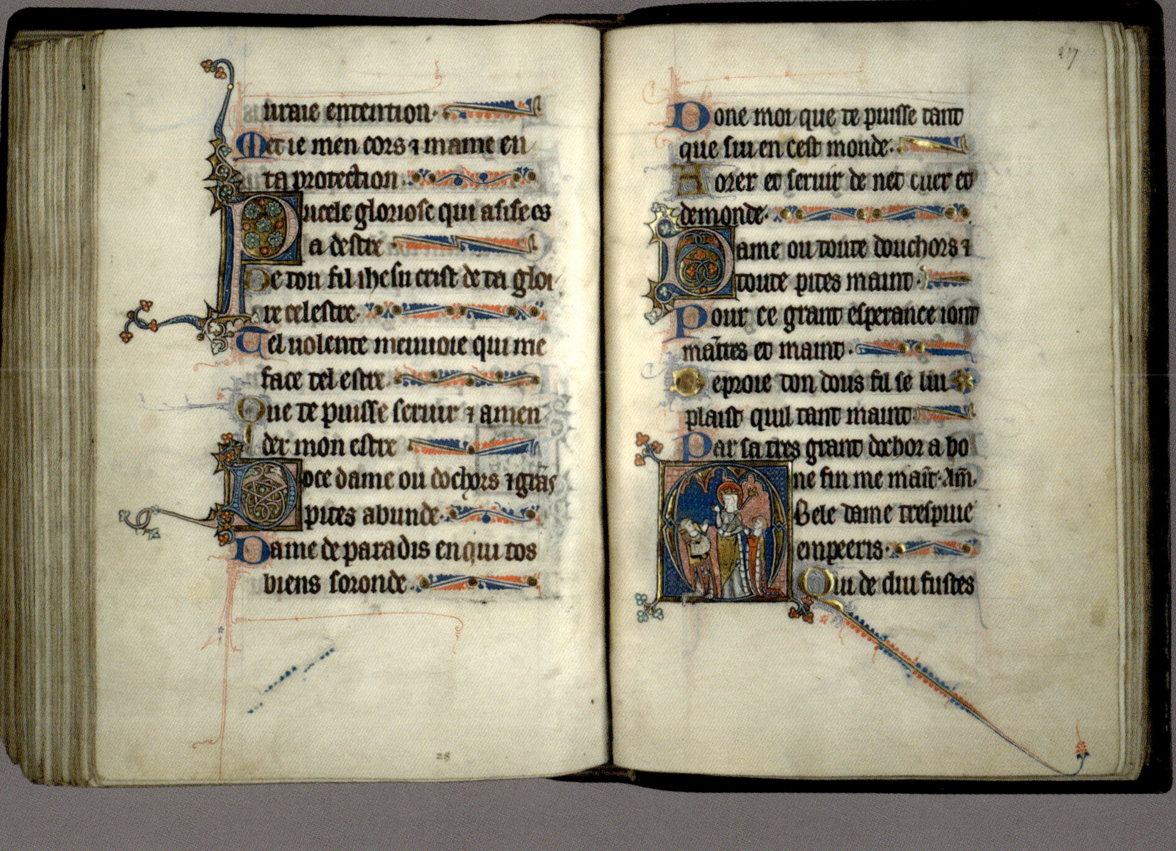

Cambrai, MM, MS. 87, Book of Hours, ff. 216v-217, Donors Kneeling before the Crowned Virgin

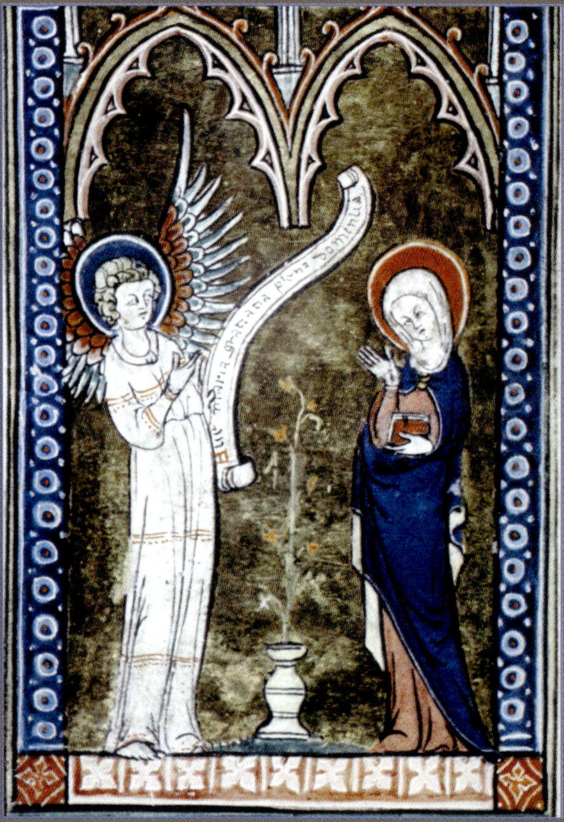

Oxford, Bodleian Library, MS Laud. 84, Psalter, f. 19, Annunciation

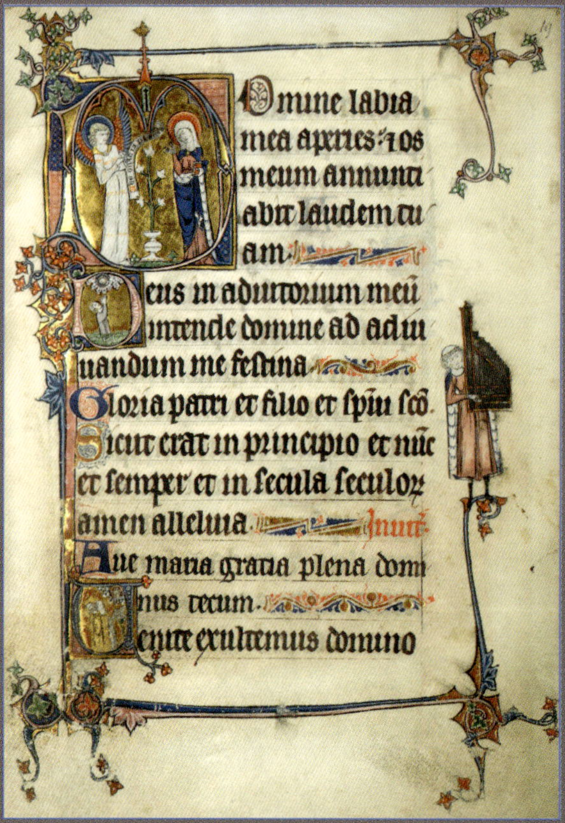

Cambrai, MM, MS. 87, Book of Hours, f. 19, Annunciation, Figure Playing an Instrument

Facing page, f. 7, Annunciation

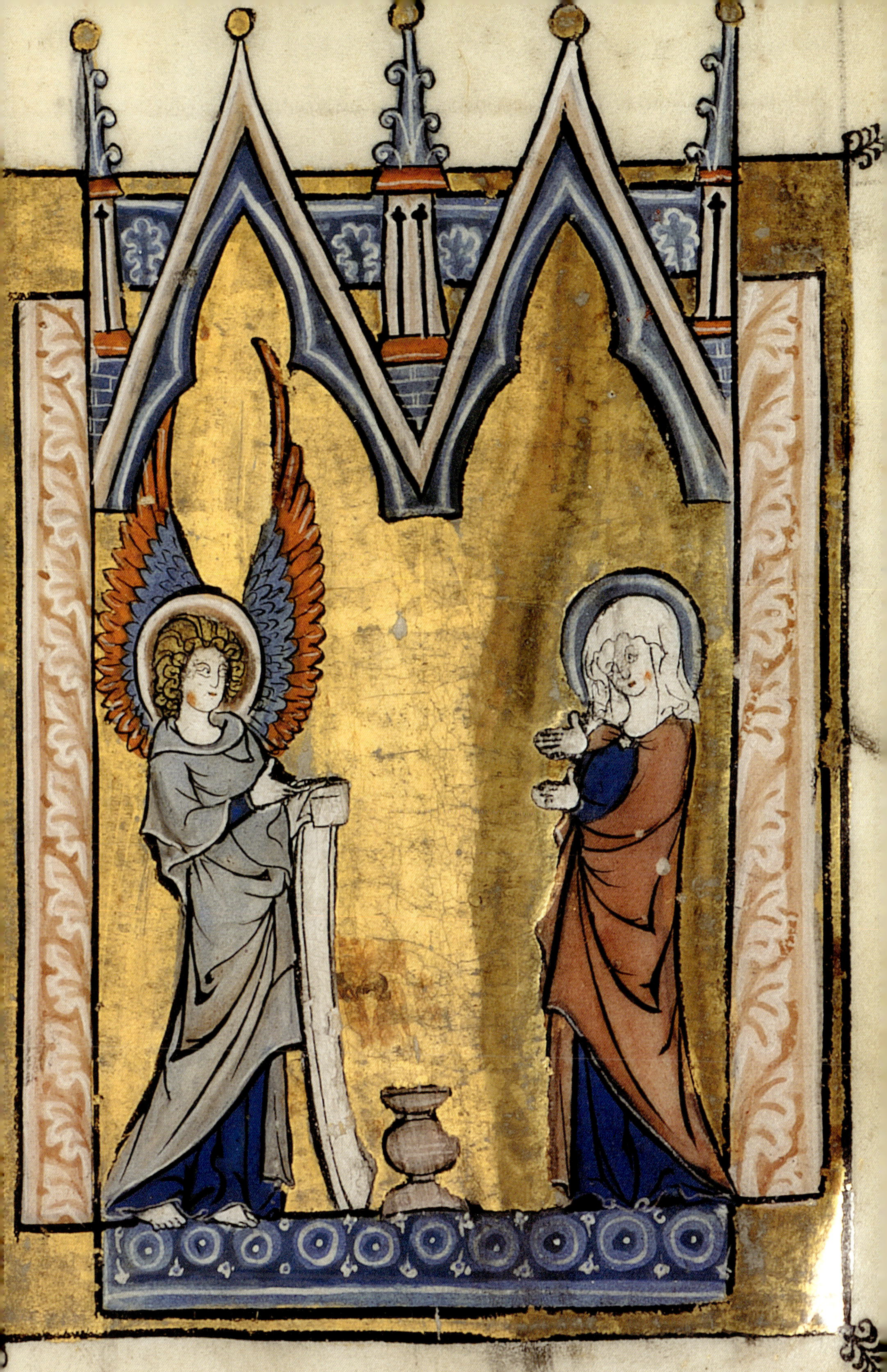

lorum. conuerte me iugiter
ac tuere per uictoriam mar
tirum. guberna me p fidem
confessorum. salua me per
deprecationem uirginum.
subueni michi semper 7 par
ce per intercessioné omni
um sanctorum qui tibi pla
cuerunt ab initio mundi.
Oret pro me sanctus abel
qui primus coronatus est
martirio. poscat pro me
sanctus enoch qui ambula
uit coram te et translatus
est de mundo. Interueniat
pro me beatus noe qué ser
uasti in diluuio propter in

3

Prayerbook of Giangaleazzo Visconti and Francesco Sforza

In Latin, illuminated manuscript on parchment
Italy, Pavia or Milan, c. 1389-1395 and c. 1455
Decorated borders and initials by Pietro da Pavia; added borders by Belbello da Pavia

This is an important manuscript both historically and stylistically. Although not a Book of Hours *per se*, this Prayerbook is nonetheless a private devotional book made for the *Signore* of Milan, Giangaleazzo Visconti (1351-1402). Promoted first Duke of Milan by the Holy Roman Emperor Wenceslaus in 1395, Giangaleazzo was the great founding patron of the Certosa di Pavia, also completing the Visconti Castle at Pavia and further contributing to work on the Duomo of Milan. His sudden rise to absolute power was one of the sensations of medieval Italy. On the verge of occupying Florence and Umbria, Giangaleazzo died suddenly in 1492, leaving his famous library ... and this elegant little Prayerbook. The latter was subsequently passed on to Francesco Sforza (1401-1466), who had wed in 1441 Bianca Maria Visconti, grand-daughter of Giangaleazzo Visconti, daughter of Filippo Maria Visconti. When the Duke Filippo Maria died, Francesco Sforza usurped the dukedom, and inherited the present book to which he added his personal emblems.

Destined for individual prayer, Giangaleazzo's Prayerbook contains prayers attributed to Saints Ambrose and Augustine, illuminated by Fra Pietro da Pavia, an Augustinian monk from the monastery of San Pietro in Ciel d'Oro (active in the last quarter of the fourteenth century) and completed by Belbello da Pavia, one of the great names in Lombard book illumination (active in Lombardy and Veneto, c. 1430 to c. 1470). The manuscript does not figure in the 1426 inventory ordered by Filippo Maria Visconti which listed 988 codices in the library of the Visconti, suggesting that it was kept elsewhere with books and objects for private devotion (see Pellegrin, 1955, pp. 41-52; Sutton, 1993, p. 90; E. Welch, in Bollati, ed., p. 29).

The collection of books owned and increased by different members of the Visconti family, housed in the princely Castle at Pavia, has long fascinated both bibliographers and art historians alike. There have been a number of studies and monographs, including the important study by Pellegrin (1955) dedicated

Facing page, f. 2, Text-page, illuminated by Belbello da Pavia, border with Sforza emblems

to the Visconti library at Pavia. However, as K. Sutton rightly underscores, it appears that Giangaleazzo Visconti certainly possessed one of the largest princely libraries of the Middle Ages, but that his additions were largely the result of purchases and confiscation of books belonging to other collectors. It seems that Giangaleazzo himself commissioned very few actual codices which contain his arms. Amongst the manuscripts certainly commissioned by him and that contain his arms in the original decoration (there are eight codices listed in Sutton, 1993, pp. 90 and 92), there are only two, perhaps three, codices that can actually be considered to be made for his own private use. These are the famous Visconti Hours, the present Giangaleazzo Visconti Prayerbook, and perhaps the Isabella Hours in the Hague (Koninklijke Bibliotheek, Ms. 76.F.6; Manzari, 2012; and König, 2012, pp. 18-27).; the other codices with his arms are actually manuscripts copied to be offered as gifts to Milanese religious foundations (see Sutton, 1993, p. 90).

The Visconti Hours, or *Offiziolo Visconteo*, is one of the most famous codices in the Biblioteca Nazionale in Florence (Florence, BN, Banco Rari 397 and MS Laudau Finaly 22; the two volumes were reunited in 1959). Made for Giangaleazzo Visconti, the two volumes were decorated first by Giovannino and Salmone dei Grassi and continued by Belbello da Pavia who took over the decoration of the second volume (and finished the first) in the 1430s during the reign of Gianaleazzo's son Filippo Maria. This second campaign was completed by Belbello da Pavia in a style markedly different from that of Giovannino dei Grassi (see the latest scholarship, Bollati, ed., 2003).

The present manuscript commissioned for and by Giangaleazzo Visconti contains a number of heraldic and emblematic elements that confirm his patronage and original ownership. The opening initial of the manuscript (f. 1) encloses a burnished gold sun with eight rays (*radia magna*) with at its center a small white dove carrying a scroll with the French motto "a bon droit." This is the device that Giangaleazzo used thoughout his life. It is probable that the missing leaf at the beginning of the Prayers attributed to Augustine contained the same heraldic emblems (wanting between ff. 64-65). The motto "a bon droyt" is repeated on small scrolls mounted on a burnished gold staff, up to fourteen times (f. 12v): at the bottom of this same leaf once figured the "radia magna" (the *radia magna* and dove also found on f. 43v in the infill of the decorated initial). The Visconti arms (viper shields or *biscia* escutcheons) with a silver shield emblazoned with the *biscia*, a red baby swallowed by a large blue viper, are found in the lower margin of f. 116. The presence of these unquartered arms allows for a dating before 1395 for this Prayerbook, since that year Charles VI of France had granted the right to quarter the Visconti arms with the fleur-de-lys of France (Sutton, 1993, p. 93). Also, although partially effaced, one can still clearly make out the cheetah with a red collar (leopard?) in the lower margin of the first leaf, another personal emblem of Giangaleazzo (see F. Manzari, in Bollati, ed., 2003, p. 153: "Il leopardo con il collare rosso compare nei libri sicuramente commissionati da Gian Galeazzo: nell'Offiziolo, nell'Messale per l'Incoronazione e anche nel Libro di preghiere Fogg").

When the manuscript was passed on the Francesco Sforza, after his wedding to Bianca Maria Visconti, other personalizing elements were added. These include the cheetah with the red collar, an emblem adopted by descendants and appearing in the later Breviary of Bianca Maria Visconti (Chambéry, BM, MS 4). Francesco's ownership is resolutely asserted on two leaves (ff. 2 and 4): as an outward sign of legitimacy and to lend a sense of continuity to Milan's Visconti past, Franceso adopted many of the heraldic devices of his wife's family, including the the crowned black "nodo visconteo" emblem with the palm and laurel (found in white in Florence, BN, MS Landau Finaly 22, f. 62v; reproduced in Welch, in Bollati ed., 2003, p. 21, fig. 6). He also added unambiguous Sforza emblems such as the three intertwined diamond rings, two horse bits, and a "scopetto" – a type of brush – accompanied with the Sforza motto "merito et tempore" (f. 2).

Patronage also must account for the idiosyncratic textual content of our Visconti-Sforza Prayerbook, including prayers attributed (sometimes erroneously) to the Church Fathers Ambrose and Augustine. The book is divided into two sections of prayers, with forty-three prayers attributed to Ambrose and twenty-four to Augustine. Indeed both Ambrose (the revered patron saint of Milan) and Augustine of Hippo were venerated locally and held an important place for the Milanese. Ambrose was Bishop of Milan at the time of Augustine's conversion. Even in images, the two saints were frequently associated, and there are even codices directly related to the Visconti that also privilege the association of the two saintly men (for instance, see Modena, Biblioteca Estense e Universitaria, MS Lat. 842, *Libro d'ore di Balzarrino*, f. 18v, and again f. 171, with two historiated initials portraying the two saints). The patron of the Modena

Hours was Balzarrino da Pusterla, cavaliere at the service of Bernabò Visconti and who was wed to Beatricina Visconti in 1405 (see F. Manzari, in Bollati, ed., 2003, pp. 107-109, fig. 52 and 54; see Sutton, 1989, p. 139; Zambrelli, 1989, pp. 51-56). There are two instances in the Visconti Hours itself where Ambrose and Augustine are represented, in the initial T introducing the *Te Deum*, a hymn frequently believed to have been composed by Saints Ambrose and Augustine (Florence, BN, Banco Rari 397, f. 148v; see Meiss and Kirsch, 1972, BR 148v) and again in a recurring *Te Deum* initial (Florence, BN, MS Laudau Finaly 22, f. 17; see Meiss and Kirsch, 1972, LF 17). Both leaves were painted during the Giovannino dei Grassi fourteenth-century phase of illumination, hence under Giangaleazzo's patronage. Thus, for Giangaleazzo, it was quite natural to select prayers from the works of Ambrose and Augustine for his personal prayerbook. Giangaleazzo Visconti is also credited with the building of the Duomo in Milan, built on top of former churches and baptisteries, where Saint Augustine was baptized by Saint Ambrose: he must have fostered a particular veneration for the pair of saints. In addition, we know that Giangaleazzo Visconti owned a very precious manuscript, the oldest in fact in his library, of Sermons by Augustine, Ambrose and Jerome (now Paris, BnF, MS lat. 3790, first half of the twelfth century; see Pellegrin, 1955, p. 1, item 517; see also, K. Sutton, 1993, p. 96, note 39: "The library did include the sermons of Saints Ambrose and Augustine and several books containing prayers but none with an incipit or explicit that correspond with the prayers here"). Finally, Giangaleazzo apparently fostered sympathy towards the Augustinians as suggested by the entries in his will in their favor (see Welch, in Bollati, ed., 2003, p. 29) and the ties he developed with the monks of San Pietro in Ciel d'Oro. The fact that Pietro da Pavia, the main illuminator of this Prayerbook, was an Augustinian is most certainly not fortuitous.

This Prayerbook is delicately decorated and adorned, in keeping with the International Gothic Style practiced in Lombardy in the last quarter of the Trecento and first half of the Quattrocento. The ornamentation of this book is simplified and without any miniatures or historiated initials. Each prayer opens with a large initial that has staves of blue, pink or red with white decoration and a flower or foliage spray in the infill painted against a ground of burnished gold, and each page with the beginning of a prayer is decorated with a full-page border (see Sutton, 1993, p. 92). The same author described the effect as one of "scintillating prettiness" (Sutton, 1993, p. 93). The artist of the greater part

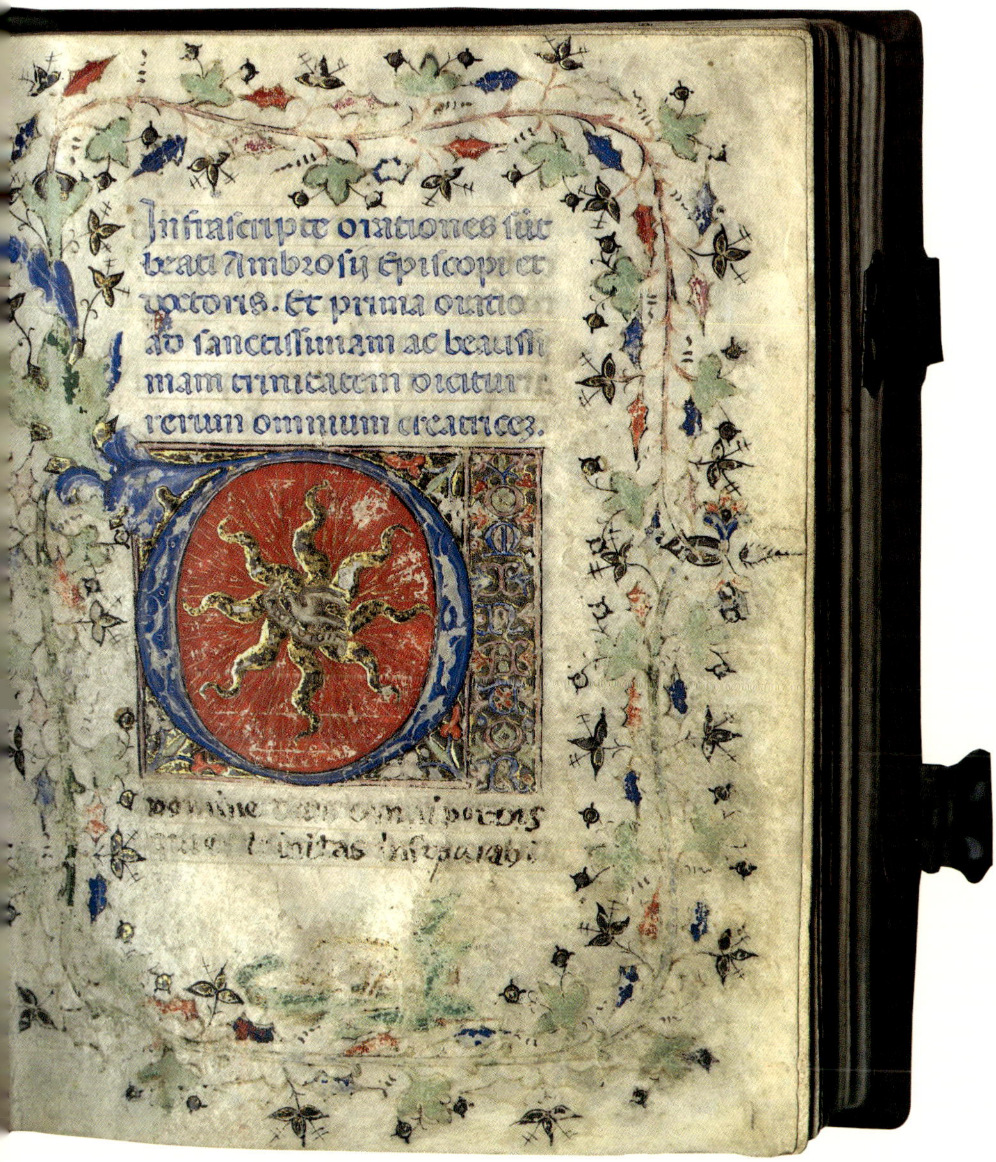

f. 1, Opening leaf, illuminated by Pietro da Pavia, border and initial D with Visconti emblem of radiating sun (raza) and dove; cheetah, in the lower margin, emblem of Giangaleazzo Visconti

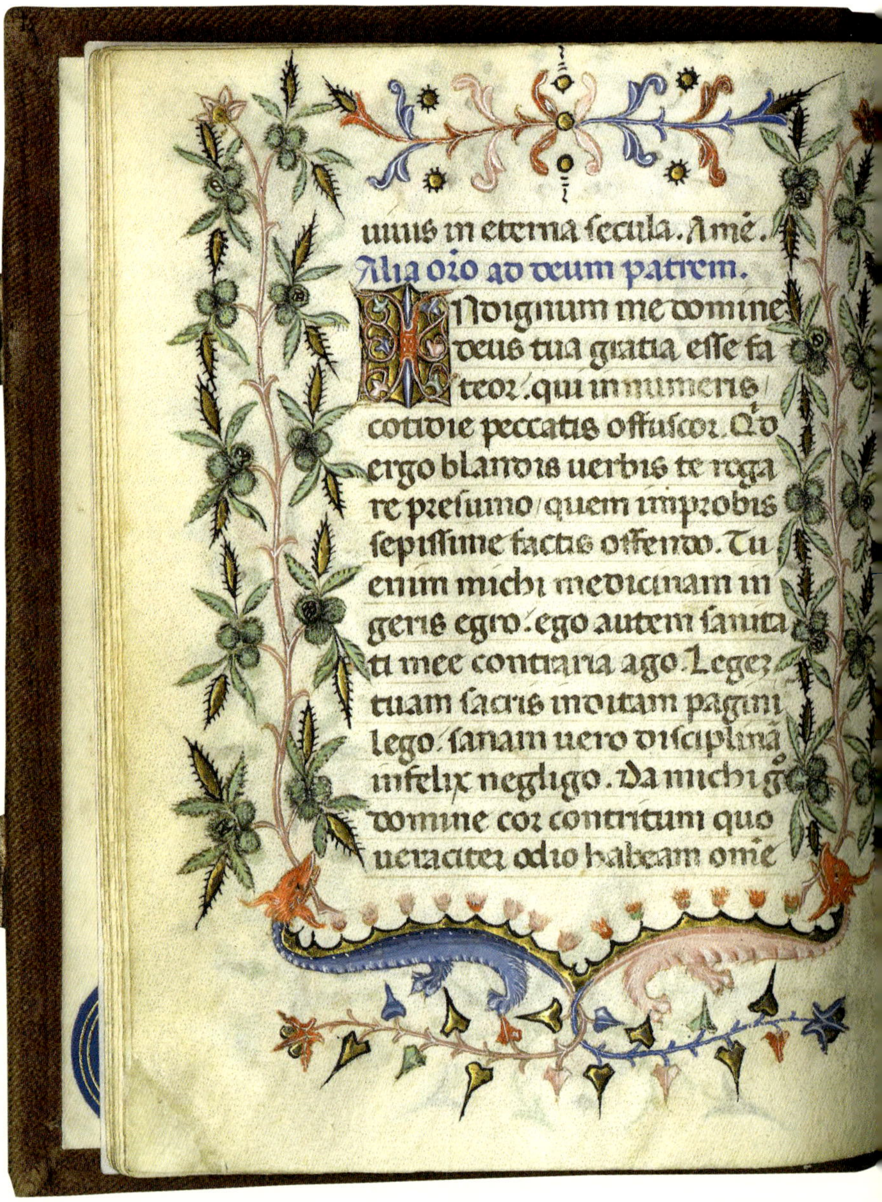
uiuis in eterna secula. Amē.
Alia orō ad deum patrem.
[I]ndignum me domine
deus tua gratia esse fa
teor. qui innumeris
cotidie peccatis offuscor. Quo
ergo blandis uerbis te roga
re presumo quem improbis
sepissime factis offendo. Tu
enim michi medicinam in
geris egro. ego autem sanita
ti mee contraria ago. Lege
tuam sacris inditam pagini
lego. sanam uero disciplinā
infelix negligo. Da michi q
domine cor contritum quo
ueraciter odio habeam omē

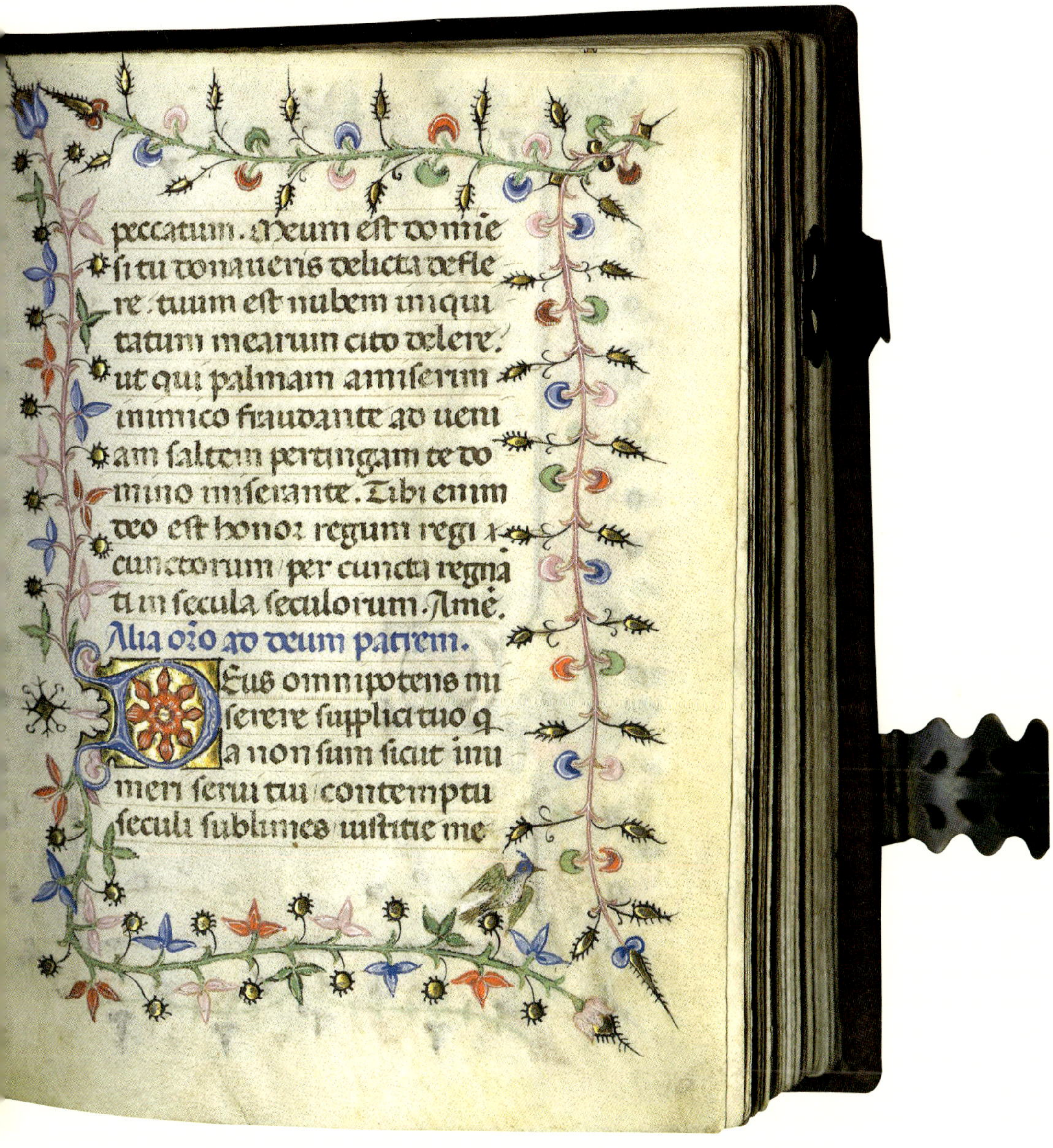
peccatum. Meum est domine
si tu donaueris delicta defle
re: tuum est nubem iniqui
tatum mearum cito delere.
ut qui palmam amiserim
inimico fraudante ad ueni
am saltem pertingam te do
mino miserante. Tibi enim
deo est honor regum regi et
cunctorum per cuncta regna
ti in secula seculorum. Amen.
Alia oro ad deum patrem.
Deus omnipotens mi
serere supplici tuo q
a non sum sicut inu
men serui tui contemptu
seculi sublimes iustitie me

ff. 9v-10, Illuminated by Pietro da Pavia, borders and decorated initials

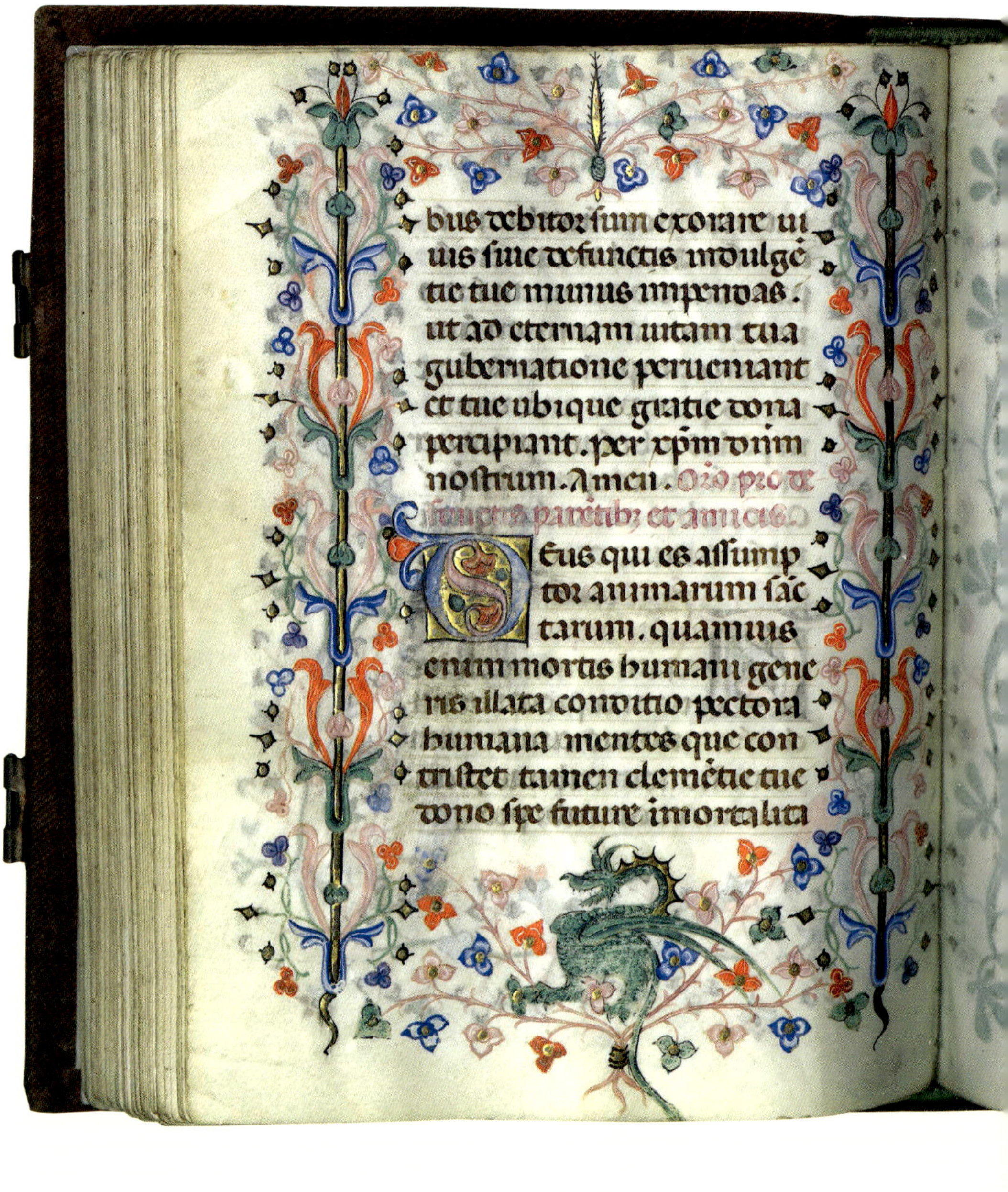

f. 56v, Illuminated by Pietro da Pavia, border and decorated initial

of the decorated borders and initials is Pietro da Pavia, an Augustinian hermit and the favorite illuminator of Giangaleazzo's chancellor Pasquino Capelli. The borders here are very close to those found in a Pliny, *Naturalis Historia* (Milano, Bibl. Ambrosiana, MS E. 24. inf.), illuminated by Pietro da Pavia for Pasquino Capelli and datable to circa 1389 (see Sutton, 1993, p. 93; Bollati, 2003, p. 140). It is in this manuscript that one finds also a dated self-portrait of the illuminator (1389). The borders of the Giangaleazzo Prayerbook also contain a variety of flowers; birds, such as a goldfinch (f. 17v), jay (ff. 51 and 102), swallow (f. 75v), and egret (f. 58v); dragons, and insects. For instance, a very delicate dragonfly is painted in the upper margin of f. 14v, reused from the same motif in the Pliny, in the opening leaf of the chapter "On insects" (see Sutton, 1993, p. 93). Also noteworthy, the mise-en-page and hierarchy in the decoration of the New York Prayerbook (Pierpont Morgan Library, MS M 944) and of the present Giangaleazzo Prayerbook are very close and sometimes even strikingly similar (see Castelfranchi Vegas, 1996, fig. 7-8). Illuminated circa 1405, the Morgan Prayerbook is attributed to Michelino da Besozzo, an artist trained by Pietro da Pavia and active in the first part of his career in Pavia, tied to the same convent of San Pietri in Ciel d'Oro (see F. Lollini, in Bollati, 2004, pp. 764-765). The present Prayerbook (painted before in the Trecento) and the Morgan Prayerbook (painted at the start of the Quattrocento) present common decorative and floral elements, underscoring the ties between Pietro da Pavia and Michelino da Besozzo, both active in Pavia.

The style of the second illuminator of the book, the celebrated Belbello da Pavia, stands out in marked opposition to the delicacy and softness of Pietro da Pavia. Belbello's emphatic manner and strong color range, the ample place secured for vigorous heraldic emblems, his strong tones of green, blue and purple, almost metallic colors contrast with the soft tones of Pietro da Pavia. It is interesting to recognize Belbello once again as an artist called upon to "finish," as in the Visconti Hours, with a second campaign of illumination in the 1430s attributed to him; or to "augment" previous codices, for example the Breviary of Marie de Savoie (Chambéry, BM, MS 4), a Franciscan Breviary illuminated for Marie de Savoie, second wife of Filippo Maria Visconti (married in 1428), largely illuminated by the Master of the Vitae Imperatorum and his workshop-collaborators in the 1430s, but showing the participation of Belbello da Pavia for a certain number of leaves (ff. 435-438v; see A. Ritz, in Heid-Guillaume and Ritz, 1998, p. 37 and p. 38; see also A. Heitz, Thesis, 2007). In the our

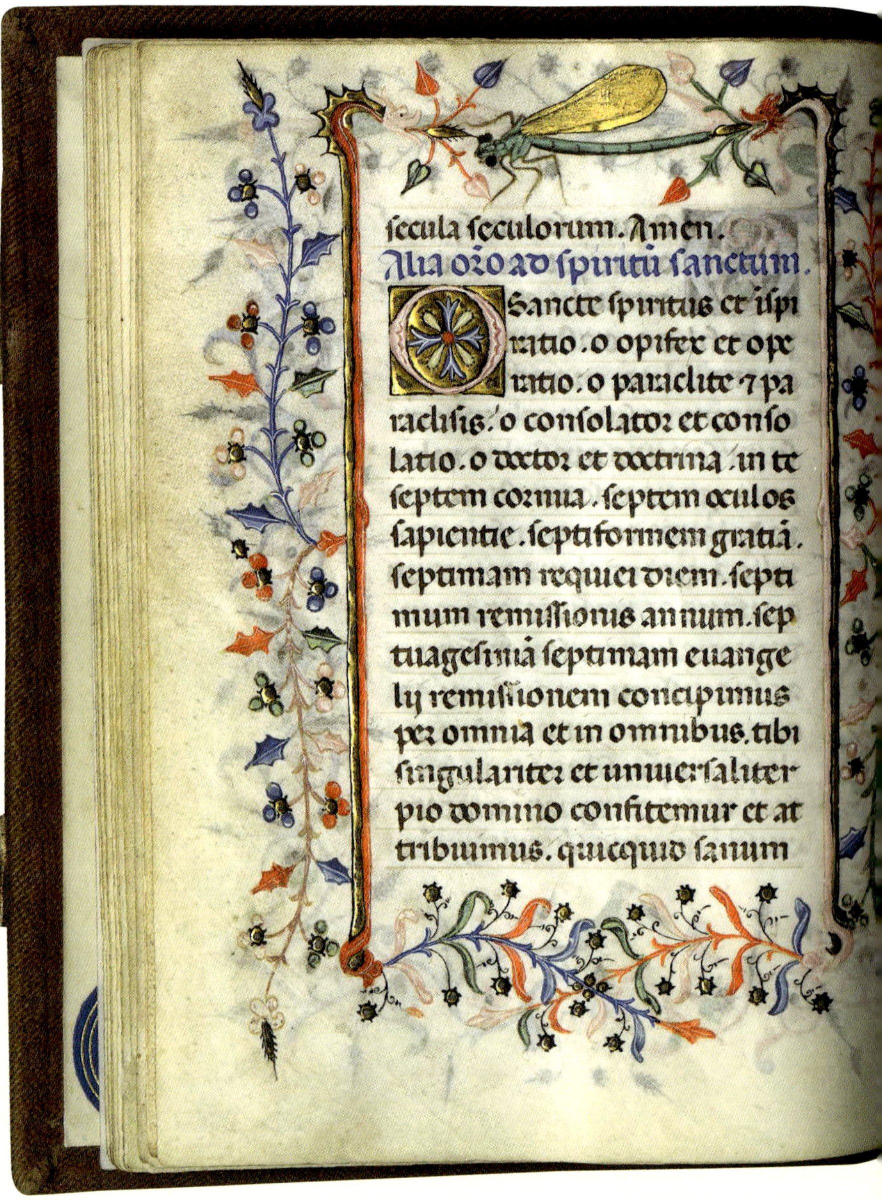
secula seculorum. Amen.
Alia orō ad spiritū sanctum.
O Sancte spiritus et īspi
ratio. o opifex et ope
ratio. o paraclite 7 pa
raclisis. o consolator et conso
latio. o doctor et doctrina. in te
septem cornua. septem oculos
sapientie. septiformem gratiā.
septimam requiei diem. septi
mum remissionis annum. sep
tuagesimā septimam euange
lij remissionem concipimus
per omnia et in omnibus. tibi
singulariter et uniuersaliter
pio domino confitemur et at
tribuimus. quicquid sanum

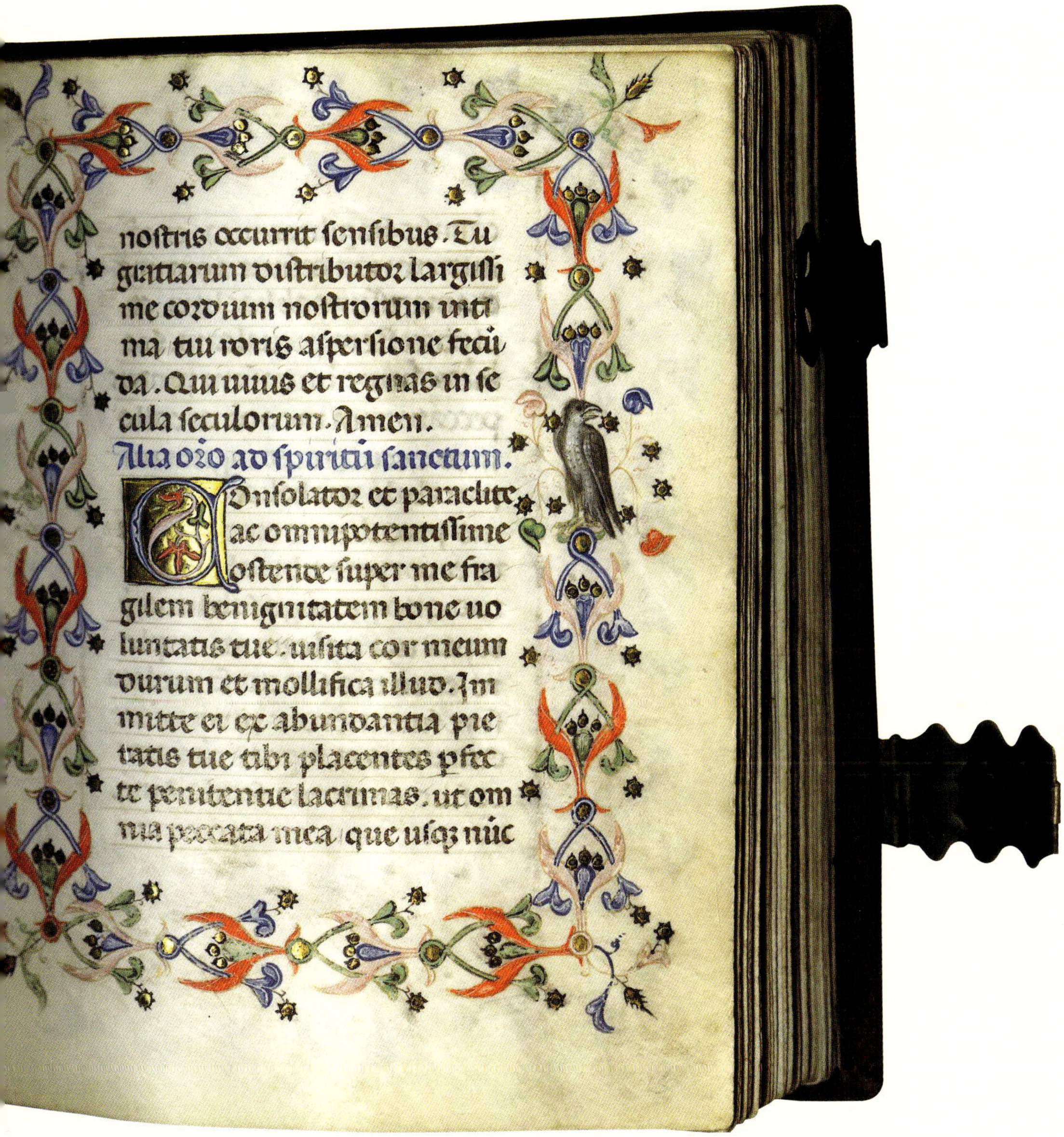

ff. 14v-15, Illuminated by Pietro da Pavia, borders and decorated initials

Visconti-Sforza Prayerbook, Belbello da Pavia was once again called upon to "add to" a previously illuminated codex for its new owner, Francesco da Sforza. The keen interest in beasts and birds reflects the movement towards naturalism initiated in the northern Italian centers around the year 1400: note, the very elegant birds on f. 4 painted by Belbello da Pavia.

Recent research by F. Manzari has embarked on outlining a "typology of devotional instruments in Trecento Lombardy" (Manzari, in Bollati, 2003, pp. 53-217; Manzari, 2012). The Prayerbook of Giangaleazzo belongs to a newly emerging category of devotional books used for daily devotions. It is related to a number of other Prayerbooks that are not Horae per se, and the question of the status of these books is subject to some debate. Are they incomplete Horae, portions or fragments of larger Horae, or another type of devotional book? The Morgan Prayerbook (Pierpont Morgan Library, MS M. 944), whose miniatures and decoration are attributed to Michelino di Besozzo, poses similar problems. The relation between text and image in the Morgan Prayerbook has been studied by MacDonald (1991), who has identified all the prayers. It would be important to identify properly all the prayers included in our Visconti-Sforza Prayerbook, which turn out to be not only by Augustine and Ambrose, but also by Anselm (and perhaps other authors, see Wilmart, 1932); they were clearly carefully chosen for a book that was tailormade for the magnificent Signore of Milan, soon to be Duke, and decorated with "scintillating prettiness."

PHYSICAL DESCRIPTION: 118 ff., preceded and followed by a single modern parchment flyleaf, wanting a leaf between ff. 64-65 (collation: i-v^{10}, vi^{8} (10-2, wanting a bifolium, with i and x likely cancelled blanks), vii^{4}, viii^{2}, ix^{5} (6-1, missing i), x-xiii^{10}, xiv^{8}), written in a fine rounded Gothic script in brown ink, on up to 17 lines per page, rubrics in blue and/or pale red ink, paragraph marks in pale red, list of contents in blue, decorated initials painted in colors and highlighted in white on burnished gold grounds with floral infills, large 9-line high opening initial D in blue with white tracery on a burnished ground, with a radiating sun and dove emblem in the infill, the word "[D]ominus" spelled out vertically, borders with a wide variety of colorful sprays of flowers, leaves and fruit, interspersed with birds and beasts, insects and dragons (none duplicates another), colors of the border always clear and light, burnished gold used for leaves or as disks scattered though the sprays, two leaves with borders painted by a different artist (ff. 2 and 4), a number of annotations in the margin in brown ink (15th c.), some pen trials or later drawings imitating the decorated original borders. Modern binding of brown suede over wooden boards, back sewn on 4 raised bands, brass clasps and catchplates, gilt edges (Bound in England by James Brockman), manuscript fitted in a box made to measure (Some leaves with ink fading; opening leaf rubbed; the manuscript was rebound in 1991 and the two lists of contents copied in blue which had been misbound within the prayers of St. Ambrose, were placed between the sections of prayers. The original intention must have been for each to have preceded the relevant section). Dimensions 150 x 110 mm.

TEXT: ff. 1-58v, Prayers of Saint Ambrose, rubric, in blue, *Infrascripte orationes sunt beati Ambrosii episcopi et doctoris. Et prima oratio ad sanctissimam ac beatissimam trinitatem dicitur rerum omnium creaticem*; incipit, "Dominator domine deus..."; following rubrics (in blue), *Alia oratio ad sanctam trinitatem* (f. 5), incipit, "Summa et incomprehensibilis natura..." (f. 5v); *Alia oratio as sanctam trinitatem* (f. 9v), incipit, "Quicquid ego indignus miser..." (f. 9v); last rubric and prayer (in red), *Oratio ad castitatem impetrandam* (f. 57v), incipit, "Rex virginum amator castitatis..."; explicit, "[...] sanctorum angelorum tuorum in circuitu me o qui vivis et regnas in secula seculorum amen. *Explicit orationes beati Ambrosii episcopi et confessoris*"; ff. 59-61v, Table of prayers of Saint Ambrose (43) with incipits, copied in blue, "Infrascripti tituli orationum beati ambrosii episcopi..."; ff. 62-62v, blank leaves; ff. 63-64v, Table of prayers of Saint Augustine (24) with incipits, copied in blue, "Infrascripti tituli orationum beati Augustini episcopi..."; ff. 65-118v, Prayers of Saint Augustine (wanting beginning); incipit, "[...] - tas locorum angustat nec receptacula..."; first rubric (in blue), *Oratio ad deum patrem*, incipit, "Ad te domine lacrimabiliter..."; last rubric (in blue) *Oratio impetrandi a deo omne bonum ac virtutem*, incipit, "Deus patrem omnipotens et bone domine..."; explicit, "[...] meum plenum sit in te quod es vita eterna. Amen. *Expliciunt orationes beati Augustini episcopi et confessoris*"; added prayer in a cursive contemporary or near-contemporary hand, in brown ink: "Domine iesu christe mundi redemptor quod spineam coronam in capite dignatis...";

ILLUSTRATION: The decorated initials and full-page borders by Pietro da Pavia are on ff. 1, 5v, 9, 9v, 10, 10v, 11, 12v, 14, 14v, 15, 16, 16v, 17, 17v, 18, 19, 20, 21, 22, 33v, 35, 36, 37, 37v, 41v, 43v, 48v, 49v, 50, 51, 51v, 52v, 53, 53v, 54v, 55, 56, 56v, 57v, 65v, 66v, 68v, 72v, 75v, 77v, 80v, 87, 87v, 89, 94, 97, 99, 100, 101v, 102, 103, 104, 109, 116, 117. - The full-page borders with the emblems of Francesco Sforza painted by Belbello da Pavia are on ff. 2 and 4.

OWNERSHIP: 1. Copied and illuminated for Giangaleazzo Visconti, Signore of Milan, before he took the title of Duke of Milan. The scribe is not identified, but the decorated borders and initials were painted by Fra Pietro da Pavia (active in Pavia, c. 1385-1412). - 2. Subsequently owned by Francesco Sforza with two leaves painted by Belbello da Pavia (active in Lombardy from 1425 to the 1470s). The illumination added by Belbello (ff. 2 and 4) contribute to the personalization of the book, with added arms and emblems tied to the Sforza clan. - 3. Some pentrials and marginal annotations in a 15th c. hand are found throughout. An added prayer is copied at the end of the Prayerbook, in Latin, also in a tight 15th c. hand. It is tempting to see here an addition made by someone in the entourage of Francesco Sforza, its owner in the second half of the 15th c.- 4. North American Private Collection.

LITERATURE: Published in Bollati et al., 2003, p. 28, pl. 10; pp. 139-141, pl. 76, and p. 153; p. 347; Bollati, 2004, [Pietro da Pavia], p. 865: "Un libro di preghiere appartenuto a Gian Galeazzo Visconti (collezione privata)"; Sutton, 1993, pp. 89-96; and Manzari, 2012. - Bollati, Milvia. *Il libro d'ore Visconti. Commentario al codice,* 2 vols., Modena, Panini, 2003. - Bollati, Milvia (ed.). *Dizionario biografico dei miniatori italiani. Secoli IX-XVI*, Milan, 2004. - Cadei, A. *Belbello miniatore lombardo, artisti del libro alla corte dei Visconti*, Bulzoni, 1976. - Castelfranchi Vegas, L. "La formazione e gli esordi di Michelino da Besozzo miniatore," in *Prospettiva* 83-84 (1996), pp. 116-127. - Heid-Guillame, C. and A. Ritz, *Manuscrits médiévaux de Chambéry*, Turnhout, Brepols, 1998 (on Chambéry, BM, MS

4, Bréviaire de Marie de Savoie, pp. 30-43). - Kirsh, E. W. *Five Illuminated Manuscripts of Giangaleazzo Visconti*, University Park and London, 1991. – König, Eberhard. *Devotion from Dawn to Dusk: The Office of the Virgin in Books of Hours in the Koninklijke Bibliotheek in The Hague*, Leiden, Primavera Pers, 2012; -MacDonald, K. "Et verbum caro factum est: The Prayer-book of Michelino da Besozzo," in *Medieval Texts and Images. Studies of Manuscripts from the Middle Ages*, ed. M. M. Manion and B.J. Muir, Sydney, 1991, pp. 201-206. – Manzari, Francesca. "Italian Books of Hours and Prayer Books in the Fourteenth Century," in *A New Look at Books of Hours*, eds. Sandra Hindman and James Marrow, Turnhout, Brepols/ London, Harvey Miller, 2012 (forthcoming). - Meiss, M. and E. W. Kirsch. *The Visconti Hours. National Library Florence*, New York, George Braziller, 1972. - Pellegrin, E. *La bibliothèque des Visconti et des Sforza, ducs de Milan, au XVe siècle*, Paris, 1955 (supplément, Florence and Paris, 1969). - Ritz-Guilbert, A. *Autour du Bréviaire de Marie de Savoie (Chambéry, Bibliothèque municipale, ms. 4): étude sur l'enluminure en Lombardie dans la première partie du XVe siècle* [Thesis], Lille, 2007. - Sutton, Kay. "Codici di lusso a Milano: gli esordi," in *Il Millennio Ambrosiano, ed. C. Bertelli, III. La nuova città, dal Commune alla Signoria*, Milano, 1989, pp. 110-139. - Sutton, Kay. "Giangaleazzo Visconti as Patron. A Prayer Book illuminated by Pietro da Pavia," Apollo, Feb. 1993, pp. 89-96. - Wilmart, A. Auteurs spirituels et textes dévôts du Moyen Age, Paris, 1932. - Zambrelli, C. "Balzerrino Pusterla, Beatrice Visconti e il Libro d'ore di Modena," in Quaderni Utinensi 7 (13/14), pp. 51-56.

ONLINE RESOURCES:

Francesca Manzari on Books of Hours in Italy
http://www.palaeographia.org/glm/glm.htm?art=manzari

Facsimile of the Visconti Hours
http://grandiopere.fcp.it/facsimili/il-libro-dore-visconti/

On Lombard illuminators including Pietro da Pavia, Michelino da Besozzo and Belbello da Pavia
http://www.storiadimilano.it/Arte/miniatori.htm

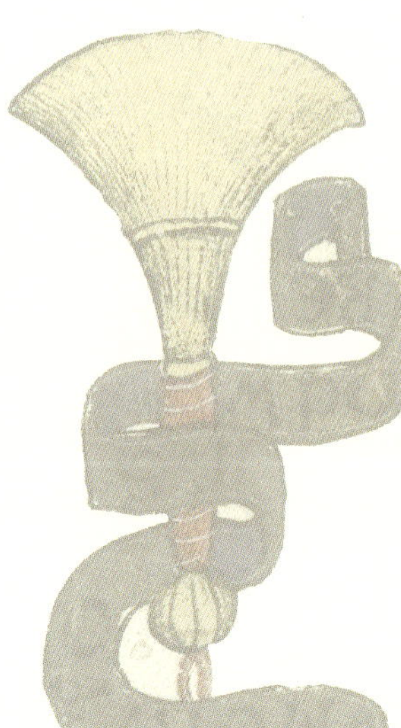

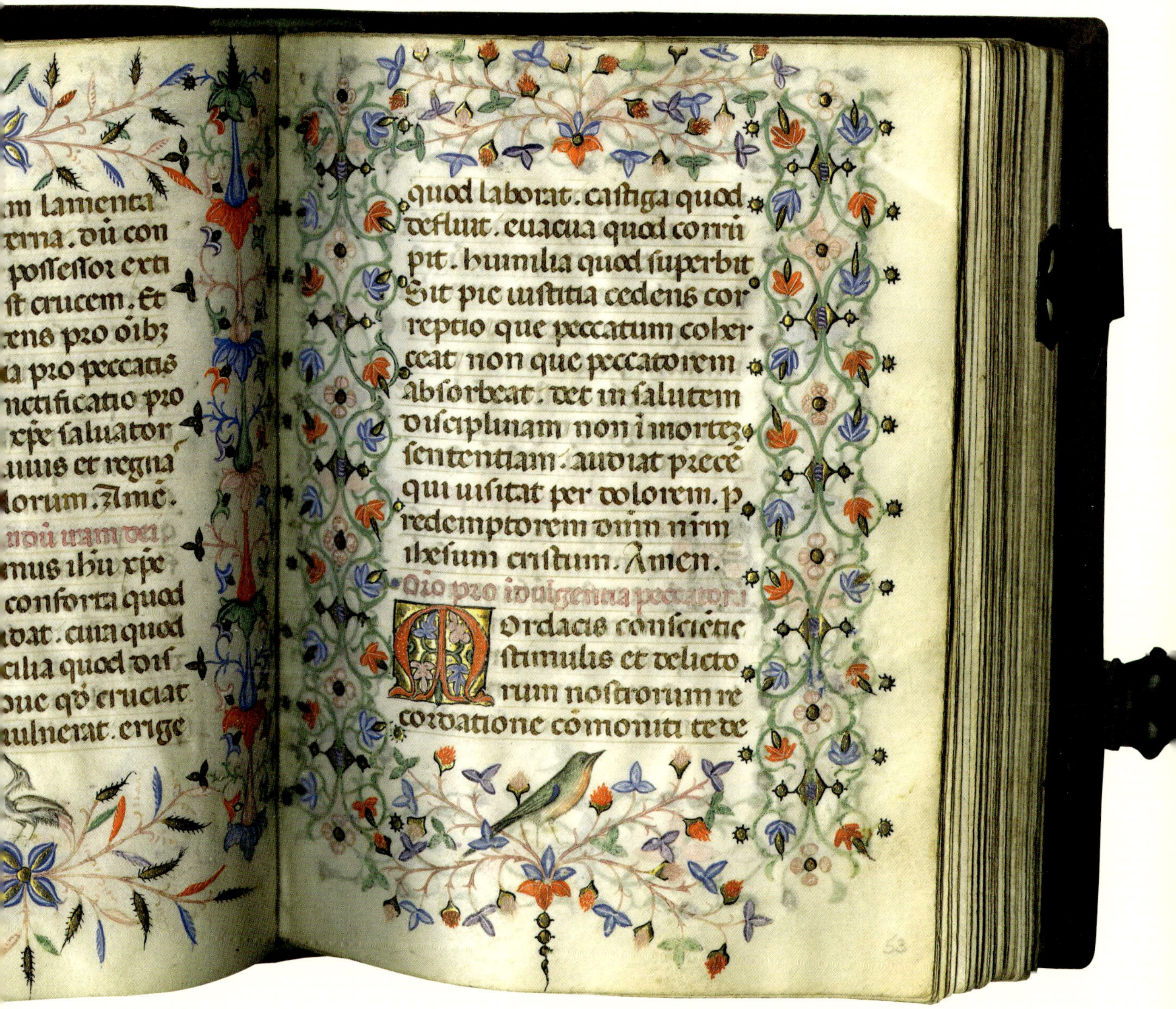

ff. 52v-53, Illuminated by Pietro da Pavia, borders and decorated initials

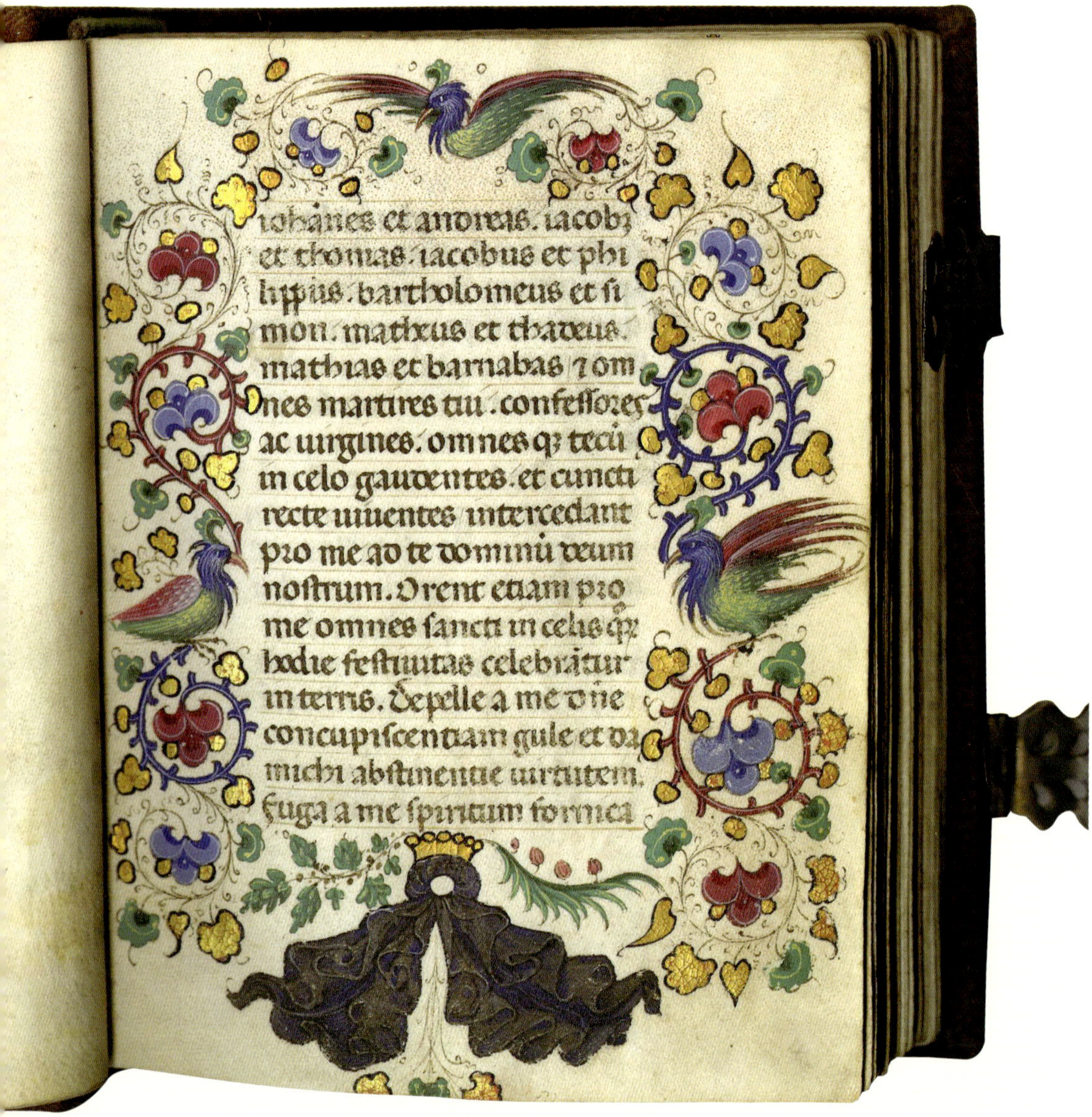
iohānes et andreas. iacobꝫ
et thomas. iacobus et phi
lippus. bartholomeus et si
mon. matheus et thadeus.
mathias et barnabas ⁊ om
nes martires tui. confessores
ac uirgines. omnes qꝫ tecū
in celo gaudentes. et cuncti
recte uiuentes intercedant
pro me ad te dominū deum
nostrum. Orent etiam pro
me omnes sancti in celis qꝫ
hodie festiuitas celebratur
in terris. Depelle a me dn̄e
concupiscentiam gule et da
michi abstinentie uirtutem.
Fuga a me spiritum fornica

f. 4, Text-page, illuminated by Belbello da Pavia, border with Visconti emblem of the crowned "nodo visconteo" (nodo in black) with palm and laurel (emblem adopted by Francesco Sforza)

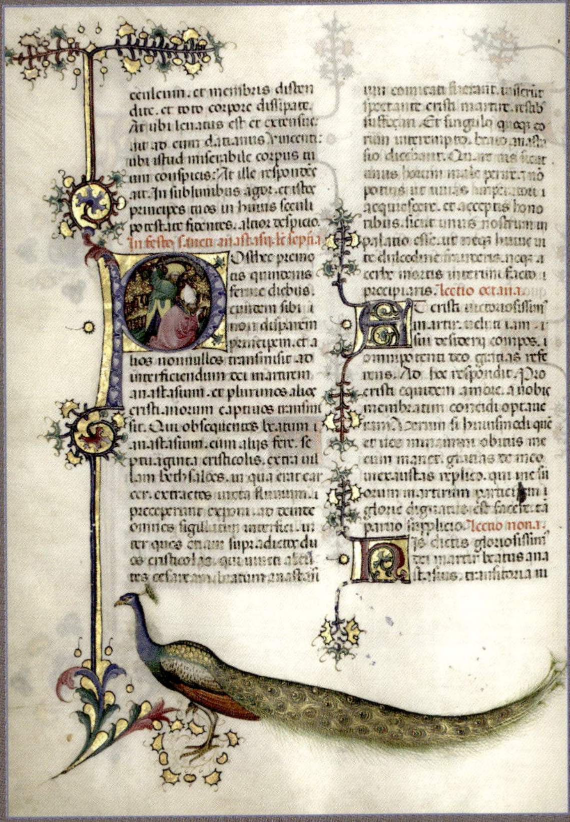

Chambéry, BM, MS 4, Breviary of Marie de Savoie, f. 436v, Initial P, Martyrdom of saint Anastasius (illuminated by Belbello da Pavia)

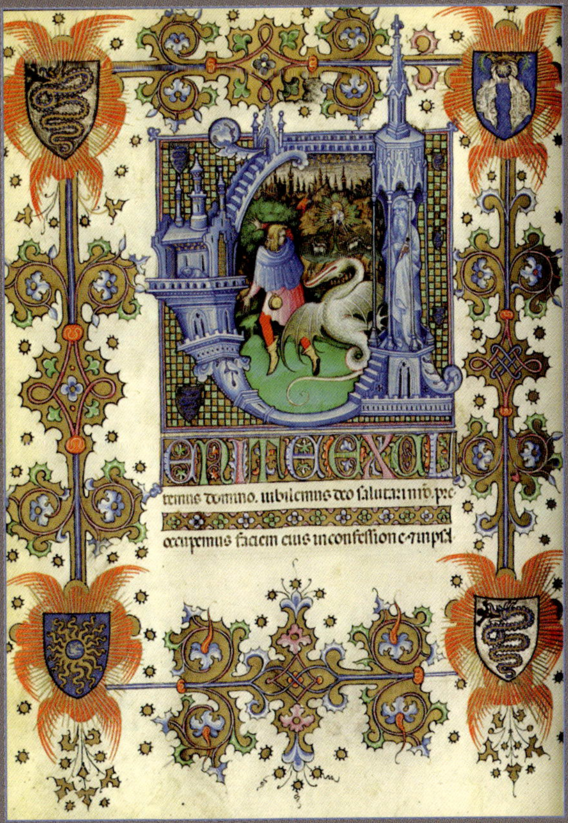

Florence, BN, MS Landau Finaly 22, Visconti Hours, f. 85v, Historiated Initial V, Rod of Moses Changed to a Serpent

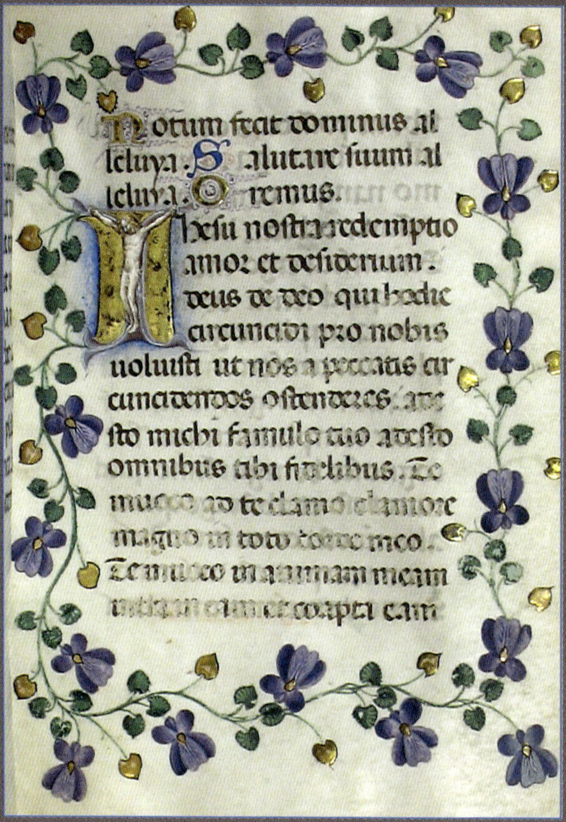
Notum fecit dominus al
leluya. Salutare suum al
leluya. Oremus.
Jhesu nostra redemptio
amor et desiderium.
deus de deo qui hodie
circumcidi pro nobis
voluisti ut nos a peccatis cir
cumcidendos ostenderes. pre
sto michi famulo tuo atque
omnibus tibi fidelibus. Te
invoco ad te clamo clamore
magno in toto corde meo.
Te invoco in animam meam

New York, Morgan Library and Museum, MS M. 944,
Prayerbook decorated by Michelino da Besozzo, f. 5

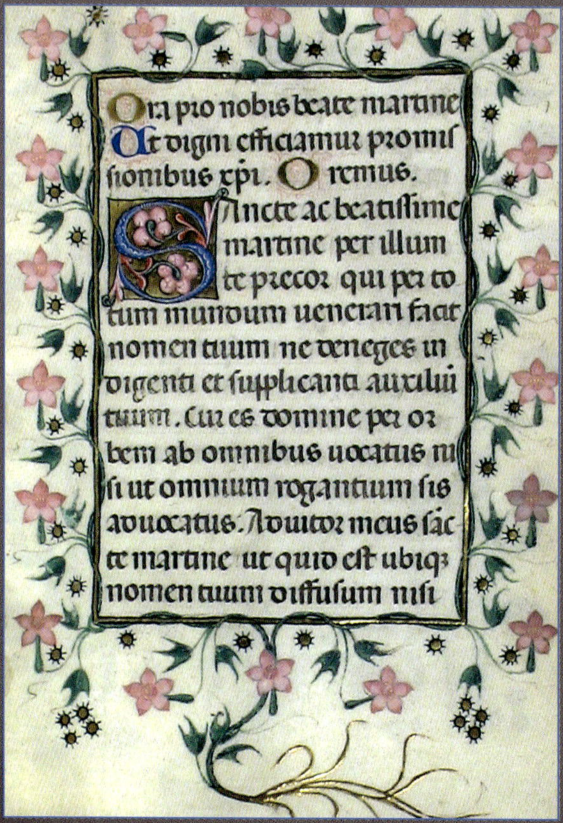
Ora pro nobis beate martine
Ut digni efficiamur promis
sionibus xpi. Oremus.
Sancte ac beatissime
martine per illum
te precor qui per to
tum mundum venerari fecit
nomen tuum ne deneges in
digenti et supplicanti auxiliu
tuum. Cum es domine per or
bem ab omnibus vocatus m
si ut omnium rogantium sis
advocatus. Adiutor meus sac
te martine ut quod est ubiq;
nomen tuum diffusum nisi

New York, Morgan Library and Museum, MS M. 944,
Prayerbook decorated by Michelino da Besozzo, f. 81

Facing page, f. 103, Illuminated by Pietro da Pavia, border and decorated initial

id est ad sempiternam salutem
anime mee quod a te quero.
Nunc conforta me obsecro te ut
indubitanter possim credere ut
a te accipiam quod a te quero. Si
in petendo querendo atque pul
sando persistam. Per intercessi
ones atque adiumenta beato
rum confessorum tuorũ quos
omnes ad laudem tuam inuo
co atque in auxilium meũ do
mine deus meus. Qui uiuis ⁊
regnas in secula seculor. Amẽ.

Oro ad deũ per intercessionem
sanctarũ uirginum.

Deus qui es credenti
bus in te sempiternũ

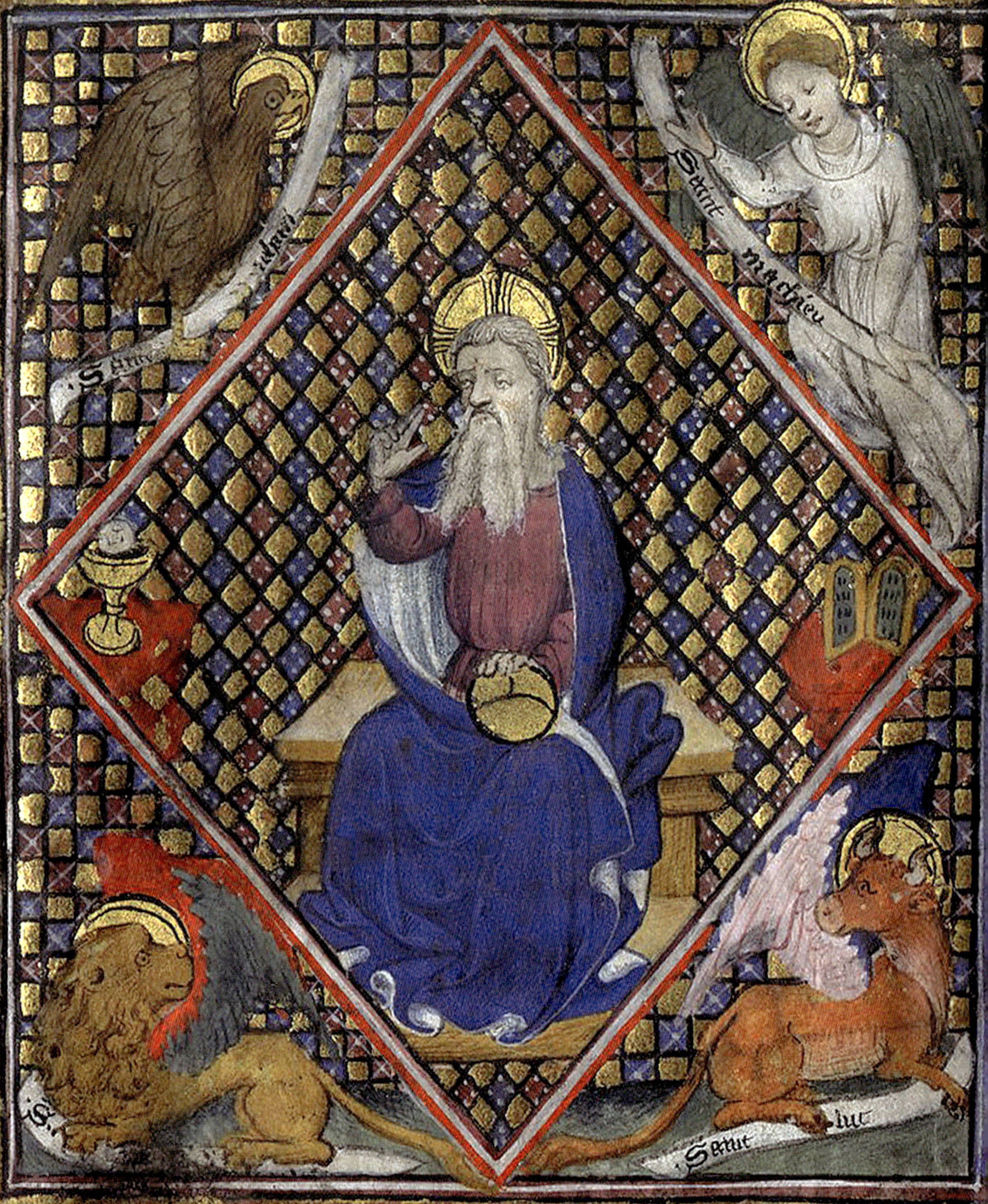

Domine ne in furore
tuo arguas me neq
in ira tua corripias
me.

4

Book of Hours (Use of Paris)

In Latin and French, illuminated manuscript on vellum

France, Paris, c. 1410

14 large miniatures from the Workshop of the Luçon Master

Already in the early fourteenth century, Dante (died 1321) in the *Divine Comedy* paid tribute to Parisian manuscript illumination when he mentioned "the art in Paris they call illumination." This charming codex is a fine example of the Golden Age of manuscript illumination in Paris in the first quarter of the fifteenth century under the reign of King Charles VI (1380-1422) and during the time of the court patronage of the Dukes of Berry, Burgundy, and Orleans, all avid bibliophiles who assembled fine libraries. In manuscript illumination, the period is characterized by the influx of foreign artists flocking towards Paris – mostly Flemish and Dutch but also some Italian – generating profound changes in the palette and a different approach to spatial and temporal settings. One of the earliest artists that marks this shift in aesthetic is the Master of Luçon, active in the last decade of the fourteenth century until circa 1417 (see A. Châtelet, 2000, "Le Maître de Luçon," pp. 123-129; F. Avril, "Grands et petits maîtres," in *Paris 1400*, 2004, pp. 276-277).

The miniatures, with their minutely patterned diapered backgrounds and simplified, pared-down compositions, are the work of a close associate of the Luçon Master, working in Paris around 1410. A leading exponent of the established Late Gothic style, the Luçon Master was first christened by Millard Meiss in 1956 (p. 193, note 23) after the cycle of miniatures that illustrates a Missal-Pontifical commissioned by Étienne Loypeau, Bishop of Luçon, which later passed to Jean, the Duke of Berry (c. 1405-1407; Paris, BnF, MS lat. 8886; see Avril, in *Paris 1400*, 2004, pp. 279-280, no. 171). The artist's works, which date from between 1401 and 1417, are distinguished by elegant, sinuous figures and subtle tonalities. They also manifest a certain conservatism and adherence to long-established models. Some of his more deluxe compositions show a lavish use of burnished and tooled goldleaf. Although he did illuminate a number of secular texts and moral treatises (he is at the summit of his art when he paints parts of the codex known as *Térence des ducs,* Paris, Bibl. Arsenal, MS 664, see Avril, *Paris 1400*, 2004, no. 145 B), the Luçon Master spe-

Facing page, f. 64, God the Father Enthroned

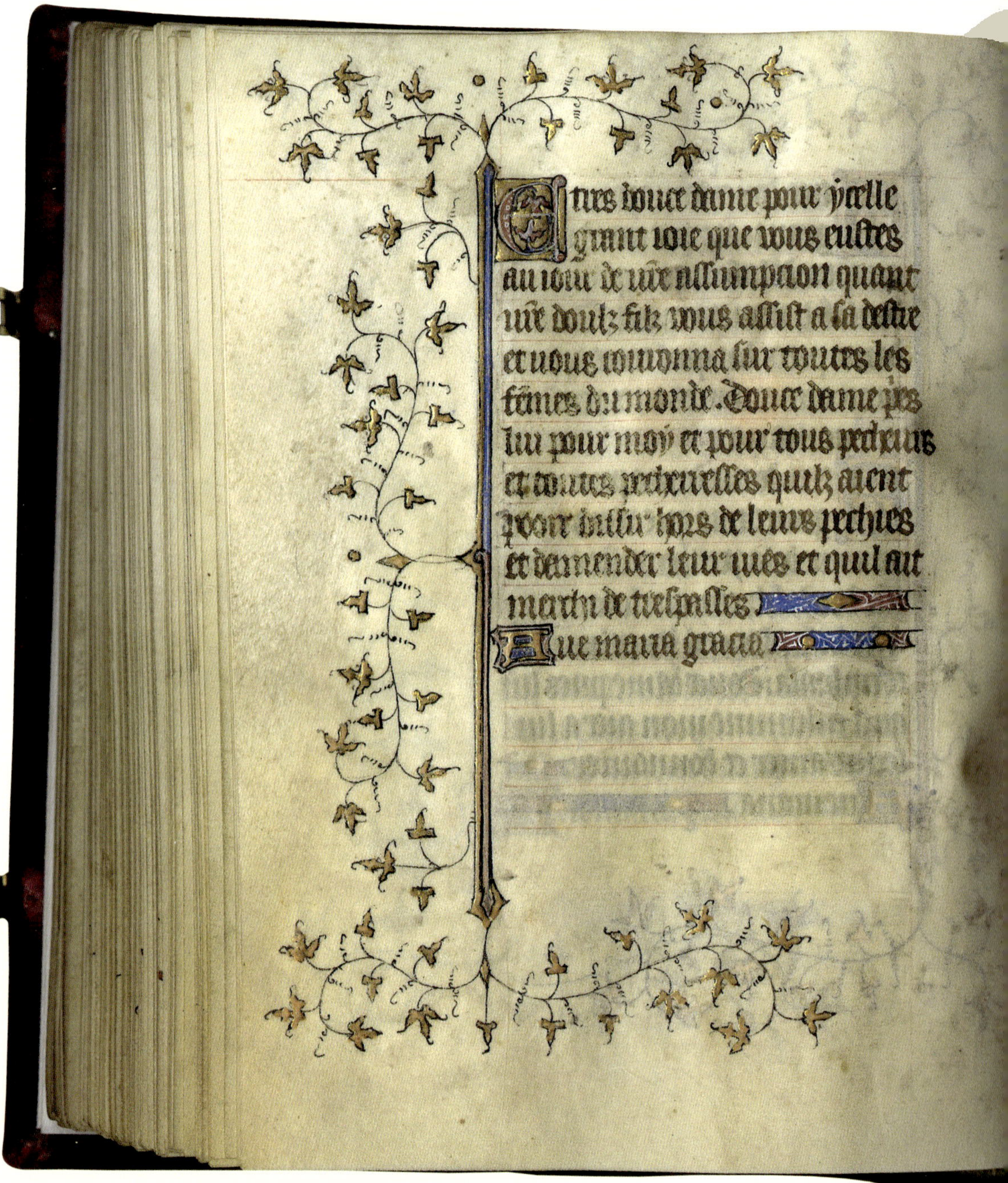

Tres doulce dame pour ycelle
grant ioie que vous eustes
au iour de vostre assumpcion quant
vostre doulz filz vous assist a sa destre
et vous couronna sur toutes les
femmes du monde. Doulce dame pries
lui pour moy et pour tous pecheurs
et toutes pecheresses quilz aient
pooir dissir hors de leurs pechies
et de amender leur vies et quil ait
merci de trespasses
Ave maria gracia

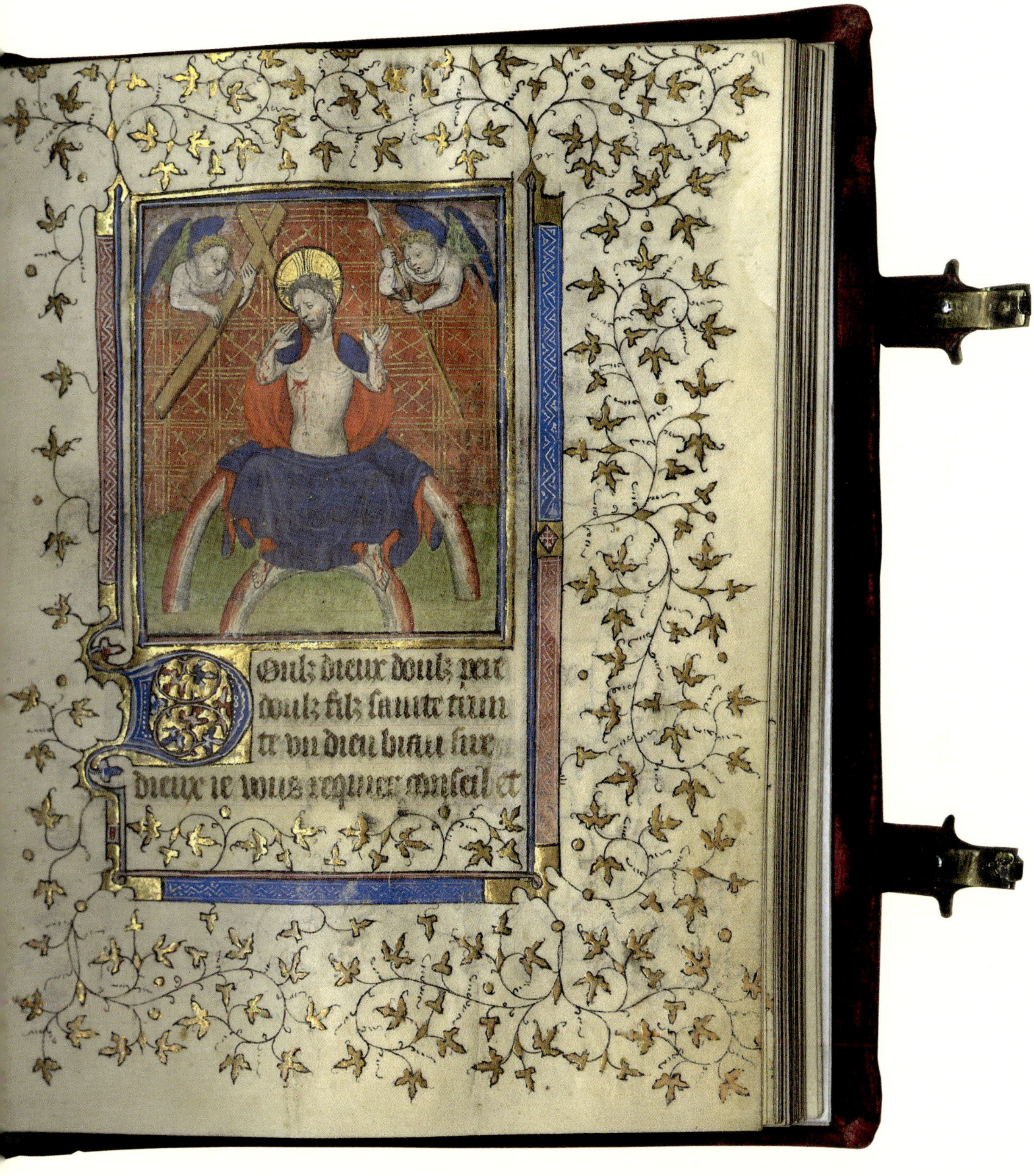

ff. 90v-91, Christ as Judge

cialized in the production of Books of Hours, as suggested by the twenty-one examples enumerated by Meiss (1974), found mostly in public collections. He evidently headed a prolific workshop, from which this book stems. The miniatures in the present book thus offer a playful variation on some of the Luçon Master's standard compositions, replicated with varying degrees of skill and imagination.

Certain miniatures in the present book, including the Visitation (f. 27), Annunciation to the Shepherds (f. 41), and Flight into Egypt (f. 52), also betray the influence of the Boucicaut Master, whose approach to landscape elements and spatial recession, typified by the famous Flight into Egypt from the Boucicaut Hours, heralded a more forward-looking and experimental trend in French manuscript illumination of the early fifteenth century. Accordingly, these miniatures depict scenes from the Infancy narrative set on grassy pastures in front of rocky outcroppings, from which small shrub-like trees sprout. Also indicative of this more progressive current are the haloes seen from behind on the right-hand-side group of apostles in the Pentecost miniature (f. 83), which have no equivalent in other works by the Luçon Master. We date the present manuscript closer to c. 1410 than earlier in the century on account of some of these more progressive features. While the artist did not go so far as to exchange the traditional diapered background for an atmospheric sky, the introduction of landscape elements was nonetheless a decisive event in the development of the spatially convincing, full-format miniature. Although it would reach its fullest manifestation much later in the century with the work of the great Jean Fouquet, the trend toward naturalistic landscape settings had its roots in Parisian illumination.

In drawing both from traditional schemas and more recently devised ones, the book's miniatures closely resemble a number of scenes found in two Book of Hours by the Luçon Master workshop now in Baltimore, Walters Art Museum MS W. 231 and MS W. 232, which Meiss dated to c. 1405 and 1407 respectively. The scenes of the Visitation (f. 42v), Nativity (f. 53v), and Adoration of the Magi (f. 64) in the latter are especially close to those found in the present book, although ours are more simplified and executed with less precision and incidental detail. Nevertheless, the adoption of more convincing landscape settings sets our book in marked contrast to other more refined but perhaps more conservative products of the Luçon Master's workshop, for example

Paris, Bibliothèque Mazarine MS 491, whose Visitation (f. 41) and Flight into Egypt (f. 67), while quite close in composition, display none of the dynamism engendered by the figures being positioned within a landscape setting.

This is an artist who merits a full study of the sort that Christine Geisler Andrews has undertaken for the Boucicaut Master. Such a study would entail an examination of the inclusion of specific texts, as well as their illustrations and the models for them, to determine how members of the workshop collaborated, amongst themselves and with other artists in Paris, to produce large numbers of Books of Hours for the market that they could also personalize in economically efficient ways. It would also account for the many manuscripts, such as the present one, that have appeared since Meiss completed his census of the artist's production and that of his followers and workshop.

PHYSICAL DESCRIPTION: 129 ff., complete (collation i^6, ii^2, $iii\text{-}vii^4$, viii^3, $ix\text{-}xi^4$, xii^3, $xiii\text{-}xvi^4$, xvii^2), written on 16 lines, in a fine gothic liturgical script in dark brown ink between 2 vertical and 17 horizontal lines ruled in light pink (justification 98 x 63 mm.), calendar written in brown and red ink, rubrics in red, capitals touched in red, line fillers and versal initials throughout in liquid gold on blue and pink grounds with white tracery, one-line initials in liquid gold on alternating grounds of pink and blue, two-line initials throughout in gothic ivy-leaf designs in pink and blue on liquid gold grounds with full-length bar borders sprouting into three margins into gold ivy leaves on hairline black tendrils, three-line initials in pink and blue on liquid gold grounds infilled with colored ivy leaves, 14 full borders consisting of gold ivy-leaf rinceaux with hairline black tendrils filling outer margins and area below text, 14 large miniatures in rectangular compartments above 3- and 4 lines of text (some slight abrasion or flaking, mostly insignificant), offset from pilgrim badge on f. 129v. Modern binding of old red velvet over boards, parchment pastedowns and flyleaves. Dimensions 171 x 130 mm.

TEXT: ff. 1-12v, Calendar, with feasts for every day, mostly for Paris, major feast days in red, the others in brown; ff. 13-17v, Gospel Sequences; ff. 18-63, Hours of the Virgin (use of Paris), with Matins (ff. 18-26v), Lauds (ff. 27-35v), Prime (ff. 36-40v), Terce (ff. 41-44), Sext (ff. 44v-47v), None (ff. 48-51), Vespers (ff. 51v-57), Compline (ff. 57v-63); f. 63v, blank; ff. 64-79v, Seven Penitential Psalms and Litany (ff. 75-79); ff. 80-82v, Short Hours of the Cross; ff. 83-85v, Short Hours of the Holy Spirit; ff. 86-92v, Fifteen Joys of the Virgin; ff. 91-93, Seven Requests to Our Lord; f. 93v, blank; ff. 94-129, Office of the Dead (use of Paris).

ILLUSTRATION: There are 14 large miniatures, each with illuminated borders: f. 18, Annunciation; f. 27, Visitation; f. 36, Nativity; f. 41, Annunciation to the Shepherds; f. 44v, Adoration of the Magi; f. 48, Presentation in the Temple; f. 51v, Flight into Egypt; f. 57v, Coronation of the Virgin; f. 64, God the Father Enthroned; f. 80, Crucifixion; f. 83, Pentecost; f. 86, Virgin and Child; f. 91, Christ as Judge; f. 94, Funeral Service.

OWNERSHIP: 1. Copied and illuminated in Paris, based on the script and style of miniatures, in the first quarter of the fifteenth century. The liturgical use for Paris suggests these Horae were copied for a Parisian or Ile-de-France patron. - 2. North American Private Collection.

LITERATURE: Unpublished. - Andrews, Christine Geisler. "The Boucicaut Master and the Commerce of Books of Hours in Early Fifteenth-Century Paris," Unpublished Doctoral Dissertation, Northwestern University, 2006. - Châtelet, A. *L'âge d'or du manuscrit à peintures en France au temps de Charles VI*, Paris, 2000. - [Exhibition Catalogue]. *Paris 1400: les arts sous Charles VI*, Paris, Fayard, 2004. - Meiss, Millard. *French Painting in the Time of Jean de Berry: The Limbourgs and Their Contemporaries*, 2 vols., New York, Braziller, 1974, pp. 351-352, 393-397. - Meiss, Millard. "The Exhibition of French Manuscripts of the XIII-XVIth-Centuries at the Bibliothèque Nationale," *Art Bulletin* 38 (1956), pp. 187-196. - Randall, Lilian M.C. *Medieval and Renaissance Manuscripts in the Walters Art Gallery*, Vol. 1, *France, 875-1420*, Baltimore, Johns Hopkins University Press, 1989, cat. nos. 84-85, pp. 228-235.

ONLINE RESOURCES:

British Library, Yates Thompson MS 37 (by the Luçon Master)
http://bl.uk/catalogues/illuminatedmanuscripts/

Harvard University Library, Richardson MS 45 (by the Luçon Master)
http://hcl.harvard.edu/libraries/houghton/collections/

Luçon Master, comparisons:
http://employees.oneonta.edu/farberas/arth/marginal_matters/lucon_comparisons.htm

Liber Floridus, Paris, Bibliothèque Mazarine, MS 491 (attributed to the Luçon Master)
http://liberfloridus.cines.fr/textes/biblio_fr.html

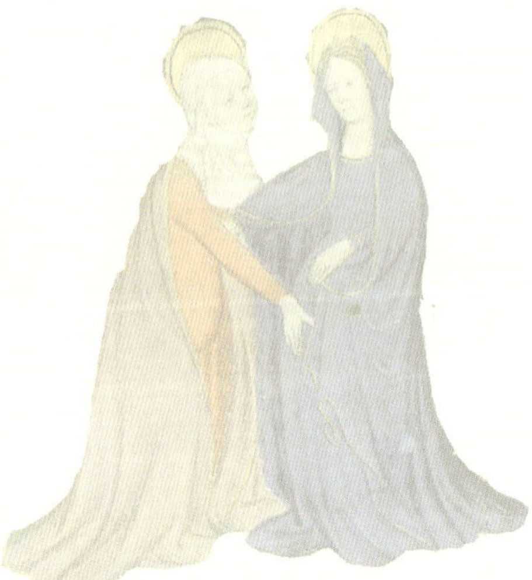

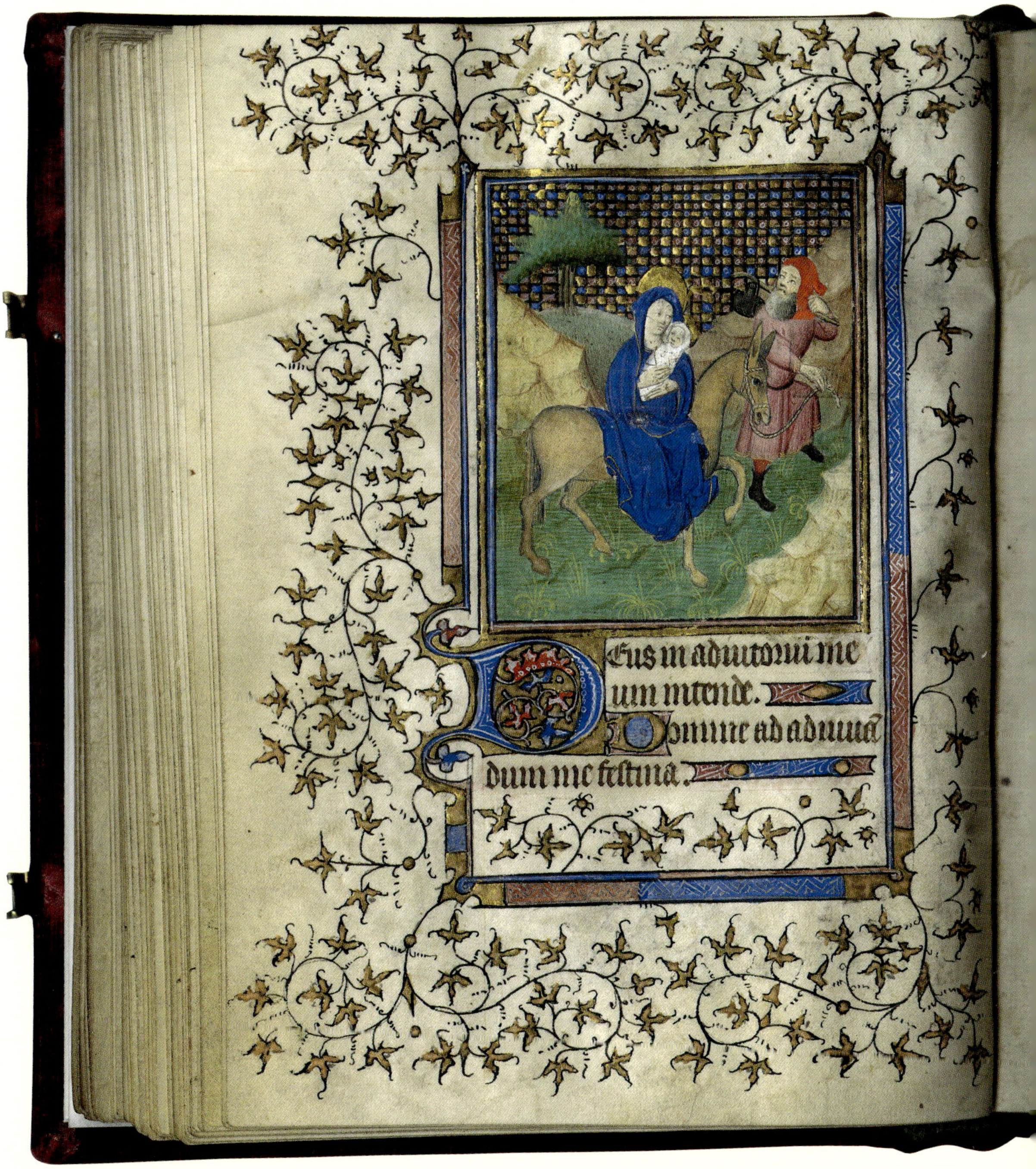

f. 51v, Flight into Egypt

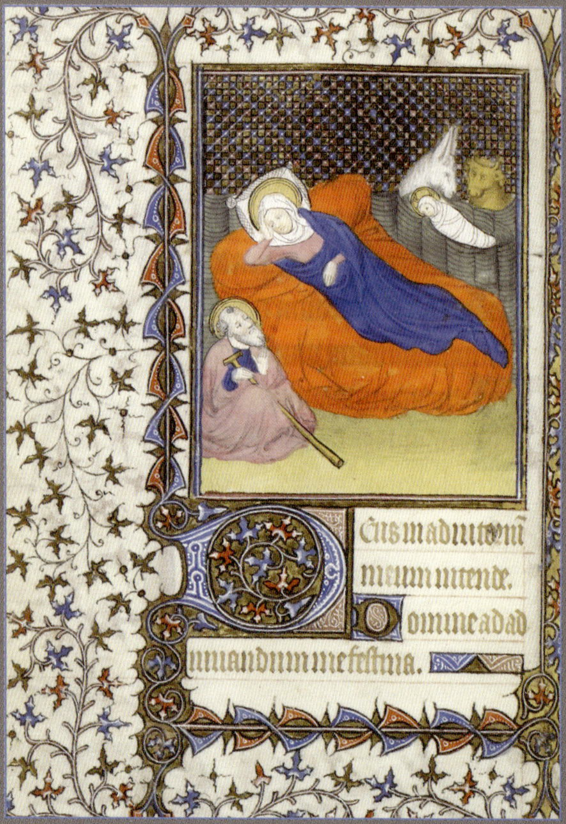

Baltimore, Walters Art Museum, MS W. 232,
Book of Hours, f. 53v, Nativity

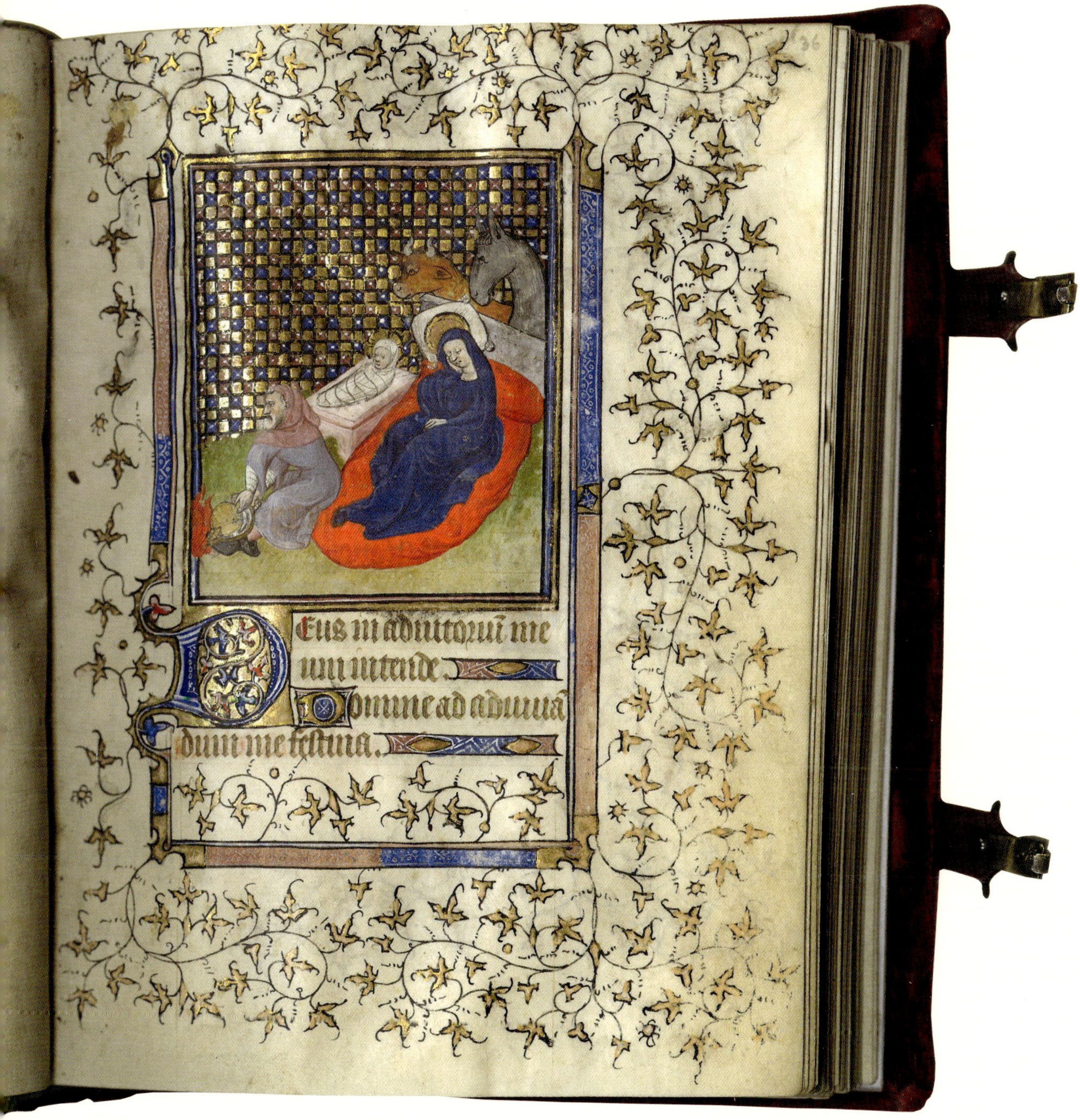

f. 36, Nativity

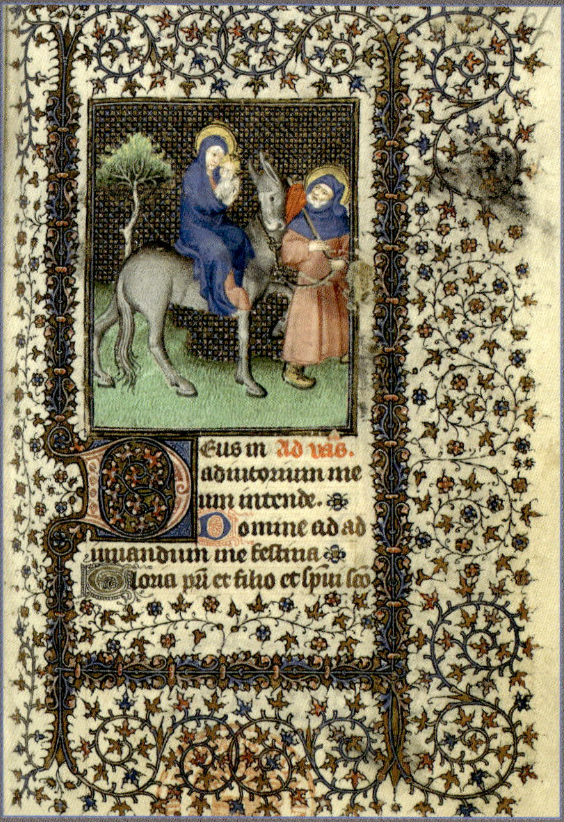

Paris, Bibliothèque Mazarine, MS 491,
Book of Hours, f. 67, Flight into Egypt

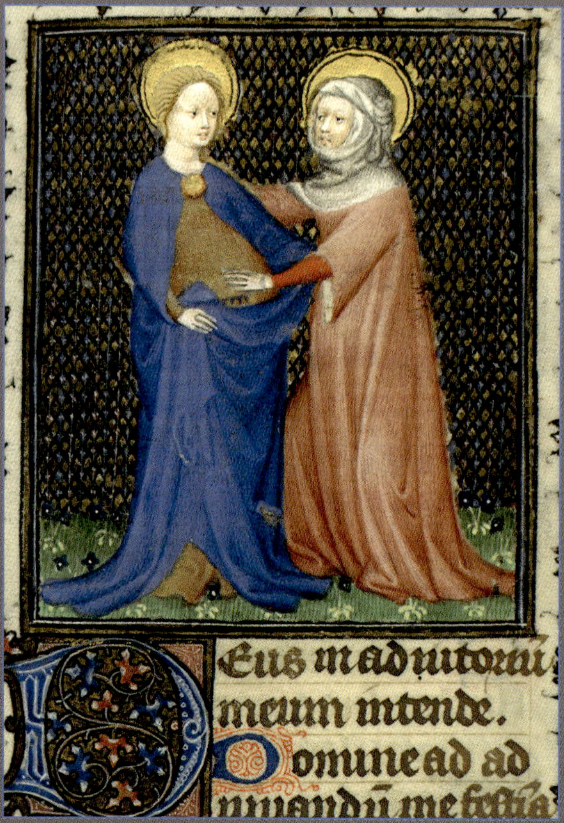

Paris, Bibliothèque Mazarine, MS 491,
Book of Hours, f. 41, Visitation

Facing page, f. 27, Visitation

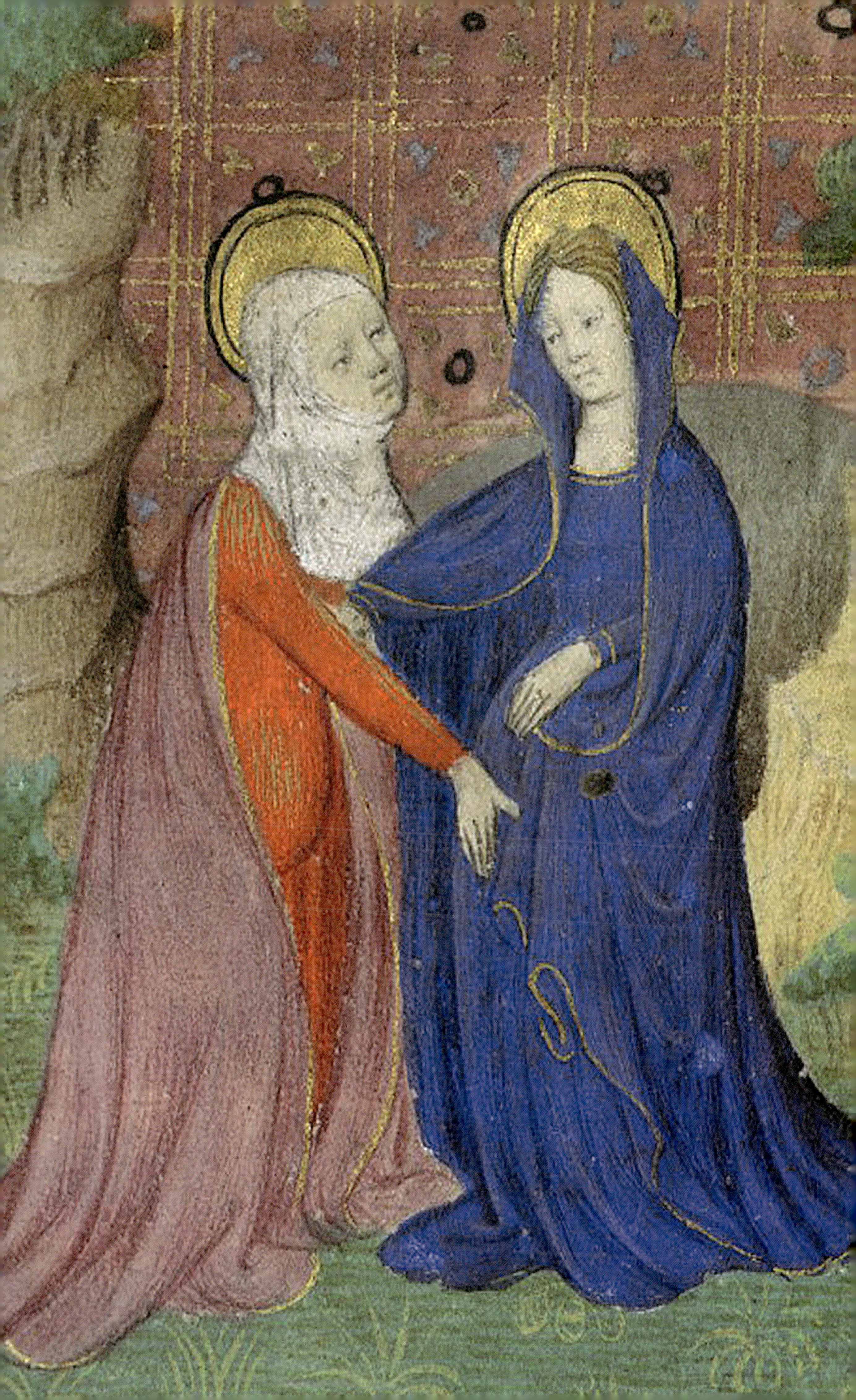

ghetide lese ic niet goe
der devocien. op dattu die
ghelovighe sielen. wilt
ste glorificeeren met dy
re heiligher bescouwin
ghe. Benedien wi den he.
God heb lof Amen. Des
dinxdaghes vande heili
ghe gheeste. Te mettē tijt

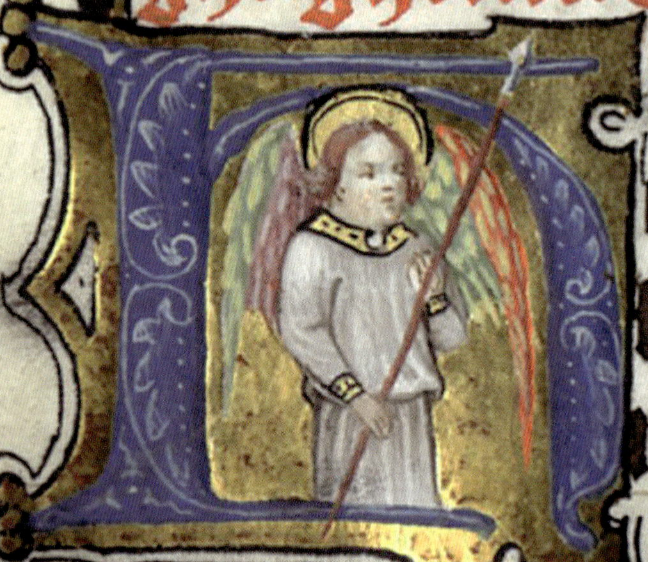

ere du selte
op doen mijn
lippen ende
mijn mont

5

Book of Hours (use of Utrecht)

In Dutch, illuminated manuscript on parchment
The Netherlands, Utrecht, c. 1425
9 historiated initials by the Masters of Zweder van Culemborg and another hand (the Masters of Otto van Moerdrecht?)

The production of Dutch Books of Hours is distinguished from that of neighboring countries, largely by the existence in the vernacular of the text of the Book of Hours (some ninety percent of extant Books of Hours from the Northern Netherlands are in Dutch). Translated by Geert Grote (died 1384), a reformer largely responsible for the eflloresence of the Devotio Moderna, the Dutch version of the Book of Hours rendered the prayerbook accessible to all literate people, not just those schooled in Latin. Just after Grote's death, the beginning of the fifteenth century marks the emergence of a distinctly Dutch tradition of manuscript illumination probably based in Utrecht but also surely practiced in other centers. One of the new currents of the "golden age" of Dutch manuscript illumination promoting pictorial naturalism is represented by the relatively rare artist (or artists), the Masters of Zweder van Culemborg, whose patrons included some of the leading families in the Northern Netherlands.

As of 1990, about twenty manuscripts by the Masters of of Zweder van Culemborg were identified, and a few more have come to light since that date (see Defoer, et al., 1990, p. 98). The artist takes his name from a Missal made around 1425 made for Zweder van Culemborg, one of the contenders for the bishopric of Utrecht (Bressanone, Biblioteca del Seminario Maggiore, Ms C 20; see E. Scheiber, 1992), and his style dominated Dutch manuscript illumination in the 1420s and 1430s. The artist may have been not a single person, but a group of illuminators working together with a common style in one atelier in Utrecht during these decades. Whether practiced by one or a group of illuminators, the progressive style of the Zweder Masters, inspired simultaneously by the Parisian illumination of the Limbourg Brothers and the panel paintings by Jan van Eyck, has earned them a place among "the most important representatives of Northern Netherlandish manuscript painting" (Defoer et al., 1990, p. 99).

The naturalistic spatial and luminous effects of style of the Zweder Master are achieved through a new subtelty of modeling, simulating the appearance of atmospheric light. The tiny figures in the present manuscript follow closely patterns seen in the eponymous Missal, including the very idiosyncratic formula for the crown of thorns. On this very small scale, the historiated initials in the present manuscript show a greater use of line to detail and define the soft brush strokes so characteristic of the artists. Size probably explains the only significant difference from the Missal in the motifs and design of the borders: the wider vertical bars in the Missal are divided into separate bands of gold, pink and blue with white patterning on the pink and blue. All other aspects of the decoration in this codex are extremely close to those in the Missal, including the shaping and outlining of the large illuminated initials and the penwork of the flourished initials.

With its idiosyncratic texts for the Hours of the Days of the Week, the present manuscript, which is textually complete, was perhaps commissioned to accompany a conventional Book of Hours with the full Office of the Virgin and the Office of the Dead. Its modest yet beautiful program of historiated initials follows the Instruments of the Passion through the weekday Hours, irrespective of their subject. It then opens a prayer to Christ with a historiated initial of the Man of Sorrows and a prayer to the Virgin with an initial of the Virgin and Child. Offsets show that at some point the pictorial content was supplemented by pasting illustrations on the original blanks opposite ff. 14 and 90 and adding new blank leaves to carry illustrations before ff. 114 and 140. It has been suggested that these sheets were for added prints, but it is possible they included full-page miniatures, later removed. On f. 90, black lines of the diapered background and the outlines of the nimbus of an unidentified saint are visible. Such traces, especially if they result from added prints, offer a fascinating insight into the changing role of the book: from aid to devotion to art object, when the added prints were removed either for a print collector or for a manuscript collector, who felt printed material interrupted the integrity of a finely crafted handmade book.

Innovative and very compelling are the poignant angels holding Arma Christi that adorn the historiated initials of the present Book of Hours. The closest stylistic comparisons with our angels are found in the Book of Hours in The Hague (KB, MS 133 M 131) attributed to a precursor of the Masters of

Zweder van Culemborg or else to a representative of his early style (Defoer, et al., 1990, p. 102 and Online Resources, below). Other angels in historiated initials occur in four different Zweder manuscripts (Cambridge, Fitzwilliam Museum, MS 289; Frauenfeld, Kantonsbibliothek, MS Y 25; Philadelphia, Free Library, MS Lewis E 188; and Sotheby's, London, 6 July 2000, lot 72). Typically, they are either just simply praying or playing musical instruments. Half-length angels holding Instruments of the Passion do occur in the borders of a manuscript in The Hague (KB, MS 79 K 2, f. 86r). But, the use of angels holding the Instruments of the Passion and placed in historiated initials, where they have a direct relationship to the text, appears to be entirely unique to the present manuscript. Through this device, surely prompted by the emphasis on meditation on the Passion in the milieu of the Devotio Moderna, these initials help promote a contemplative response on the part of the reader-viewer, leading him or her to read the accompanying prayers with quietude and sadness.

Perhaps the initials depicting the Virgin Mary and the Christ Child and the Man of Sorrows are painted not by the Zweder Master but by one of his collaborators, the Masters of Otto van Moerdrecht. The Zweder Master collaborated with the Moerdrecht Masters for example in the Egmont Breviary (New York, Pierpont Morgan Library, M.87). Compare also a Man of Sorrows in a Missal in Düsseldorf (Düsseldorf, Hauptstaatsarchiv, MS G III 3, f. 140).

PHYSICAL DESCRIPTION: 176 ff., including 2 blanks + vellum binding fragment from a fourteenth-century Breviary, apparently complete (collation with gatherings mostly of 8 leaves: i^{8} [ff. 1-9]; ii^{8} wants 6-8, excised after f. 13 [ff. 9-13]; iii^{8} (probably missing an inserted full page miniature before f. 14) [ff. 14-21]; iv-xi^{8} [ff. 22-85]; xii^{6} wants 5-6, excised after f. 89 [ff. 86-89]; xiii^{8} (probably missing an inserted full page miniature before f. 90) [ff. 90-97]; xiv-xv^{8} [ff. 98-113]; xvi^{8} (probably missing an inserted full page miniature before f. 114) [ff. 114-121]; xvii^{8} [ff. 122-129]; xviii^{8} (probably missing an inserted full page miniature before f. 130, stub visible) [ff. 130-137]; xix^{8} [ff. 112-145]; xx-xxii^{8} [ff. 146-169]; xxiii^{6} [ff. 170-175], xxiv^{2} wants 2, excised after f. 176 [f. 176]), ruled in brown (single bounding lines, full across) for one column of 13 lines between two verticals and 14 horizontals (the Calendar ruled for 15 lines) (justification 78/79 x 49/50 mm), prickings visible in some margins, written in textura, capitals stroked with red, red rubrics, some red underlining in the Calendar, added texts on ff. 170-171 and on ff. 171v-172v are in two different hands, 1-line high initials alternate blue on red pen-flourish fields with gold on blue pen-flourish fields, 2-line high initials are in gold alternating on blue or red pen-flourish fields, 4-7 line high initials commencing hours or major new texts are blue with white tracery on gold fields, in all nine historiated initials, the initial commencing Prayers to Mary on fol. 114 encloses painted foliage and flowers, leaves with 4. to 7- line high initials have painted and gold baguettes along the outer lateral side of the text column, gold bar-baguettes in the upper and lower margins, border decoration in all four margins of ink sprays, green tear-drop leaves, and painted and gold petals and tri-petals. Binding of 17th-century plain vellum over pasteboard (upper cover partly detached); holes in the upper and lower covers for two ties, now lacking (occasional smudges or light stains, face of angel on f.14 smudged, initial on f. 90 slightly rubbed, some rubbing to burnished gold; slight offsetting opposite the cancelled blanks at four openings). Dimensions 122/124 x 89 mm.

TEXT: ff. 1-13v, Calendar for Utrecht in red and brown, full, "S. Jeroens dach" is a later addition to the entry of the Octave of St. Lawrence on August 17; ff. 14-22, Sunday Hours of the Trinity: *Des sonnendaghes vander heiligen drievoudicheit*, ff. 22-35v, Monday Hours of the Dead: *Des manen daghes voer alle ghelovighe sielen die ghestorven sijn*; ff. 35v-46, Tuesday Hours of the Holy Spirit: *Des dinxdaghes vanden heilighen gheeste*; ff. 46-54v, Wednesday Hours of All Saints: *Des woensdaghes van allen helighen*; ff. 54v-66v, Thursday Hours of the Sacrament: *Des donredaghes vanden heilighen sacramente*; ff. 66v-78, Friday Hours of the Cross: *Des vridaghes vanden heilighe cruce*; ff. 78-89v, Saturday Hours of the Virgin: *Des saterdaghes van onser liever sueter vrouwen*; ff. 90-106, Prayers to Christ, with ff. 90-96, *O ewighe alemachtighe alre coninghen* and ff. 96v-106, *O alre sueste here ihesus christe die gheseynt biste wt*; ff.106-111, Prayer to God the Father: *Voer die voeten dijnre hoechste almachtighe vader legghe ic*; ff.111-113, Prayer to the Three Persons of the Trinity: *O du hemelsche vader aelmachtich god ontferm di over mi arme sondaer*; [f. 113v frame ruled, unwritten]; ff. 114-145, Prayers to Mary, with ff.114-124v indulgenced prayer to be said before an image of the Virgin: *O edel coninghinne der hemeenl ende reyne maghet*; ff.125-127v, Prayer to the Virgin to be said for thirty days: *Oc bidde w vrouwe sinte maria doer die vruechde die ghi hadt*; ff.127v-129v, Prayer to the Virgin: *O maechdelike moeder des almachtigen Godssoen*; ff.130-136v, Prayer to be said daily to the Virgin to ensure warning of death: *O heilighe ende sonder smette maghet ende moeder des levenden gods sone*; ff.136v-140v, Prayers to the Virgin: *O onbeulekte ende ewelike ghebenedide eenpaerlike...*; ff.141-141v, *Fonteine der duechden sonder ghelijt*; ff. 141v-145, Two Suffrages to St. Michael, ff.141v-144 Here god weset mi arme mensche goedertieren and ff.144-145, *O sinte Michael heilighe weerde*; [f. 145v lined, unwritten]; ff. 146r-160v, Suffrages, with ff.146-148, Suffrage of Saint Erasmus: Heer sinte herasmus martelear gods...; ff.148-151v, Suffrage to the Three Kings: *O heilighe drie coninghe Jasper Melchior ende balthaser*; ff.151v-152v, Suffrage to St. George: *O edele martelaer ende ridder ons heren*; ff.152v-156v, Prayer to Christ attributed to St. Jerome: *Here ihesu christe aendenke huden aen mi ende*; ff.157-158, Suffrage to Saint Sebastian: *O heilighe sebastiaen groot is dijn ghelove*; ff.158v-159v, Suffrage to Mary Magdalene: *O heilighe maria Magdalena*; ff.159v-160v, Suffrage to St. Barbara: *Siet en wise ionfrouwe*; ff. 161-169, Two Blessings, with ff.161-162 marked for signing with the cross: *Die keiserlike moghentheit gheven...*; ff.162-163v, *Die benedixi des vaders...*); ff. 163v-167, Two Prayers to One's Guardian Angel, with ff.163v-166, *Ic bidde u heilighe weerde enghel*; ff.166-167, *Heilighe enghel dien ic bevolen bin...*; ff.167-169, Seven Verses of St Bernard; [f. 169v frame ruled, unwritten]; ff. 170r-172v , Added Prayers, with ff. 170v-171, Prayer to Christ sent by Boniface VI to King Philip of France, a Dictum of St. Augustine (added Hand 1): *O heer ihesu christe die aen naemste*; ff. 171v-172v, The Magnificat (added Hand 2): *Mijn siel maect groot den heer*; [ff. 173-176, lined, unwritten excepts for added ownership of Van der Laen and Assendelft inscriptions on ff. 175v-176v].

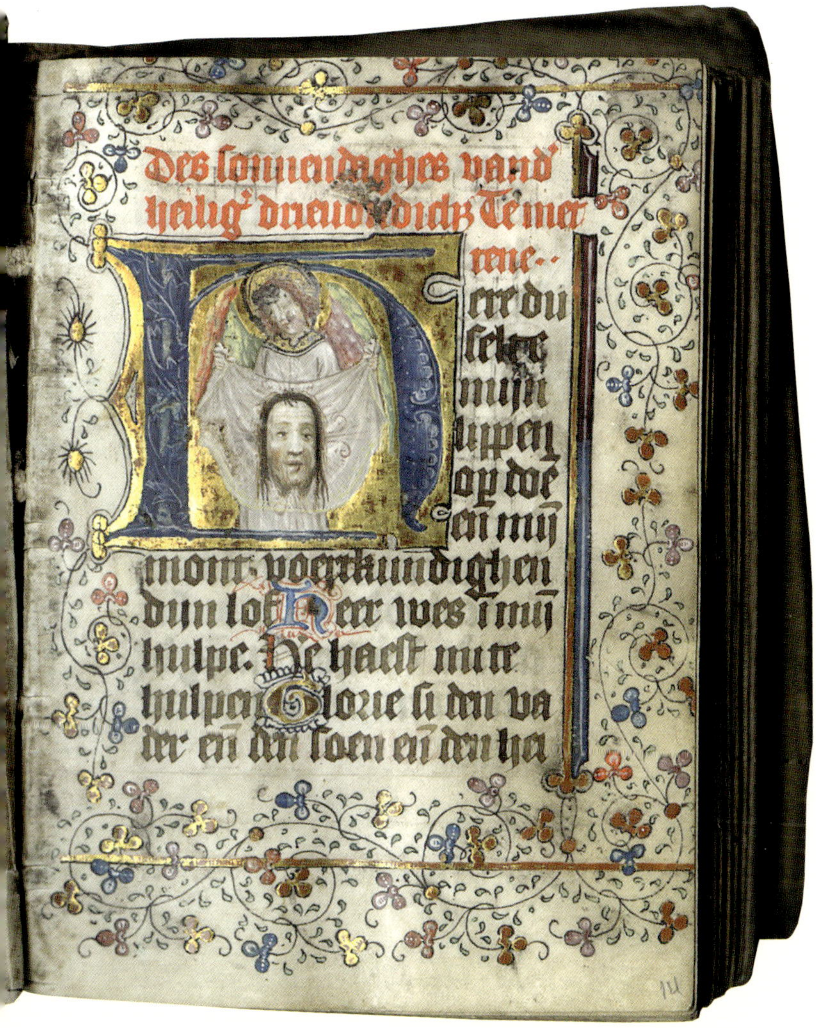

Des sonnendaghes vand'
heilig' drievoudich Te met
tene..
Heer du
selve
mijn
lippen
op doe
en mijn
mont voerkundighen
dijn lof Heer wes in mijn
hulpe. He haest mi te
hulpen Glorie si den va
der en den soen en den hei

f. 14, Angel Holding the Sudarium

ILLUSTRATION: There are nine historiated initials ranging from 4-7 lines in height: f. 14, Angel holding the Sudarium (7-line H, 42 mm. x 50 mm. for the Sunday Hours of the Trinity); f. 22, Angel holding the Column of the Flagellation (4-line L, 25 mm. x 31mm. for the Monday Hours of All Souls); f. 35v, Angel holding the Spear of the Crucifixion (4-line H, 31 mm. x 34 mm., for the Tuesday Hours of the Holy Spirit); f. 46, Angel holding a Lance with the Sponge of the Crucifixion (4-line H, 25 mm. x 34 mm., for the Wednesday Hours of All Saints); f. 54v, Angel holding the Hammer of the Crucifixion (4+ line H, 36 mm. x 27mm., for the Thursday Hours of the Holy Sacrament); f. 66v, Angel holding the Nails of the Crucifixion (4-line H, for the Friday Hours of the Cross); f. 78, Angel holding the Crown of Thorns (5-line H, for the Saturday Hours of the Virgin); f. 90, The Man of Sorrows emerging from a Tomb in half-length (5-line O: Prayer to Christ); f. 130, Madonna and Child in half length (4-line O, 26 mm. x 33 mm., introducing a Prayer to Mary).

OWNERSHIP: 1. The saints in red in the Calendar and the style of illumination and flourishing all place the origin of this Hours in Utrecht. St Jeroen, patron saint of Noordwijk and venerated throughout the county of Holland has been added to the calendar (17 August), perhaps for the van der Laen family of Leiden. - 2. According to 16th-century notes on ff. 175v-176v , these Horae belonged to Diewer or Dieber van der Laen, daughter of Gerrit van der Laen (c.1480-1568), who moved from Haarlem to Leiden, and wife of Hendrik van Assendelft, the son of Barthout van Assendelft, secretary to the Court of Holland, and Alijt de Vriese Nicolaesdr. He died on 10 February 1573 and was buried in the Oude Kerk in Amsterdam. His widow returned to Leiden, where she died 19 November 1600 and was buried in St Peter's Church. On f. 176, Diewer recorded her husband's death and on f.175v is a record of her death: "ons moeder Joffrou[w] diwer van der lan veduwe van Jo[n]cker hendrick van Assendelft is in den heere gerust op den negentienden novenbris tuschen negent ende achten Smorgens Anno sestien hondert ende leijt begraven inde piters kerck achter het hoge oulter tot Leiden alwaer wij het graf gekoch hebbe. God geef de zijl rust ende vrede." They apparently had children, who inherited the book, since these accounts are labeled "our father" and "our mother." Further notes on f. 176v record the deaths of Diewer's brother and sister: "Joffrou Anna van der Lan weduwe van Joncster Johan van basserode is inder heer gerijst opdy xxix mart Anno sestien hondeet ende? vijf [in a different hand: 1605] smiddag het half elffs Jonckheer hendrick van der lan is in der heer geriist opdy ix may Anno xvi c acht? ontrent negen vrey inder hage ende is begraven tot Voorhout in de capel van der van der Lan." Anna van der Laen married Johan van Bassenrode, drossaert van Montfoort, son of Willem van Bassenrode and Margriete van Montfoort, who had died by May 1601, when his inheritance was settled and Hendrik represented his sister's interests. The inscription gives her death date as 29 March 1605. Her heir, Hendrik van der Laen, born 1537/8 in Leiden, recognized as noble in 1566, married Maria Suys and died in The Hague on 9 May 1608. He was buried in the Van der Laen chapel at Voorhout. - 3. H. F. von Aussem, no 40, his signature in an 18th-century hand on pastedown. If his numbering related only to manuscripts he had a significant collection, of which the following have been identified: a Delft Book of Hours of c.1470, his no 18 (Cambridge, Fitzwilliam Museum, MS Mc Clean 97), a German manuscript Prayerbook now in The Hague (KB, MS 134 C 63), a devotional text (The Cornelius J. Hauck Collection, Christie's, New York, 16 June 2006, lot 136), a 16th-century Psalter text from St. Amand (Gaebelein collection) and a 15th-century German Missal (McGill University), see de Ricci, *Census*, II pp.1672, 2205. - 4. Walter Hirst, his bookplate, by descent.

LITERATURE: Unpublished. – Defoer, Henry et al, eds. *The Golden Age of Dutch Manuscript Illumination*, New York, 1990, pp. 98-116. - Scheiber, E. *Niederländische Buchmalerei, die Miniaturen des Culenborch-Missales in Brixen*, 1992

ONLINE RESOURCES:

Exhibition The Hague KB MS 79 K 2 by Zweder Master
http://www.kb.nl/galerie/stijl/071culemborg-en.html

Book of Hours, The Hague, KB MS 133 M 131
http://www.kb.nl/manuscripts/search/

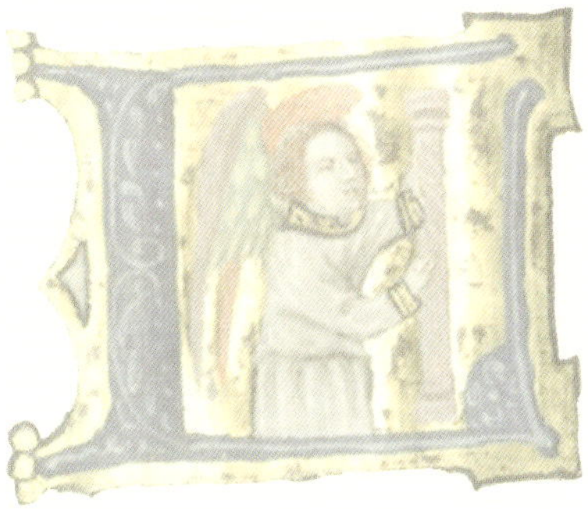

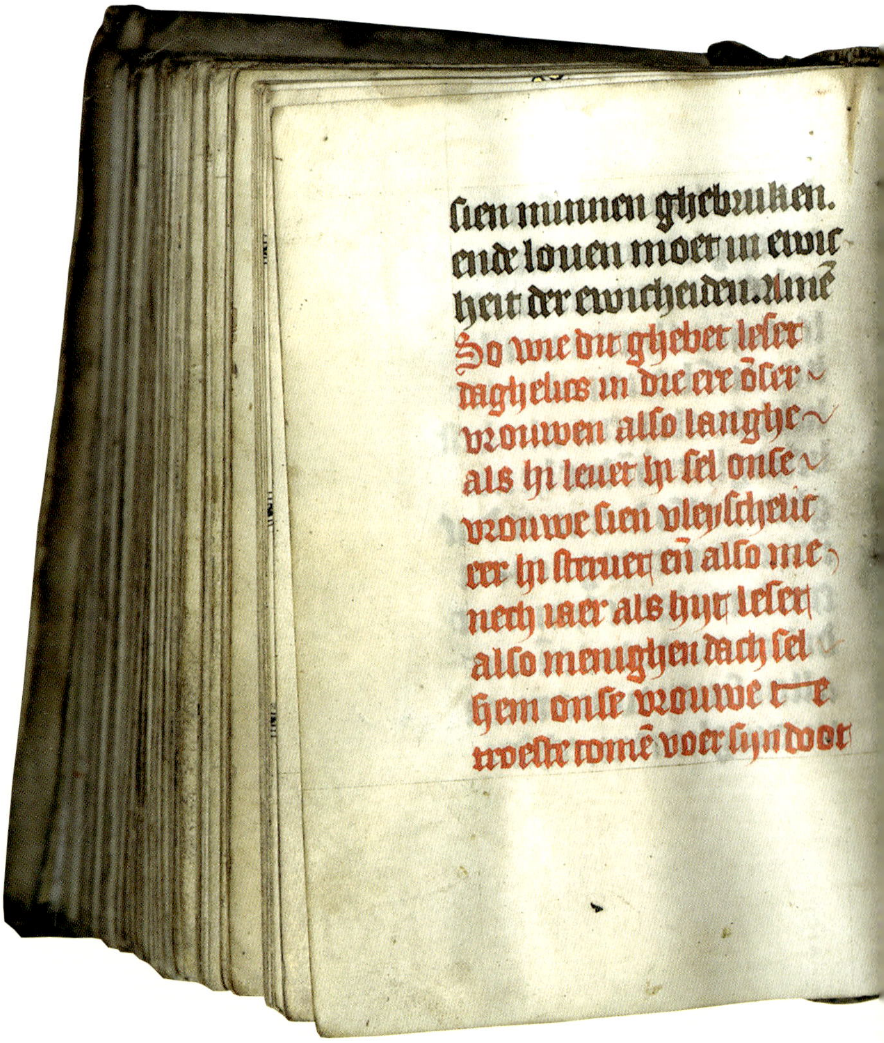
sien minnen ghebruken.
ende louen moet in ewic
heit der ewicheiden. Amē
So wie dit ghebet leset
daghelics in die ere ōser
vrouwen also langhe
als hi leuet hi sel onse
vrouwe sien vleyschelic
eer hi steruet eñ also me-
nech iaer als hyt leset
also menighen dach sel
hem onse vrouwe te
troeste comē voer syn doot

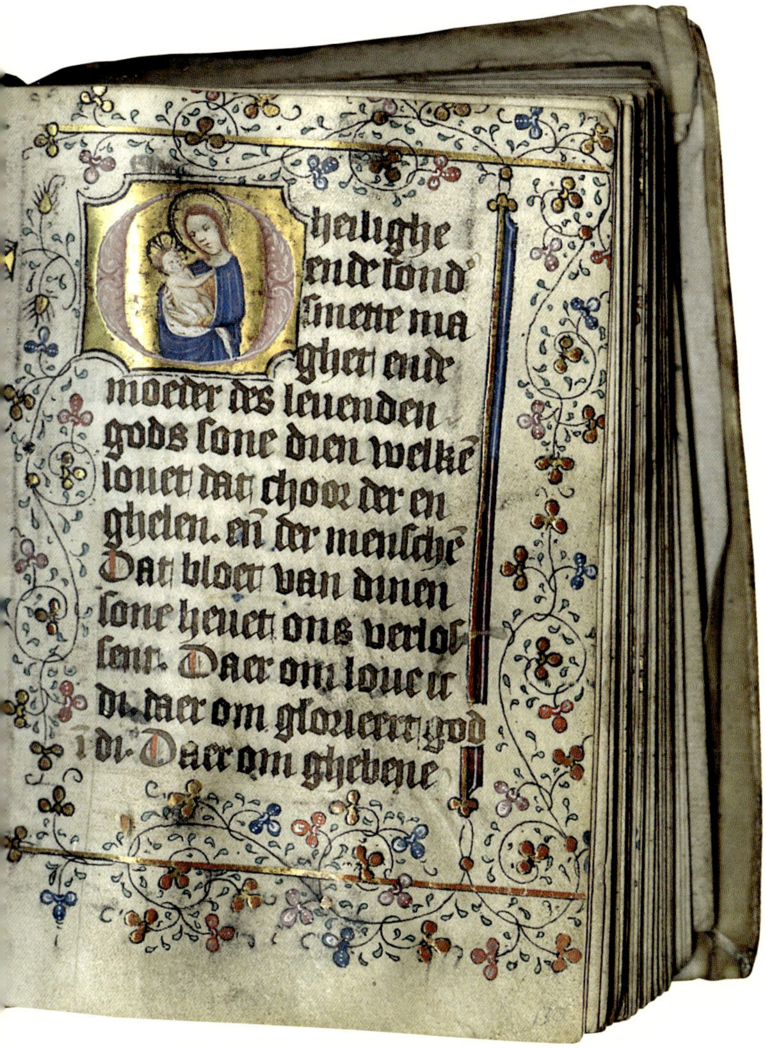

helighe
ende sond
smette ma
ghet ende
moeder des leuenden
gods sone dien welke
louet dat choor der en
ghelen. en der mensche
Dat bloet van dinen
sone heuet ons verlos
sent. Daer om loue ic
di. daer om glorieere god
i di. Daer om ghebene

ff. 129v-130, Madonna and Child in Half Length

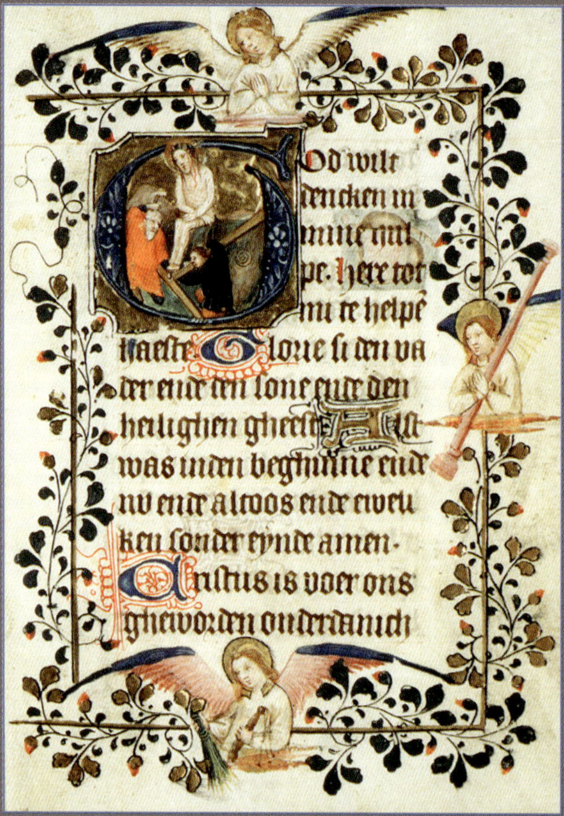

The Hague, Koninklijke Bibliotheek, 79 K 2,
Book of Hours, f. 80, Preparation for the Crucifixion

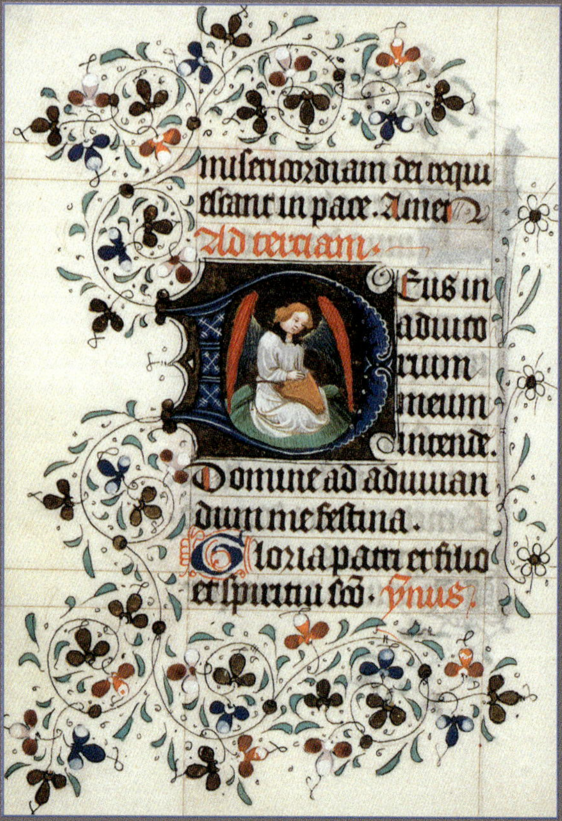

The Hague, Koninklijke Bibliotheek, 133 M 131,
Book of Hours, fol. 113v, Angel Playing Instrument

Facing page, f. 22, Angel Holding the Column of the Flagellation

mi vter goedertierenheit.
vleen volcomelic te ghe
louen. Amen. Benedien
wi den here god heb lof.

Des manen daghes voer
alle ghelouighe sielē die
ghestoruen syn. Temet
ten tijt.

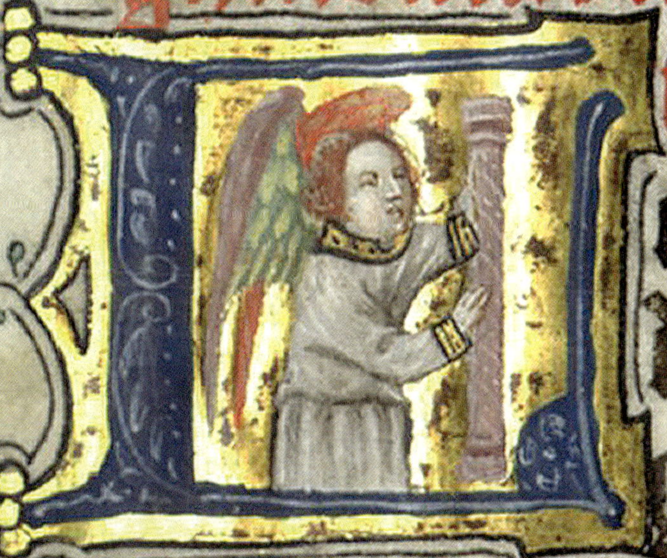
aet ons bid
den voer alle
ghelouighe
sielen. Heer verleen hē
allen die ewighe ruste.

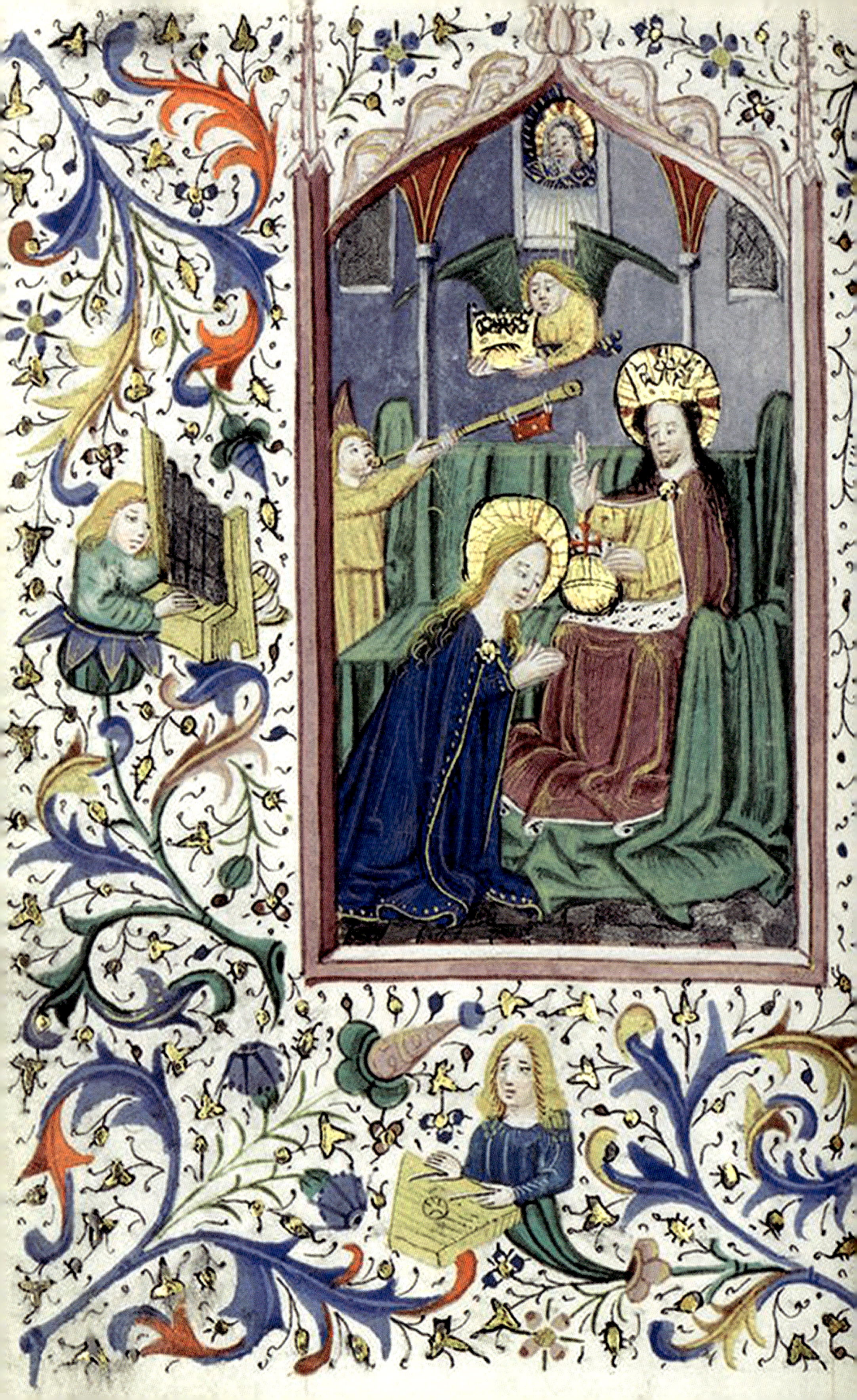

6

Book of Hours (Use of Rome)

In Latin, illuminated manuscript on parchment
Southern Netherlands, Bruges, c. 1450
37 full-page miniatures, 13 small miniatures, and 8 historiated initials by the Gold Scrolls Painter of Berlin, Kunstbibliothek, MS Grisebach, 4

First coined by F. Winkler in 1925, the Masters of the Gold Scrolls is now thought to refer to a style practiced by a group of artists, not to a single hand, active between about 1415 and 1455 probably in Bruges (see the recent assessment, [Exhibition], Brussels and Paris, 2011, pp. 140-147). Named for the dominant use of gold scrolls on flat, often burnt orange grounds in the backgrounds of many of the miniatures, the style is also characterized by the presentation of figures with oval doll-like faces, the nose, mouth, and eyes summarily treated. They are drawn with supple, unbroken lines and make stereotyped gestures. The prevailing colors are green, blue, red and orange. The style of these artists is formed by a combination of influences. There is a manuscript begun by the Boucicaut Master and finished by the Gold Scrolls Masters, the Hours of Joseph Bonaparte (Paris, BnF, MS lat. 10538), and at the same time in some of the early production there is also the influence of the "ars nova" or pre-Eyckian artists, such as the Master of the Beaufort Saints. By the end of the lengthy span of production, the artists collaborate with those of the generation of Willem Vrelant, for example on the Montfort Book of Hours (Vienna, ÖNB, Cod. s.n. 12878). The hypothesis that Vrelant actually took over the "workshop" of the Gold Scrolls Master when he arrived in Bruges has been advanced. Certainly the refined Vrelant of the 1450s owes much to the Gold Scrolls painters of the 1430s and 1440s; indeed, his style grows directly out of theirs.

The discovery of any significant manuscript from the workshop presents a welcome opportunity to sort out further questions of the production of the Masters of the Gold Scrolls. The present manuscript, although modest in height and width, is exceptionally rich both in ancillary texts (it is almost 400 folios thick) and in illustration, including nearly sixty pictures. Beginning with a Calendar, followed by two special Suffrages, nearly the whole first third of the manuscript is made up of the relatively unusual Hours of the Days of the Week (from the Sunday Hours of the Trinity to the Friday Hours of the Cross). These

Facing page, f. 171v, Coronation of the Virgin

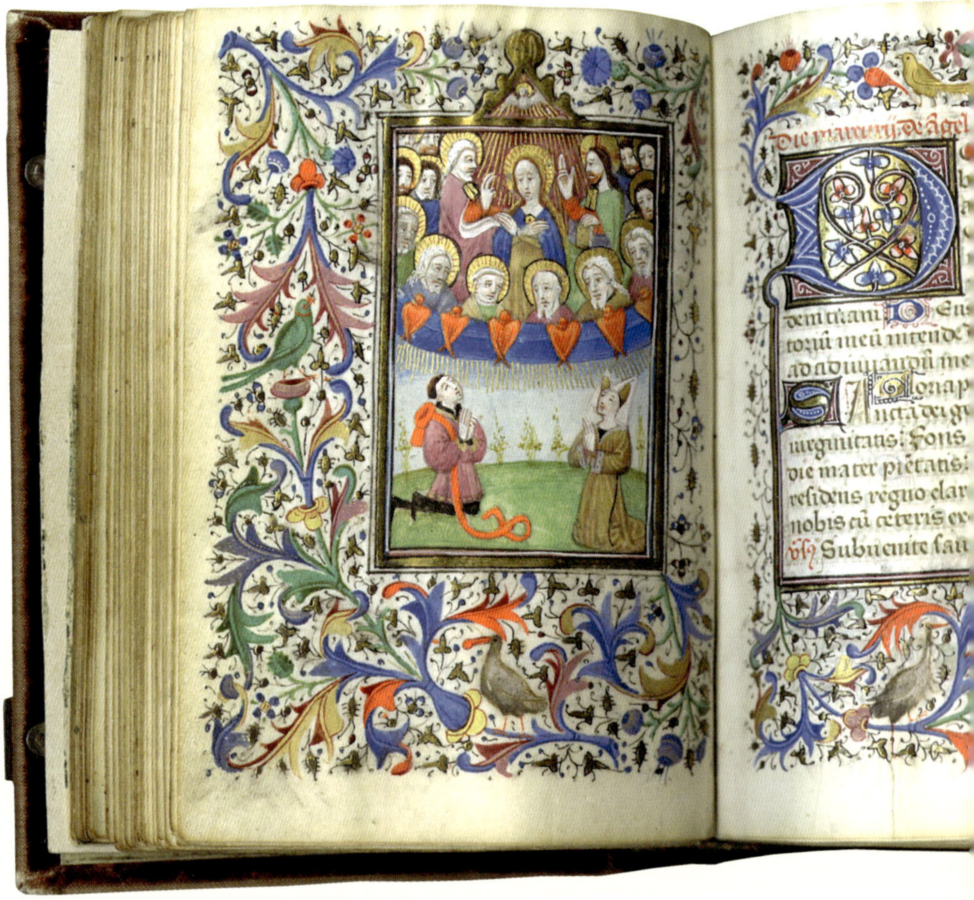

f. 65v, Patron & Patroness beneath All Saints

are followed by the traditional Hours of the Virgin, the Hours of the Passion, the Penitential Psalms, and the Office of the Dead, and then by a large number of Suffrages, mostly addressed to male saints. The presence of two different versions of the "O intemerata," a prayer requesting the Virgin's intercession, is especially remarkable. The "Obsecro te" and both versions of the "O intemerata" are written in the masculine form, and there is a paucity of female saints in the Suffrages, which suggest that the patron was a man.

Indeed, the unusual emphasis on Louis of Toulouse and Francis of Assisi, with their Suffrages occupying a place of honor at the beginning of the book just after the Calendar and before any of the Hours, suggests that our book's patron was a member of the Third Order of Saint Francis. Saint Louis of Toulouse, cadet of the royal house of Anjou, was embraced by the Franciscans. The Franciscan Tertiaries included both congregations of vowed men and women and fraternities of men and women, who lived standard lives in the world usually married. Otherwise unidentified, the original owner is represented twice in the manuscript, once with his wife on f. 65v and once alone on f. 105v (the full-page armorials on f. 3 are unfinished and were added, in any event, in the later fifteenth century).

Our codex appears specifically to have been painted by one of the Masters of the Gold Scrolls who illuminated a Book of Hours in the Kunstbibliothek in Berlin (MS Grisebach 4; Achten 1980, cat. 48). One of the ten full-page subjects in the much less richly illustrated Berlin codex also occurs in our manuscript. Of the nine, only our and the Berlin Men of Sorrows (ff. 220v and 61v, respectively) and Depositions of Christ (ff. 212v and 14v, respectively) hew closely to the same models. The Last Judgments in our book (f. 251v) and the Berlin Hours (f. 70v; Achten 1980, ill. 14) differ only in the addition of the Hell mouth in the Berlin representation. In the remaining six subjects, however, our painter studiously avoids compositional repetition. The Annunciations in our book (f. 116v) and in the Berlin Hours (f. 17v; Finke s.d., frontispiece), for example, present the same physiognomic types, the same haloes embellished with red rays, and the same charming detail of God the Father looking in on the scene through an aperture in the wall on the left. The two interiors, on the other hand, are largely different.

Likewise, the furnishings and fenestrations of Jerome's study in our and the Berlin codex (ff. 307v and 122v, respectively) have been completely relocated and reimagined. In the depictions of Christ before Pilate in our codex (f. 200v) and in the Berlin Hours (f. 32v; Finke s.d., Abb. 4), Jesus is positioned differently and the settings have been subtly altered. Save the wattle fences that enclose the figures, our and the Berlin Arrest of Christ (ff. 195v and 44v, respectively) share few points of resemblance, and the Funeral Services (ff. 269v and 92v, respectively) are entirely different.

Both the present manuscript and the Berlin codex share similar border styles. While the frames of the Berlin miniatures are simply arched, however, the apices of ours are peaked, gabled, crocketed, and otherwise more inventively shaped; frequently those apices also house the figure of God the Father. Their tiny size notwithstanding, the landscapes in our codex are also surprisingly and delightfully deep, with middle grounds bisected by waterways and brightly roofed townscapes set atop distant hillocks.

The dense borders that adorn nearly every page are often inhabited by birds, animals, and figures, further enhancing the extraordinary richness of the pictorial program. While not all of the marginal figures on the pages with full-page miniatures relate to or comment on the subjects they enframe, there are many exceptions. In addition to those described under Illustrations below, these include the third laywoman who looks on from the outer margin at the monstranced host on f. 86v; the winged angel in the outer margin who holds a chalice to catch the Savior's blood to the left of the Crucifixion (f. 92v); the mitred half-length hybrid with another gift of gold for the baby Jesus to the right of the Adoration of the Magi (f. 147v); the distressed angels in the outer and lower margins who witness Christ brought before Pilate (f. 200v); the doleful angels below and to the right of the Entombment of Christ (f. 216v); the two mourning clerics just beyond the Funeral Service (f. 269v); and the angel who holds the text that Jerome copies on f. 307v.

The compelling comparisons summarized here establish a distinct subgroup composed of the Berlin Hours and the present manuscript within the vast oeuvre of the Masters of the Gold Scrolls, which represents the dominant style in Bruges and West Flanders in the second quarter of the fifteenth century. Little advance has been made to date in sorting out the various artists,

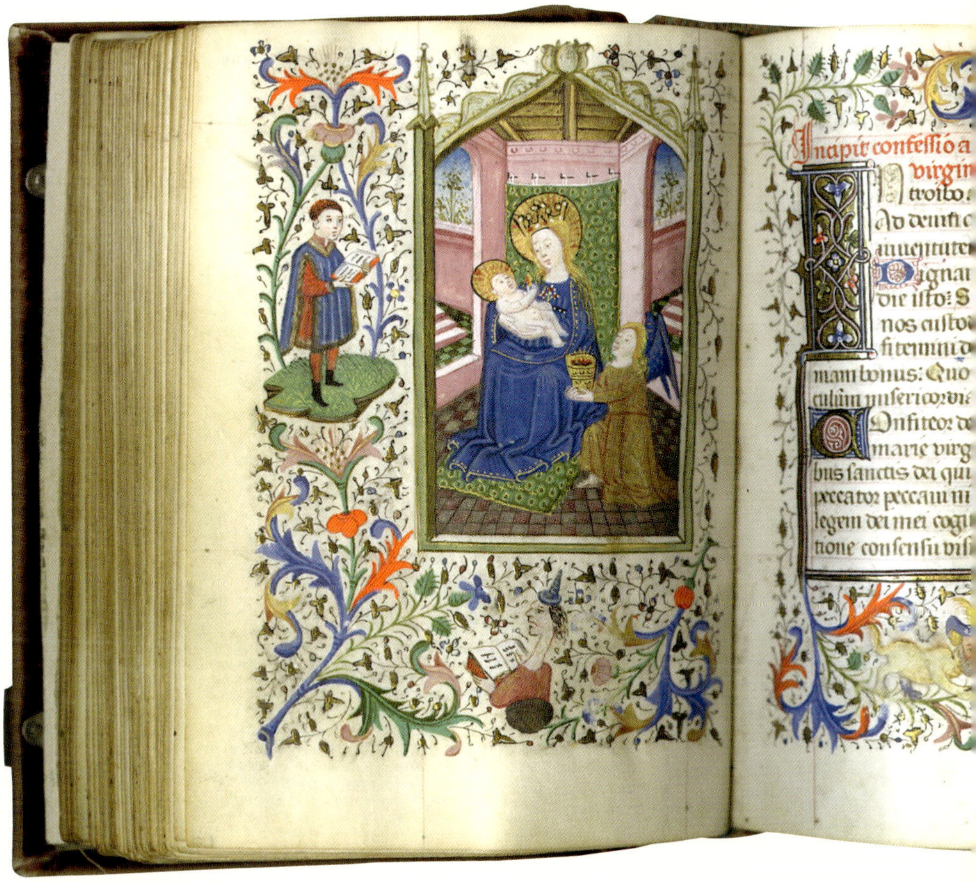

f. 105v, Enthroned Virgin & Child with Donor in the Margin

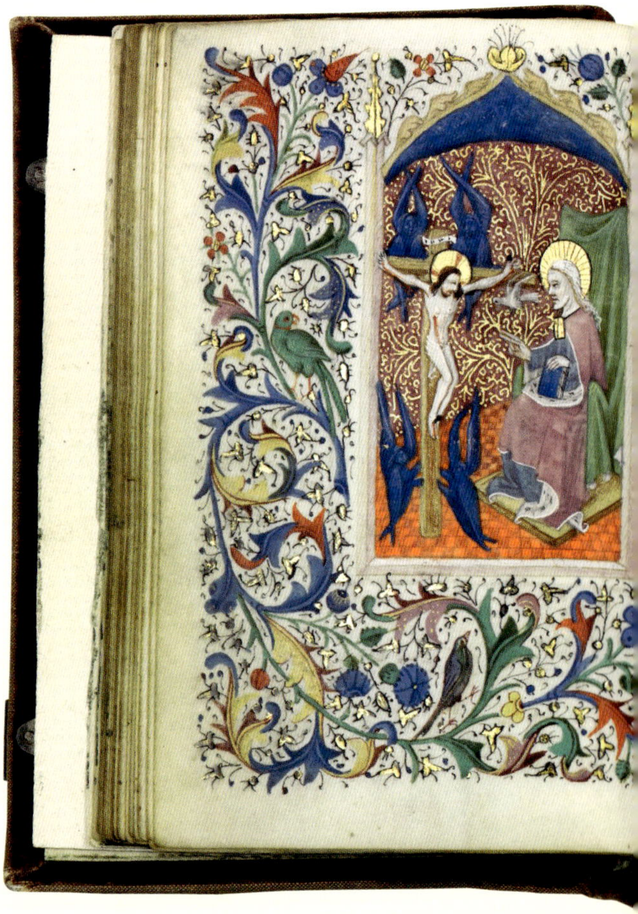

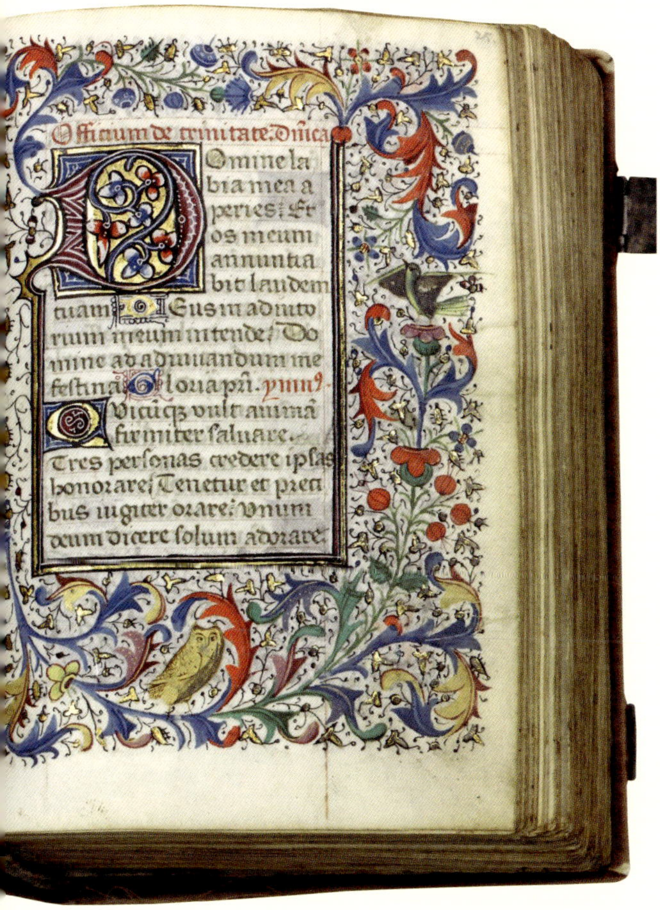

f. 24v, Trinity, with enthroned God the Father

as the group provides such a convenient catch-all into which all manuscripts generically in this style are classed. Only through careful and complete analyses of the texts, the models for the illustrations, and the circumstances of production taken decade by decade over the forty-year span of activity of the artists can we hope to arrive at a better understanding of the actual identity and contribution of the Gold Scrolls illuminators in the history of Flemish manuscript illumination. Our manuscript, with its splendid and rich sequence of miniatures and borders, will occupy a central place in such a rewritten history.

PHYSICAL DESCRIPTION: 395 ff., complete (all full-page miniatures on singletons, some joined to text singletons to form bifolia: i^{3} (1-3, 3 inserted), ii^{12} (4-15), iii^{6} (16-21, 16-21 and 18-19 manufactured bifolios), iv^{10} (22-31, 22 and 24 inserted), v^{6} (32-37, 32 inserted, blank at 37-38 cut), vi^{7} (38-44, 38 inserted), vii^{7} (45-51, 45 inserted, catchword on 49v, some leaves out of order?), viii^{10} (52-61, 52 and 58 inserted, catchword on 60v, some leaves out of order?), ix^{14} (62-75, 65-72 manufactured bifolio), x^{15} (76-90, 79 and 86 inserted, blank at 78-79 cut?), xi^{8} (91-98, 92 inserted, blank at 98-99 cut), xii^{6} (99-104, 99-104 manufactured bifolio), xiii^{7} (105-111, 105 inserted), xiv^{9} (112-120, 116 inserted), xv^{9} (121-129, 126 inserted), xvi^{9} (130-138, 137 inserted), xvii^{10} (139-148, 142 and 147 inserted), xviii^{8} (149-156, 152 inserted, blank at 151-52 cut), xix^{10} (157-166, 157 and 165 inserted), xx^{9} (167-175, 171 inserted), xxi^{10} (176-185), xxii^{9} (186-194, 186 inserted), xxiii^{11} (195-205; 195, 200, and 203 inserted), xxiv^{15} (206-220; 206, 209, 212, 216, and 220 inserted), xxv-xxvii^{8} (221-244), xxviii^{7} (245-251, 251 inserted), xxix^{5} (252-256, 252 inserted), xxx^{8} (257-264), xxxi^{9} (265-273, 269 inserted), xxxii-xxxv^{8} (274-305), xxxvi^{9} (306-314, 307 inserted), xxxvii- xliv^{8} (315-378), xlv^{6} (379-84), xlvi^{8} (385-92), xlvii^{3} (393-95, 395 inserted); catchwords at ends of gatherings ix, xiii-xvii, xix-xx, xxiii, xxv-xxvii, xxx-xxxiv, xxxvi-xliv, and xlvi); ruled in pale red ink, on 17 lines, written in dark brown ink in hybrida formata (written space 56/58 x 38/40 mm.), rubrics in red; geometric line endings in blue, 1-line initials in gold with penwork in black, 1-line initials in blue with penwork in red, 2-to-3 line initials in burnished gold on colored grounds with white tracery, 6-to-8-line initials in gothic ivy-leaf designs in colors with white tracery on burnished gold grounds; 3-sided borders with pen-and-ink rinceaux, multicolored acanthus leaves, small colored flowers and fruits, and bezant sprays on all text pages with 2-3-line initials in burnished gold (90 x 55 mm.); 4-sided borders with pen-and-ink rinceaux, multicolored acanthus leaves, small colored flowers and fruits, bezant sprays, and marginal figures on all pages with full-page miniatures, small miniatures, and historiated initials as well as on text rectos facing full-page miniatures (95/100 x 68/70 mm.); 37 full-page miniatures (55/60 x 40 mm.), 13 small miniatures 6- to 7-line high, and 8 historiated initials 6- to 7-line high, all in colors and liquid gold within narrow burnished-gold frames (unfinished full-page armorials on f. 3v; some rubbing on some pages, but generally in good condition). Modern (19th-century?) worn red velvet over boards, metal clasps and catches (one clasp missing), gilt edges, modern parchment endleaves. Dimensions 110 x 82 mm.

TEXT: ff. 1-2v, modern parchment flyleaves with added notes in pencil on f. 2; ff. 3-3v, added late 15th-century parchment leaf with unfinished armorial on f. 3v; ff. 4-15v, Calendar, with relatively sparse entries that include the southern Netherlandish saints Silvinus (15 Feb.), Bavo of Ghent in red (1 Oct.), and Donatian of Bruges (14 Oct.); ff. 17-17v, Suffrage to Louis of Toulouse; ff. 19-19v, Suffrage to Francis of Assisi; ff. 23-23v, Ten Commandments; ff. 25-29v, Sunday Hours of the Trinity; ff. 33-37v, Sunday Mass of the Trinity; ff. 39-44v, Monday Hours of the Dead; ff. 46-51v, [Monday] Mass of the Dead; 53-57v, [Tuesday] Hours of the Holy Spirit; ff. 59-64v, [Tuesday] Mass of the Holy Spirit; ff. 66-70, Wednesday Hours of All Saints; ff. 73-78v, "In die martis missa de angelis" [=Wednesday Mass of All Saints?]; ff. 80-85, Thursday Hours of the Sacrament; ff. 87-91v, Thursday Mass of the Sacrament; ff. 93-98v, Friday Hours of the Cross; ff. 100-104, Friday Mass of the Cross; ff. 106-111, [Saturday] Mass of the Virgin; ff. 111v-115v, Gospel Sequences; ff. 117-169v, Hours of the Virgin "secundu[m] usum curie romane" (use of Rome), with Matins (f. 117), Lauds (f. 127), Prime (f. 138), Terce (f. 143), Sext (f. 148), Nones (f. 153), Vespers (f. 158), and Compline (f. 166); ff. 170-170v, Salve regina; ff. 172-184v, Hours of the Virgin at Advent; ff. 187-219v, Hours of the Passion, with Matins (f. 187), Lauds (f. 196), Prime (f. 201), Terce (f. 204), Sext (f. 207), Nones (f. 210), Vespers (f. 213), and Compline (f. 217); ff. 221-230v, Passion Sequence from John; ff. 230v-231, Suffrage to Francis of Assisi; ff. 231-231v, Suffrage to Louis of Toulouse; ff. 231v-249v, prayers to Christ and the Virgin; ff. 252-268v, Penitential Psalms and litany (the latter with Lambert of Liège among martyrs); ff. 270-306v, Office of the Dead (use of Rome); ff. 308-324v, Psalter of St. Jerome; ff. 325-328v, Suffrages to God the Father (f. 325), Trinity (f. 326), Holy Spirit (f. 327), and the Cross (f. 327v); ff. 328v-331, Seven Last Words of Our Lord; ff. 331-343, Suffrages to Archangel Michael (f. 331), John the Baptist (f. 332v), Peter (f. 333), Paul (f. 333v), John the Evangelist (f. 334v), Andrew (f. 335), James Major (f. 335v), Stephen (f. 336), Lawrence (f. 337), Christopher (f. 337v), Dionysius (f. 338), Nicholas (f. 339), Martin (f. 339v), Anthony Abbot (f. 340), Mary Magdalen (f. 341), Katherine (f. 341v), and Cecilia (f. 342v). ff. 343-344, "Ave maria gratia plena dominus tecum ita sis semper mecum nunc et in hora exitus mei"; ff. 344v-347, "O intemerata" (short version, in masculine form); ff. 347-350v, "Obsecro te" (in masculine form); ff. 350v-355, "O intemerata" (long version, in masculine form); ff. 355v-384, "Ave mundi spes maria ave mitis ave pia," followed by other prayers and texts; ff. 385-394, Athanasian Creed, followed by other prayers and texts; ff. 394v-395v, ruled blanks.

ILLUSTRATION: The subjects of the 37 full-page miniatures are: f. 16v, Louis of Toulouse standing in an ecclesiastical interior (full-page); f. 18v, Francis of Assisi receiving the stigmata in a landscape (full-page); f. 22v, Moses receiving the Tablets of the Law in a landscape as the Children of Israel look on (full-page); f. 24v, Trinity, with enthroned God the Father looking at crucified God the Son opposite him, the dove of the Holy Spirit between them (full-page); f. 32v, Throne of Mercy in an ecclesiastical interior (full-page); f. 38v, Triumph of Death in a landscape, with winged Death on horseback firing arrows at men and women of different classes and social stations (full-page); f. 45v, Raising of Lazarus, in a churchyard with a landscape visible over a coped wall (full-page); f. 52v, Baptism of Christ, in a broad river Jordan in a full landscape (full-page); f. 58v, Pentecost, in a vaulted interior (full-page); f. 65v, Kneeling patron and patroness in a landscape beneath a heavenly apparition of All Saints (full-page); f. 72v, Standing Angels in a vaulted interior (full-page); f. 79v, Procession of the Sacrament, with four angels supporting a canopy over a cleric holding a

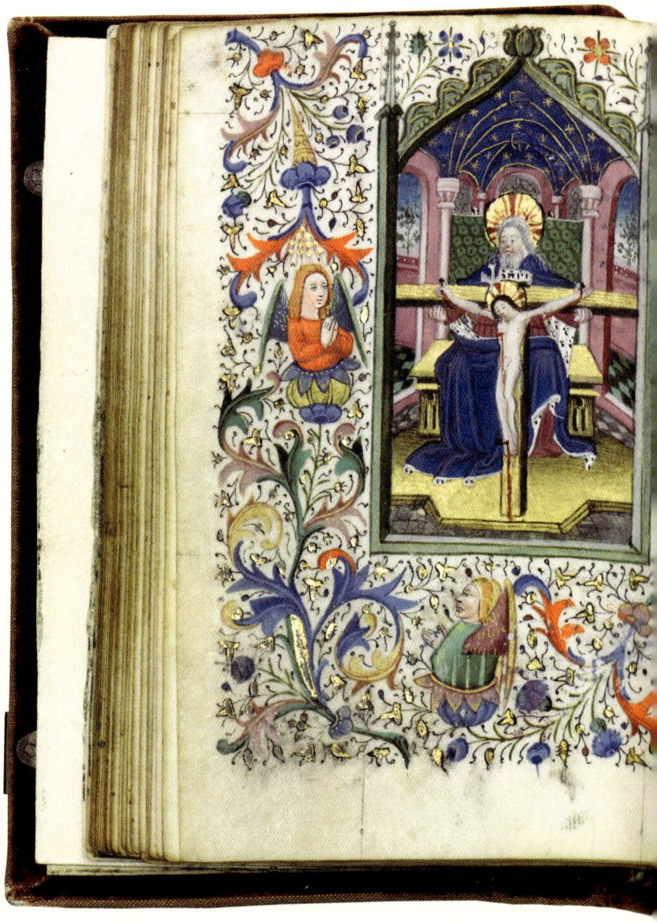

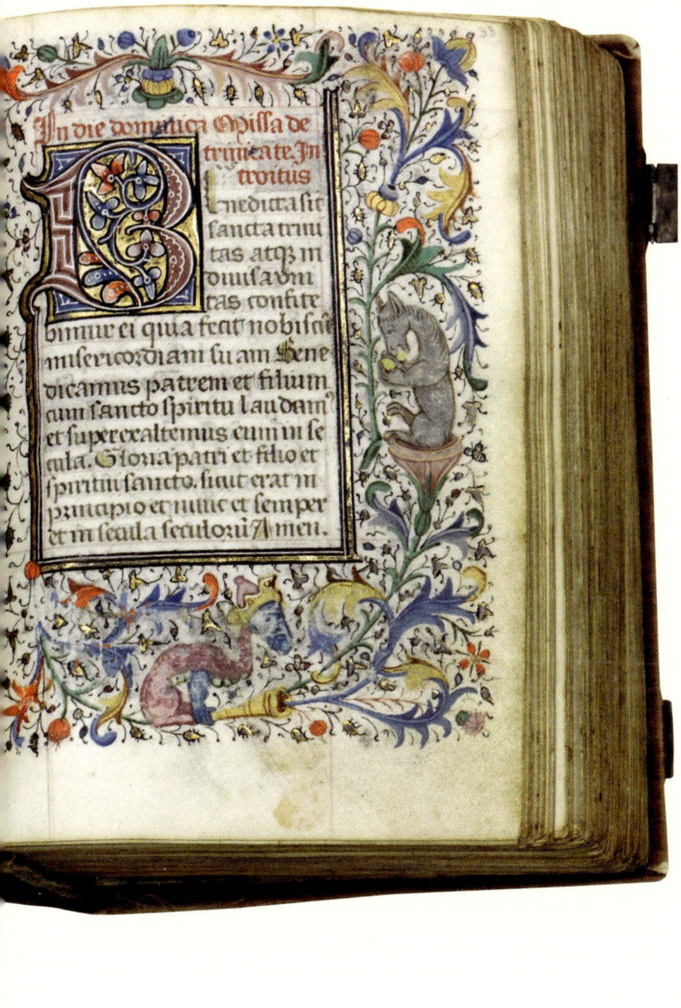

f. 32v, Throne of Mercy in an Ecclesiastical Interior

monstranced host (full-page); f. 86v, Laypeople kneeling before monstranced host on an altar in an ecclesiastical interior (full-page); f. 92v, Crucifixion, with Christ, the Virgin, John the Evangelist, and onlookers (full-page); f. 99v, Helen overseeing disinterment of True Cross, in a deep landscape (full-page); f. 105v, enthroned Virgin and Child in loggia, an angel proffering fruit, the standing patron reading from an opened book in the outer margin (full-page); f. 116v, Annunciation, in a chapel, with God the Father looking on through an aperture in the wall (full-page); f. 126v, Visitation, before a wattle fence, in a deep landscape (full-page); f. 137v, Nativity, before a wattle fence, with Joseph holding a candle (full-page); f. 142v, Annunciation to the Shepherds, before a wattle fence, in a deep landscape (full-page); f. 147v, Adoration of the Magi, in a shed (full-page); f. 152v, Presentation in the Temple (full-page); f. 157v, Massacre of the Innocents, in Herod's vaulted throne room (full-page); f. 165v, Flight into Egypt, in a deep landscape, with a toppling idol in the outer margin (full-page); f. 171v, Coronation of the Virgin, in a vaulted throne room, with an angel playing a psaltery in the lower margin and another angel playing a portative organ in the outer margin (full-page); f. 186v, Christ on Gethsemane, set within a wooden palisade (full-page); f. 195v, Taking of Christ, set in a deep landscape (full-page); f. 200v, Christ before Pilate, in Pilate's throne room (full-page); f. 203v, Flagellation of Christ, in a vaulted chamber (full-page); f. 206v, Christ Carrying the Cross, in a deep landscape (full-page); f. 209v, Christ Nailed to Cross on a foreground rise (full-page); f. 212v, Christ Deposed from the Cross on a foreground rise (full-page); f. 216v, Entombment of Christ in a deep landscape (full-page); f. 220v, Man of Sorrows with Arma Christi before a blue-sky backdrop (full-page); f. 251v, Last Judgment, with an angel carrying a soul in a white cloth in the outer margin (full-page); f. 269v, Funeral Service, in a church choir (full-page); f. 307v, St. Jerome in His Study (full-page). - There are 13 small miniatures: f. 326, Throne of Mercy before gold-scroll backdrop (6-line-high small miniature); f. 327, Pentecost (6-line-high small miniature); f. 327v, Crucifixion with Mary and John before gold-scroll backdrop (6-line-high small miniature); f. 332v, Standing John Baptist in Landscape (6-line-high small miniature); f. 333v, Paul standing before diapered ground (6-line-high small miniature); f. 334v, John the Evangelist standing before coped wall (7-line-high small miniature); f. 335, Andrew standing before gold-scroll backdrop (6-line-high small miniature); f. 335v, James Major standing before gold-scroll backdrop (6-line-high small miniature); f. 336, Stephen standing before coped wall (6-line-high small miniature); f. 337, Laurence standing before coped wall (6-line-high small miniature); f. 337v, Christopher Carrying Child (6-line-high small miniature); f. 339v, Martin Dividing Cloak in Landscape (6-line-high small miniature); f. 341, Mary Magdalene Standing in Landscape (6-line-high small miniature). - There are 8 historiated initials: f. 325, Standing God the Father before coped wall (6-line-high initial D); f. 331, Standing Archangel Michael in Landscape (6-line-high initial O), with souls emerging from the earth in lower and outer margins; f. 333, Standing Peter in Landscape (7-line-high initial P); f. 338, Dionysius Standing before gold-scroll backdrop (6-line-high initial D); f. 339, Nicholas Standing before gold-scroll backdrop (6-line-high initial B); f. 340, Anthony Abbot Standing in Landscape (6-line-high initial V); f. 341v, Katherine Standing before gold-scroll backdrop (6-line-high initial V); f. 342v, Cecilia Standing before gold-scroll backdrop (6-line-high initial V).

OWNERSHIP: 1. Written ca. 1450 in Bruges, for male use (ff. 344v-347, 347-350v, and 350v-355), probably for the man represented on ff. 65v and 105v. - 2. Unidentified owner who had inserted the late 15th-century singleton (f. 3) with the never completed quartered armorials on f. 3v (quarters 1 and 4: or, a cross pattée fitchée at bottom point gules, between the four 1 and 4 a fleur-de-lis sable, 2 and 3 a rose heraldic lilac; quarters 2 and 3: empty). - 3. "De la Collection de M. Schlumberger Ribeauville" and to right "R / 1941 / Fors. No. 10:" (modern pencil notes on verso of ultimate back paper flyleaf). - 4. Bookplate of Madeleine and René Junod (inside front cover).

LITERATURE: Unpublished; compare Achten, Gerd. *Das christliche Gebetbuch im Mittelalter*, Berlin, 1980. - [Exhibition]. Brussels, Bibliothèque Royale and Paris, Bibliothèque Nationale de France. *Miniatures flamandes 1404-1482*, eds. Bernard Bousmanne and Thierry Delcourt, Brussels and Paris, 2011, pp. 140-142. - Cardon, Bert. "The Illustrations and the Gold Scrolls Group, Typologische Tafeleren uit het Leven van Jesus [Typological scenes from the Life of Christ]: A Manuscript from the Gold Scrolls Group (Bruges, c. 1440) in the Pierpont Morgan Library, New York, MS Morgan 649," *Corpus of Illuminated Manuscripts from the Low Countries*, i, ed. M. Smeyers, Leuven, 1985, pp. 119-204. - Dogaer, Georges. *Flemish Miniature Painting in the 15th and 16th Centuries*, Amsterdam, 1987, pp. 27-31. - Finke, Ulrich, ed. *Katalog der mittelalterlichen Handschriften und Einzelblätter in der Kunstbibliothek*, Berlin, s.d. [c. 1967]. - Smeyers, Maurits. *Flemish Miniatures from the 8th to the mid-16th Century. The Medieval World in Parchment*, Louvain, Davidsfonds, 1999. - Winkler, Friedrich. *Die flämische Buchmalerei des XV.und XVI. Jahrhunderts*, Leipzig, 1925 (repr. Amsterdam, 1978), pp. 25-27.

ONLINE RESOURCES:
"Gold Scrolls Group" in the Dictionary of Art
http://www.oxfordartonline.com/public/book/oao_gao

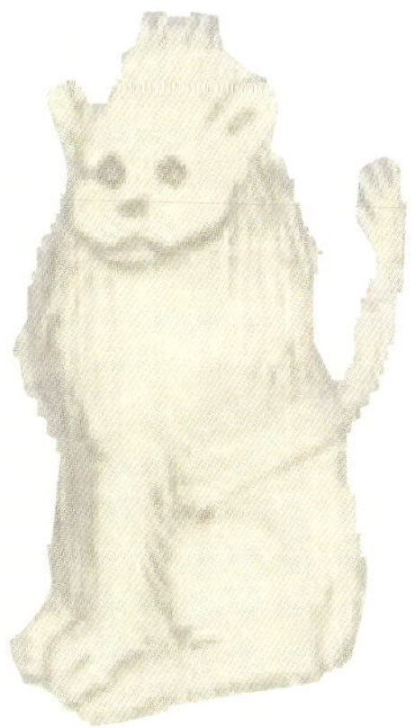

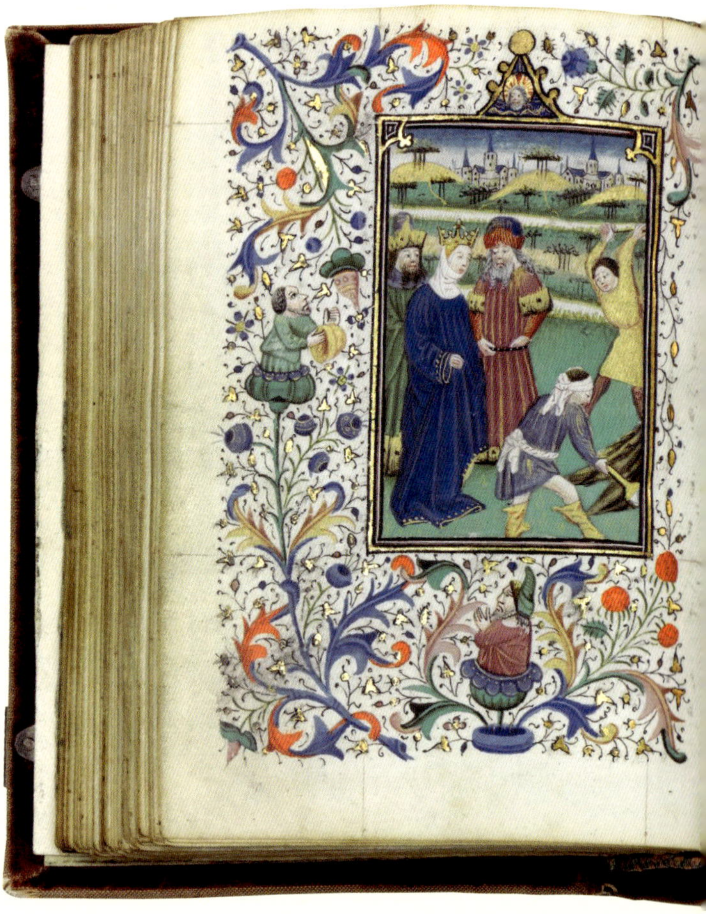

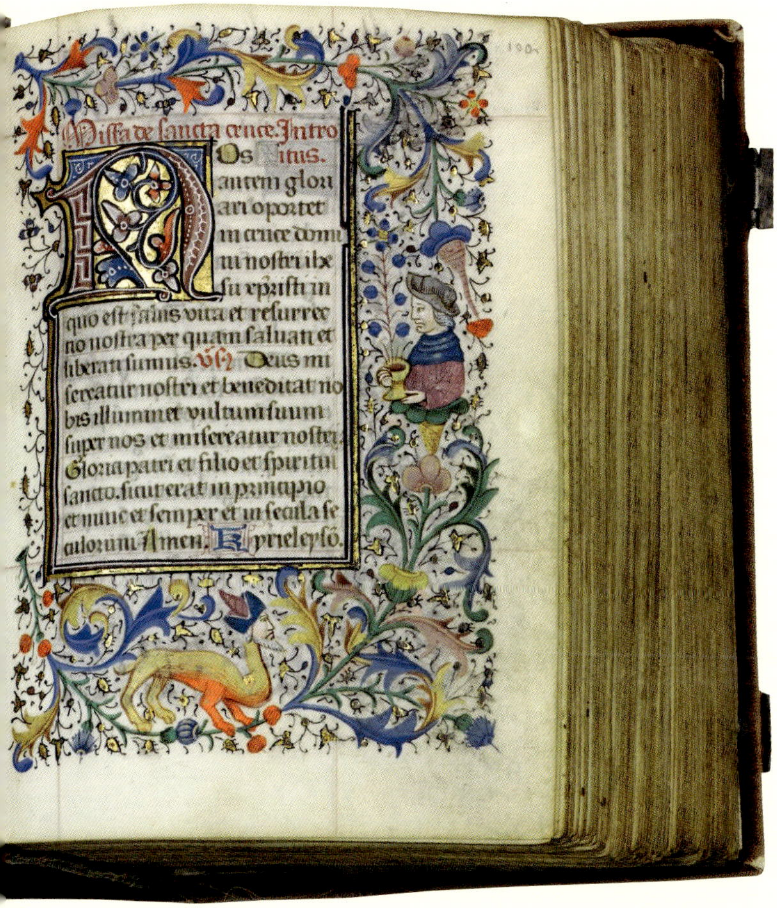

ff. 99v-100, Helen Overseeing Disinterment of True Cross

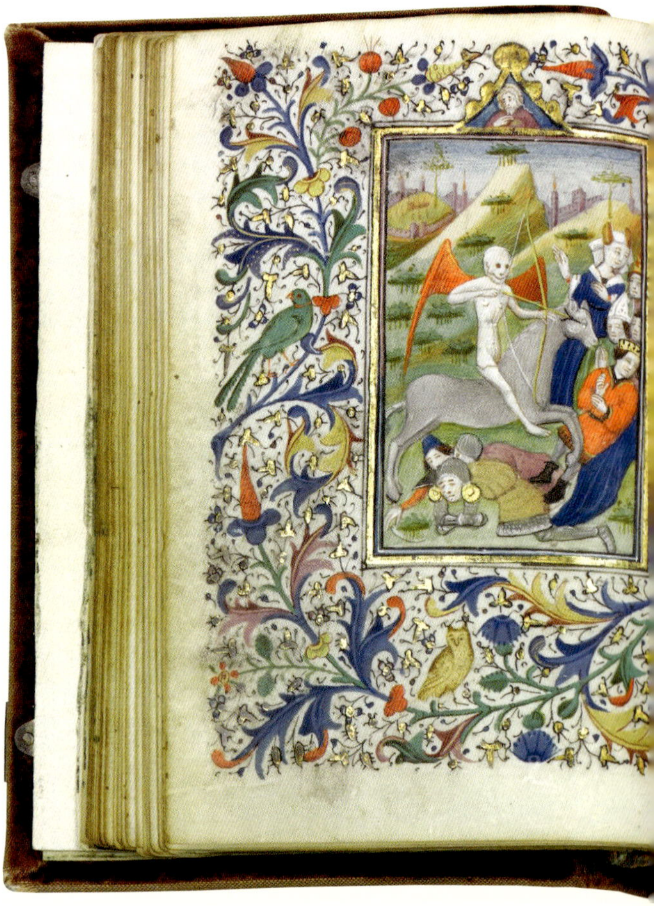

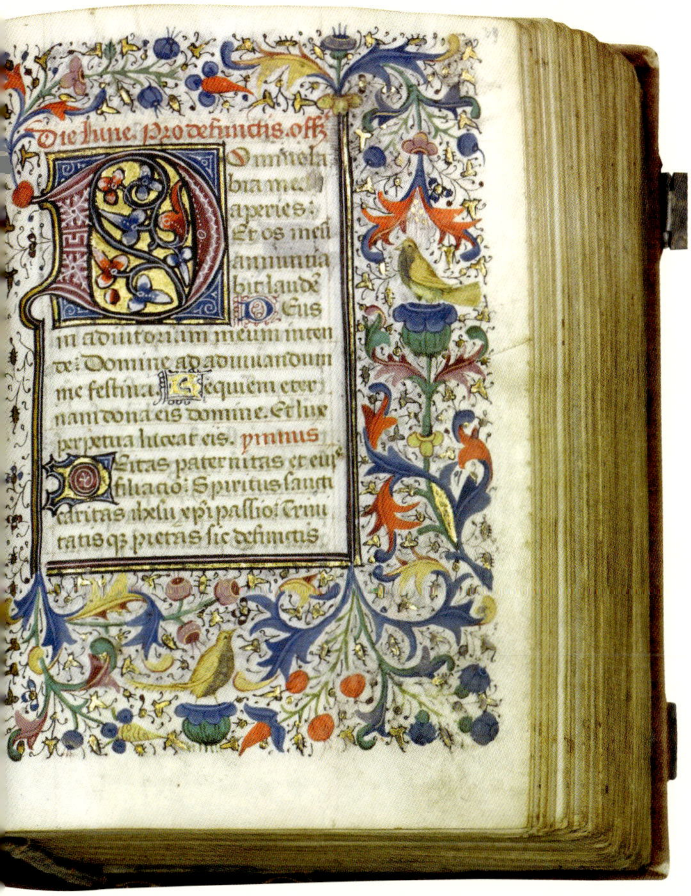

ff. 38v-39, Triumph of Death

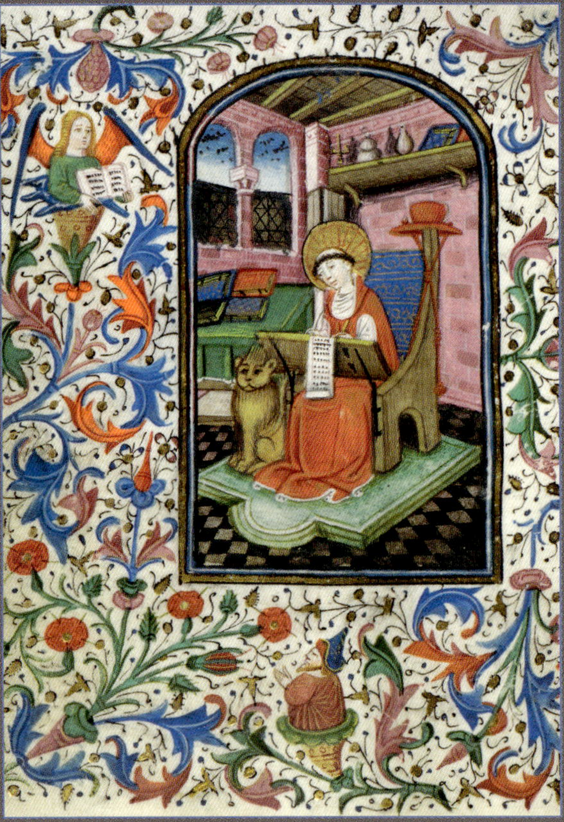

Berlin, Kunstbibliothek, MS Grisebach 4,
Book of Hours, f. 122v, Saint Jerome in His Study

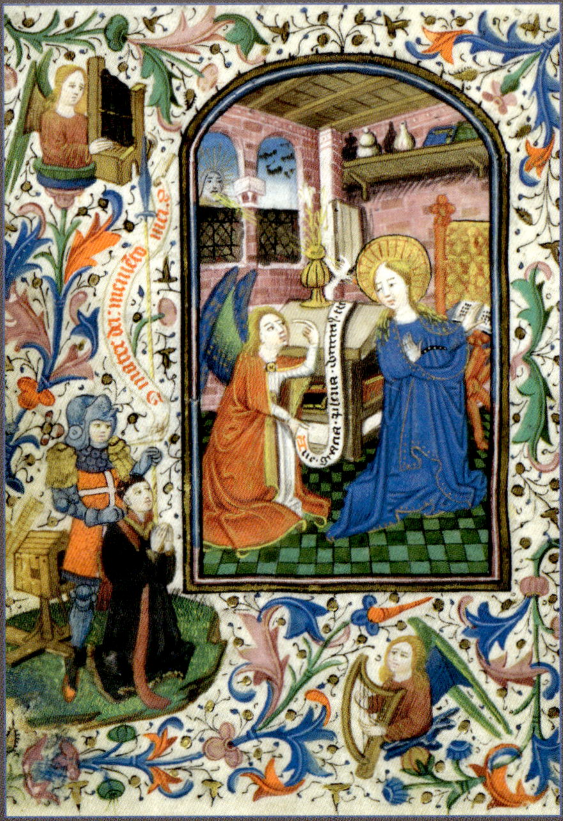

Berlin, Kunstbibliothek, MS Grisebach 4,
Book of Hours, f. 17v, Annunciation

Facing page, f. 307v, St. Jerome in His Study

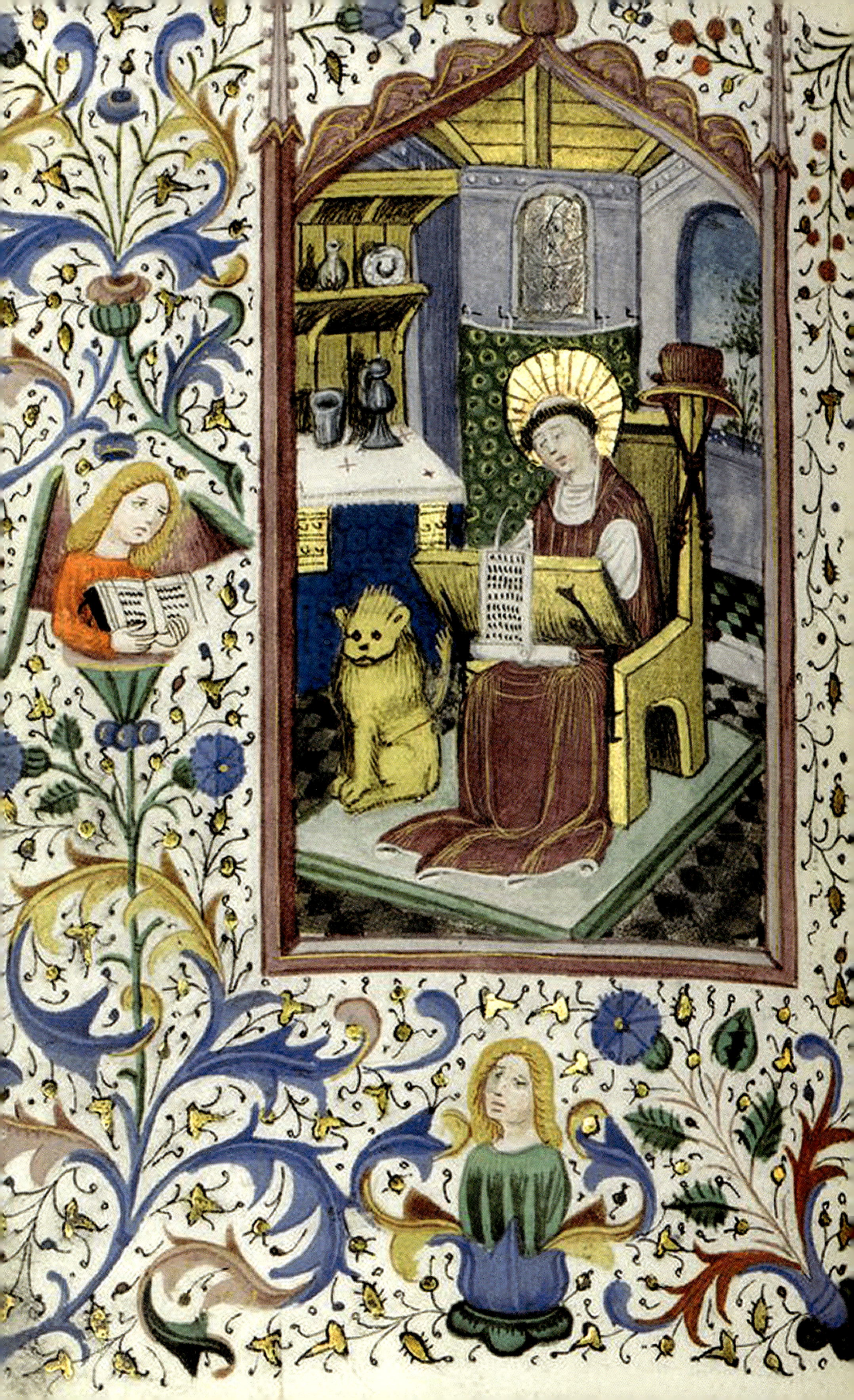

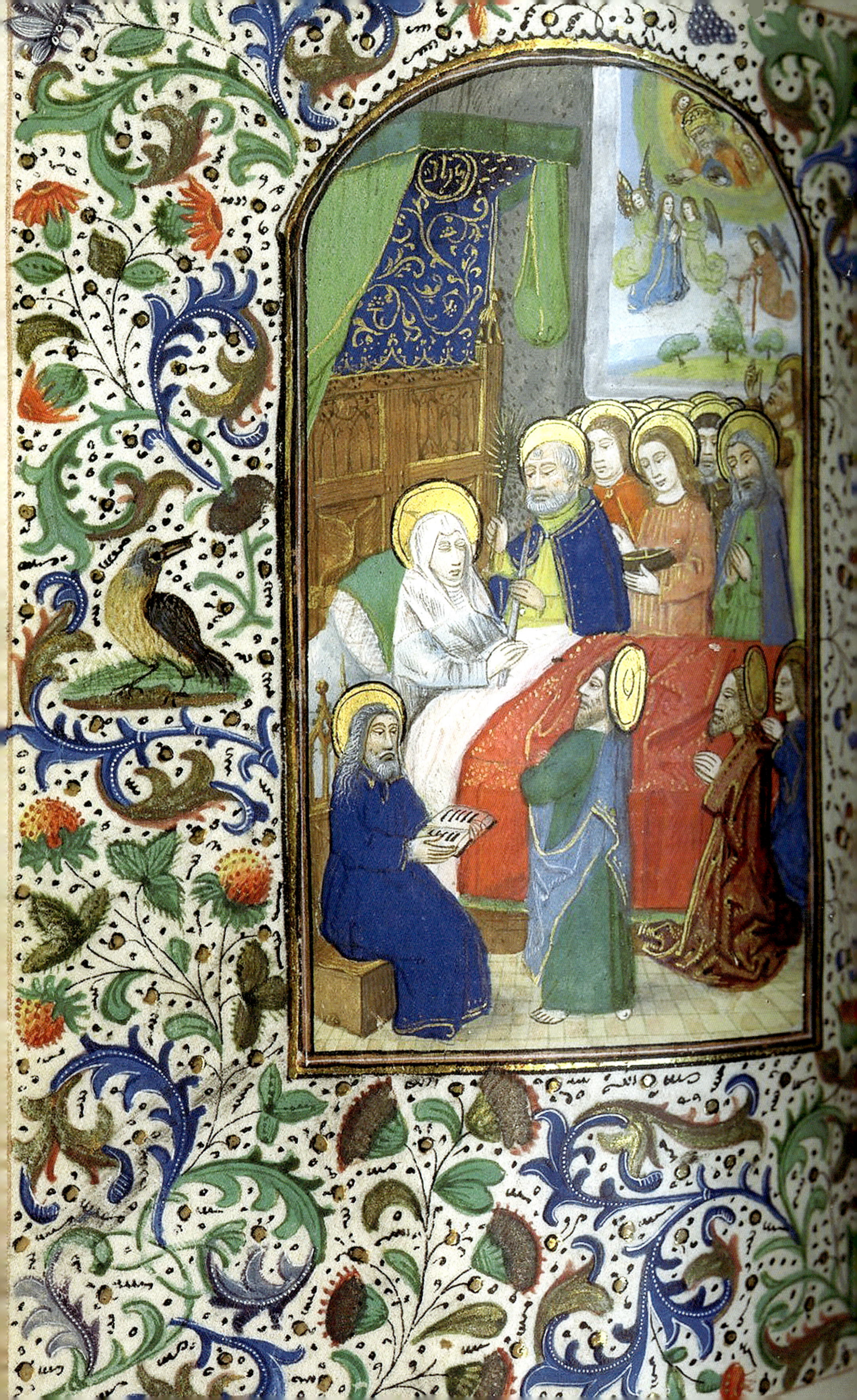

7

Book of Hours (Use unknown)

In Latin with Dutch and French, illuminated manuscript on parchment
Southern Netherlands, probably Bruges or Ghent, c. 1470-1480
5 miniatures from the circle of Willem Vrelant

In the fifteenth and sixteenth centuries the city of Bruges became a European art capital, rivaling Paris in the production of Books of Hours. Its European-wide importance derived not only from its flourishing cloth markets and its central position within the Hanseatic League, which promoted trade with England and elsewhere, but from Duke Philip the Good's establishment of the court of Burgundy in the city and its surroundings. Active in Bruges, a succession of great Flemish panel painters began with Jan van Eyck (died 1441) and continued through Gerard David (died 1523). Illuminators during roughtly the same time include a group of pre-Eyckian artists, mostly anonymous, such as the Beaufort Master, and continue through the Master of Mary of Burgundy and finally the great Simon Bening (died 1561). When Willem Vrelant moved to Bruges around mid-century, it must have been to take advantage of the opportunities posed by the thriving market for illuminated manuscripts.

Stylistically typical of Bruges painting in the third quarter of the century, this manuscript is an unusual, thick, and beautifully preserved Flemish Book of Hours with wonderful illuminated borders on most pages and remarkably fine full-page miniatures. It does not contain the Hours of the Virgin. Instead it includes Hours of the Days of the Week with the virtually unique Hours of the Purification of the Virgin, which suggests that it was a special commission for a client to supplement a "normal" Book of Hours or a monastic Breviary. Indeed this elaborate volume was doubtless planned as a special commission and perhaps as a supplement to a Book of Hours or to a monastic Breviary. There are Sunday Hours of the Trinity, the Wednesday Hours of All Saints, and the Thursday Hours of the Sacrament, rare in any manuscript. There is also the extremely rare Hours of the Purification recorded by Leroquais only in a single manuscript (Paris, BnF, MS lat. 1077, Liège, thirteenth century). The iconography of the first miniature included here is also very rare. The Gathering of Manna occurs in the Hours of Catherine of Cleves (Plummer, 1966, pl. 74), but we know of nothing comparable in Bruges books. The figure of Moses may be taken from a pattern of Christ in Gethsemane.

Facing page, f. 228v, Death of the Virgin

The principal decoration of this manuscript consists of five miniatures that stand stylistically midway between Willem Vrelant and the Master of Raphael de Mercatellis. Willem Vrelant was the most prolific illuminator in Bruges in the third quarter of the fifteenth century and the principal illuminator of his generation (Bousmanne, 1997). Vrelant (or Wyelant as he is called in some of the documents) moved from Utrecht to Bruges before 1454, when his name first appears in the guild. He sponsored three or four illuminators in the guild during the course of his long career (he died in 1481/82). The introduction of new compositions and iconography, sometimes based on the panel paintings of earlier and contemporary Bruges panel painters, such as Jan Van Eyck and Hans Memling, was one characteristic of Vrelant's contribution. There is still considerable confusion regarding Vrelant's role in the artistic production that bears his name, that of his workshop, or his followers (Farquhar, 1974). Both the volume and the widely varying quality of the production ascribed to him strongly suggest that by the 1460s Vrelant had evolved into an entrepreneur who subcontracted to other book painters adept at adhering to his signature style (Clark, 1997, pp. 106-9). The consensus today seems to be that, while maintaining a workshop, Vrelant also functioned as a sort of *libraire* or stationer, gathering together artists, scribes, decorators, and binders for diverse commissions and possibly also for ready-made manuscripts.

The name of the Master of Raphael of Mercatellis describes a number of anonymous miniaturists working in Bruges, Ghent, or both, who illuminated a body of manuscripts for Raphael, abbot of Saint Bavo in Ghent from 1478 up until his death in 1508 (Dogaer 1987, pp. 150-55). A Book of Hours in the style of the Raphael de Mercatellis Master – later owned by Jean-Jacques Charron de Menars (1643-1718) – was first identified in 1990 by Eberhard König (König 1990, pp. 362-77, cat. 32). To these Horae may be added a second one in the Fitzwilliam Museum in Cambridge (MS McClean 98; Morgan & Panayotova 2009, pp. 196-97, no. 228). In the present Horae, on the one hand, the profiled male heads and the zigzag white lines that highlight the trees and bushes in our Dormition of the Virgin (f. 228v) invite comparison with those in the McClean Crucifixion (f. 14v). On the other hand, the less linear modeling of the physiognomies in our manuscript recalls that of figures painted in the Vrelant style in the 1460s and early 1470s. Although Vrelant died in 1481, his signature style seems to have run its course by the mid-1470s. By contrast, König dated the Charron de Menars Hours to about 1480, and Morgan and Panayotova placed McClean 98 between about 1480 or 1490. All of this suggests a date in the 1470s for our codex, when Vrelant was still active. Bruges or Ghent seems the most likely place of manufacture for the extant five miniatures.

Whoever the actual painter of the miniatures in our manuscript and whatever his precise relationship was with Willem Vrelant, the soft colors and dreamy landscapes echo Dutch manuscripts of the mid-century, as in the Montfort Book of Hours in Vienna (Österreichische Nationalbibliothek, ser. nov. 12878). The Montfort Hours is ascribed to Vrelant before he left Utrecht to settle in Bruges in 1456 (see Thoss, 1987, no. 7, with further references). The Dutch links recur in the final parts of the present book. Gatherings 37-41 (except for its first leaf, f. 293) are in a second style (ff. 294-332) and gatherings 42-44 and 46-51 are in a similar but third style (ff. 333-352 and 357-end). Borders here are in formal archaic prickly ivy-leaf patterns atypical of the southern Netherlands but certainly current in Utrecht in the early decades of the century (see H. Defoer, et al., 1989, color pls. I.1a, I.3a-3b, I.6, I.7, etc.). The leaves here may have been salvaged from a much earlier book brought to Bruges and adapted and updated in the Vrelant shop. Three of the miniatures are on added sheets. The intended position of one was marked before its insertion by a Dutch guideword "vieronik" [Veronica] (f. 368v) and a similar word "marie" suggests a lost insertion after f. 379v.

PHYSICAL DESCRIPTION: 397 ff., text complete, likely missing some inserted miniatures (collation: i^{12}, $ii\text{-}xv^{8}$, xvi^{8+1}, $xvii\text{-}xx^{8,}$ xxi^{4}, xxii^{8+1}, $xxiii\text{-}xviii^{8}$, xxix^{8+1}, $xxx\text{-}xxxv^{8}$, xxxvi^{8+1}, xxxvii^{8}, xxxviii^{8+1}, xxxix^{8}, xl^{8+1}, xli^{6}, $xlii\text{-}xliv^{8}$, xlv^{2+1}, xlvi^{8}, xlvii^{8+1}, xlviii^{2+1}, xlix^{8}, 110), full-page miniatures on tipped-in singletons, text on up to 17 lines, ruled in pale red ink (justification: 91 x 54 mm.), written in dark brown ink in a very skillful gothic liturgical hand, rubrics in red, contemporary foliation in Roman numbers in red ink on ff. 13–290 (i–cclxxv, omitting added sheets), capitals touched in yellow, line-fillers in blue and red and burnished gold, versal initials throughout alternately burnished gold and dark (or pale) blue with penwork in red or black, 2-line initials in quires 37–51 in burnished gold on red and blue grounds with white tracery, 3-line initials elsewhere in highly burnished gold on red and blue grounds with delicate white tracery and with marginal sprays with gold ivy leaves and some colored petals on hairline stems, four large 3-line initials with thick ivyleaf borders extending into all margins, 28 large initials with half or three-quarter borders, the initials mainly 3-line (five 5-line, one on f. 235 one-line) in ivy-leaf designs in colors on highly burnished gold grounds, the borders in designs of colored acanthus leaves and flowers and fruit infilled with tiny black dots, 13 very large initials with full borders, the initials mostly 5-line (one 6-line) and the borders often including grotesque animals and birds, etc., 5 full-page miniatures in arch-topped compartments within full borders. Bound in mid-

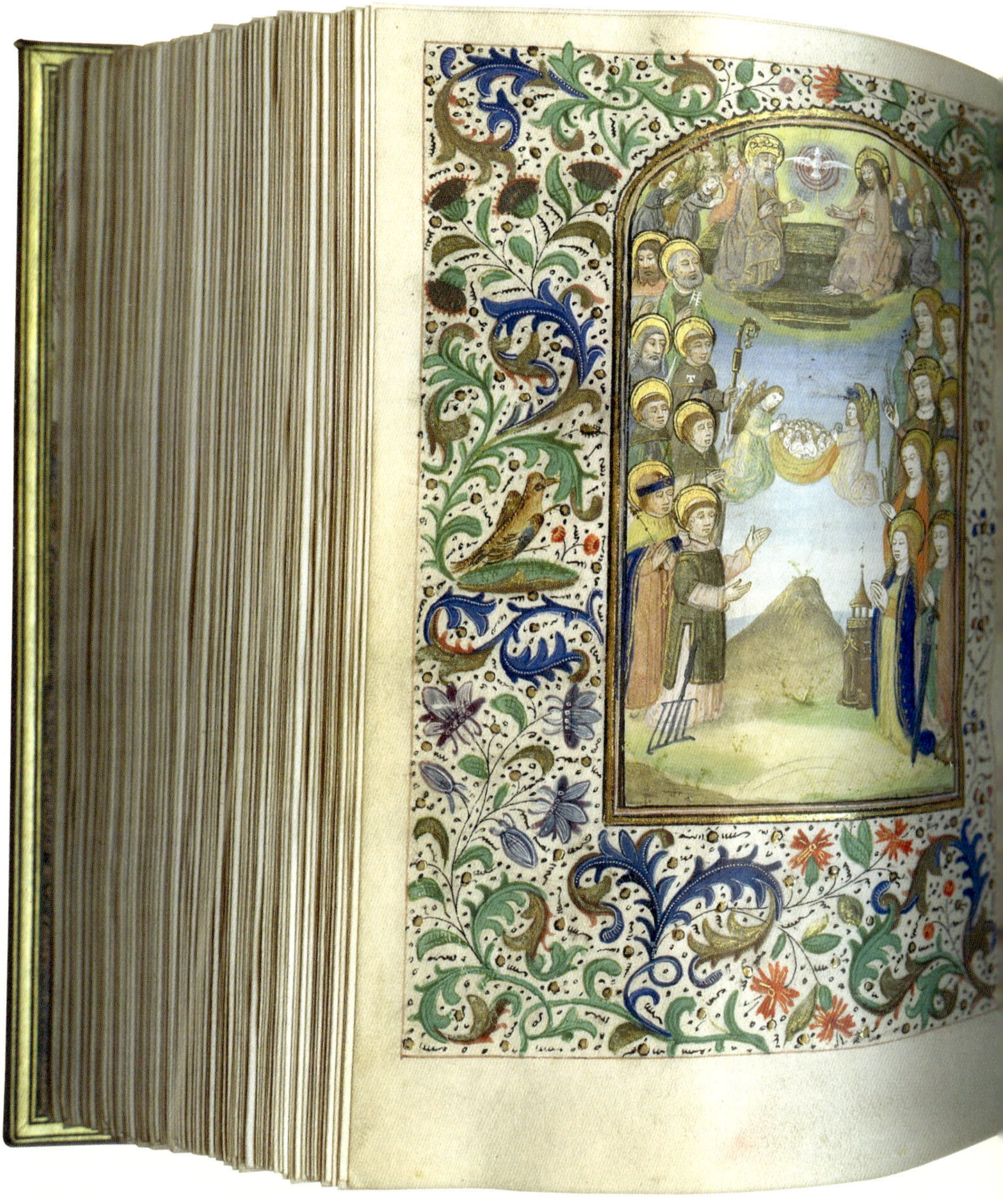

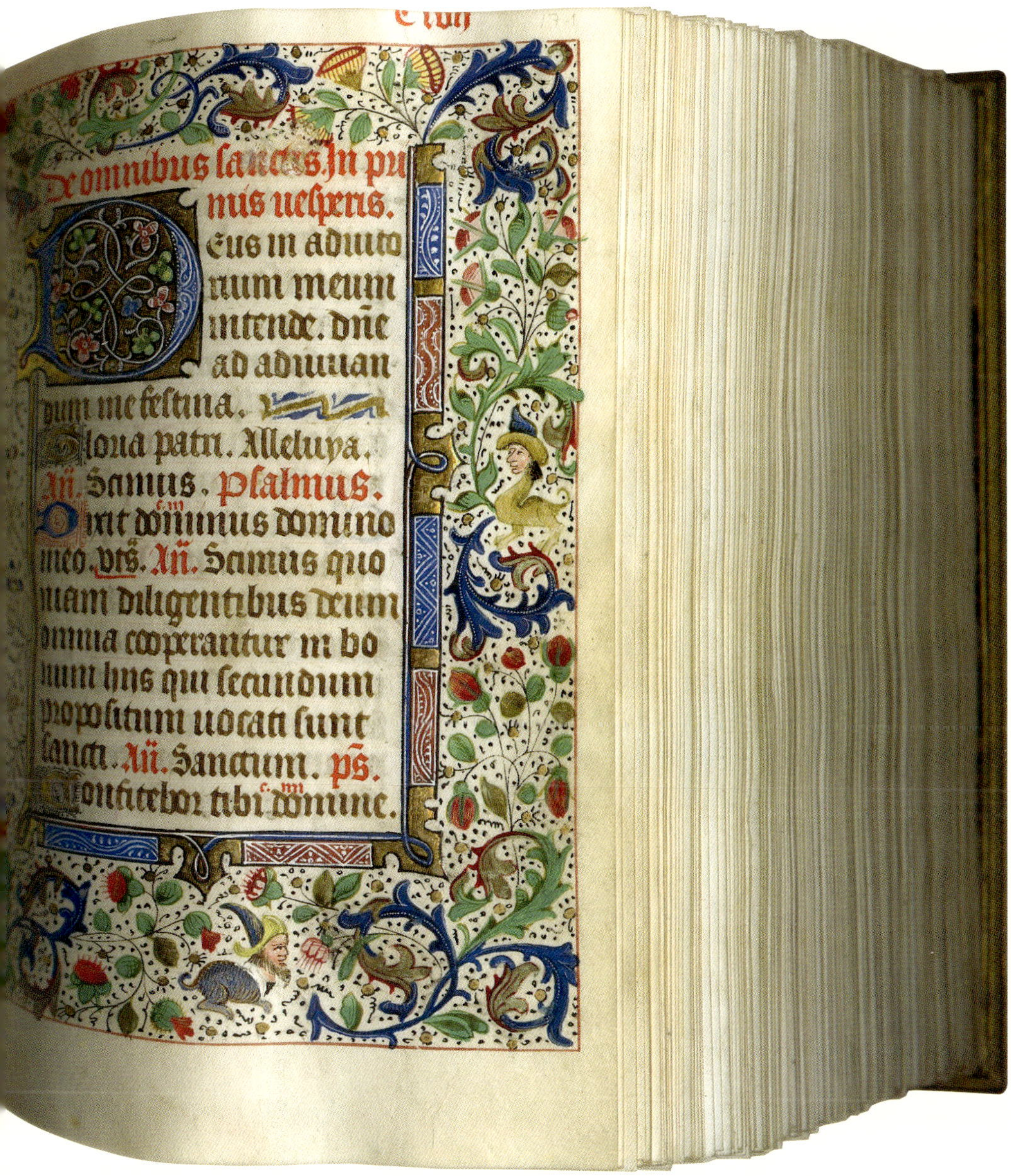

ff. 170v-171, All Saints

nineteenth-century Parisian dark brown morocco profusely gilt, spine in compartments profusely gilt, green morocco mosaic doublures inset with decorative strapwork designs in black and gilt, marbled endleaves, green silk marker, gilt edges (Bound by Niedrée (1803–circa 1856), signed along inner edge of the inside upper cover). (Some contemporary folio numbers partly cropped, occasional slight smudging and rubbing of illumination, a few minor marks here and there, generally in very fine fresh condition with sparkling gold and wide clean margins). Dimensions 156 x 98 mm.

TEXT: ff. 1-12v, Calendar; ff. 13-124v, Hours of the Trinity, in full, with first Vespers (f. 13), Compline (f. 24), Matins (f. 33), Lauds (f. 64v), Prime (f. 77), Terce (f. 95), Sext (f. 101), None (f. 108v) and second Vespers (f. 115); ff. 126-169v, Hours of the Holy Sacrament, in full, with first Vespers (fol. 126), Compline (fol. 130v), Matins (f. 133), Lauds (f. 157v), Prime (f. 160), Terce (f. 162), Sext (f. 164), None (f. 166) and second Vespers (f. 166); ff. 171-227, Hours of All Saints, in full with first Vespers (f. 171), Compline (f. 176), Matins (f. 179), Lauds (f. 213), Prime (f. 217), Terce (f. 218v), Sext (f. 221), None (f. 223) and second Vespers (f. 225); ff. 229-291, Hours of the Purification of the Virgin, in full, with first Vespers (f. 229), Compline (f. 235), Matins (f. 238), Lauds (f. 268), Prime (f. 271v), Terce (f. 272v), Sext (f. 275v), None (f. 277v) and second Vespers (f. 279v), followed by the hymn for the dedication of a church (f. 291v); ff. 293-332v, Office of the Dead, with Vespers (f. 293), Matins (f. 299) and Lauds (f. 321); ff. 333-342v, "Salvo te sancta maria" and other hymns to the Virgin and Christ, including a prayer of St. Augustine (begins f. 343v); ff. 349-349v, rubric in Dutch, *Dit ghebet maete sinte augustijn ende soe wie datse* ..., incipit, "O crux gloriosa"; ff. 350-368v, Prayers, "Ave mundi spes maria ..." with collects, followed by prayers for peace, "Pax illa celestis ..."; to the Virgin, "Immolate integra et ..." (f. 355); "O intemerata ..." (f. 356v); "Obsecro te" (f. 359v); rubric *Soe wat meinschen die dese bedinghe seghet alle daghe* ..., incipit "Maria virgo virginum ..." (f. 363); ff. 370-371, "Salve sancta facies ..."; ff. 371-379v, Indulgences; Hundred Names of Christ (f. 377v); Psalms for the deliverance of souls from purgatory (f. 380v), and other prayers (all with rubrics in Dutch).

ILLUSTRATION: f. 125v, Children of Israel in the Wilderness of Sinai, Manna falling from Heaven; f. 170v, All Saints; f. 228v, Death of the Virgin; f. 348v, Symbols of the Passion, rectangular miniature (85 x 48 mm.); f. 369v, St. Veronica, rectangular miniature (85 x 48 mm.).

OWNERSHIP: 1. Doubtless illuminated in Bruges. The Calendar singles out in red saints Amand and Vedast, Basilius Archbishop, Boniface, Bavo and Remigius, and Donatian. The text has rubrics frequently in Dutch and rarely in French (e.g., ff. 377v-378r), suggesting use on the border between the two cultures. There are faint plummet inscriptions in an italic hand on ff. 151 and 206, "Quis sit quare. Vive bourgoingne, 1593, 15 Aug." – 2. Ignace de Coussemaker, of Bailleul, near Dunkerque, historian, with his nineteenth-century armorial bookplate; perhaps from the Coussemaker sale in Brussels, 17 April 1877. – 3. Sale in Paris, *Précieux manuscrits et livres anciens*, Galantaris, Nouveau Drouot, 19 December 1986, lot 62, with color plate; resold Sotheby's, 1 December 1987, lot 57, to Tenschert. – 4. Joost R. Ritman (born 1941), a businessman from the Netherlands and founder of the library Bibliotheca Philosophica Hermetica in Amsterdam, purchased from Tenschert, *Leuchtendes Mittelalter*, I, cat. 21, 1989, pp. 219-222, no. 37 (190,000 DM). – 5. Sold Sotheby's Ritman Sale, *A Selection of Illuminated Manuscripts from the 13th to the 16th Centuries, The Property of Mr. J. R. Ritman*, 6 July 2000, lot 24. – 6. Private North American Collection.

LITERATURE: Bousmanne, Bernard. *"Item a Guillaume Wyeland aussi enlumineur" Willem Vrelant, Un aspect de l'enluminure dans les Pays-bas meridionaux*, exh. cat., Brussels, Bibliothèque Royale, 1997. - Exhibition Brussels, Royal Library of Belgium, and Paris, BnF, *Miniatures flamandes 1404-1482*, Brussels and Paris, 2011. - Clark, Gregory T. *The Hours of Isabel la Católica:The Facsimile Edition – Commentary*, Madrid, 1997.- Defoer, Henri et al. *The Golden Age of Dutch Manuscript Illumination*, New York, 1989. - Dogaer, Georges. *Flemish Miniature Painting in the 15th and 16th Centuries*, Amsterdam, 1987.- Farquhar, James D. "The Vrelant Enigma: is the Style the Man?," *Quaerendo* 4 (1974), pp. 100-108. - König, E. *Leuchtendes Mittelalter II* (Antiquariat Heribert Tenschert, Katalog 25), Rotthalmünster (D) & Ramsen (CH), 1990. - Morgan, Nigel, and Stella Panayotova, eds., *Illuminated Manuscripts in Cambridge:A Catalogue of Western Book Illumination in the Fitzwilliam Museum and the Cambridge Colleges. Part I*, Volume 2: *The Meuse Region [and the] Southern Netherlands*, London & Turnhout, 2009.- Plummer, John. *The Hours of Catherine of Cleves,* New York, 1966. - Thoss, Dagmar. *Flämische Buchmalerei,* exh. cat., Vienna, Österreichische Nationalbibliothek, 1987.

ONLINE RESOURCES:

William Vrelant, at the J.P. Getty Museum:
http://www.getty.edu/art/gettyguide/artMakerDetails?maker=1077

Turning the pages, William Vrelant, BnF
http://expositions.bnf.fr/flamands/livres/heures/index.htm

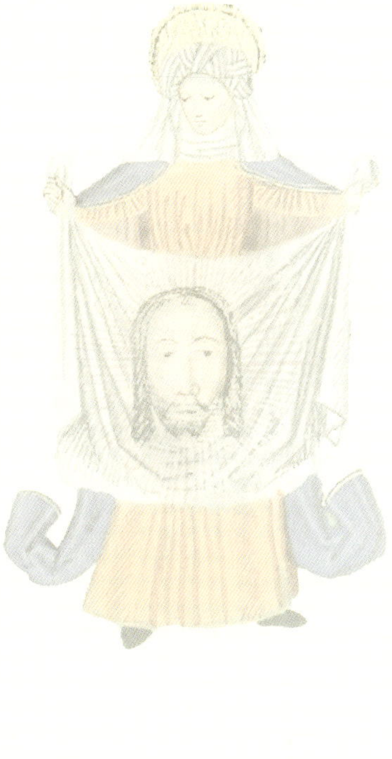

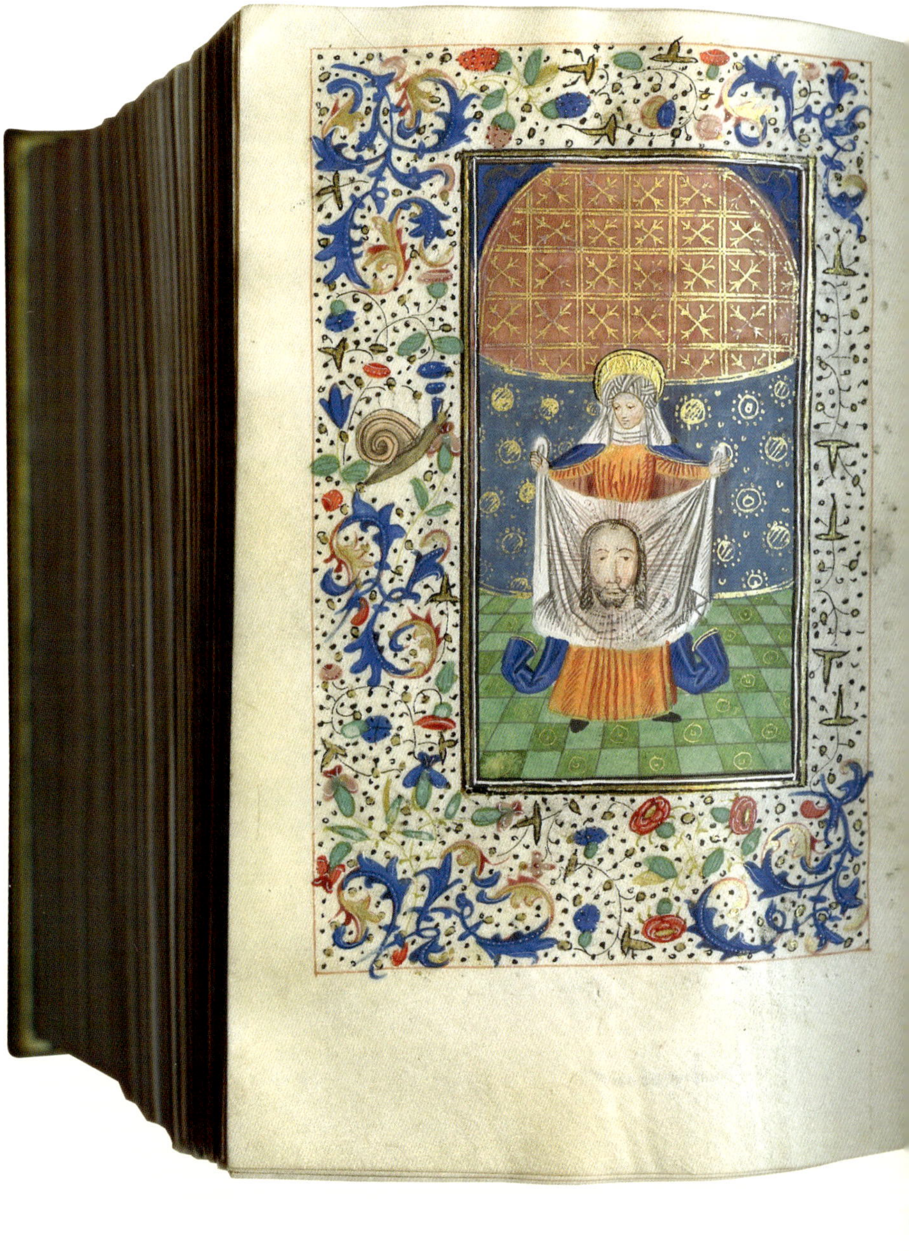

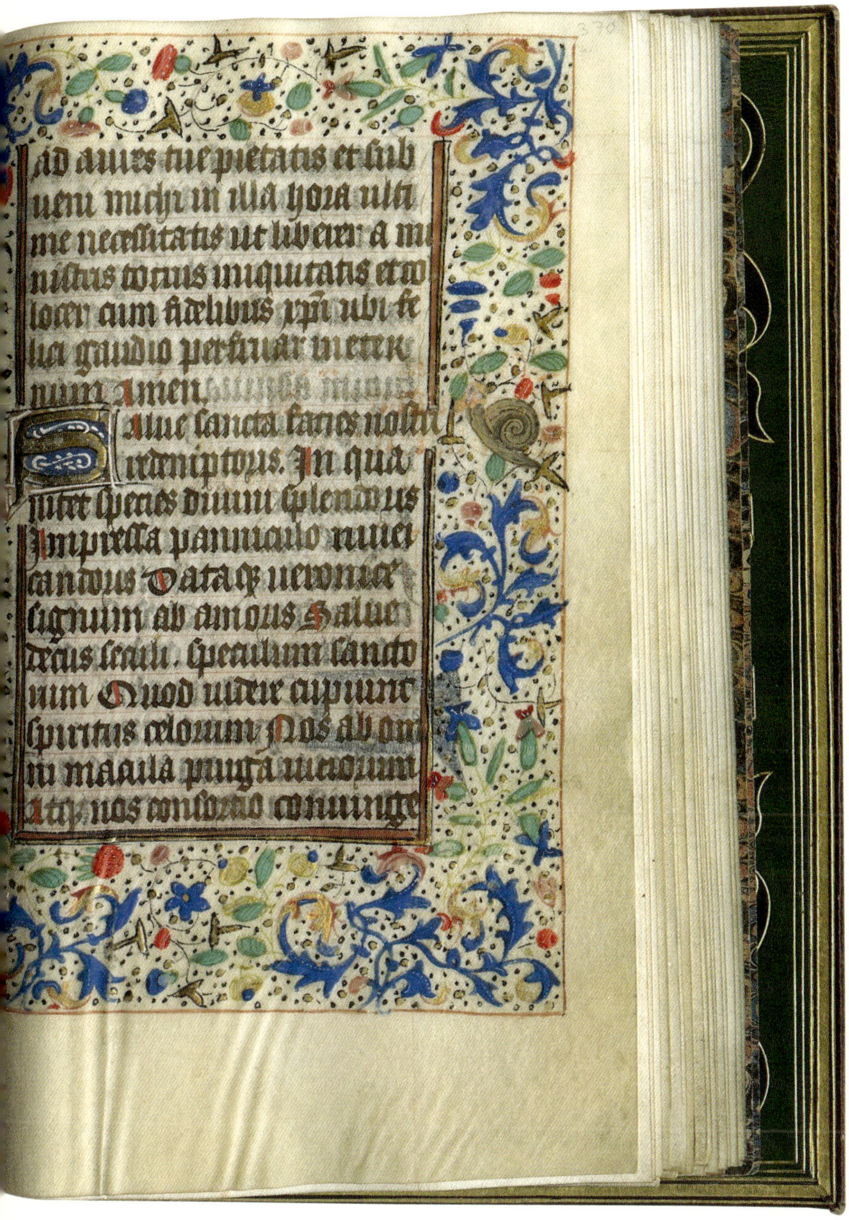
ad aures tue pietatis et sub
ueni michi in illa hora ulti
me necessitatis ut liberer a mi
nistris totius iniquitatis et col
locer cum fidelibus xpi ubi fe
lici gaudio perfruar in etter
num Amen.
Salue sancta facies nostri
redemptoris. In qua
nitet species diuini splendoris
Impressa panniculo niuei
candoris Dataque ueronice
signum ob amoris Salue
decus seculi. Speculum sancto
rum Quod uidere cupiunt
spiritus celorum Nos ab om
ni macula purga uiciorum
Atque nos consorcio coniunge

ff. 369v-370, St. Veronica

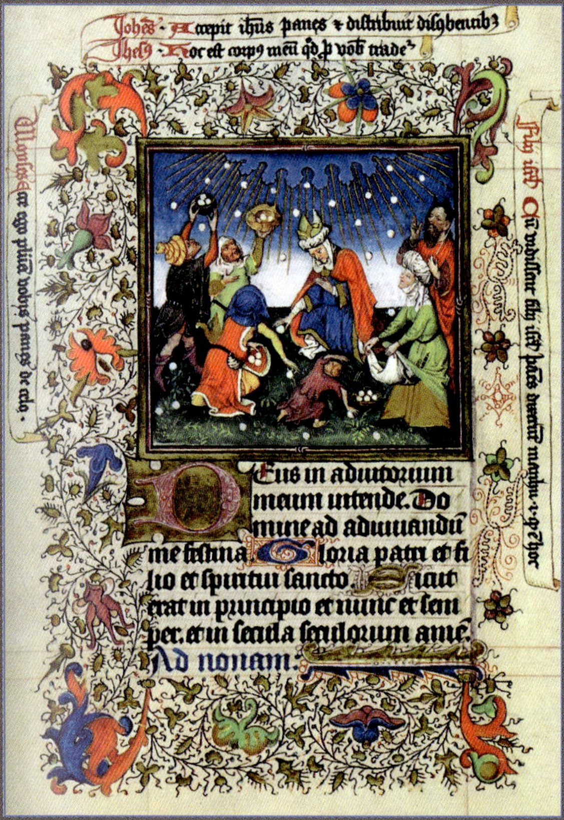

New York, Morgan Library and Museum, MS M. 945,
"Hours of Catherine of Cleves," f. 137v, Gathering of Manna

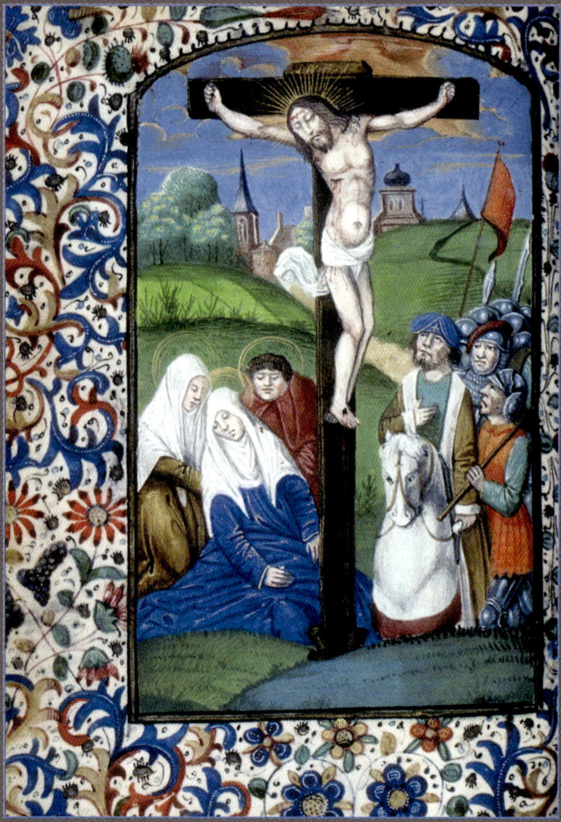

Cambridge, Fitzwilliam Museum, MS McClean 98,
Book of Hours, f. 14v, Crucifixion

Facing page, ff. 125v, Children of Israel in the Wilderness of Sinai

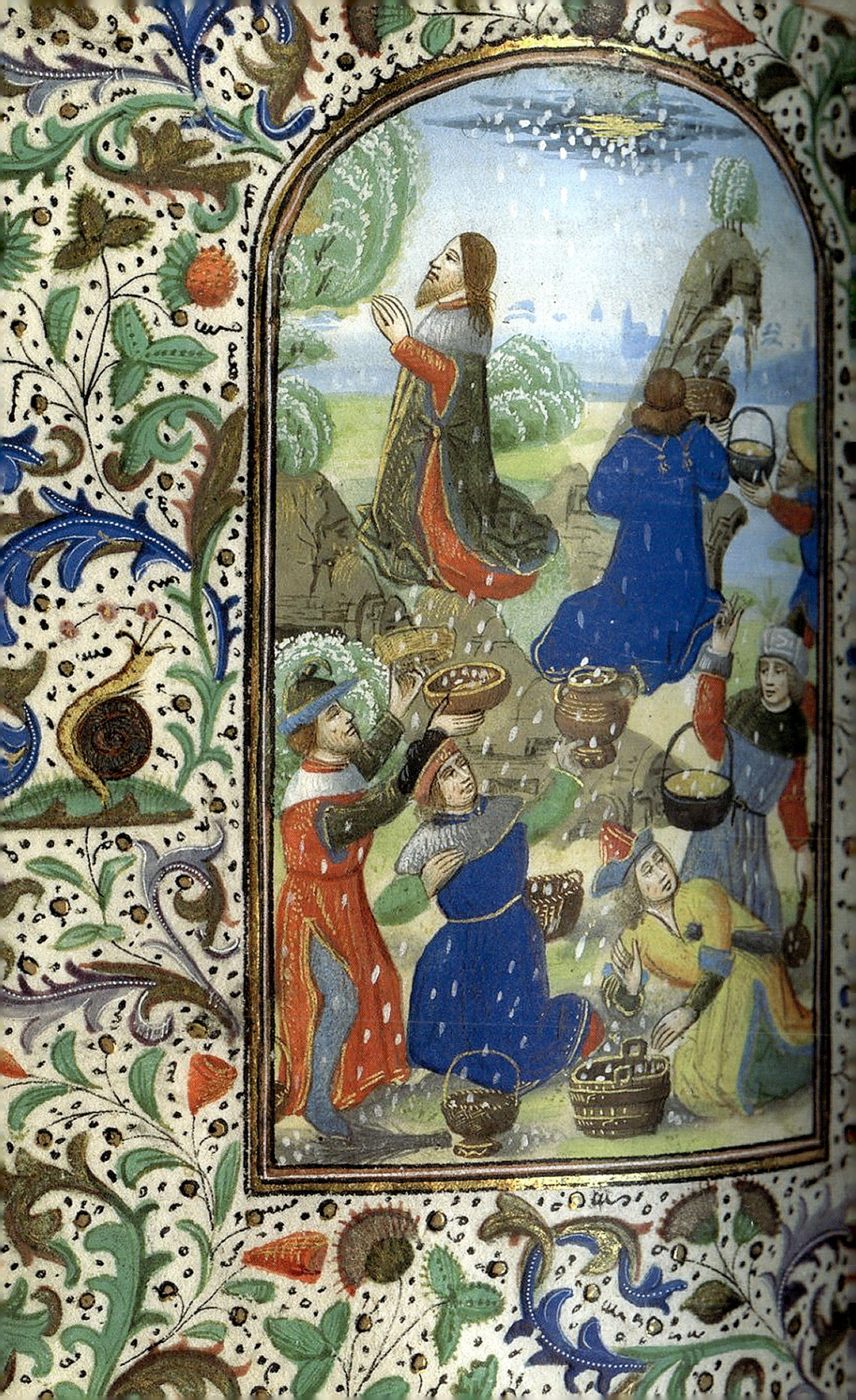

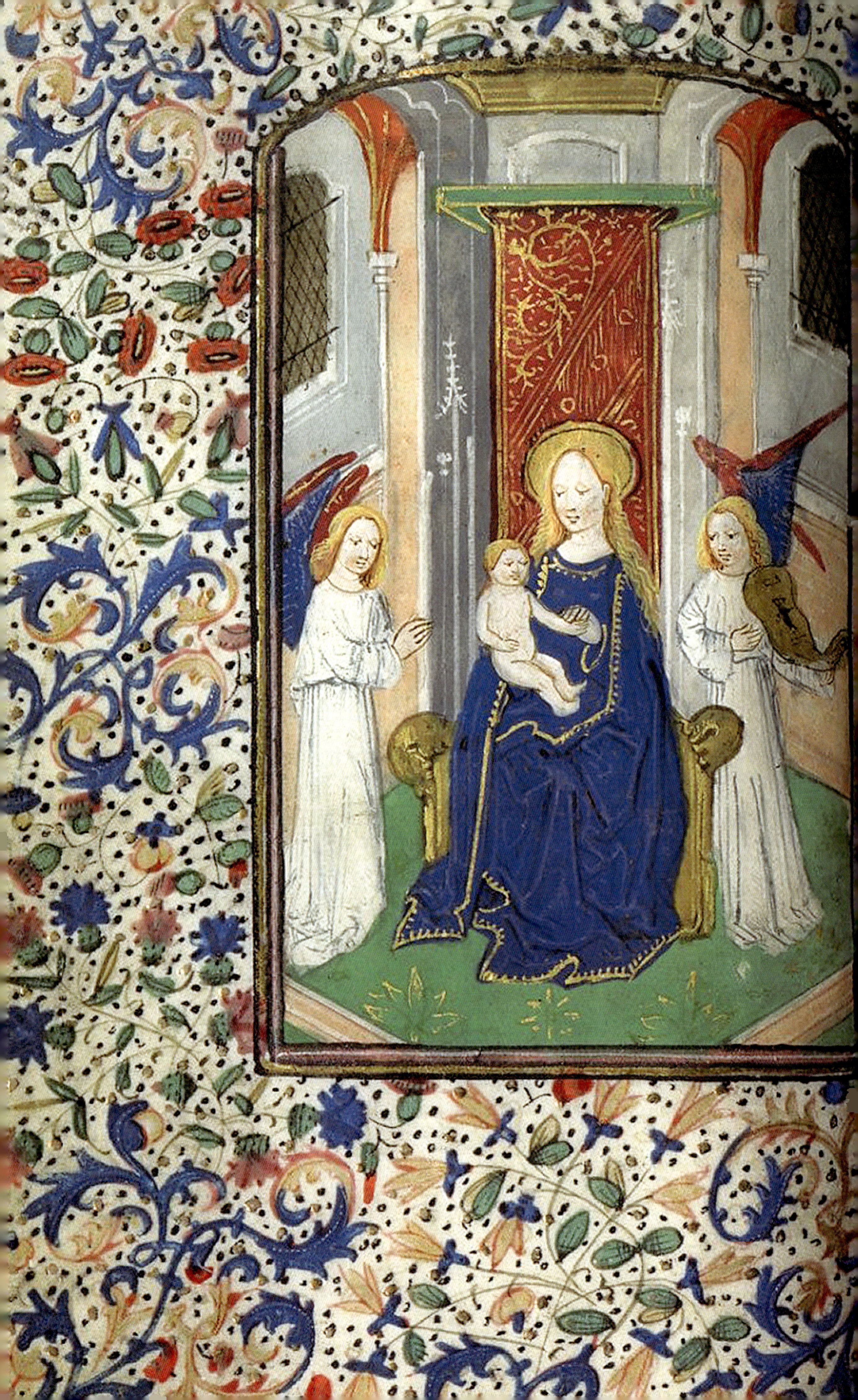

8

Book of Hours (Use of Rome)

In Latin, illuminated manuscript on parchment
Southern Netherlands, Bruges, 1460s
14 miniatures in the style of the Mildmay Master

When Willem Vrelant moved to Bruges in 1454, he would have settled in a dynamic mercantile city with a cultivated court which offered local artists incomparable opportunities for patronage. Vrelant and his associates and followers certainly took advantage of opportunities provided by ducal patronage, for a document in 1468 specifies payment to Vrelant for miniatures in a volume of the *Chroniques de Hainaut* (Brussels, Bibliothèque Royale, MS 9243) and another in 1469 paid "Guillaume de Vrelant" for miniatures in a *Vita Christi* (perhaps Valenciennes, BM MS 240). The oeuvre of Vrelant has thus been established based on his stylistic contributions to the Chronicles. Even a glimpse at the large body of work now recognized as being by Vrelant and his circle shows that these artists also responded to prospects offered by the presence of international merchants in the city and the prosperous import-export trade, by producing Books of Hours for export especially to England and the Mediterranean.

This charming small manuscript, complete, and entirely homogenous In its style and decoration is attributed to the Mildmay Master (Rogers, 1982). Rogers has named this artist the Mildmay Master after his work in a Book of Hours now in Chicago that contains early ownership notes by the English family Mildemaye (Newberry Library, MS. 35; Chicago 1969, cat. 5; and Saenger, 1989). On an intimate scale, the miniatures evoke Bruges panel painting of the day, especially those of Hans Memling. The Virgin and Child with Music-Playing Angels, the Annunciation, and the Presentation in the Temple (ff. 27v, 34v, 79v) all echo models by Memling. The rounded script of Italianate character and an early ownership note in Spanish suggest that the book may have been made for export to southern Europe.

The Mildmay Master worked in the style of his contemporary Willem Vrelant of Bruges (died 1480/1481) who, while maintaining a workshop, may also have functioned as a sort of *libraire* or stationer, gathering together artists, scribes, decorators, and binders for diverse commissions and possibly also for

Facing page, f. 28v, Virgin and Child with Music Playing Angels ready-made manuscripts (this is the view of Farquhar, 1974; Bousmanne, 1997; Clark, 1997). The deep reds and blues and wide palette of greens are all typical of Vrelant and his associates and followers, and many of the compositions here repeat well-known Vrelant patterns, such as the Pentecost, the Nativity, and the Massacre of the Innocents (see Bousmanne, p. 181, fig. 163; p. 114, fig. 97; and p. 120, fig. 108, respectively).

Extraordinarily productive, the Mildmay Master specialized in Books of Hours for both the continental and English market. He also worked on secular manuscripts, one of the most impressive of which was the *Légende dorée* made for Jean IV, sire and baron d'Auxy, chamberlain and counselor to Philip the Good, duke of Burgundy, and now divided between Mâcon (BM., MS 3) and New York (New York, Pierpont Morgan Library, M.672-75; Bousmanne 1997, pp. 271, 281-83). Ascribed by Bernard Bousmanne to the Master of the Vraie Cronicque descose, illuminations in the Morgan-Mâcon *Légende dorée* such as the Assumption of the Virgin (New York, Pierpont Morgan Library, M.675, f. 1), like the miniatures in our manuscript (f. 52v), lack the harsh linearity that identifies the hand of the Vraie Cronicque Master (Brussels and Paris 2011, pp. 256-58). Instead, the illuminations in the *Légende dorée* and our codex are characteristic of the Mildmay Master, who favored figures with markedly blushed cheeks and women and young men with slightly pointed chins.

The Mildmay Master's collaborators in the Morgan-Mâcon *Légende dorée* include the mature Willem Vrelant, the Master of the Chroniques de Pise (for example, New York, Pierpont Morgan Library, M.672, f. 55; Exhibition Brussels and Paris 2011, pp. 259-61), and the Master of Anthony of Burgundy (for example, New York, Pierpont Morgan Library M.675, fol. 74v; Exhibition Brussels and Paris 2011, pp. 310-22). While Vrelant and the Chroniques de Pise Master were working in Bruges already in the 1450s, the Anthony of Burgundy Master did not appear on the Bruges scene until the mid-1460s. Given all of this, a date in the 1460s and a manufacture in Bruges for the Morgan-Mâcon *Légende dorée* and our Horae seem most likely.

Our manuscript joins an ever-growing group of manuscripts in the Vrelant circle, which has become a kind of "catch-all" for the conservative trend of manuscript illumination in Bruges in the third quarter of the fifteenth century (Exhibition Brussels and Paris, 2011, p. 242). An alternative to the complex commercial operation proposed by Bousmanne, Clark, and others, would be the existence of a small family structure, in which certain anonymous hands, such as the Master the Vraie Cronicque descose, were actually members of Vrelant's family (Van Buren, 1999; Brussels and Paris, 2011, p. 241). Under the terms of such a hypothesis, the Master the Vraie Cronicque descose could actually be identified with Marie Vrelant, the widow of Willem, who continued to pay dues to the guild until 1490-1491. The place of the Mildmay Master, with his appealing colorful style, in this "Vrelant" group – be they professional collaborators or family members – has yet to be sorted out satisfactorily.

PHYSICAL DESCRIPTION: 173 ff. + 2 added parchment leaves at end, complete (i-ii^{6}, iii^{8+2}, iv-v^{8+1}, vi^{8}, vii-viii^{8+1}, ix-x^{8+2}, xi-xii^{8+1}, xiii^{2}, xiv^{8+1}, xv^{8} xvi^{8+1}, xvii-xx^{8}, xxi^{8+1}), with all full-page miniatures on inserted singletons, ruled in very pale ink, on 16 lines, written in dark brown ink a small rounded gothic bookhand (justification 60 x 41 mm.), rubrics in purplish red, capitals touched in yellow, versal initials throughout in blue or burnished gold with penwork in red or black, 2-line high initials through in blue or burnished gold with penwork in red or black, 20-line high initials throughout in burnished gold on red and blue grounds with white tracery, 14 large initials with full illuminated borders, 5-line high initials in gothic ivy-leaf designs in colors on burnished gold grounds, the borders with blue and liquid gold acanthus leaves and small colored flowers and strawberries infilled with black dots and tiny gold besants, fourteen full-page miniatures in arch-topped compartments (65 x 42 mm.), in colors and liquid gold within narrow burnished gold frames and full borders, early sixteenth-century additions on pages added at end. Modern (19th-century?) pale brownish-pink velvet over pasteboards, pierced silver clasps and catches, gilt edges, parchment endleaves, in a fitted brown morocco case, title gilt upper (Outer extremities of final leaves fractionally nibbled, some thumbing sometimes affecting full borders, border on f. 34v a little smudged, generally in good condition). Dimensions 112 x 75 mm.

TEXT: ff. 1-12v, Calendar, with relatively sparse entries including in black St. Donatian, patron saint of Bruges on 7 August, St. Bertin on 5 September, venerated in the north of France; ff. 14-20, Short Hours of the Cross; ff. 22-26v, Short Hours of the Holy Spirit; ff. 28-33v, Mass of the Virgin, with the Gospel Sequences (beginning f. 32r); ff. 35-97v, Hours of the Virgin "secundum consuetudinem romane curie" (use of Rome), with Matins (f. 35), Lauds (f. 53), Prime (f. 65), Terce (f. 70), Sext (f. 75), None (f. 80), Vespers (f. 85), and Compline (f. 93); ff. 99-106v, Advent Office; ff. 108-127v, Penitential Psalms and Litany (ff. 119-121v); ff. 129-169v, Office of the Dead (use of Rome); ff. 170-173v, "Obsecro te" (in masculine form); ff. 173v-176v, added texts written in two hands with hymns (without musical notation), in a later sixteenth-century hand.

ILLUSTRATION: The subjects of the miniatures are: f. 13v, Crucifixion; f. 21v, Pentecost; f. 27v, Virgin and Child with Music-Playing Angels; f. 34v, Annunciation; f. 52v, Visitation; f. 64v, Nativity; f. 69v, Annunciation to the Shepherds; f. 74v, Adoration of the Magi; f. 79v,,

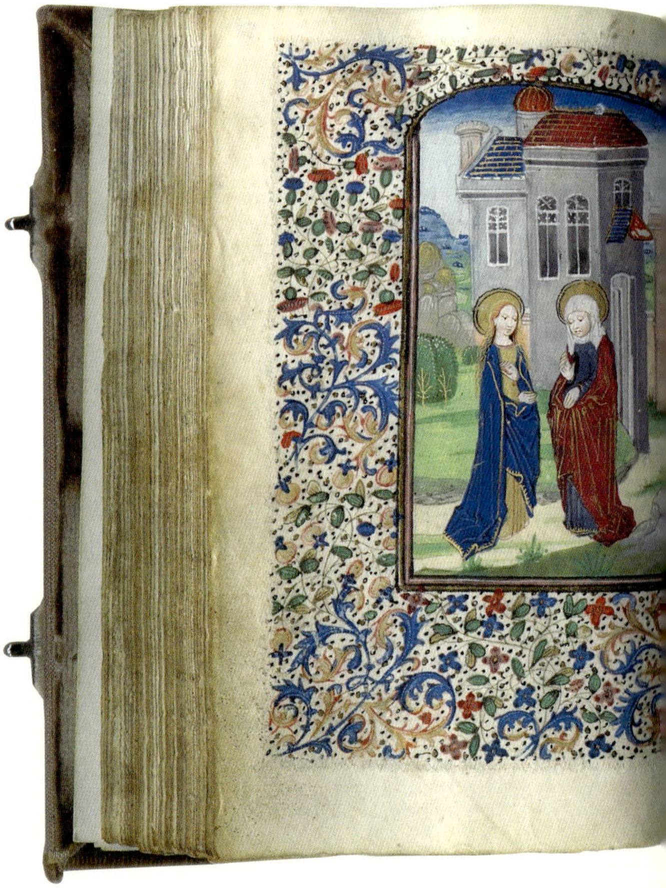

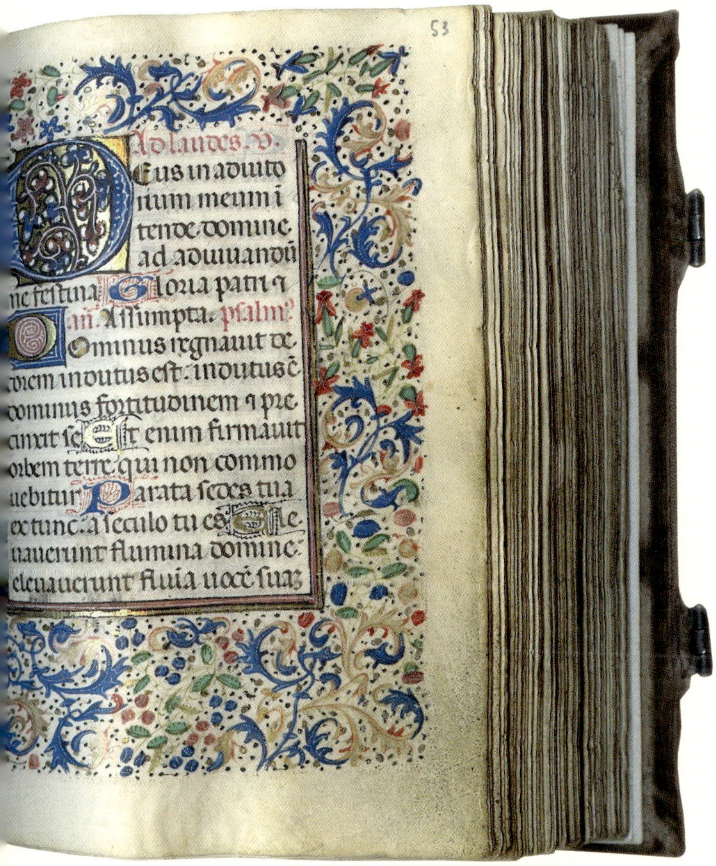

ff. 52v-53, Visitation

Presentation in the Temple; f. 84v, Massacre of the Innocents; f. 92v, Flight into Egypt; f. 98v, Coronation of the Virgin; f. 107v, King David in Prayer; f. 128v, Funeral Mass.

OWNERSHIP: 1. Written in Bruges, for male use (f. 172v), probably for export to Spain or Portugal, not earlier than 1450, since the Calendar includes St. Bernardinus, canonized in that year. – 2. There is a sixteenth- or early seventeenth-century signature in Spanish (or Iberic tongue) on f. 1, "fray gregorio de ahla." – 3. Joel and Maxine Spitz, Glencoe, Illinois, MS 513, their bookplate "Trail-Tree/ from the library of Maxine and Joel Spitz Glencoe Illinois" on inside front cover, MS 6 written below the bookplate, bought in 1946 from Wallach, New York (C.U. Faye and W.H. Bond, *Supplement to the Census of Medieval and Renaissance Manuscripts in the United States and Canada*, 1962, p. 166, no. 6). – Private North American Collection.

LITERATURE: Bousmanne, Bernard. *"Item a Guillaume Wyeland aussi enlumineur." Willem Vrelant, Un aspect de l'enluminure dans les Pays-bas méridionaux*, exh. cat., Brussels, Bibliothèque Royale, 1997. – [Exhibition]. Brussels, Royal Library of Belgium, and Paris, BnF, *Miniatures flamandes 1404-1482*, Brussels and Paris, 2011. – [Exhibition]. Chicago, Newberry Library, *French and Flemish Illuminated Manuscripts from Chicago Collections*, Chicago, 1969. – Clark, Gregory T. *The Hours of Isabel la Católica: The Facsimile Edition – Commentary*, Madrid, 1997. – Defoer, Henri et al. *The Golden Age of Dutch Manuscript Illumination*, New York, 1989. – Dogaer, Georges. *Flemish Miniature Painting in the 15th and 16th Centuries*, Amsterdam, 1987. – Farquhar, James D. "The Vrelant Enigma: is the Style the Man?," *Quaerendo* 4 (1974), pp. 100-108. - Rogers, Nicholas John. "Books of Hours Produced in the Low Countries for the English Market," M. Litt. Diss., University of Cambridge, 1982. – Saenger, Paul. *Catalogue of the Pre-1500 Western Manuscript Books at the Newberry Library*, Chicago, 1989. – Thoss, Dagmar. *Flämische Buchmalerei*, exh. cat., Vienna, Österreichische Nationalbibliothek, 1987. – Van Buren, Ann. "Willem Vrelant. Questions and Issues," *Revue belge d'archéologie et d'histoire de l'art. Belgisch tijdschrift voor oudheidkuunde en kunstgeschiedenis*, 68 (1999), pp. 3-30.

ONLINE RESOURCES:

William Vrelant, at the J.P. Getty Museum:
http://www.getty.edu/art/gettyguide/

Turning the pages, William Vrelant, BnF
http://expositions.bnf.fr/flamands/livres/heures/index.htm

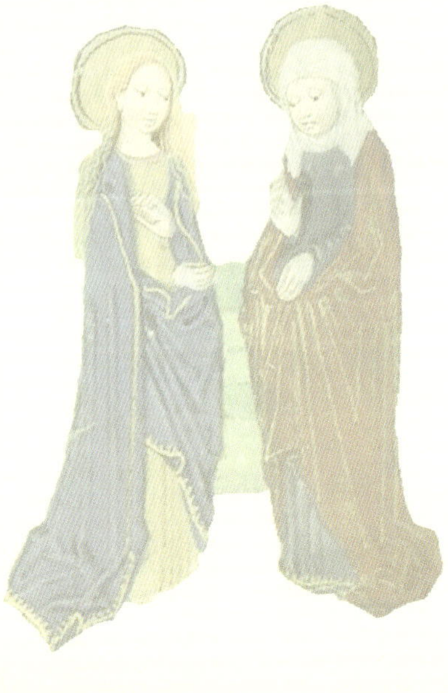

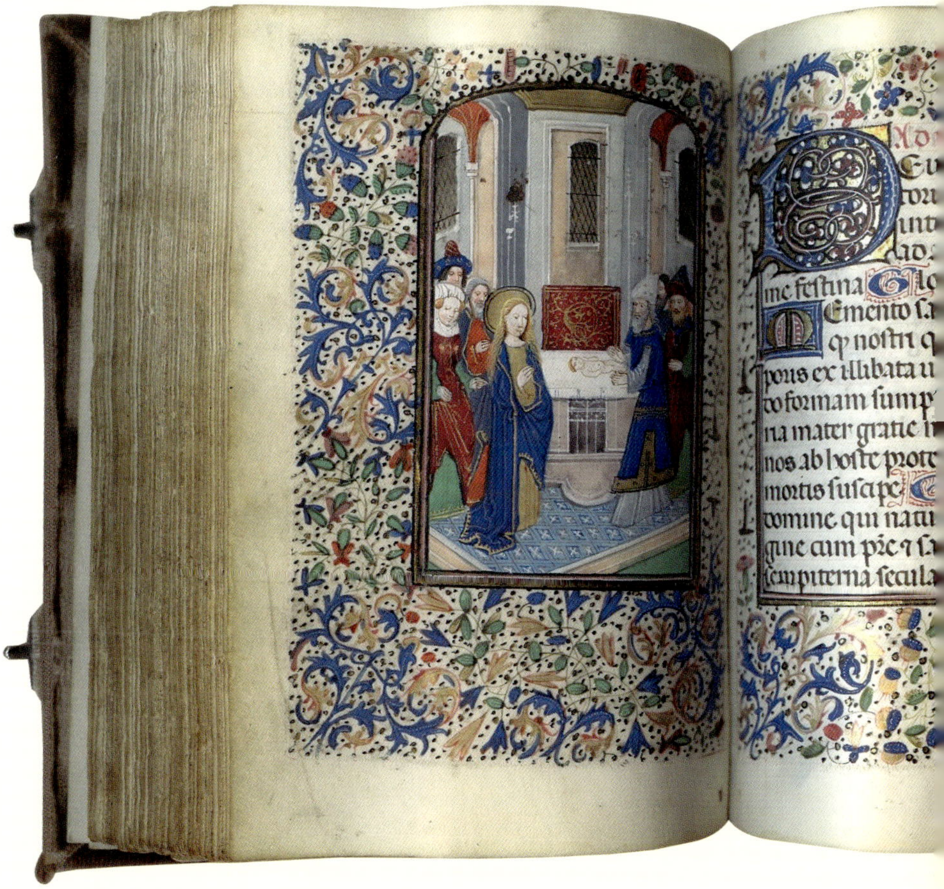

f. 79v, Presentation in the Temple

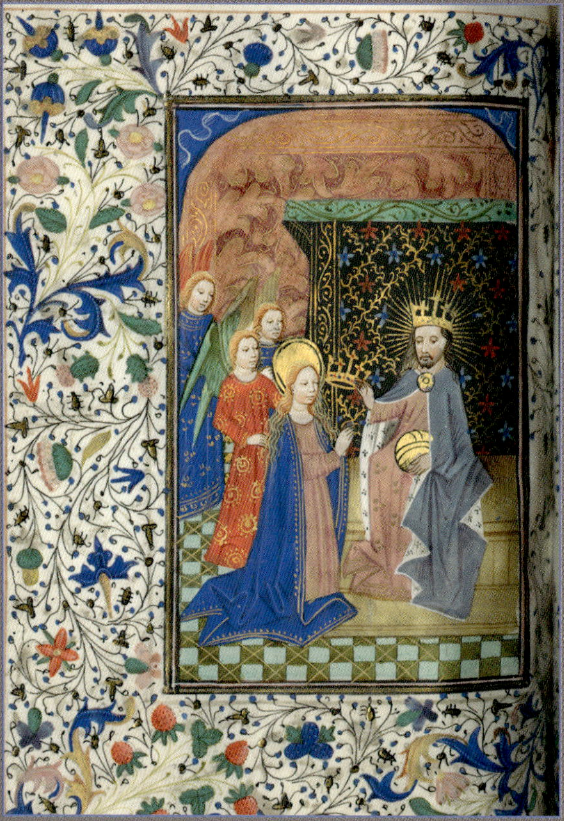

Chicago, Newberry Library, MS. 35,
Book of Hours, f. 77v, Coronation of the Virgin

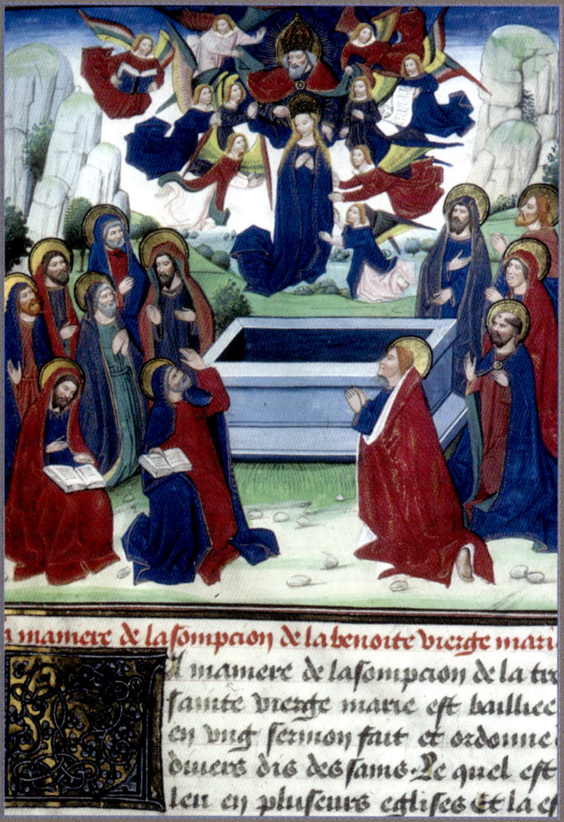

New York, Morgan Library and Museum, MS M. 675,
Book of Hours, f. 1, Assumption of the Virgin

Facing page, f. 99v, Coronation of the Virgin

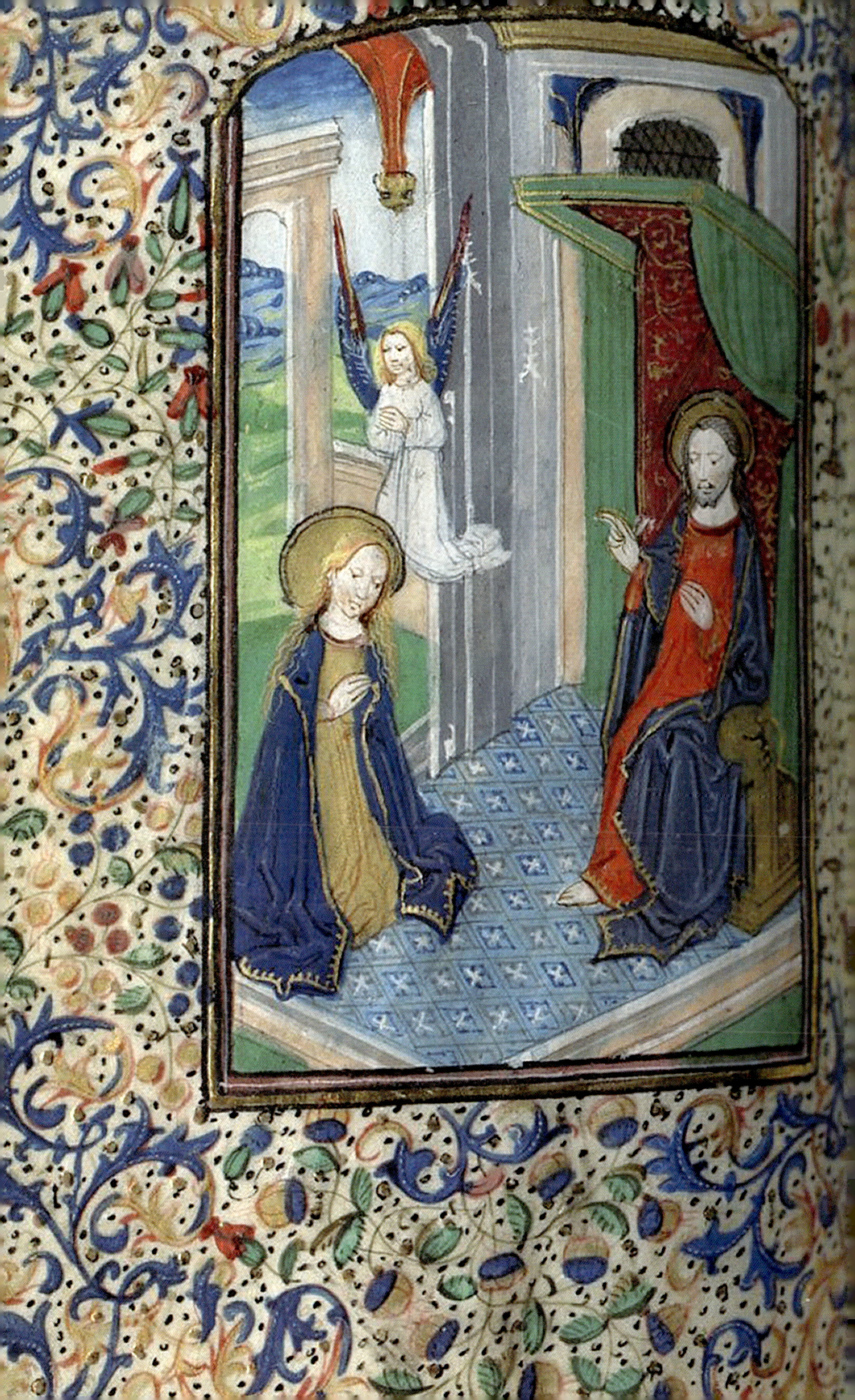

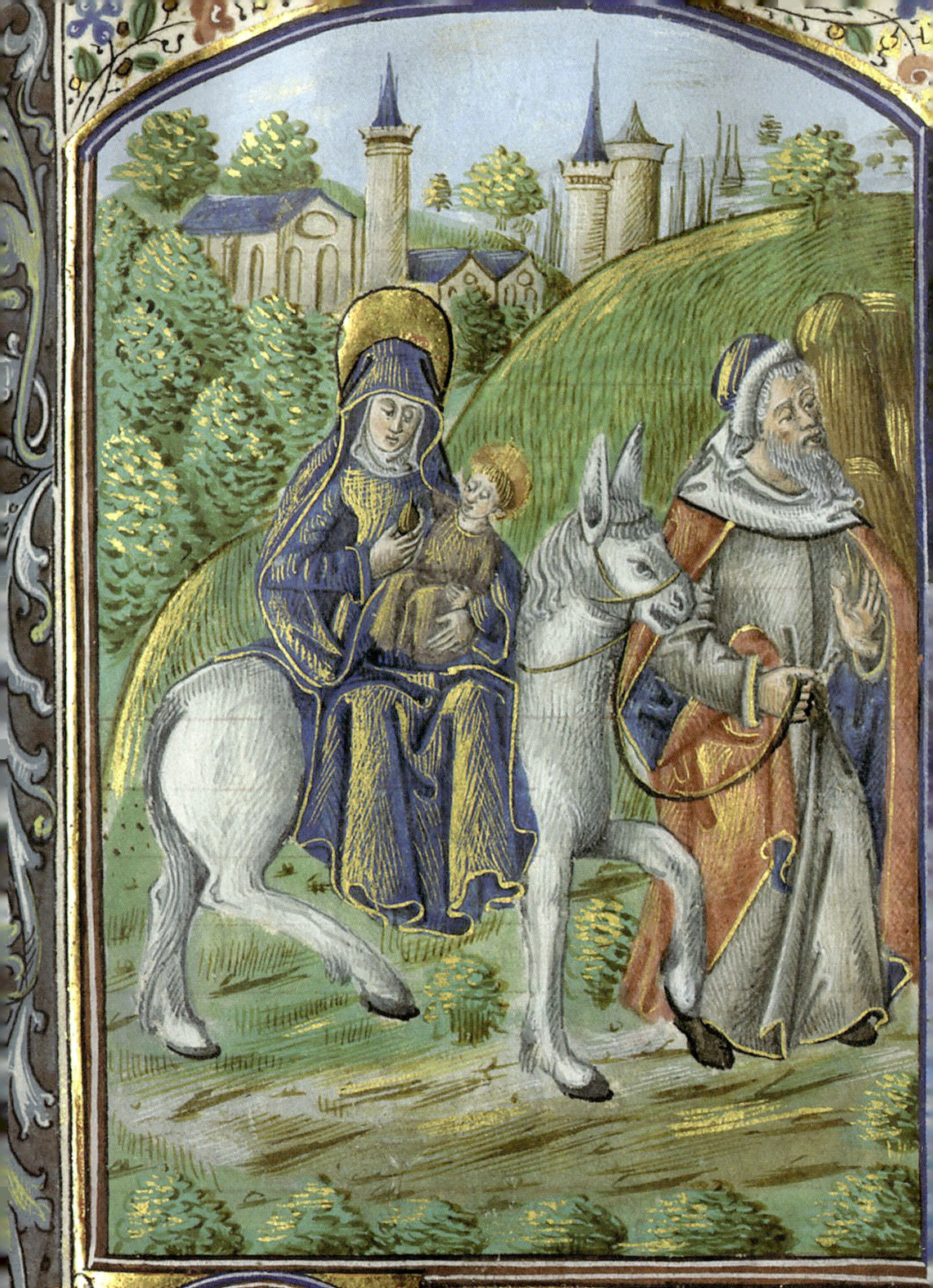

Deus in adiutorium meum in
tende. Domine a
adiuuandum me festi

9

Book of Hours (Use of Rouen)

In Latin and French, illuminated manuscript on parchment
France, Normandy (Lisieux, Sées?), c. 1480
6 historiated initials, 7 small miniatures, 8 square miniatures, 10 arch-topped miniatures, 1 full-page miniature by two unidentified artists

"Familiar yet puzzling" would best qualify the present Horae. Familiar because the liturgical use is not problematic and clearly points to Rouen, puzzling because the style of the two hands that painted the numerous miniatures and the borders is difficult to pin-point and tie to a specific school of illumination. This is precisely what makes Books of Hours interesting and exciting, the issues and uncertainties that they raise, the possibilities they suggest. This large and striking manuscript, richly illuminated with a remarkable series of miniatures, presents a number of intriguing questions, and is quite deserving of future study.

The present book is uniformly Rouennais in its liturgical features. The Calendar however is more complex and is certainly not a common Rouen calendar. It contains a large number of saints — some actually quite rare — related to Normandy but also Brittany such as Vincent, honored in Rouen (in red, 22 Jan.), Honorine, patron saint of Graville, near Le Havre (27 Feb.) (see Réau, 1958, III, 2, pp. 657-658), Opportuna, of Sées, abbess of Montreuil, near Argentan, south-east of Rouen (22 April) (see Réau, 1958, III, 2, pp. 1010-1011), Célérin (in the Calendar Scelerin, 7 May), a rare saint, related to the town of Saint-Célérin, in the Sarthe, mid-way between Le Mans and Chartres, Désir, of Lisieux (23 May); Turien [or Thuriau] (13 July, archbishop of Dol-de-Bretagne, Brittany) (see Réau, 1959, III, 3, pp. 1281-1282), Samson of Dol (28 July), a Breton saint but also very much honored in "Basse-Seine" including Ouistreham in Normandy but also honored in Clermont-en-Beauvaisis (near Beauvais) (see Réau, 1959, III, p. 1181), Lubin of Chartres (15 Sept.), Mellon (22 October, first bishop of Rouen), and Ursin (30 Dec., usually honored 9 Nov. but also celebrated in Lisieux on 30 Dec.). Oddly, absent here is the patron saint of Rouen, Romanus. If the book had been for use in Rouen proper, surely Romanus would have been included in the Calendar, in the Suffrages or in the Litany. Nonetheless, the liturgical use for the Office of the Virgin is clearly Rouen, as well as for the Office of the Dead.

We would like to suggest tentatively that these Horae were made for use in one of the suffragan dioceses that surrounded Rouen, that of Lisieux, Évreux or Sées, all south or south-east of Rouen. Because of the presence of typically Breton saints (Thuriau, Samson of Dol), one might be tempted to look towards regions bordering Brittany and Normandy to suggest a place of production for these Horae, but still within the diocese of Rouen. More plausibly, one should explore the southern parts of the archdiocese of Rouen, bordering the diocese of Chartres, towards the regions of the "Perche," stretching a bit towards Le Mans. This would account for the Chartres or Le Mans related saints (such as Lubin, Saint-Célérin) but also explain the numerous "southern" Norman saints (Opportune, Désir, Ursin). There is of course something of a "grey" divide between Brittany and Normandy, and many saints honored in eastern Brittany would also be popular in western Normandy.

Textually, these Horae contain some interesting and rare texts, surely specially ordered by the female patron and her daughter (?), who appear in the miniature of the Pietà on f. 3v. Meriting further study, these texts include the Hours of St. Barbara (found in other Horae, but not common, probably the donor's patron saint), as well as the Gospel excerpts chosen to celebrate the Conception of the Virgin, the Purification of the Virgin, the Annunciation, and finally the Assumption. These texts are also the pretext for an interesting (and unusual) series of miniatures replacing the traditional representations of the Evangelists before the start of the Hours of the Virgin. Each miniature is preceded by a rubric that clearly associates a Gospel reading with one of the events in the Marian cycle. The Hours of the Cross present here, but oddly positioned after the Litany, are illustrated with an unusual full sequence of historiated initials, opening with a large miniature representing Christ on Gethsemane (f. 51). The Hours of the Cross are not usually as fully illustrated, and it would be interesting to find other examples of the Hours of the Cross illustrated with a full sequence of historiated initials in French Horae of the period. The Hours of the Holy Spirit do not receive such treatment.

Style matters here (as often!) and stylistically the present Horae are hard to localize. They do not present the typical Rouennais features one usually immediately recognizes in Books of Hours illuminated in Rouen, with such ateliers active in the fifteenth century as the Master of Sir John Falstoff or the Master of the Échevinage de Rouen, the latter generating a non-negligible number of followers and related workshops well into the fifteenth century (see Avril, in Avril and Reynaud, 1993, p. 169; see Rabel, 1984 and 1989; on the Master of the Échevinage and his workshop and followers, see this catalogue no. 10). Other artists emerge towards the very end of the fifteenth century such as Robert Boyvin, mentioned in archival sources. If indeed the present Horae were painted in Rouen, it would be another example of the very large and important production of Book of Hours in Rouen from the 1460s onwards. Compositions circulated amongst illuminators, and Rouen established itself as a very important center of illumination, second only to Paris, catering even to export abroad, with such examples as the Playfair Hours, made for the use of Sarum for a Scottish owner (London, Victoria and Albert Museum, MS L.475-1918; see Watson, 1984).

These Horae are painted by two hands. The first hand prefers a softer palette, rounder faces (he paints miniatures on ff. 4v, 5, 7, 9, and perhaps 35v). The compositions by this first hand are sometimes surprising and offbeat, to wit the highly unusual Presentation in the Temple, with the Virgin kneeling before a bare altar (f. 7). The second hand in these Horae adopts a stronger palette with some very dark colors, more shadowed faces and eyes with heady eyelids (all the remaining miniatures, the historiated initials, and the small miniatures in the Suffrages). The borders are very diverse, with a clear intention of "mixing" styles: there is a clearly northern influence, from French-Flanders (perhaps Hainault?), with borders that include brightly illuminated panels in the Ghent-Bruges style (f. 11), some with scrolling phylacters (ff. 16v, 30, and 113). But the general style of the borders is more often than not French traditional acanthus leaves on liquid gold grounds, sometimes scrolling grisaille acanthus leaves (f. 16v) that indeed recall later Rouennais border illumination (that will triumph in late fifteenth and early sixteenth century Rouen manuscript illumination), and also quite classical colored acanthus leaves, flowers, elements from the bestiary, and small burnished gold besants and vine-leaves, all on reserved grounds (ff. 8, 9, 32 et alia). Some borders suggest they were left somewhat unfinished (for instance f. 35v): it is entirely possible there were later campaigns of illumination in the borders, some perhaps added in the sixteenth century.

With regards to the compositions, some can be found amongst the preferred compositions that circulated in Rouen. For instance, the miniature of the Four Evangelists presents the typically Rouen feature of portraying the figures

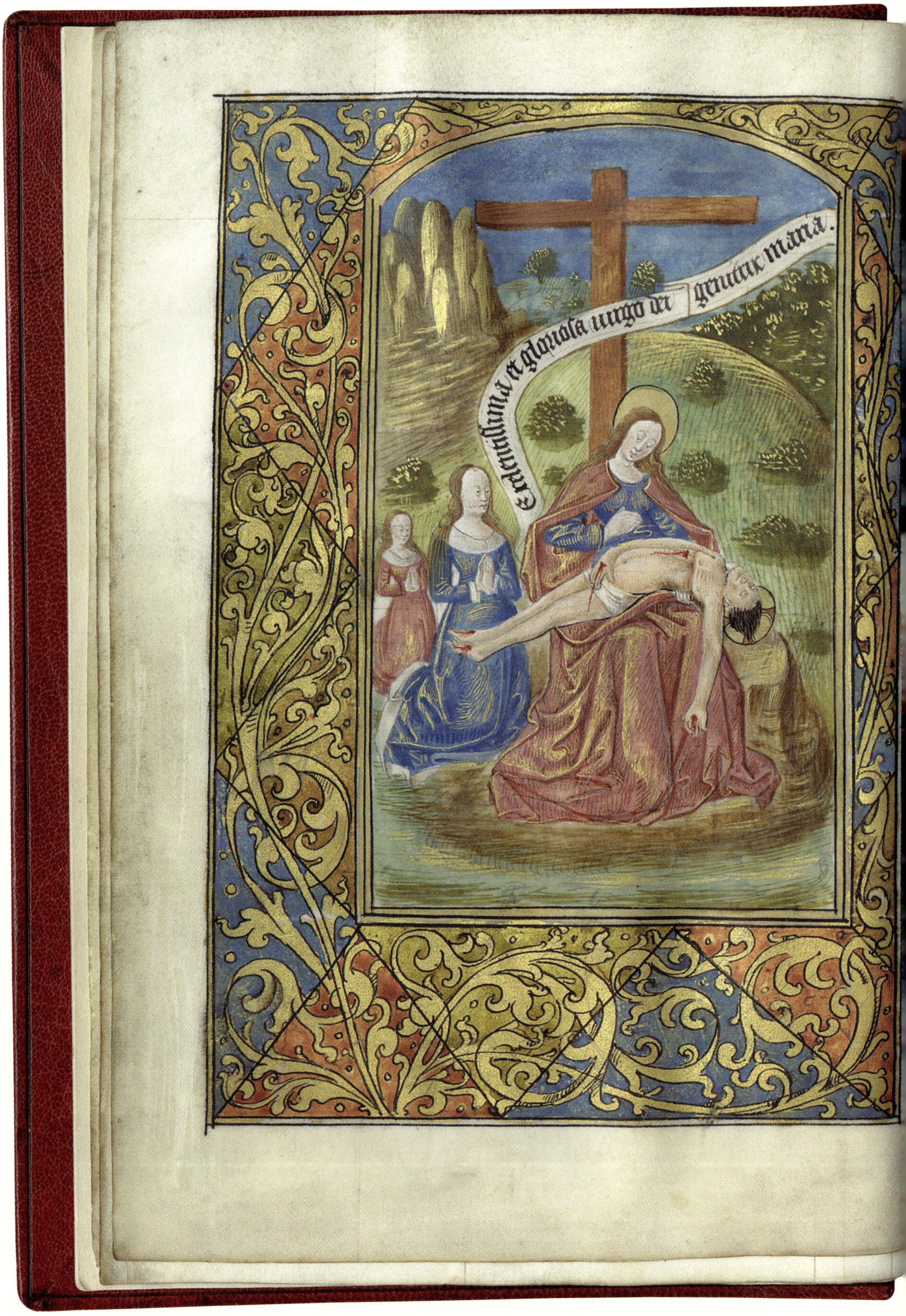
Excelentissima et gloriosa uirgo dei genitrix maria.

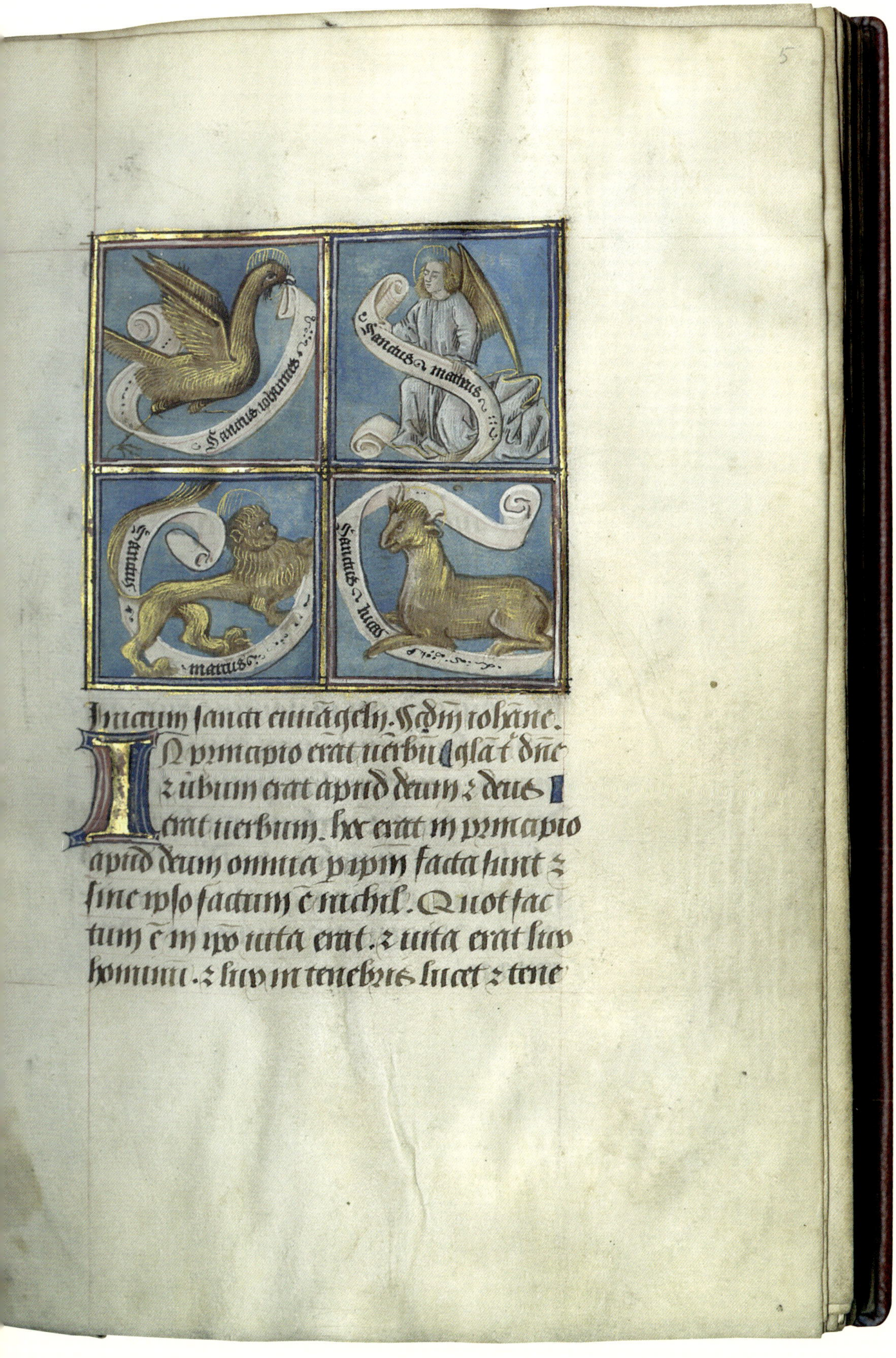

ff. 4v-5, Pietà, with a Kneeling Female Patron and her Attendant;
Four Symbols of Evangelists, each Holding a Scroll with their Names

in a half-page miniature divided by a frame into four quarters (as found for example in the Playfair Hours, London, Victoria and Albert Museum, MS L.475-1918, f. 13, see Watson, 2011, cat. no. 56, pp. 323-329; in Oxford, Bodleian, MS Douce 253, f. 13 etc.). There is a major difference though as the present miniature with the Four Evangelists in our Horae eliminates the actual Evangelists, leaving only their symbols in each quadrant. There are other characteristic marks of Rouen book illumination such as the depiction of the Assumption of the Virgin, borne by five angels (our Horae, f. 9), often found in Rouen illuminated Books of Hours (again see the Playfair Hours, f. 22) and later in printed Horae. Once again, one notes a change in the traditional iconography; the apostles who are usually witnesses of the scene are absent in our Horae. Another interesting miniature in our Horae is the depiction of the Instruments of the Passion, usually displayed around a Crucifixion scene (as in the Playfair Hours, f. 170v) and here again reduced to its "bare" essentials with only the Passion Instruments and the Cross but without Christ (f. 75v).

An additional feature nicely personalizing these Horae is the presence of a seventeenth- century "livre de raison" for the d'Abancourt family, originally from the Beauvaisis, recording the births and deaths from 1604 to circa 1654. Because these Horae escape conventions or at least depart from the traditional iconography and style adopted in Rouen in the last quarter of the fifteenth century, we can see why they would have pleased a number of discriminating book collectors such as Thomas Phillipps or more recently Baron Frederick Hesketh. It is a book for a collector who will no doubt thrill in exploring different avenues to understand better who and for whom these Horae were painted in a style that sought to go beyond the common compositions and style engrained in Rouen.

PHYSICAL DESCRIPTION: 83 ff., preceded by a single parchment and 2 paper flyleaves, followed by 2 paper flyleaves, wanting some leaves (collation: i^4, ii^7 (i a singleton, of 8, missing vii), iii^8, iv^6, $v\text{-}vi^8$, vii^2, viii^8, ix^8, x^6 (of 8? missing i and viii), xi^8, xii^4), ruled in brown and pink ink for 20 lines, prickings still visible, written in a fine lettre bâtarde in brown ink (justification: 120 x 85 mm.), some leaves with lay-out in two columns (e.g. Calendar; Litany), some capitals touched in yellow (in the Calendar), rubrics in pale red, numerous 1- and 2-line initials in gold on blue and pink grounds, some 3- to 4-line high initials in pink with white tracery and leafy infill on gold grounds (e.g. ff. 6, 8 etc.), ten 3- or 4-line initials in blue heightened with white tracery and colored leafy infill on gold grounds, six historiated initials (ff. 52, 52v, 53, 53v, 54, 54v), seven small miniatures for the suffrages (ff. 61v, 62, 62v, 63, 63v, 64, 64v), eight square miniatures (ff. 5, 8, 9, 16v, 28, 51, 58, 75v), ten three-quarter page arch-topped miniatures (ff. 7, 11, 23, 26, 30, 32, 35v, 43, 55), all miniatures (except the historiated initials and the small miniatures for Suffrages) placed in full illuminated borders of very different types, on reserved or colored grounds with a variety of ornaments (floral and foliate) and drolleries (such as a naked woman and a jester baring their bottoms at each other, drollery-creatures, birds and animal-masks, criss-crossing phylacter inscribed with Psalm 24:18, bird-headed drollery reaching between its own legs to peck at its bare bottom, a dog-like drollery with a human head et passim), one full-page arch-topped miniature (f. 4v) with full border of scrolling gold acanthus leaves on blue, pink and gold grounds. Bound in modern red morocco over pasteboards (early 20th c.), spine sewn on 5 raised thongs, gilt title on spine "Horae" and "Manuscript XV Cent.," double frame on inner boards traced in single blind filets, gilt edges (Binding in fine condition, a few internal stains but overall in very good condition with wide margins and fresh colors). Dimensions 221 x 160 mm.

TEXT: ff. 1-3v, Calendar, text in two columns, in red, blue and brown ink, in French, with a large number of Norman and Breton saints: Saints Honorine (27 Feb.), Opportuna (22 April, abbess of Montreuil, near Argentan), Célérin (in the calendar Scelerin, 7 May), a rare saint, related to the town of Saint-Célérin, in the Sarthe, mid-way between Le Mans and Chartres, Désir, of Lisieux (23 mai), Turien [Thuriau] (13 July, archbishop of Dol, Brittany), Samson of Dol (28 July), Lubin of Chartres (15 Sept.), Mellon (22 October, first bishop of Rouen), Anien [Anianus] (17 Nov.), Ursin (30 Dec., usually honored 9 Nov. but also celebrated in Lisieux on 30 Dec.); noteworthy is the absence of the patron saint of Rouen: Romanus; f. 4, blank; ff. 5-10v, Gospel readings and prayers [wanting beginning of prayers]; rubrics, *In conceptione beate marie virginis... Inicium sancti evangelii secundum matheum* (f. 6); *In purificatione beate marie virginis ... Sequentia sancti evangelii secundum lucam* (f. 6v); *In annunciacione beate marie virginis secundum lucam* (f. 8); *L'assumpcion nostre dame secundum lucam*; ff. 11-38, Hours of the Virgin, use of Rouen, with Matins (f. 11); Lauds (f. 17v); Prime (f. 23); Terce (f. 26); Sext (f. 28); None (f. 30); Vespers (f. 32); Compline (f. 35v); ff. 38-40, *Obsecro te*; ff. 40-41, *O intemerata*; ff. 41v-42v, blank; ff. 43-49, Penitential Psalms; ff. 49-50v, Litany and Prayers [wanting ending]; ff. 51-55, Hours of the Cross [beginning imperfectly]; ff. 55v-58, Hours of the Holy Spirit; ff. 58-61v, Hours of St. Barbara; ff. 61v-64v, Suffrages of Saints [wanting ending]; ff. 65-75v, Office of the Dead [beginning and ending imperfectly], apparently for the use of Rouen; f. 76, Passion of Christ according to the Gospel of John.

ILLUSTRATION: Large miniatures: f. 4v, Pietà, with a kneeling female patron and her daughter (?) to the left (full-page arch-topped miniature); f. 5, Four Symbols of Evangelists, each holding a scroll with their names (large square miniature, quartered); f. 7, Presentation in the Temple (three-quarter miniature); f. 8, Annunciation to the Virgin (three-quarter miniature); f. 9, Assumption of the Virgin (three-quarter miniature); f. 11, Annunciation to the Virgin (three-quarter miniature); f. 16v, Visitation (square miniature); f. 23, Nativity (three-quarter miniature); f. 26, Annunciation to the Shepherds (three-quarter miniature); f. 28, Adoration of the Magi (rectangular miniature); f. 30, Flight into Egypt (three-quarter miniature); f. 32, Presentation in the Temple (three-quarter miniature); f. 35v, Coronation of the Virgin (three-quarter miniature); f. 43, King David kneeling in prayer (three-quarter miniature); f. 51, Christ on Gethsemane (square miniature); f. 55v, Pentecost (three-quarter miniature); f. 58, St. Barbara (square miniature); f. 75v, Cross surrounded by the instruments of the Passion (rectangular miniature). Seven small miniatures: f. 61v, Holy Trinity; f. 62, Saint Anthony; f. 62v, Saint Christopher; f. 63, Saint Georges; f. 63v, Anne, the Virgin and Child; f. 64, Saint Michael; f. 64v, Saint John the Baptist; - Six Historiated Initials: f. 52, Arrest of Christ, initial D; f. 52v, Christ before Pilate, initial D; f. 53, Flagellation, initial D; f. 53v, Crucifixion, initial D; f. 54, Deposition of the Cross, initial D; f. 54v, Entombment, initial D.

OWNERSHIP: 1. Copied and painted in France, in a highly original and still unidentified style. The liturgical use of the Hours of the Virgin are for Rouen. There are however linguistic features that point towards a scribe with ties perhaps to the North and Flanders, with such rubrics in French as "Tierche de la vierge marie mere de dieu" (f. 25v); "De saint Michiel" (f. 64); "la seconde lechon de mors" (f. 71). Stylistically however, there are no satisfactory Flemish comparisons. The saints in the Calendar strongly suggest a southern Norman origin with saints honored in the dioceses of Lisieux and Sées. - 2. There is a *livre de raison* copied on the last leaves of these Horae for the d'Abancourt family (ff. 82-83), beginning: "Enfans de Fransois d'Abancourt, seigneur du Blancart / Memore de ma fille Elyzabet Juli ... mil six cent et quatre en viront deux eurre apres midit du douzieme de mars...." One reads on f. 83 (note the former foliation in brown ink "150" in the upper righthand corner): "Abancourt. Enfans de Pierre d'Abancourt, seigneur d'Abancourt / Ma fille Marie et venue au monde le samedy dizieme d'avril mille six sens et trente deux...." Hence the present *livre de raison* records births in the d'Abancourt family between 1604-c. 1645. A "Hail Mary" redacted in French in found on f. 82v. The d'Abancourt are a family from the Beauvaisis. François d'Abancourt is recorded in Lachesnaye-Desbois, *Dictionnaire de la noblesse*, Paris, 1770, vol. I, as "seigneur de Puiseaux, de Courcelles et de Bus-David". - 3. Formerly part of the Thomas Phillipps Collection as suggested by the small bookplate pasted on the upper pastedown: "Bibliotheca Philippica. From the collection formed by Sir Thomas Phillipps Bt., 1792-1872, purchased by private treaty by William H. Robinson Ltd., Pall Mall, London." This is Phillipps MS 2614, acquired from Thorpe, apparently from the collection of Juan de Iriarte (1702-1771), Spanish paleographer and bibliophile (see Munby, Phillipps Studies III, p. 149). - 4. Frederick Fermor Hesketh, second Baron Hesketh (1917-1955), his heraldic bookplate and motto pasted on the upper pastedown, important collector and bibliophile. He likely acquired these Horae from William H. Robinson, bookdealer.

LITERATURE: Unpublished. - Avril, François and Nicole Reynaud. *Les manuscrits à peintures en France, 1440-1520*, Paris, 1993. - Rabel-Julien, Claudia. *Les livres d'heures de Rouen peints par le Maître du Trésor génevois et les enlumineurs influencé par lui, au 3e quart du 15e siècle: essai pour une étude stylistique, iconographique et historique*, Unpublished dissertation, DEA, Paris, Université de Paris I, 1984. - Rabel, Claudia. "Artiste et clientèle à la fin du Moyen Age: les manuscrits profanes du Maître de l'échevinage de Rouen," *Revue de l'art* 84 (1989), pp. 48-60. - Réau, Louis. *Iconographie de l'art chrétien. III, 1-3. Iconographie des saints*, Paris, 1958-1959. - Watson, Rowan. *The Playfair Hours. A Late Fifteenth Century Illuminated Manuscript from Rouen*, London, Victoria and Albert Museum, 1984. - Watson, Rowan. *Victoria and Albert Museum. Western Illuminated Manuscripts. A Catalogue of Works in the National Art Library from the Eleventh to the Early Twentieth Century, with a complete account of the George Reid Collection*, London, Victoria & Albert Publishing, 2011, vol. I.

ONLINE RESOURCES: Liturgical Use of Rouen
http://www.chd.dk/use/

Calendar for Rouen (different from the present Calendar)
http://www.chd.dk/cals/

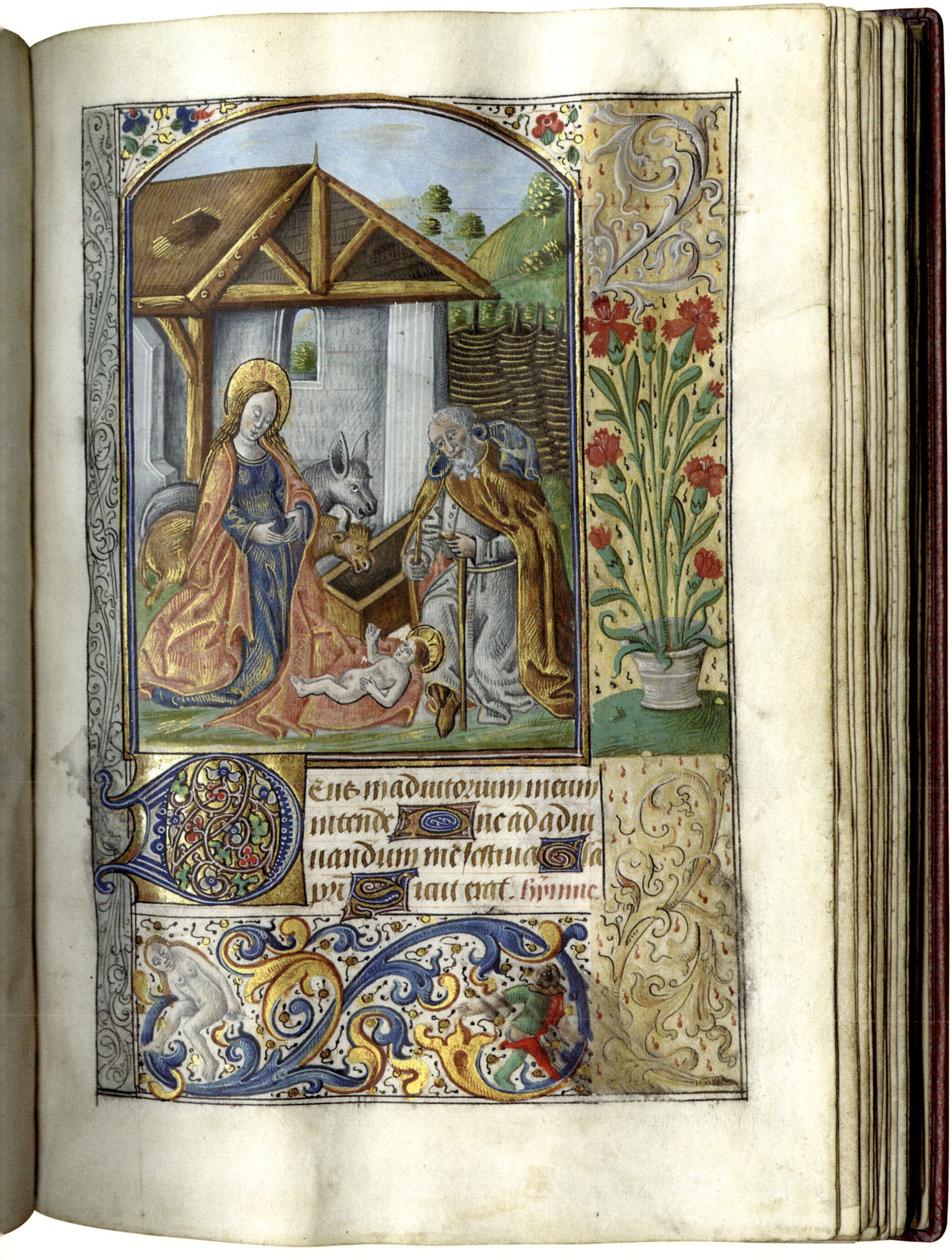

f. 23, Nativity

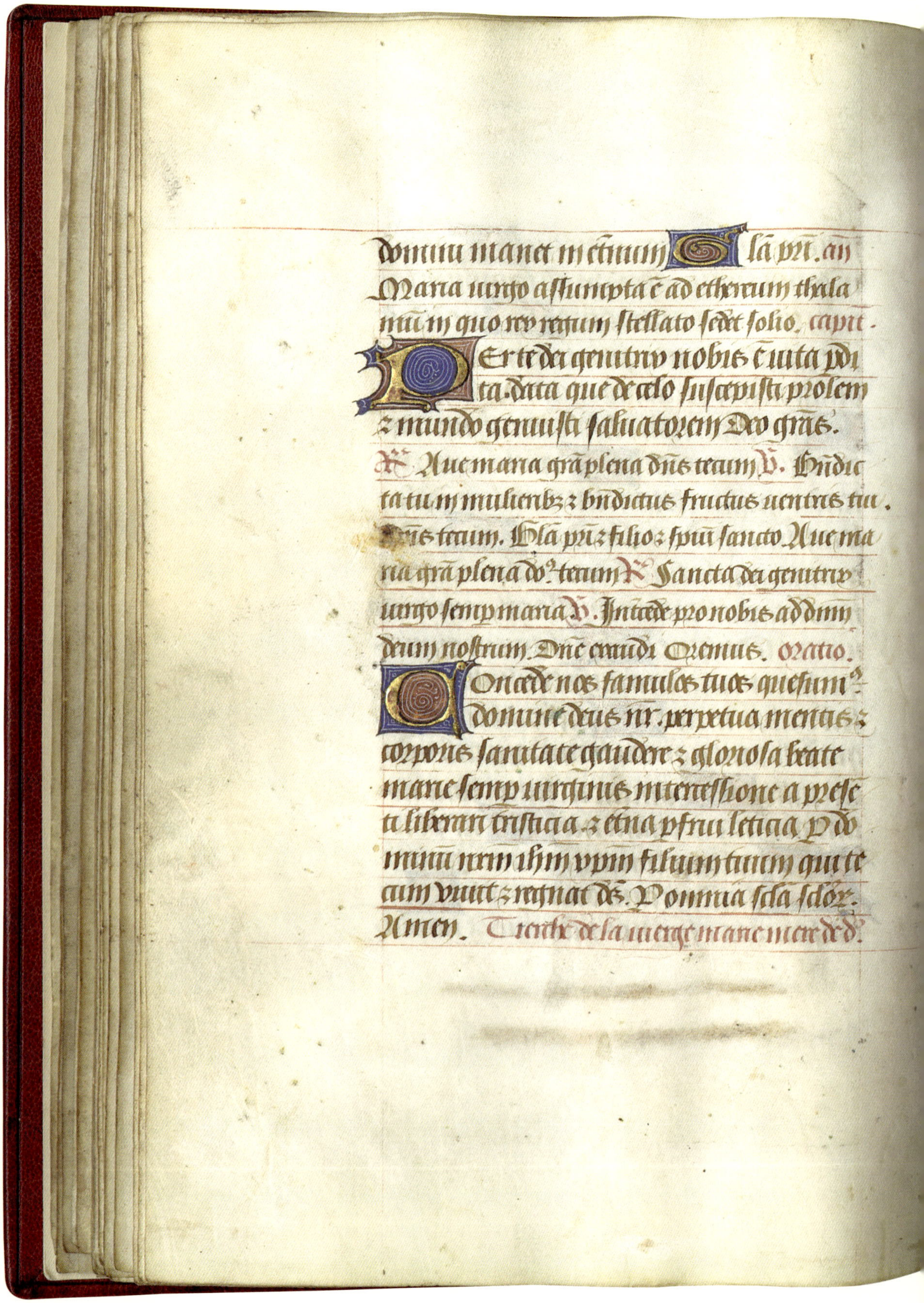
dominu manet in eternum. Gloria patri. an
Maria virgo assumpta est ad ethereum thala
mum in quo rex regum stellato sedet solio. capit
Per te dei genitrix nobis est vita perdi
ta data que de celo suscepisti prolem
et mundo genuisti salvatorem. Deo gratias.
R. Ave maria gratia plena dominus tecum. V. Benedic
ta tu in mulieribus et benedictus fructus ventris tui.
Dominus tecum. Gloria patri et filio et spiritui sancto. Ave ma
ria gratia plena dominus tecum. R. Sancta dei genitrix
virgo semper maria. V. Intercede pro nobis ad domi
num deum nostrum. Domine exaudi. Oremus. oratio.
Concede nos famulos tuos quesumus
domine deus noster perpetua mentis et
corporis sanitate gaudere et gloriosa beate
marie semper virginis intercessione a presen
ti liberari tristicia et eterna perfrui leticia. Per do
minum nostrum ihesum christum filium tuum qui te
cum vivit et regnat deus. Per omnia secula seculorum.
Amen. Tierce de la vierge marie mere de d.

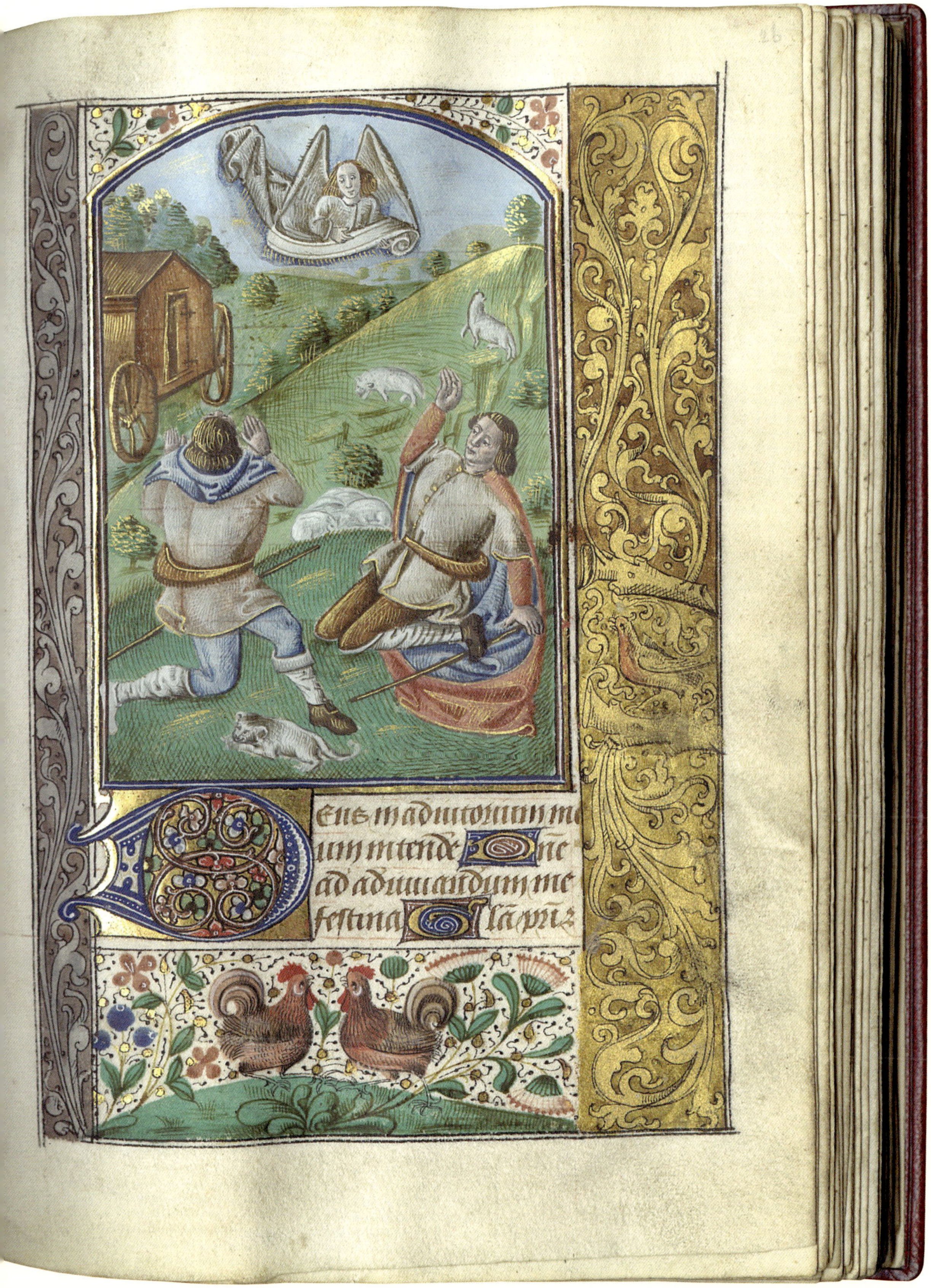

ff. 25v-26, Annunciation to the Shepherds

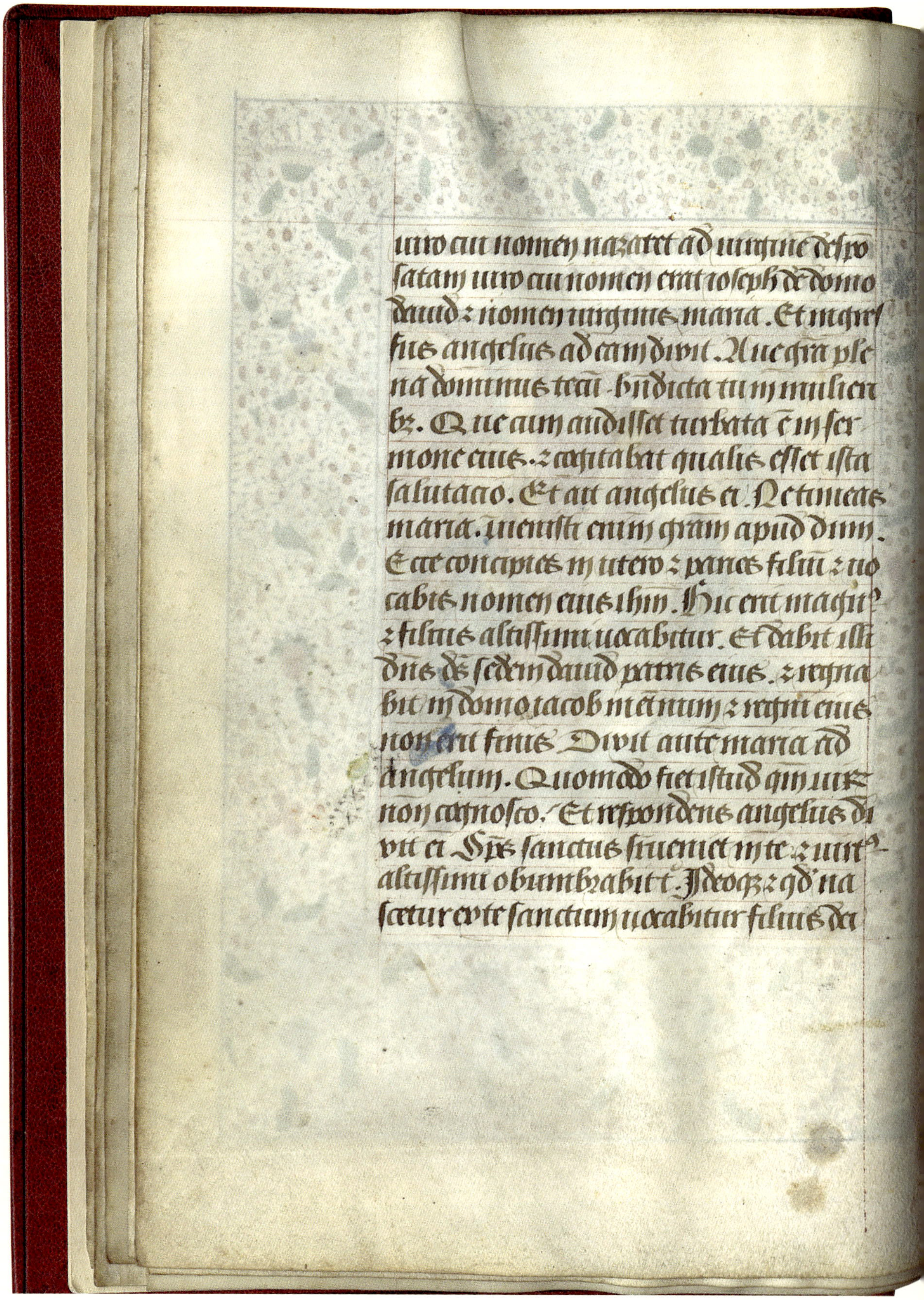
urbe cui nomen nazareth ad virginem despon-
satam viro cui nomen erat ioseph de domo
david: et nomen virginis maria. Et ingres-
sus angelus ad eam dixit. Ave gratia ple-
na dominus tecum. benedicta tu in mulieri-
bus. Que cum audisset turbata est in ser-
mone eius. et cogitabat qualis esset ista
salutacio. Et ait angelus ei. Ne timeas
maria. invenisti enim gratiam apud deum.
Ecce concipies in utero et paries filium et vo-
cabis nomen eius ihesum. Hic erit magnus
et filius altissimi vocabitur. Et dabit illi
dominus deus sedem david patris eius. et regna-
bit in domo iacob in eternum et regni eius
non erit finis. Dixit autem maria ad
angelum. Quomodo fiet istud quoniam virum
non cognosco. Et respondens angelus di-
xit ei. Spiritus sanctus superveniet in te et virtus
altissimi obumbrabit tibi. Ideoque et quod na-
scetur ex te sanctum vocabitur filius dei

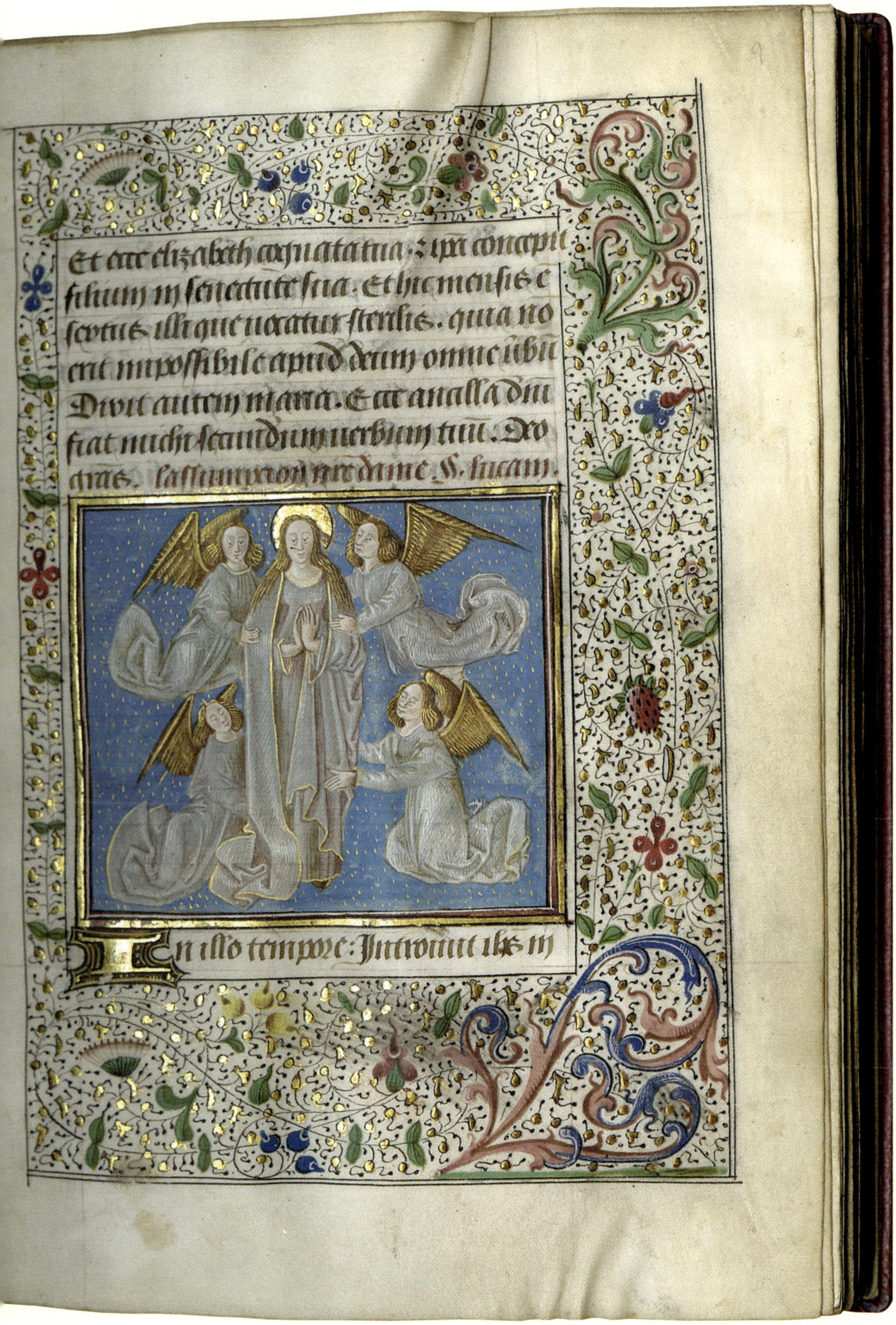

ff. 8v-9, Assumption of the Virgin

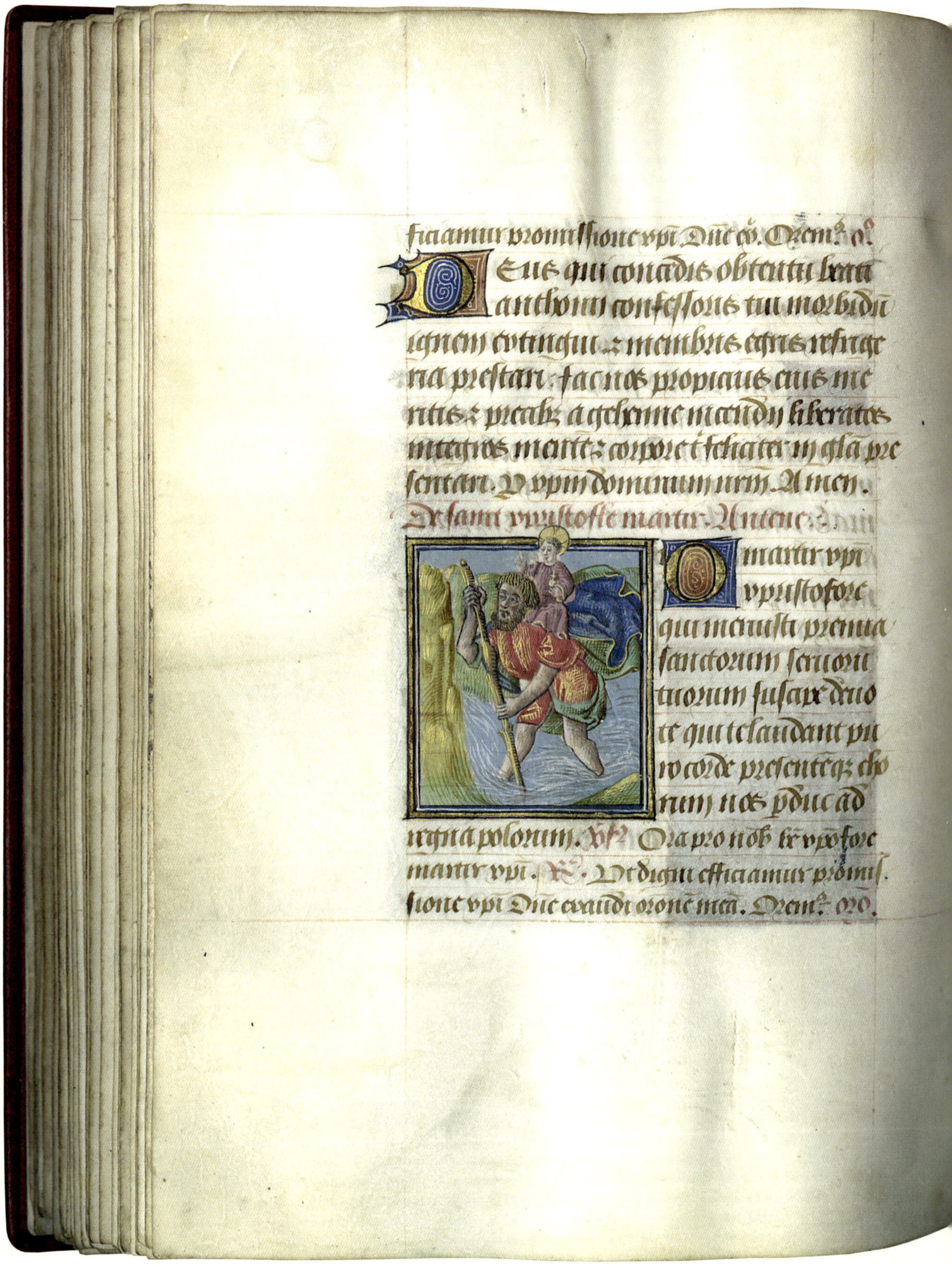

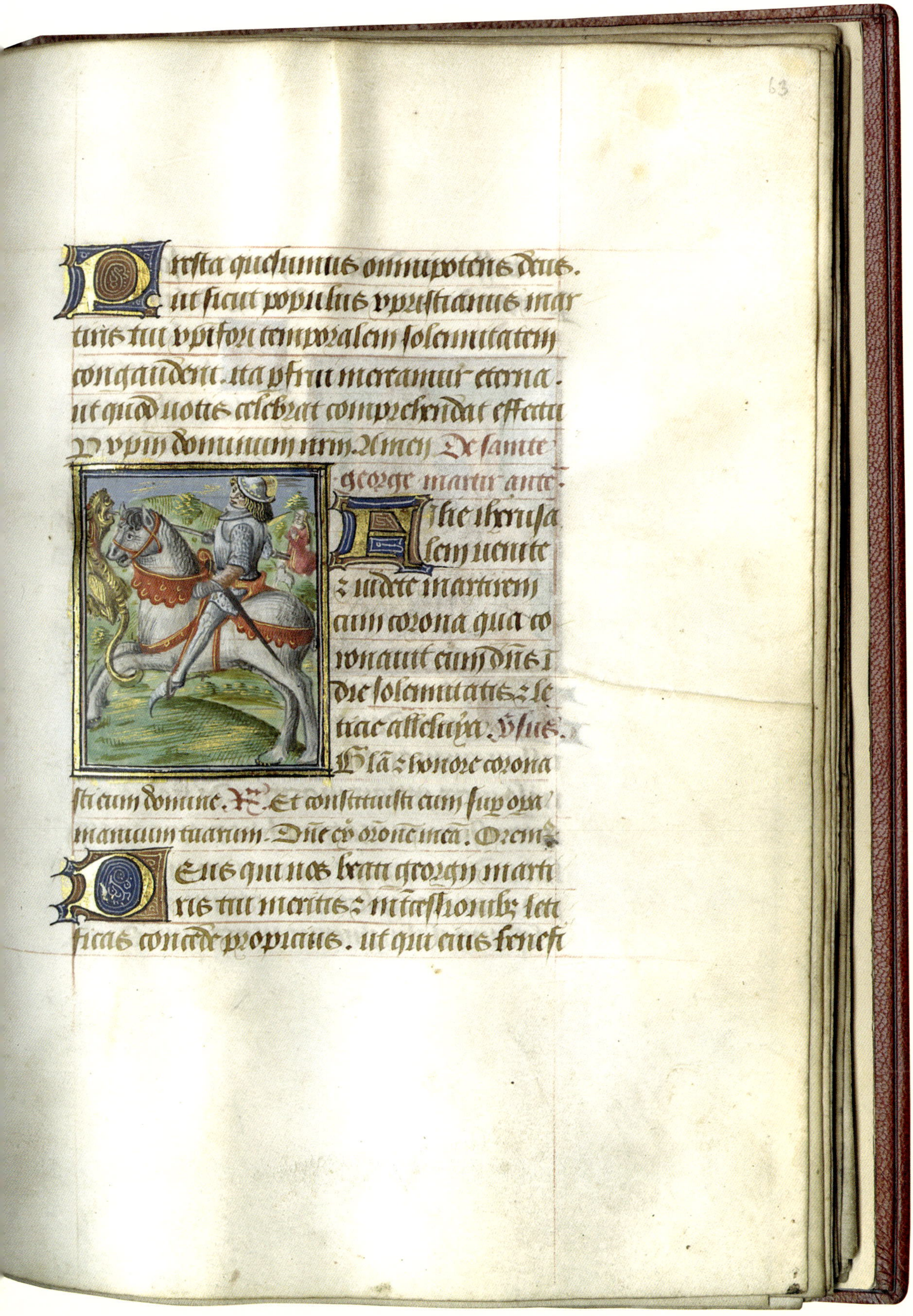
Presta quesumus omnipotens deus.
ut sicut populus christianus mar
tiris tui christofori temporalem solemnitatem
congaudent. ita perfrui mereamur eterna.
ut quod uotis celebrat comprehendat effectu.
Per christum dominum nostrum. Amen. De sancto
george martir antiphona.
Filie iherusa
lem uenite
et uidete martirem
cum corona qua co
ronauit eum dominus in
die solemnitatis et le
ticie alleluya. Versus.
Gloria et honore corona
sti eum domine. R. Et constituisti eum super opera
manuum tuarum. Domine exaudi orationem meam. Oremus.
Deus qui nos beati georgii marti
ris tui meritis et intercessionibus leti
ficas concede propicius. ut qui eius benefi

ff.62v-63, St. Christopher; St. Georges

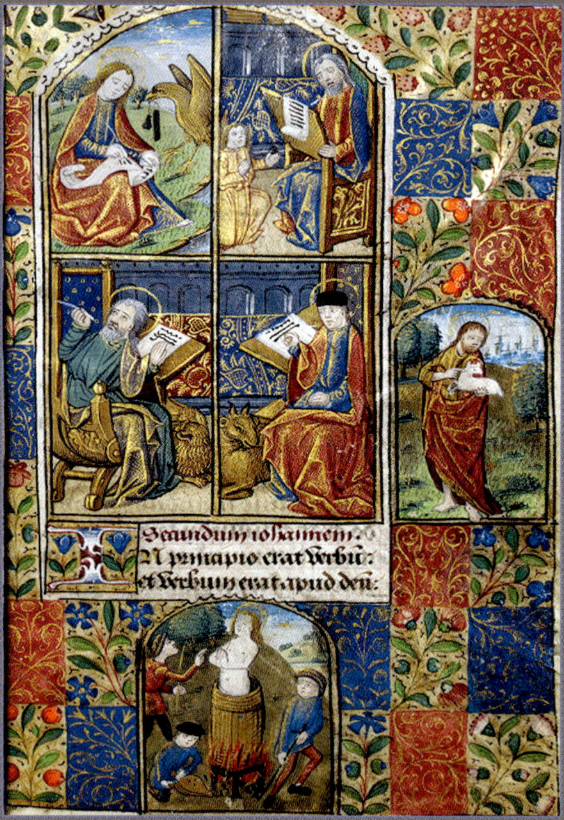

London, Victoria and Albert Museum, National Art Library, MS MSL/1918/475, "Playfair Hours," f. 13, Four Evangelists

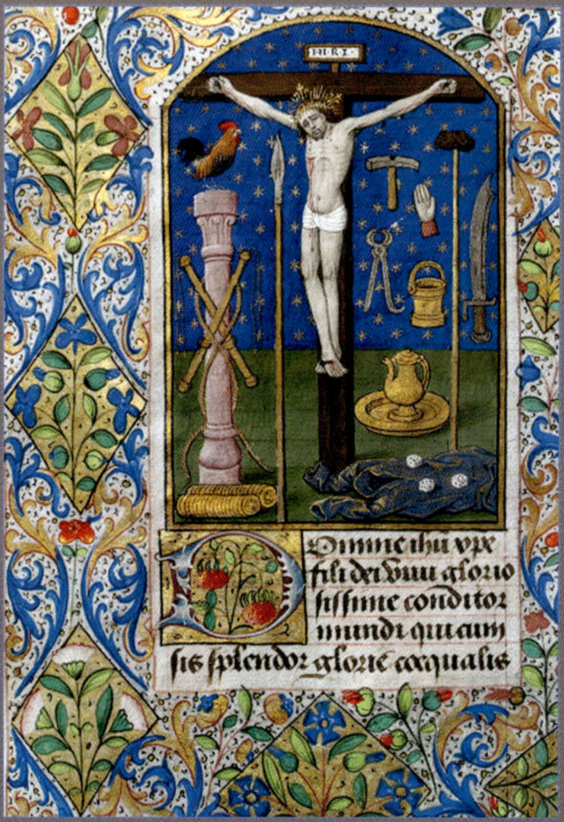

London, Victoria and Albert Museum, National Art Library, MS MSL/1918/475, "Playfair Hours," f. 170v, Crucifixion with Arma Christi

Facing page, f. 75v, Cross and Arma Christi

nibz consecrantur. Qui viuis et regnas
ds p omnia secula seculorum Amen. Requiesc
cant in pace. Amen.

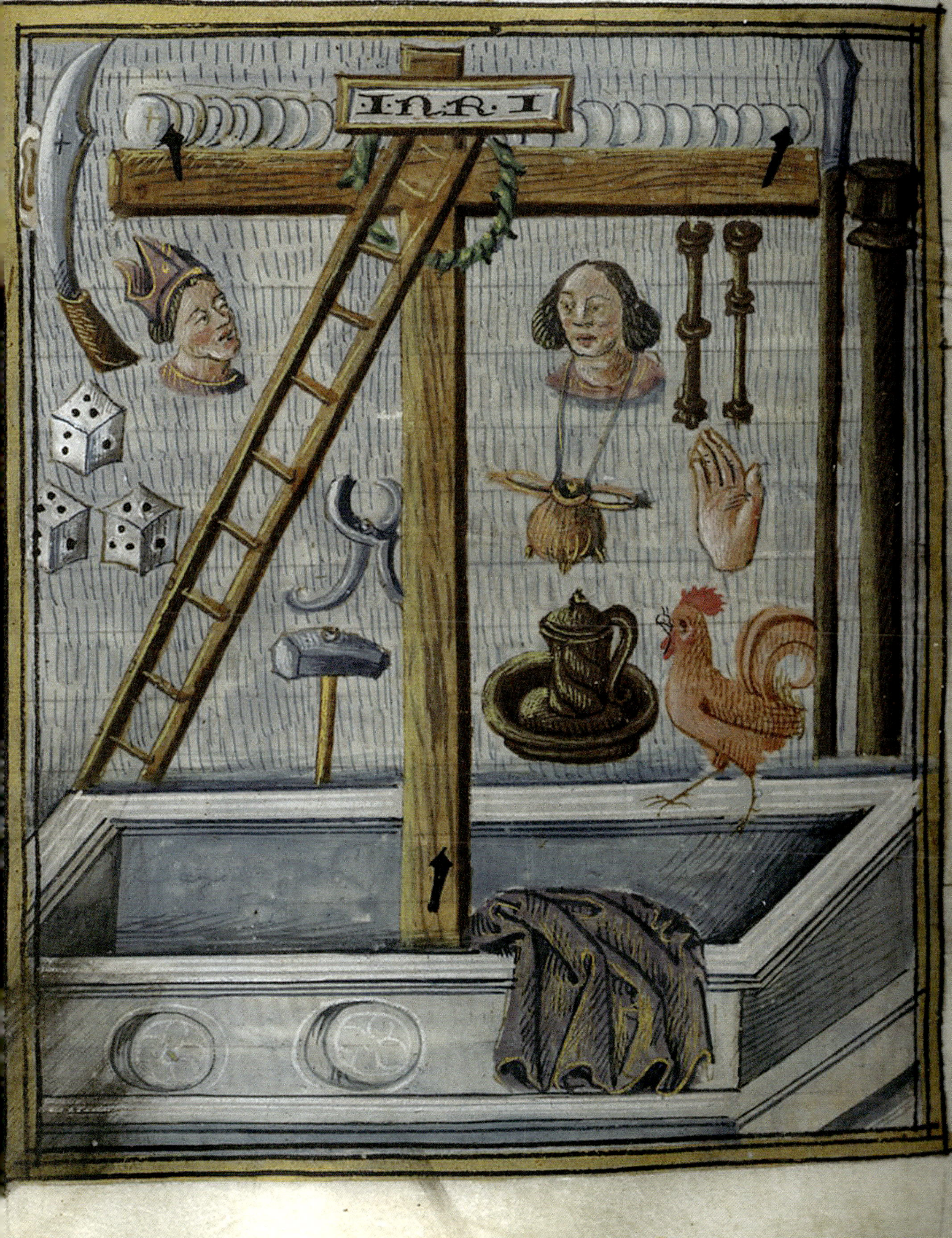

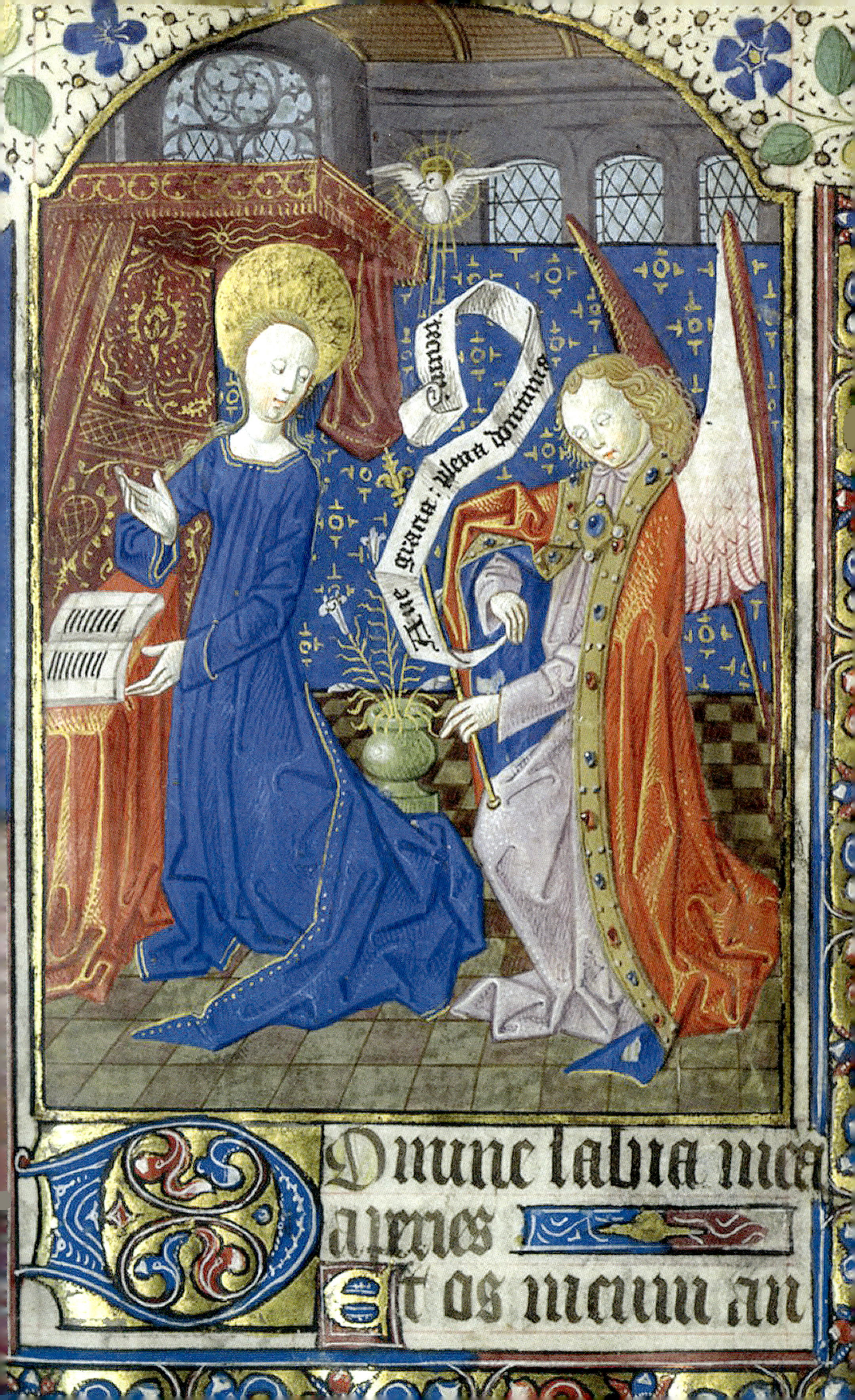
Ave gratia plena dominus tecum
Domine labia mea
aperies
Et os meum an

10

Book of Hours (Use of Lisieux)

In Latin and French, illuminated manuscript on vellum

France, Rouen, c. 1460-1470

13 large miniatures attributed to the Circle of the Master of the Échevinage de Rouen.

The death of King Charles VI in 1422 and the installation of an English king on the French throne resulted in political turmoil in the capital engendered by the quarrel of succession and the ongoing Hundred Years' War. Many artists thus fled Paris to install themselves elsewhere. This decade, the 1420s, effectively marks the origin of French regional manuscript illumination. Rouen quickly emerged as one of the most active hubs. Until 1449, Rouen was the center of the English occupation, a phenomenon that produced close ties with Normandy and England itself and led to a brisk patronage among the wealthy English and French residents of the city by artists who combined Parisian and English influences. With the departure of the English from Rouen in 1449, Rouen witnessed a second phase of activity in manuscript production, in response to growing demands from mercantile and professional clients, including an emergent bourgeois class of governmental officials. In the third quarter of the century, a larger number of manuscripts were made in Rouen than in any other city of France, with the exception of Paris (see Rabel, 1984; Watson, 1984). Rouen's dynamic book trade, its professional illuminators clustered together in the shadow of St.-Maclou and the Cathedral, was complemented by the imprints that would soon follow and exist parallel to manuscript production.

Closely related to a key artist from the second phase of Rouen manuscript illumination, the Master of the Échevinage de Rouen, these very elegant Horae were made for the uncommon use of Lisieux. Rouen produced a number of Horae for neighboring dioceses such as Lisieux and Évreux and also for export abroad (to wit, the Playfair Hours, painted in Rouen for export to Scotland, see Watson, 1984, who mentions other Rouen manuscripts destined for export and Watson, 2011, vol. I, no. 56; see also De Hamel, 1994, p. 184). Most likely an important patron in or near Lisieux (Normandy) ordered the present book from nearby Rouen, which accounts for the inclusion of a number of entries in honor of Saint Ursin in the Calendar. Saint Ursin was honored locally

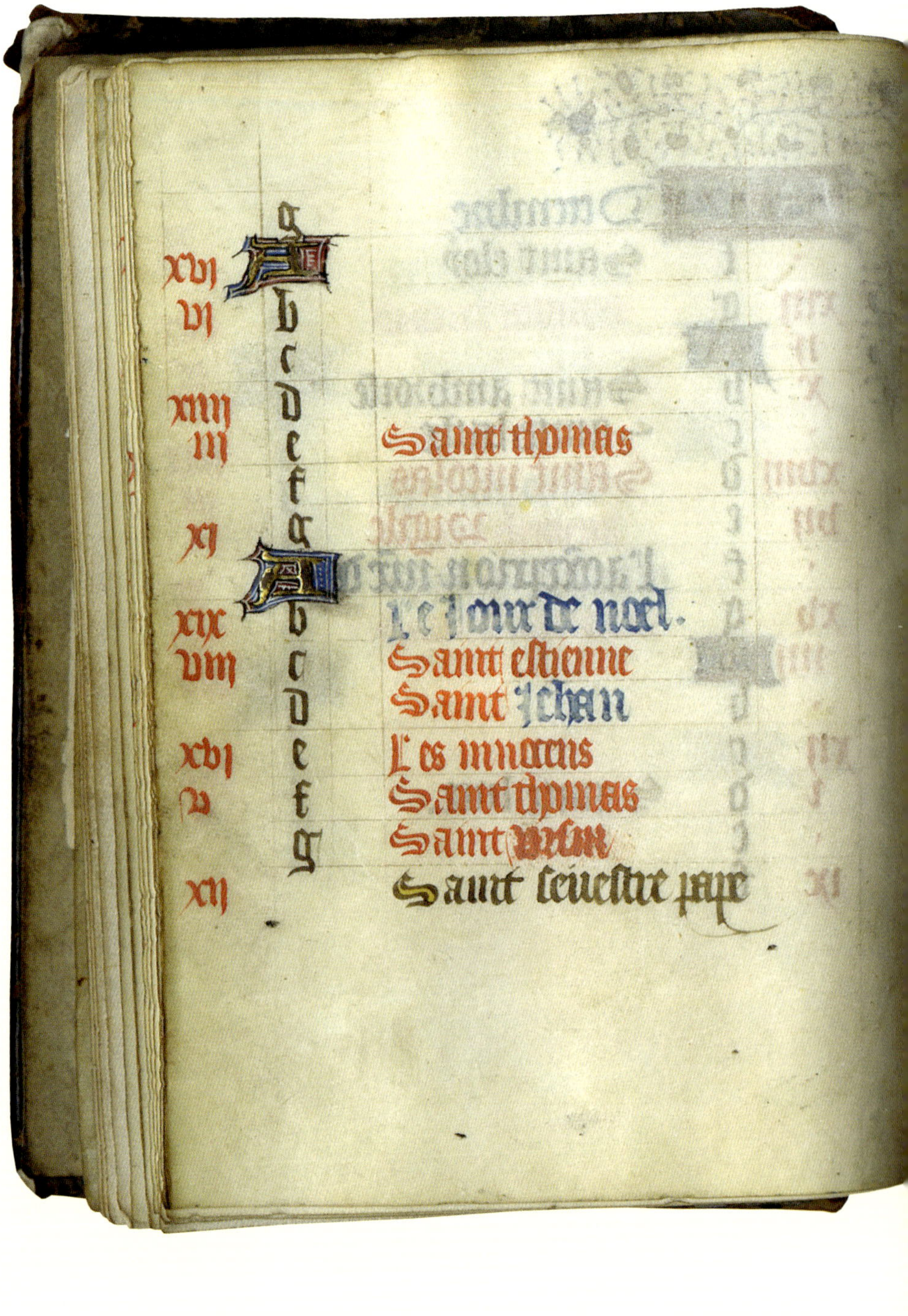
Saint thomas
Le jour de noel.
Saint estienne
Saint Jehan
Les innocens
Saint thomas
Saint sevestre pape

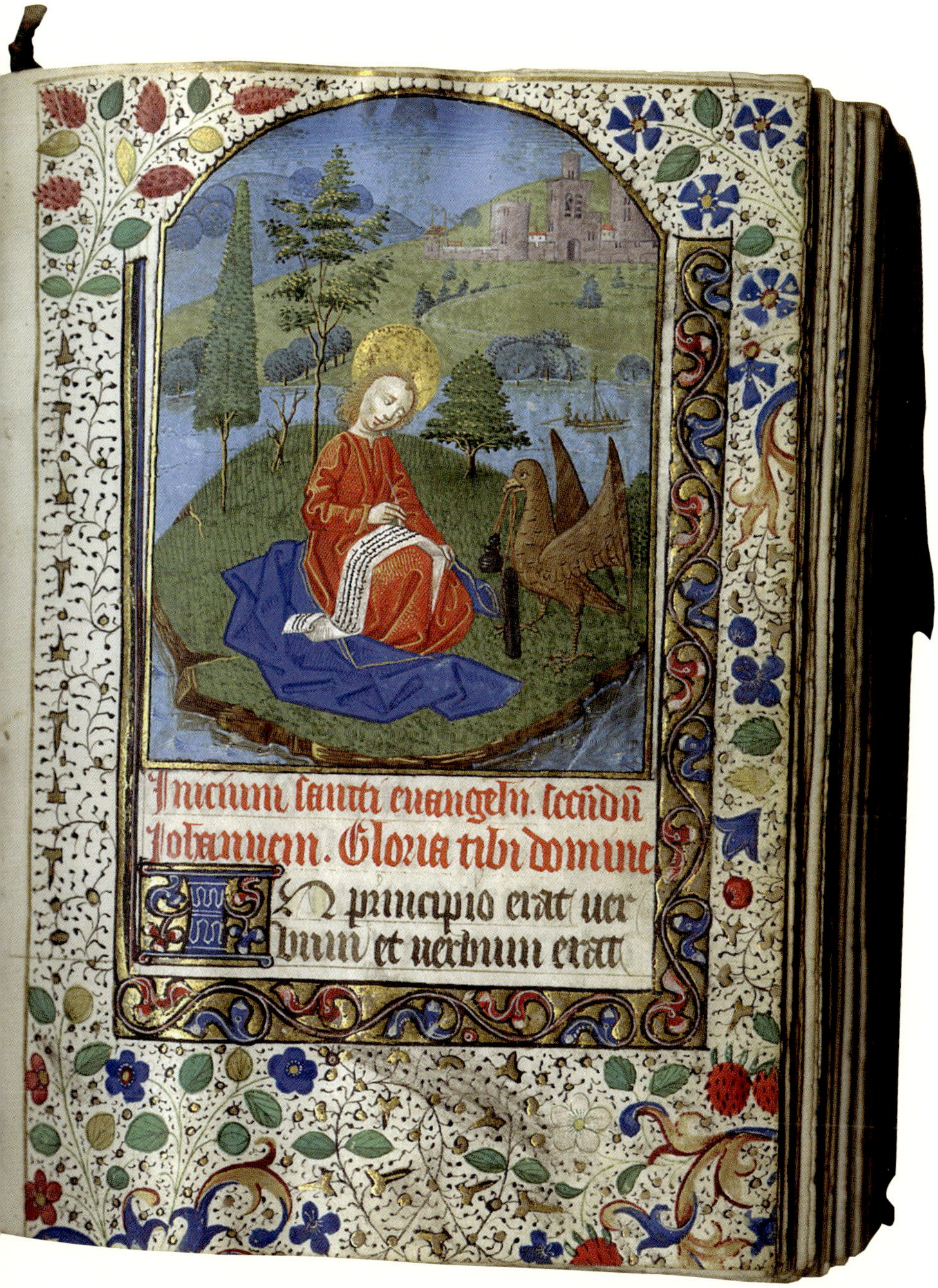

ff. 12v-13, Calendar leaf (December with Saint Ursin, in red); John on Patmos

in Lisieux where his relics are housed in the Cathedral dedicated to Saint Peter. There are four entries, some red-lettered, for Ursin (including Feasts for the Octave and the Revelation) as well as for other locally honored saints such as Patrice and Désir. The liturgical use of these Horae is very clearly Lisieux, a relatively rare use. There is only one Book of Hours recorded in Leroquais (1927, vol. I, no. 108) for the use of Lisieux (Paris, BnF, MS lat. 1395, no stylistic comparisons). We have localized only a few other Horae for the use of Lisieux, which are Châlons-en-Champagne, BM, MS 334 (no stylistic comparisons), and London, Victoria and Albert Museum, Reid 13 (see Watson, 2011, no. 55; no stylistic comparisons).

Active in Rouen from circa 1460 to 1480, the Master of the Échevinage de Rouen (formerly Master of the Geneva Latini or "Boucquechardière Master") worked, amongst other patrons, for the city aldermen (échevins) of Rouen, and the splendid manuscripts he and his workshop painted were housed in the library of the "Échevinage," whose inventory counts some 21 codices (see Rabel, 1989, p. 48). The personality of the artist who painted the miniatures of this Book of Hours, with its fine figures and vibrant colors, is complex and merits further study. The present artist is clearly influenced by two important artists who are first and foremost the above-mentioned Master of the Échevinage de Rouen (see C. Rabel, 1984, 1989 and 2011) and also to a certain extant Colin d'Amiens (see Reynaud, 1993, pp. 58-68; C. Grodecki, 1996). From the Master of the Échevinage de Rouen, whose style he follows closely, the artist of these Horae adopts the taste for profuse colored draperies (often present in the Horae painted by the Master of the Échevinage) as in the Annunciation, the Nativity, the Coronation of the Virgin, David in Prayer, even on the back of the donkey in the Flight into Egypt. One might signal also the trees in characteristic clusters in bright shades of green. The composition of David praying on his terrace is found in Hours attributed to the Master of the Échevinage de Rouen and his workshop (compare for example in the Hours of Chrétienne de France, Paris, Bibl. Arsenal, MS 562, f. 77; see Avril, 1993, no. 91, p. 172), harking back to compositions attributed to the much earlier Master of Bedford (see for example London, Sotheby's, 13 June 1983, lot 11, f. 105). The Visitation in the Lisieux Horae is quite close to one painted by a follower of the Master of the Échevinage in a Book of Hours in Oxford, Bodleian Library, Buchanam e 13 (f. 37). Our artist shares many compositions found in Hours attributed to the Master of the Échevinage: compare for example the Flight into Egypt with a veiled Virgin figured in profile in Paris, BnF, MS lat. 18030 (f. 57) and the Flight into Egypt in the present Lisieux Horae (f. 64) (on the large corpus of Horae attributed to the Master of the Échevinage de Rouen, see Rabel, 1984).

A number of elements also reveal the Parisian influence of Colin d'Amiens (and his workshop) on the artist of the Lisieux Horae. Colin d'Amiens (formerly referred to as the Master of Coëtivy, see Reynaud, in Avril and Reynaud, 1993, pp. 58-69) or Nicolas d'Ypres was active in Paris circa 1450 till the late 1480s as a painter, illuminator, and designer of artistic programs in several media. The very bucolic figure of the shepherdess with her short-sleeved white apron on a red dress, her headband, and a sheep climbing on her lap (see Paris, BnF, MS lat. 1400, f. 88v, attributed to Colin d'Amiens), also found in another manuscript likewise attributed to a close follower of Colin d'Amiens (Sotheby's, 1 December 1987, lot. 65, f. 66; König, in Tenschert, Kat. XXI, 1989, no. 73), compares well with the sweet figure of the shepherdess in the same subject in the present Lisieux Hours (f. 49v). Other compositions in the Lisieux Horae are equally inspired by compositions adopted by Colin d'Amiens, such as the Presentation in the Temple or the Adoration of the Magi, although the coloring and style of the Lisieux Horae are closest to the more local Rouennais style of the Master of the Échevinage.

Most of the compositions found in these Horae derive from models that circulated locally in Rouen and were frequently repeated. Compare for instance the Nativity in the Lisieux Hours with four other similar compositions from four different Horae as reproduced by De Hamel, who gives four examples of quasi-duplication in Horae produced in Rouen circa 1470 (De Hamel, 1994, pp. 196-197). Nonetheless, the single artist of the Lisieux Hours is not devoid of originality and finesse: note in the Annunciation the elegance of the Virgin and the stylish gestures of the angel, where the rendering seems truly inspired by panel painting. Another Book of Hours can be attributed to this intriguing artist, an Horae for the use of Évreux, sold twice at Sotheby's (compare the Nativity; the Annunciation to the Shepherds, the Adoration of the Magi in the Évreux Hours sold at Sotheby's, 24 May 1977, lot 59; Sotheby's, 19 June 2001, lot 23; see also König, in Tenschert, Kat. XXV, 1990, n° 46; Kat. XXIX, 1992, p. 550-551). König dates these Horae, formerly owned by J. P. Getty, to circa 1450 and attributes the miniatures to the Workshop of the Master of the Échevinage de Rouen according to König (König, in Tenschert, Kat. XXV, 1990,

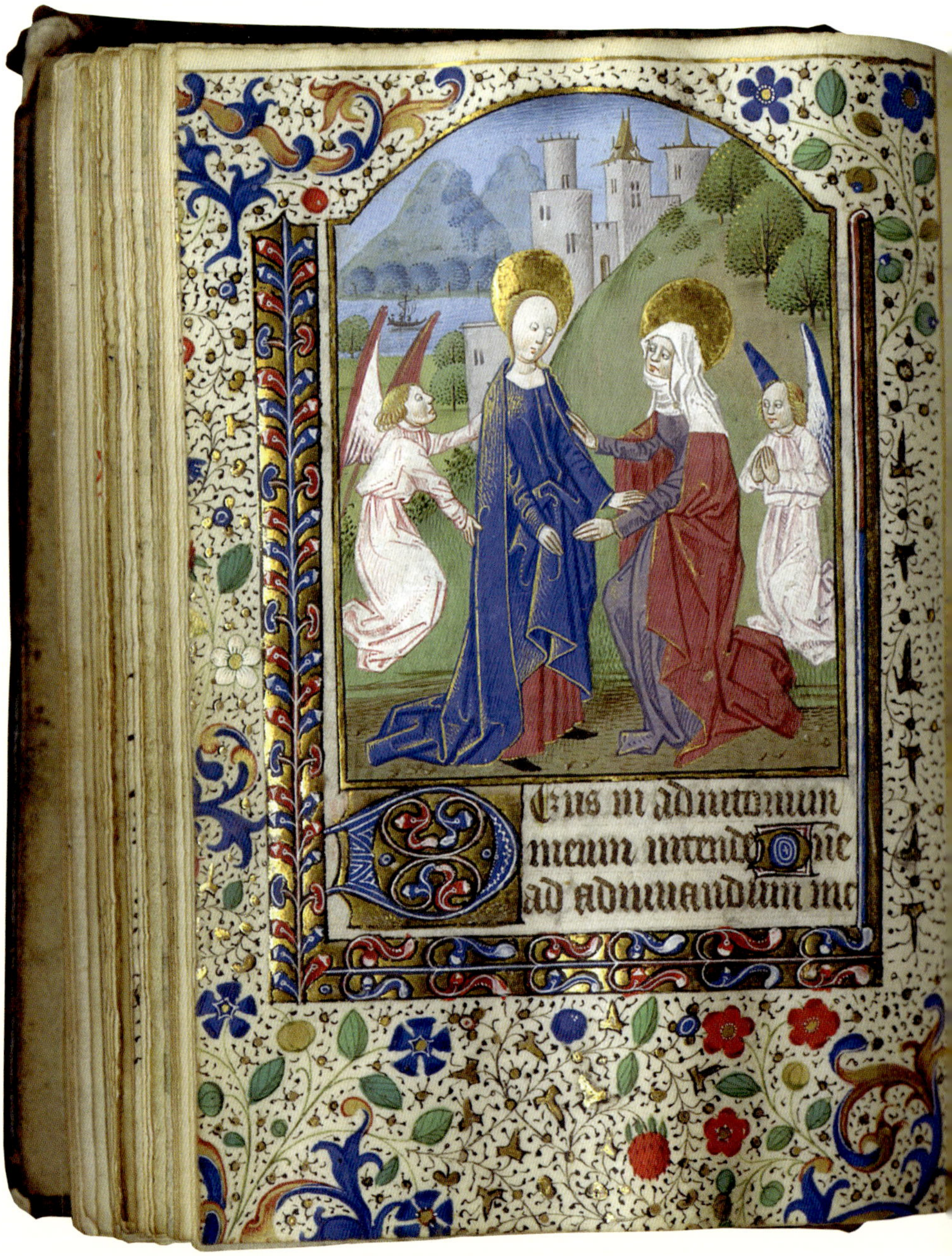

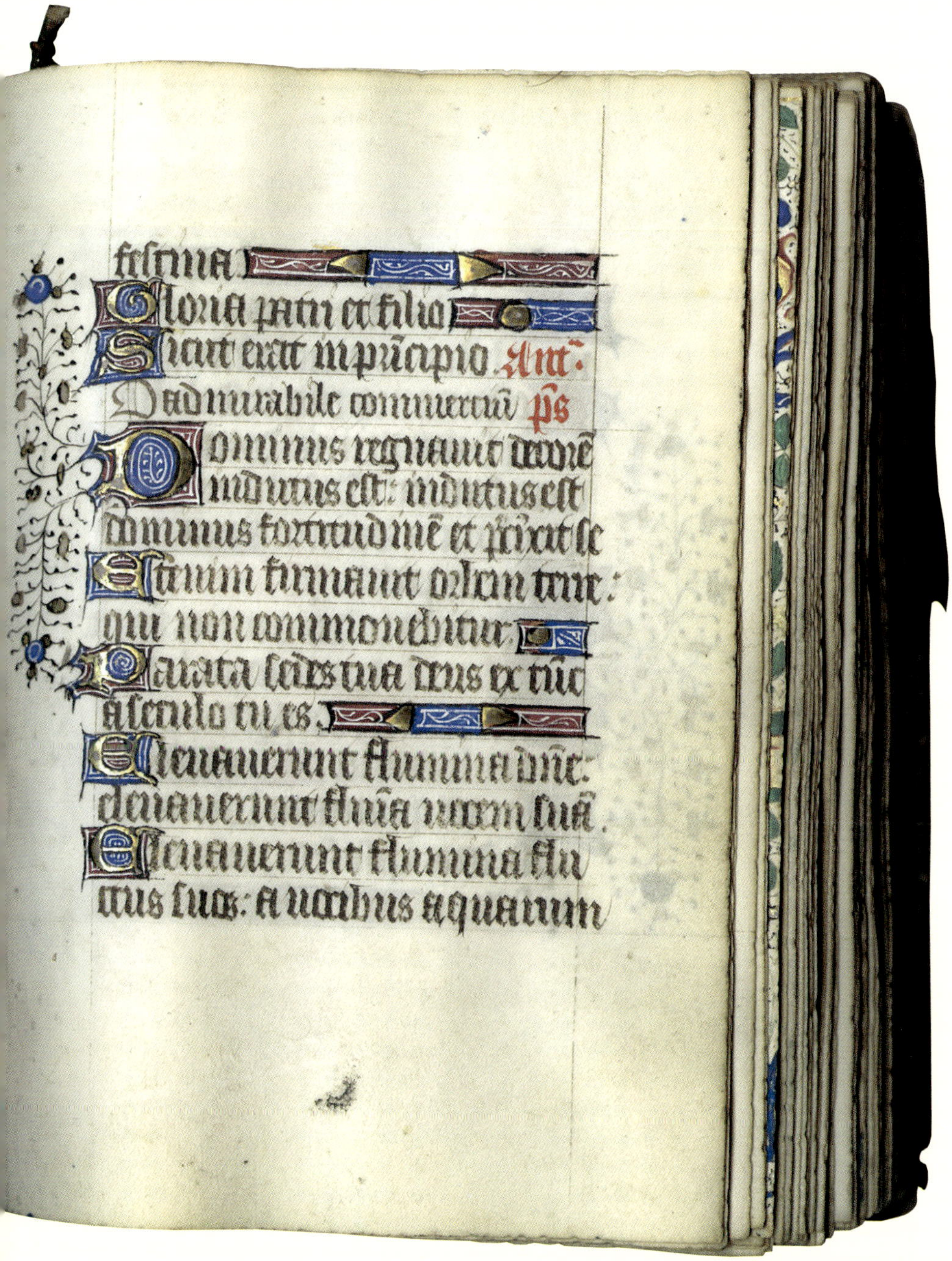

ff. 31v-32, Visitation

n° 46, pp. 530, 542 and 544). The study of this artist will surely yield other Horae painted by his hand. It would be important to map out his oeuvre and explore his ties or position within the workshop of the Master of the Échevinage de Rouen. Both the Sotheby's Évreux Hours and the present Lisieux Hours show how local patrons held the workshop of the Échevinage in high regard, turning to Rouen rather than Paris when commissioning their Books of Hours for use in smaller dioceses.

PHYSICAL DESCRIPTION: 163 ff., preceded by one parchment and four paper flyleaves, followed by four paper flyleaves, complete (collation: i-ii^6, iii-ix^8, x^6, xi^2, xii-xvi^8, xvii^2, xviii-xxii^8, xxiii^6), parchment ruled in light brown and pink ink, written in a Gothic bookhand, on up to 15 lines (justification 96 x 66 mm.), a few catchwords survive in the lower edge of some gatherings, pencil foliation, some capitals in Calendar touched in yellow, rubrics in red, line-fillers in pink and blue with burnished gold besants and white tracery, 1- and 2-line high initials in highly burnished gold on blue and pink grounds highlighted in white tracery, larger 2-line high initials with black penwork tendrils, golden ivy-leaf sprays and blue disks extending into the margin, every page with a miniature is fully-illuminated with a 3-line high initial in blue with white tracery against burnished gold grounds with colored foliage in the infill, three-sided borders with stylized and naturalistic flowers and plants, scrolling colored acanthus leaves, black hairline tendrils with sprays of golden leaves and trefoils, 13 arch-topped miniatures closely framed by illuminated bar-borders and baguettes of colored foliage on burnished gold grounds, set in full-illuminated borders as described above. Bound in sixteenth-century gilt binding of tanned calf over pasteboards, central oval cartouche where once were gilt letters (now effaced, likely those of a 16th century owner) set within a larger hatched strapwork cartouche, on a semé of hermine, hatched strapwork cornerpieces, double gilt fillet border, spine gilt, sewn on four raised bands, traces of ties (now wanting), gilt and gaufered edges (Binding in need of restoration, hinges split and thongs on spine apparent due to leather wanting, outer edge of a few leaves a bit cropped, but overall very fresh internal condition). Dimensions 163 x 120 mm.

TEXT: ff. 1-12v, Calendar, in red, blue and brown ink, in French, for use in Rouen and in Lisieux, with such noteworthy saints as Romain (twice in red, 23 Oct.;18 Nov.); Les octaves saint Ursin (5 Jan.) [Lisieux], Saint Patrix (Patrice) (17 March) [Lisieux], Saint Ytrope (Eutrope), evesque (30 April), Desir (23 May) [Lisieux], Saint Ursin and Saint Benart (in red, 11 June) [Lisieux], Mellon (in brown ink, 22 Oct.), Revelation S. Ursin (in red, 9 Nov.) [Lisieux], Thomas (twice, in red, 21 and 29 Dec.), Ursin (in red, 30 Dec.) [Lisieux]; ff. 13-19, Gospel Extracts; ff. 19-20v, Salve Regina and other prayers; ff. 21-76, Hours of the Virgin, apparently use of Lisieux, with Matins (ff. 21-31), Lauds (ff. 31v-42v), Prime (ff. 43-49), Terce (ff. 49v-54), Sext (ff. 54-58, erroneous rubric), None (ff. 59-63v), Vespers (ff. 64-71), Compline (ff. 71v-76); the antiphons and capitulae are as follows: Matins: Benedicta tu / Beata es [hymnus: "Quem terra ponthus..."]; Lauds, O admirabile / In omnibus requiem [hymnus: "O gloriosa domina..."]; Prime, O admirabile / Ab inicio; terce, Quando natus / Et sic in syon; Sext erroneous rubric on f. 54 "Ad terciam", Rubum quia / Et radicavi; None, Ecce Maria / Felix namque; Vespers, Post partum virgo / Beata es virgo; Compline, Cum iocunditate / Sicut cynamonium; f. 76v, blank; ff. 77-94, Penitential Psalms and Litany; ff. 94v-102, Hours of the Cross; ff. 102v-108, Hours of the Holy Spirit; ff. 108v-112, *Obsecro te*; ff. 112v-116v, *O intemerata*; ff. 117-117v, blank leaves; ff. 118-163v, Office of the Dead, use of Rouen, with nine lessons.

ILLUSTRATION: There are 13 three-quarter page miniatures: f. 13, St. John on Patmos; f. 21, Annunciation; f. 31v, Visitation; f. 43, Nativity; f. 49v, Annunciation to the Shepherds; f. 54v, Adoration of the Magi; f. 59, Presentation in the Temple; f. 64, Flight into Egypt; f. 71, Coronation of the Virgin; f. 77, David in Prayer; f. 94v, Crucifixion; f. 102v, Pentecost; f. 118, Burial Scene.

OWNERSHIP: 1. Copied and illustrated in Normandy, likely Rouen based on stylistic evidence (Hours of the Virgin, use of Lisieux, see text below). The Office of the Dead however follows the use of Rouen. Interestingly the presence of a number of entries in the Calendar in honor of Saint Ursin confirms the use for Lisieux, where Saint Ursin was particularly venerated. There is a later inscription on f. 1 (17th century hand?) that reads "Lisieux." Another Lisieux saint also present in the Calendar is Saint Désir (23 May). Ursin was venerated locally in Lisieux and his relics were "discovered" during the renovation of the Cathedral in the eleventh century. The Cathedral itself in Lisieux is dedicated to Saint Peter. Another noteworthy Lisieux saint present in the Calendar is Saint Patrice (17 March), whose relics were also honored in the Cathedral of Lisieux. - 2. John L. Brownlowe, his heraldic bookplate pasted on the upper pastedown: "Baron Charleville and Viscount Tyrconnel in the Kingdom of Ireland" and motto: "Esse quam videri." Another bookplate on recto of first flyleaf: "Belton House." Brownlow (or Brownlow), Third Baronet (1659-1697). He inherited the Belton Estates including Belton House in 1679. He was elected to the House of Commons for Grantham, a seat he held till his death. - 3. European Private Collection.

LITERATURE: Unpublished but compare by the same artist the manuscript sold successively at Sotheby's, 24 May, 1977, lot. 59; König, Kat. XXV, 1990, no. 46; König, Kat. XXIX, 1992, pp. 550-551; Sotheby's, 19 June, 2001, lot. 23. - Avril, F. and N. Reynaud, *Les manuscrits à peintures en France, 1440-1520*, Paris, 1993. - De Hamel, C. *A History of Illuminated Manuscripts*, London, Phaidon Press, 1994. - Grodecki, C. "Le "Maître Nicolas d'Amiens" et la mise au tombeau de Malesherbes. A propos d'un document inédit," *Bulletin monumental*, 154, IV, 1996, p. 329-342.- Leroquais, V. *Les livres d'heures manuscrits de la Bibliothèque nationale*, Paris, 1927. - Pellerin, H. "Le culte de Saint Ursin à Lisieux," in *Bulletin de la Société des antiquaires de Normandie*, tome LVIII, 1965-1966. - Pellerin, E. and J. Bergeret, *La Cathédrale Saint-Pierre de Lisieux*, Lisieux, 1995.- Rabel-Julien, C. *Les livres d'heures de Rouen peints par le Maître du trésor genevois et les enlumineurs influencé par lui, au 3e quart du 15e siècle: essai pour une étude stylistique, iconographique et historique* (unpublished dissertation, DEA, Paris, Université de Paris I, 1984). - Rabel, C. "Artiste et clientèle à la fin du Moyen Age: les manuscrits profanes du Maître de l'échevinage de Rouen," *Revue de l'art* 84 (1989), pp. 48-60. - Rabel, C., "Rouen. Maître de l'échevinage de Rouen," in *Enluminures du Louvre Moyen Age et Renaissance*, Paris, Musée du Louvre, 2011, in particular, pp. 208-211, no. 106.- Sotheby's, *A Selection of Illuminated Manuscripts from the 13th to the 16th centuries, The Property of Mr. J. R. Ritman, sold for the benefit of the Bibliotheca Philosophica Hermetica, Amsterdam*, London, 6 July 2000, lot. 25. - Sotheby's, *A Second Selection of Illuminated Manuscripts from c. 1000 to c. 1522. The Property of Mr. J. R. Ritman, sold for the benefit of the Bibliotheca Philosophica Hermetica, Amsterdam*, London, 19 June 2001, lot 23. - König, *Leuchtendes Mittelalter*, II, Kat. XXV, Antiquariat Heribert Tenschert, 1990, no. 46. - König, *Leuchtendes Mittelalter* IV, Kat. XXIX, Antiquariat Heribert Tenschert, 1992, p. 550-551. - Watson, R. *The Playfair Hours. A Late Fifteenth Century Illuminated Manuscript from Rouen (V & A, L. 475-1918)*, London, 1984. - Watson, R. *Victoria and Albert Museum. Western Illuminated Manuscripts*, London, V & A Publishing, 2011, vol. 1.

ONLINE RESOURCES:

Liturgical Use of Lisieux: http://www.chd.dk/use/

Claudia Rabel, *Revue de l'art*, 84 (1989)
http://www.persee.fr/web/revues/

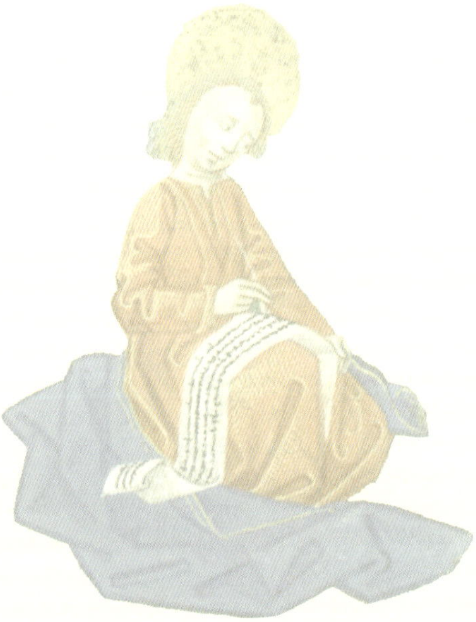

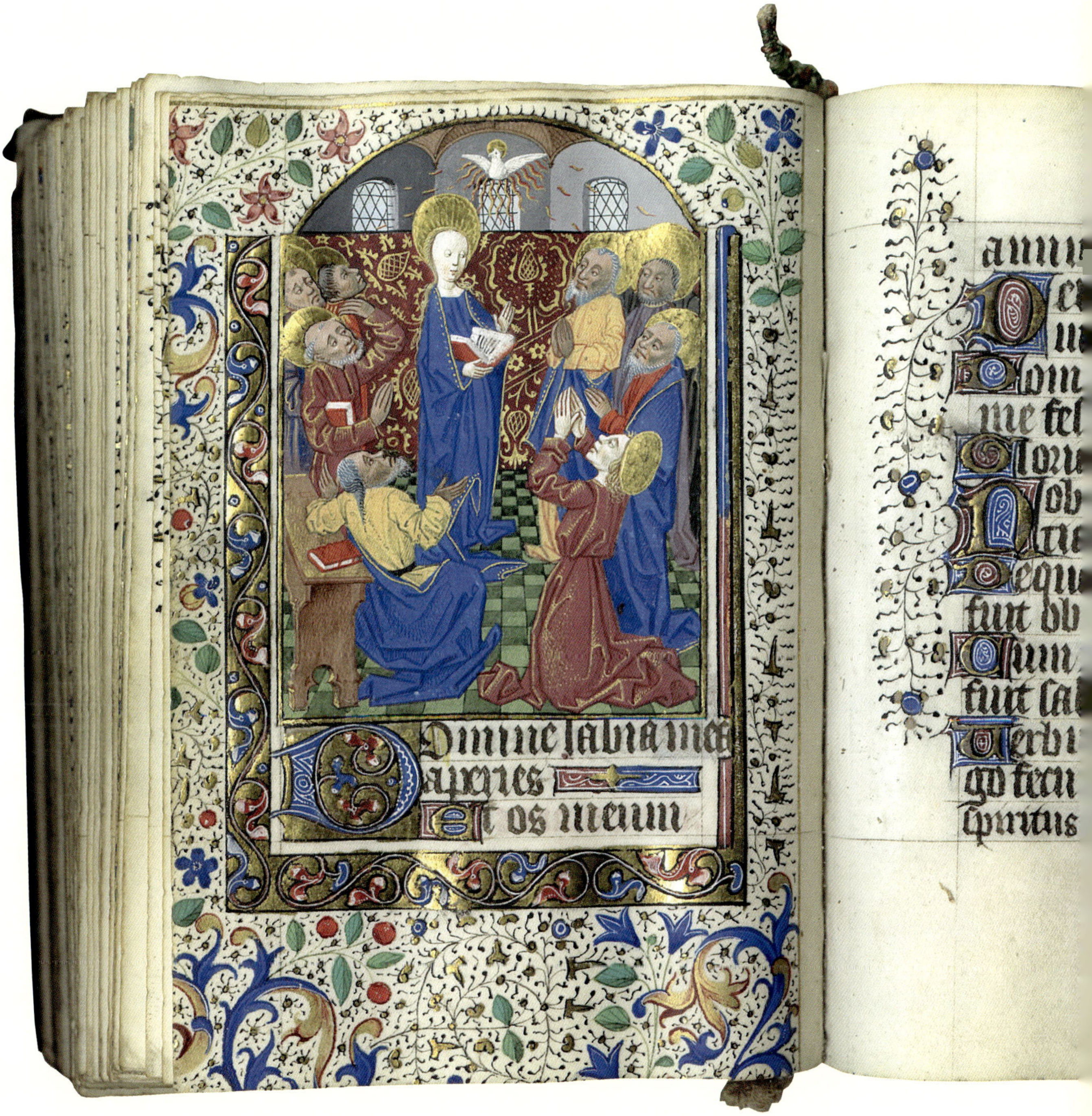

f. 102v, Pentecost

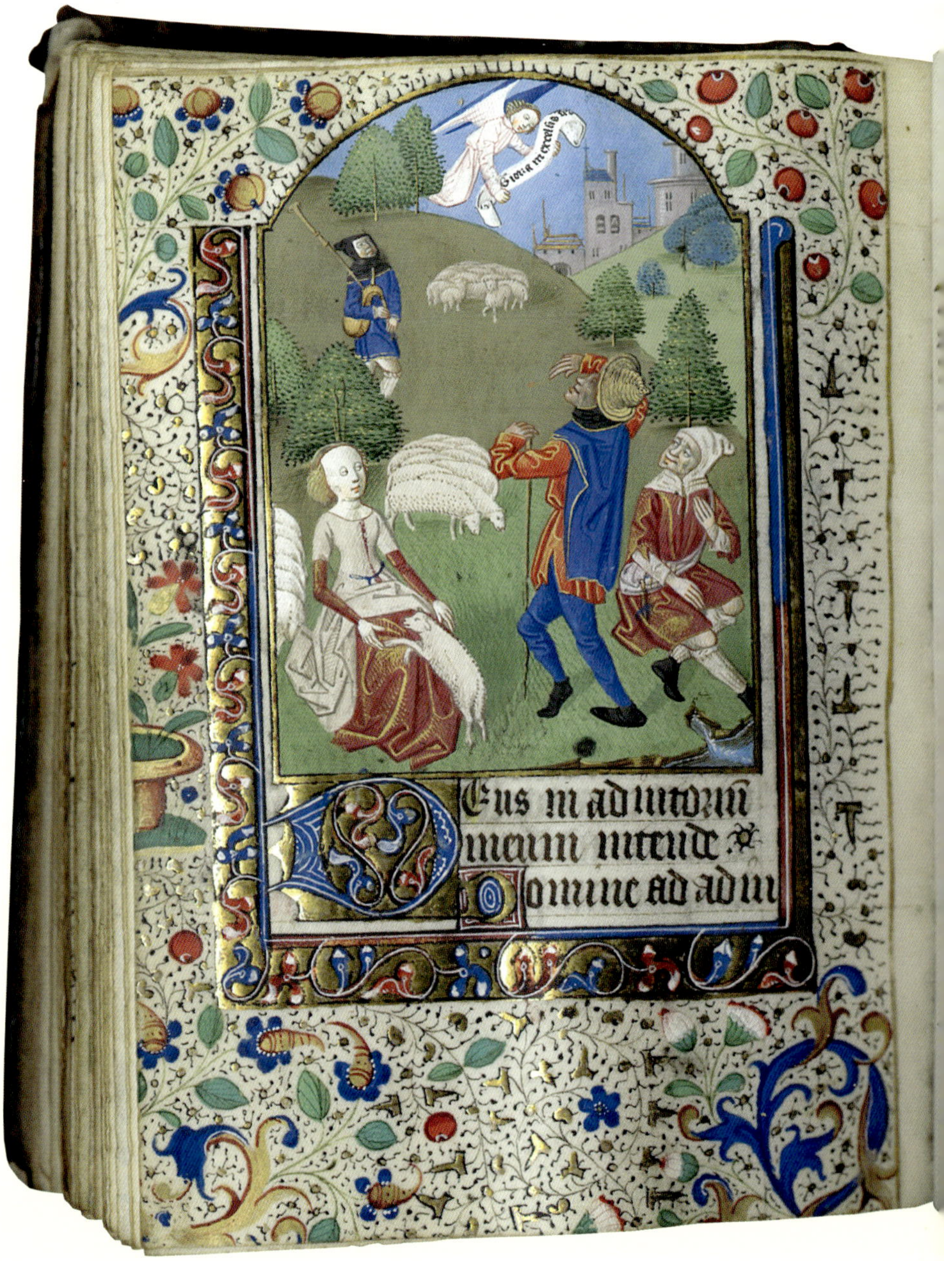

f. 49v, Annunciation to the Shepherds;

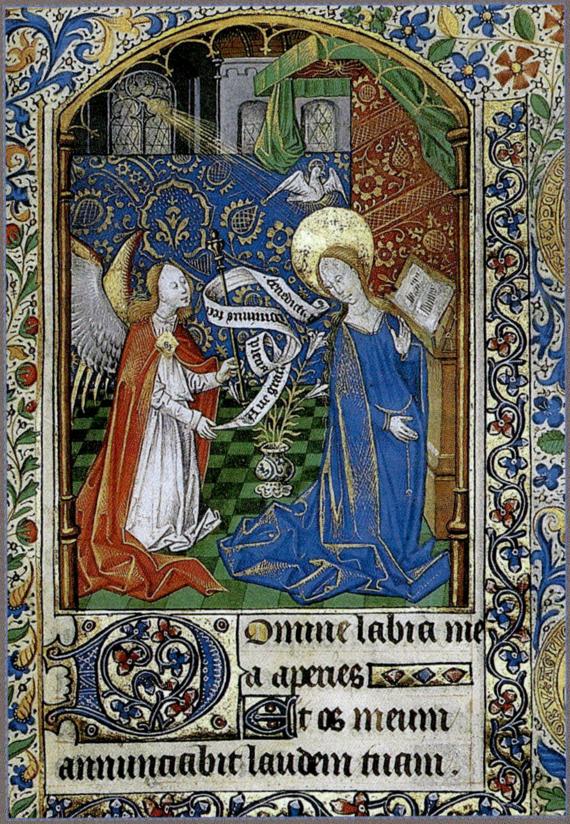

Private Collection, f. 35, Annunciation,
(formerly Sotheby's, London, 19 June 2001, lot 23, Book of Hours)

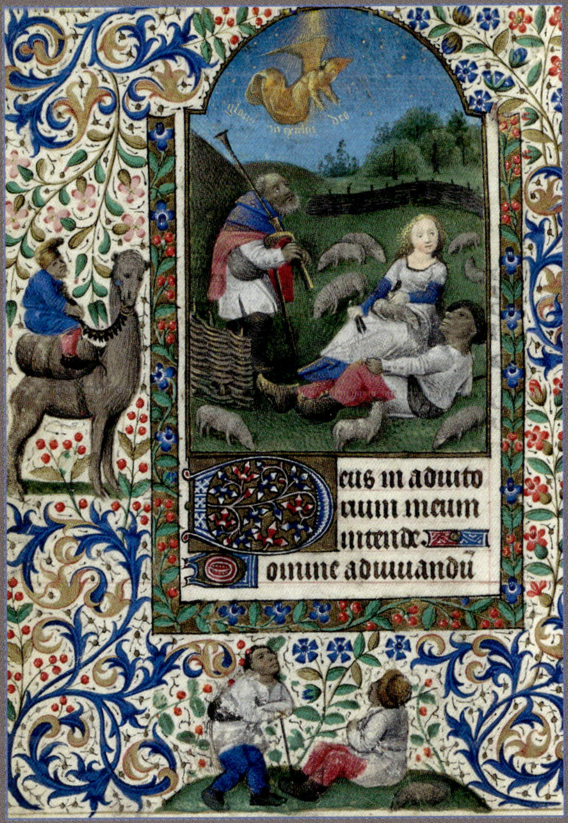

Paris, BnF, MS lat. 1400, Book of Hours,
f. 88v, Annunciation to the Shepherds;attributed to Colin d'Amiens

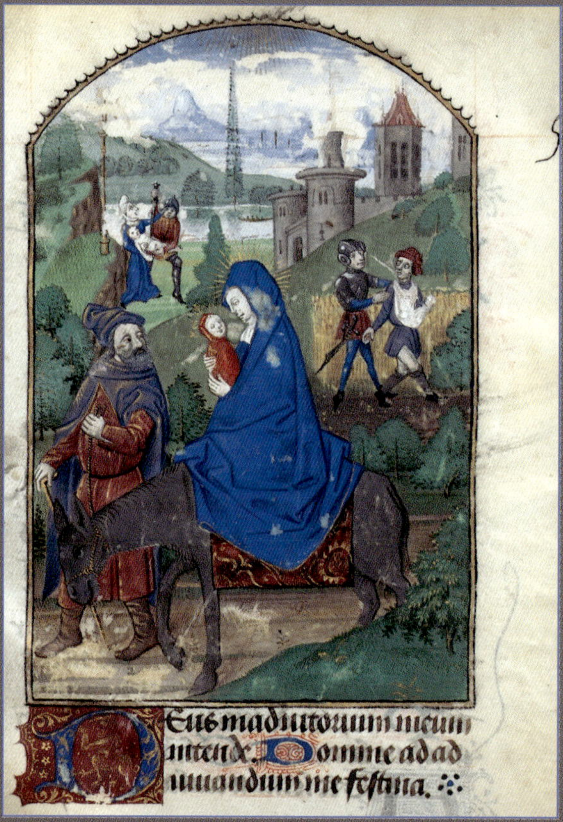

Paris, BnF, MS lat. 18030, Book of Hours,
f. 57, Flight into Egypt, attributed to the Master of the Échevinage de Rouen

Facing page, f. 64, Flight into Egypt

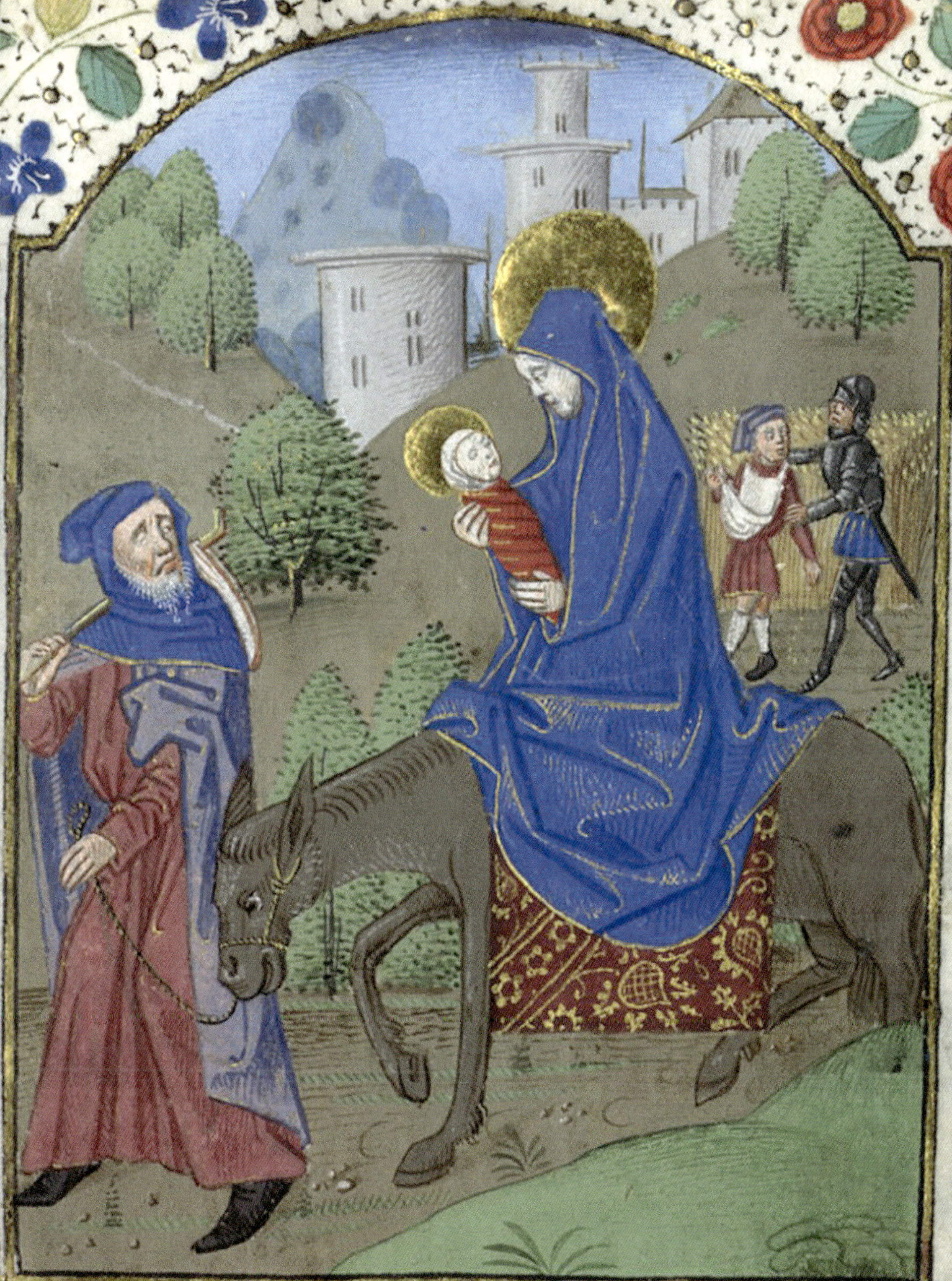

Deus in adiutorium
meum intende.
Domine ad adiuuandum

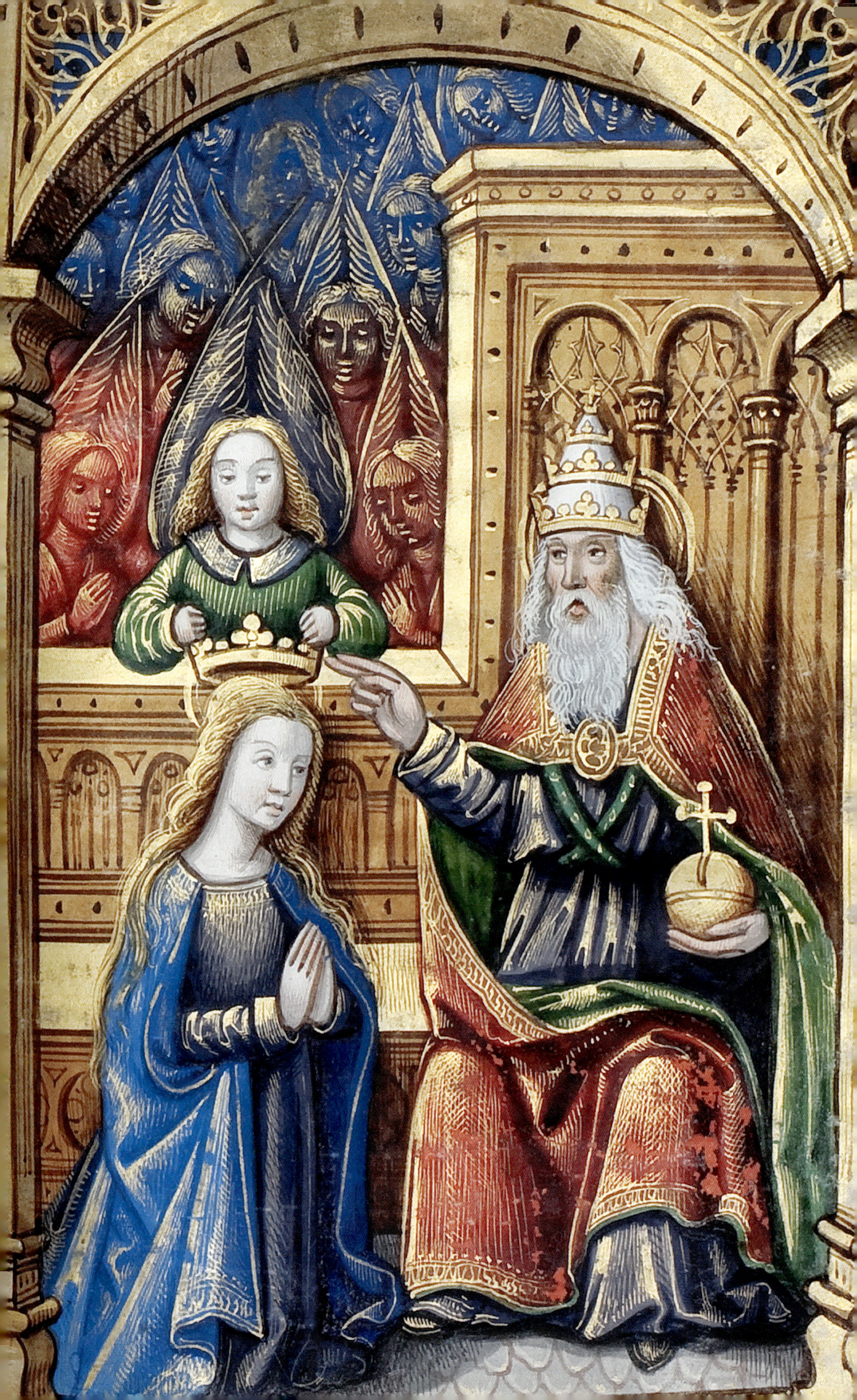

11

Book of Hours (Use of Rome)

In Latin, illuminated manuscript on parchment
France, Lyons, c. 1495-1510
11 full-page, 28 small, and 1 half-page miniatures by Guillaume II Le Roy

This handsome, richly illuminated Book of Hours is a good example of manuscript production in the age of print. It was painted by a prolific multi-talented artist, Guillaume II Le Roy, who was active as an illuminator at the same time that he supplied drawings and designs for illustrations for the printing industry and executed large-scale media (panel-painting and ephemeral art tied to royal entries or celebrations). Guillaume II Le Roy or Guillaume Le Roy the Younger was the son or nephew of the first printer established in Lyons, probably of Flemish stock given that the name sometimes occurs in archival records as "Guillaume le Flamand." Indeed well documented in the archives, Guillaume the Younger painted both secular and liturgical manuscripts for local Lyons humanists, prelates, and noblemen. His oeuvre on parchment counts some 28 (or perhaps 30) extant manuscripts and other painted printed books or cuttings (see Burin, 2001, cat. 95-136). The archives reveal that in 1523, Guillaume Le Roy lived on rue Mercière, in the center of the Lyons book trade.

It is now generally accepted that Guillaume Le Roy's career corresponded to that of a woodcutter and engraver known as the "Maître au Nombril," who produced woodcuts in imprints published between 1494 and 1529 (see A. and H. Joly, 1963; Avril, 1993, p. 362). The woodcutter was so named because of the recurring peculiar vertical line drawn from the navel to the pube on most of his nudes. Amongst the woodcuts formerly attributed to the "Maître au Nombril" and now to Guillaume II Le Roy (himself or his workshop according to his designs and guidance) there is an edition of Jean Lemaire de Belges, *Illustrations de Gaule et singularitez de Troyes* (Paris, G. de Marnef, 1513). He clearly collaborated with other printers such as Etienne Gueynard (for instance he provides the woodcuts for a *Biblia*, Lyons, 1512 and 1516) or Simon Vincent, who printed Barthélémy Chasseneux (1480-1541), *Catalogus gloriae mundi*, Lyon, 1527. The latter imprint on encyclopedic knowledge and on legal precedence is illustrated with full-page woodcuts, attributed to Guillaume II Le Roy. These woodcuts present notable similarities in figural and facial types and compositions with illuminations in our Horae. The architectural frames with the arch seen from below and the Renaissance columns and pilasters are also repeated in our

Facing page, f. 82, Coronation of the Virgin

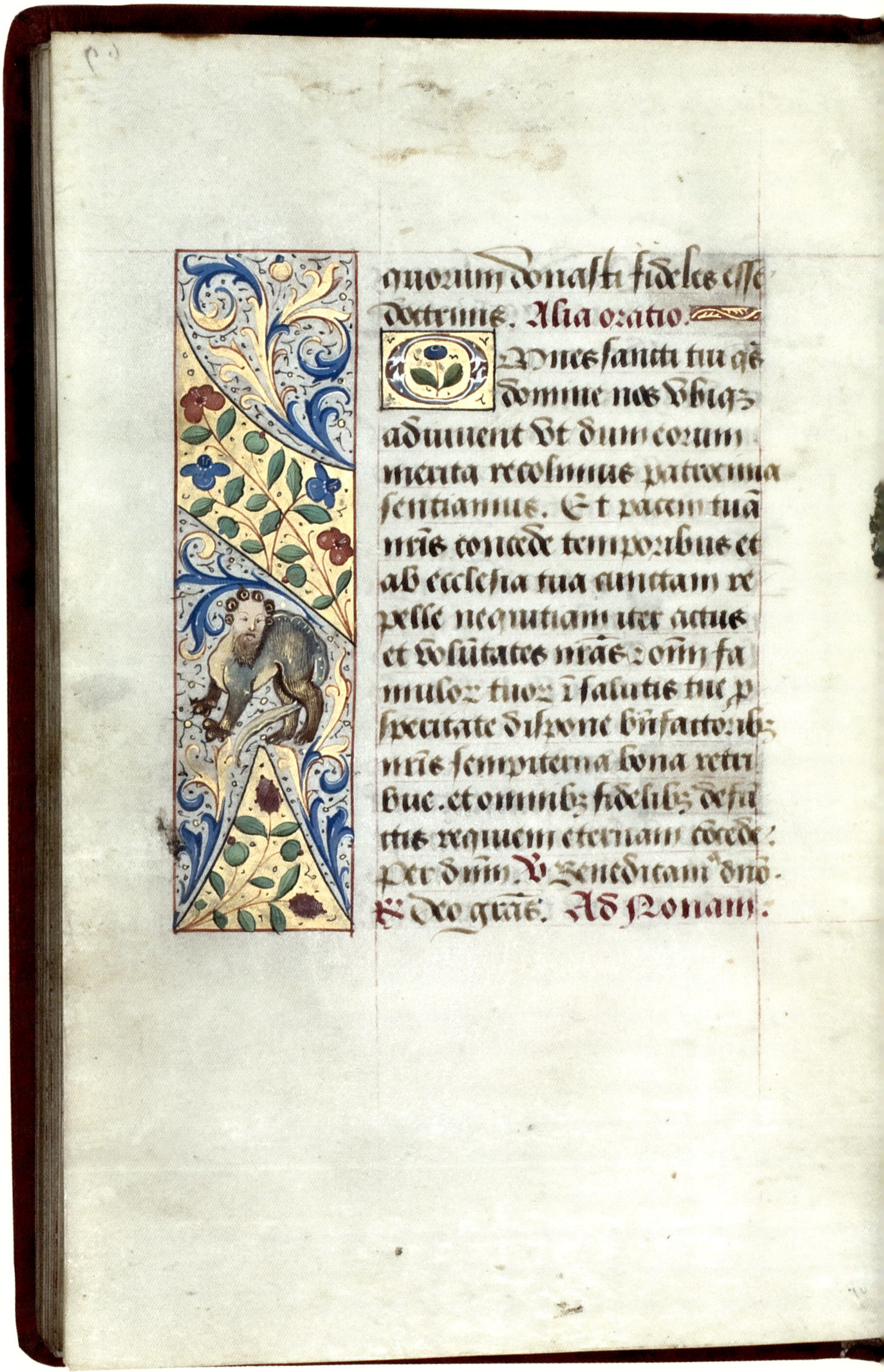

quorum donasti fideles esse
doctrinis. Alia oratio.
Omnes sancti tui quesumus
domine nos ubique
adiuvent ut dum eorum
merita recolimus patrocinia
sentiamus. Et pacem tuam
nostris concede temporibus et
ab ecclesia tua cunctam re
pelle nequitiam iter actus
et voluntates nostras et omnium fa
mulorum tuorum in salutis tue pro
speritate dispone benefactoribus
nostris sempiterna bona retri
bue. et omnibus fidelibus defun
ctis requiem eternam concede.
Per dominum. V Benedicamus domino.
R Deo gratias. Ad Nonam.

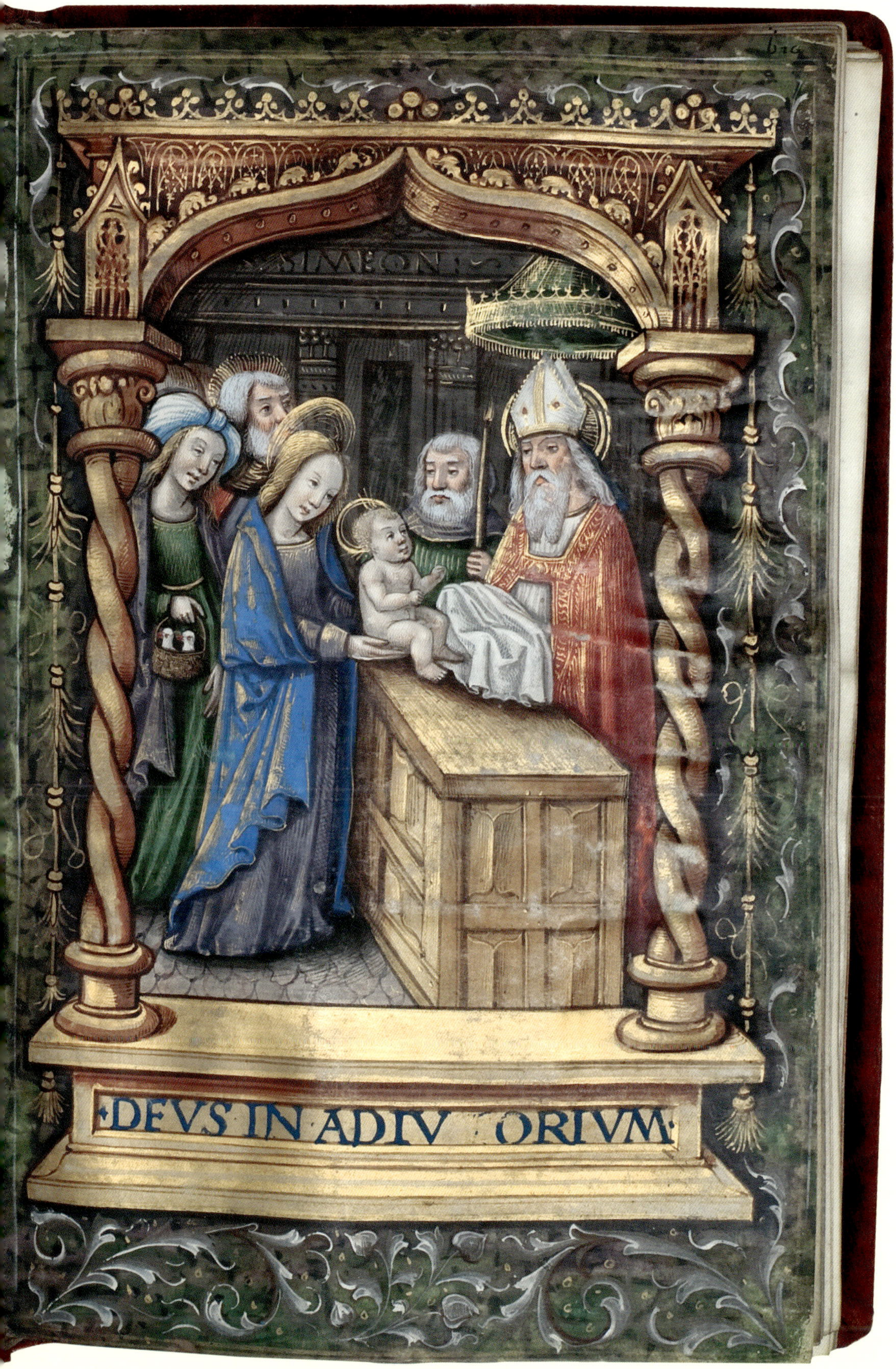

ff. 69v-70, Presentation in the Temple

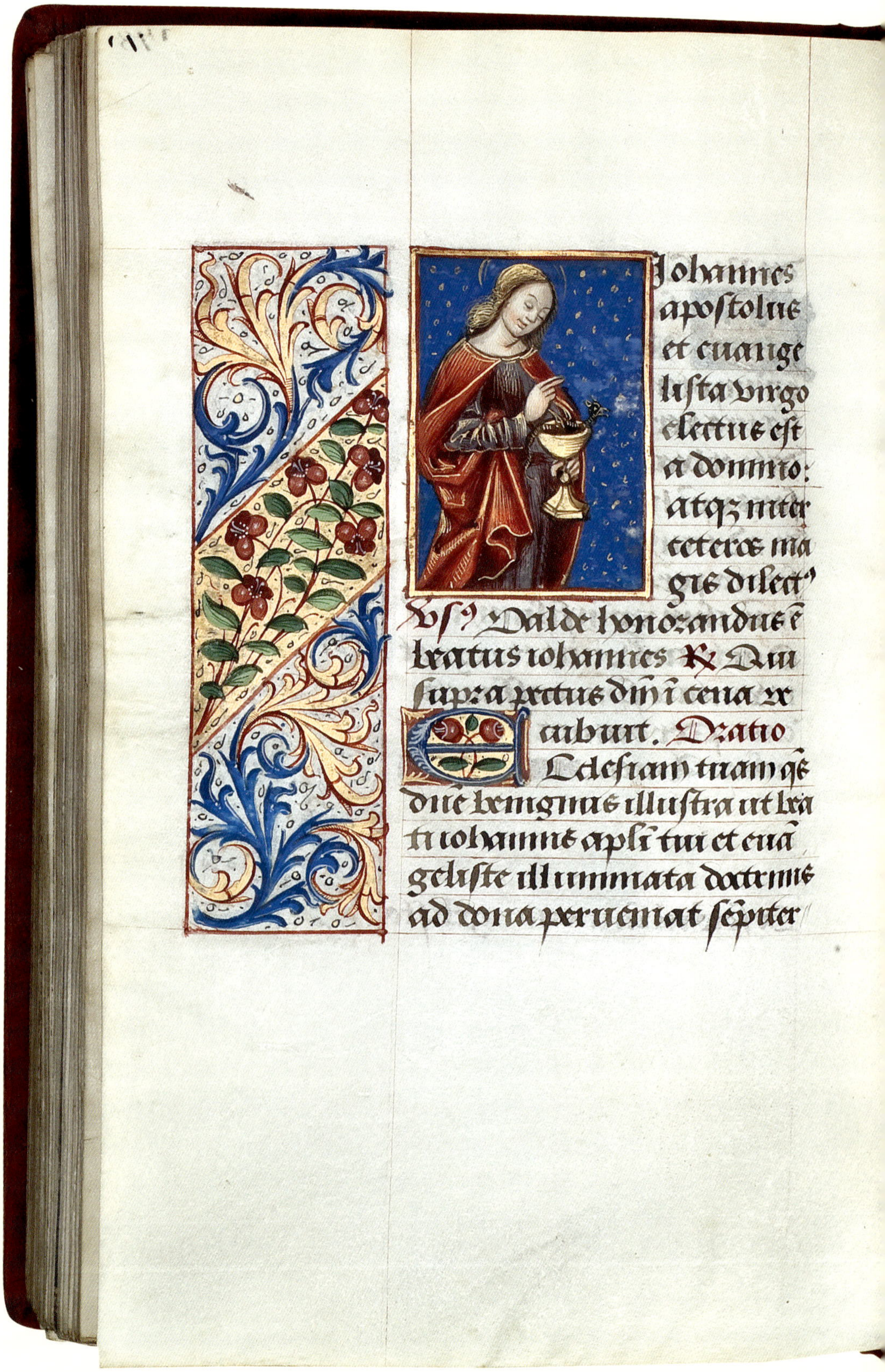
Iohannes
apostolus
et euange
lista virgo
electus est
a domino:
atque inter
ceteros ma
gis dilect'
V. Valde honorandus e
beatus iohannes R. Qui
supra pectus dni i cena re
cubuit. Oratio
Ecclesiam tuam qs
dne benignus illustra ut bea
ti iohannis apli tui et eua
geliste illuminata doctrinis
ad dona perueniat sepiter

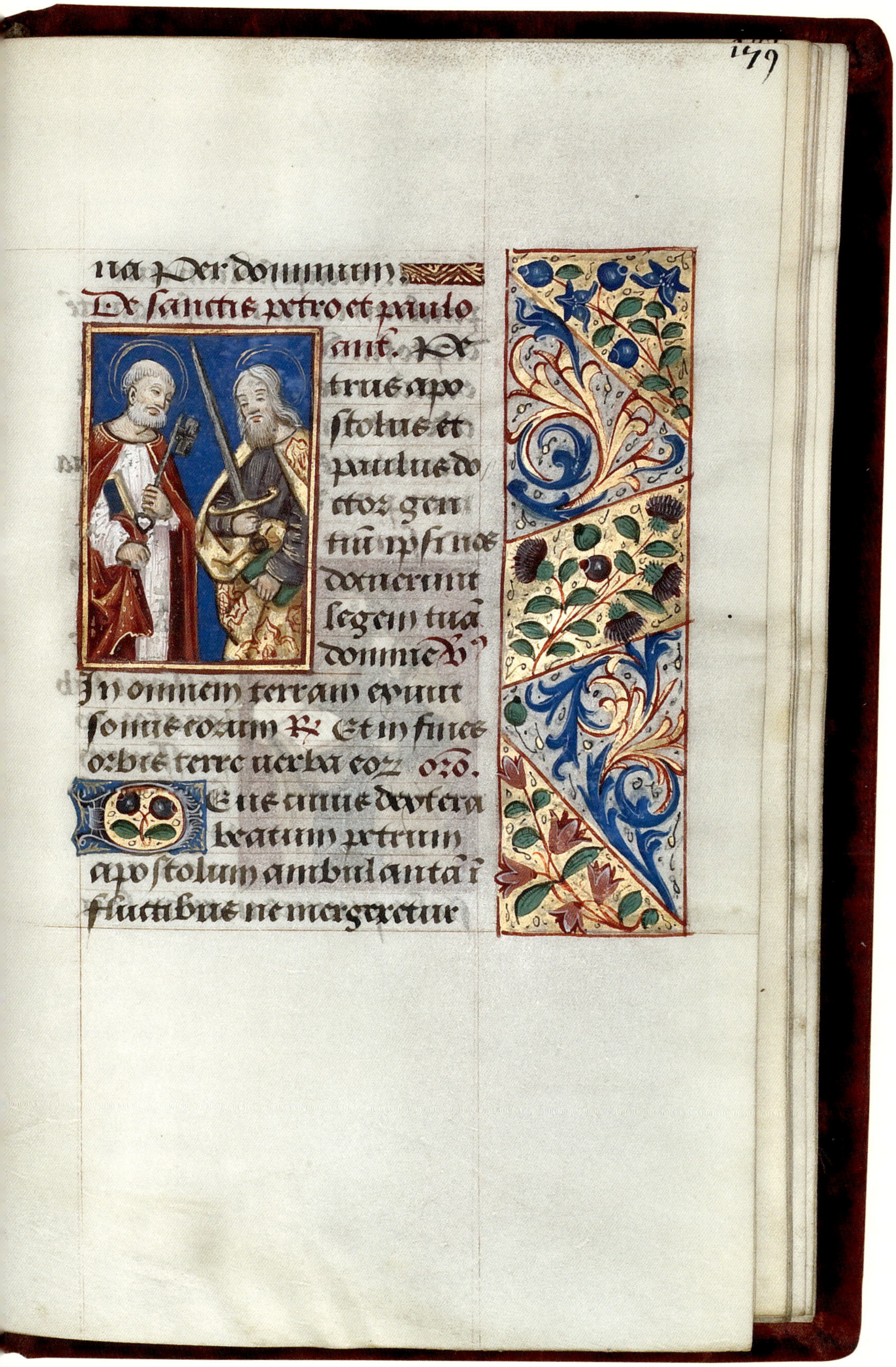

ff. 178v-179, St. John the Evangelist; St. Peter and St. Paul

Horae, as well as the ornamentation in the spandrels. On Guillaume II Le Roy and his work for the printing trade see in particular H.-J. Martin (ed.), 2000, pp. 212-219.

At the time of Guillaume II Le Roy's activity, Lyons was the third capital of the realm, and the artist undertook numerous commissions from the courts of Kings Louis XII and Francis I (see Avril and Reynaud, 1993, p. 357; and Burin, 2001). A series of literary manuscripts shows that throughout the first quarter of the sixteenth century, when prominent authors and humanists visited Lyons and the court, it was to Guillaume Le Roy that they turned to illustrate their work. His artistry is found, for example, in Johann von Morsheim's *Chronique des Rois de France* written for Louis XII in 1503 (Paris, BnF, MS all. 84), in Michel Nagonius's celebratory poem, *Prognostichon Hierosolymitanum* in honor of Pope Julius II (Vatican City, BAV, MS Vat. Lat. 1682), and in three manuscripts by his eminent contemporary, the humanist Pierre Sala (Paris, BnF, MSS fr. 584, 10420; and Vienna, ÖNB, Cod. 2618; see Avril and Reynaud, 1993, no. 205, p. 364-65; and Burin, 2001, cat. 134). To these three manuscripts for Sala, we can add another, a *Vie des philosophes*, previously unknown, by the artist (Les Enluminures, Cat. 15, no. 17).

In 1993, before Burin's study on Lyons illumination (1473-1530), Avril noted that Guillaume II Le Roy rarely painted Books of Hours and liturgical manuscripts but specialized instead in secular works popular with local humanists and the court; he cited the present manuscript as the only Book of Hours attributed to the artist (Avril and Reynaud, 2003, p. 363). Since then, Burin has assembled quite a substantial oeuvre for the artist. She identified some thirty manuscripts by him, along with six other manuscripts on which he collaborated, three single leaves, and three printed books. Among these are some nine Books of Hours, which nevertheless still take a back seat to the large number of interesting and unusual secular texts (Burin, 2001, cat. 95, 97, 98, 101, 111, 126, 128, 129, 130).

In excellent condition, this Book of Hours, with its brightly colored pictures and striking simulated porphyry borders, is one of his best and most unusual works of the genre. It is tempting to see the influence of Italian art in the use of these borders imitating the monumental use of porphyry and marble also found in manuscript illumination in Italy. Since Lyons was at the crossroads between France and Italy, and there were numerous ties between the Lyonnais and Italian book trade, it comes as no surprise that Guillaume II Le Roy was affected by Italian art and printing. Richly illuminated, with its lavish use of gold throughout, this Book of Hours bears all the hallmarks of Le Roy's style. Large, heavy figure types with wide, almost child-like faces dominate each miniature. The colorful palette used for the drapery typically includes bright enamel-like reds and blues. The figures stand out against distant landscapes with tiny towns perched on hilltops and rendered in soft blue tones. The miniature of St. John on Patmos in particular shows the artist's characteristic treatment of mid-grounds with mounds covered in dense clumps of trees and scattered tufts of vegetation, all painted in broad brushstrokes. Classicizing gold architectural frames inhabited with putti, typical of Lyonnais illumination and familiar from the workshop of the earlier illuminator Guillaume Lambert, surround each full-page miniature. All are placed on simulated porphyry grounds of green, red, grey or purple, to striking effect. The delightfully rich and varied borders on every page can be attributed to Le Roy himself. Full of invention, they contain carefully drawn naturalistic flowers, fruit, birds, frogs, grasshoppers and grotesques placed upon variously shaped grounds of liquid gold.

Our manuscript compares well with one of his masterpieces, an Horae purchased by the city of Lyons in 1995 (London, Sotheby's 20 June 1995, lot 117; now Lyons, BM, MS 6881; see Burin, cat. 101, pp. 219-222). However, the camaïeu d'or and porphyry borders in the present manuscript are highly original and quite unlike those more traditional acanthus and floral borders that decorate the Lyons manuscript. Our Annunciation is similar to a large single leaf of the same subject from an unidentified parent manuscript (see Les Enluminures, cat. 5, no. 19). Burin included the present manuscript in her catalogue and study of the artist (Burin, 2001, cat. 95, pp. 212-213). Clearly the present Book of Hours was painted for an important patron – the list of Guillaume Le Roy's patrons and clients is impressive – that further research (archival and stylistic) on this artist might eventually reveal.

PHYSICAL DESCRIPTION: 187 + [II] ff., (collation: i-ii^{6}, iii^{8}, iv-ix^{8}, x^{2}, xi-xiii^{8}, xiv^{2}, xv^{8} [originally $^{8+i}$, now lacking vi], xvi^{7} [of 8, lacking i], xvii-xxv^{8}, xxvi^{8} [v-vii blank, viii pastedown], lacking two leaves probably with miniatures), later foliation ff. 1-195, followed here, includes two paper guards and omits ff. 55, 65, 97, 102, 106-7, 128, vertical catchwords on final versos of each gathering, written on 18 long lines in brown ink in a lettre bâtarde between two verticals and 19 horizontals ruled in red (justification 108 x 66 mm.), rubrics in red, one-line decorated initials in liquid gold on alternate grounds of blue and red, similar line-endings, 2- to 3-line initials and two 5-line initials with blue or red staves with white decoration on liquid gold grounds with infills of flowers, a panel border on every page with blue and gold acanthus scrolls and sprays of flowers and fruit on variously divided fields of liquid gold or parchment inhabited with birds, creatures and grotesques, one half-page and 28 small miniatures and 11 full-page miniatures in architectural frames of camaïeu d'or inscribed with the opening words, on marbled (porphyry) grounds of purple, red or green (Some losses of pigment, for example, drapery of the angel on f. 25 and the outer borders or incipits on some miniatures, occasional smudging, including the background of the suffrage miniature on f. 178v, small tear at inner lower margin of f.56, upper half of textblock split at f. 86). Bound in old red velvet (raised bands on spine rubbed), housed in a 20th-century morocco-backed cloth box. Dimensions 215 x 142 mm.

TEXT: ff. 1-12v, Calendar; ff. 13-19, Gospel Sequences; ff. 19-22v, *Obsecro te*; ff. 22v-24v, *O Intemerata*; ff. 25-87, Hours of the Virgin, use of Rome, Matins (f. 25), Lauds (f. 44), Prime (f. 56), Terce (f. 60v), Sext (f. 66), None (f. 70), Vespers (f. 74v), Compline (f. 82), with variants for the liturgical year, ff. 87v-96v; ff. 98-101, Short Hours of the Cross; ff. 103-105, Short Hours of the Holy Spirit (lacking opening); ff. 108-127, Seven Penitential Psalms (lacking opening) and Litany; ff. 128v-169, Office of the Dead, use of Rome; ff. 169v-192, Suffrages, including the Trinity, God the Father, God the Son, the Holy Spirit, St. Veronica, St. Michael the Archangel, St. John the Baptist, St. John the Evangelist, Sts. Peter and Paul, St. James the Great, St. Stephen, St. Laurence, St. Christopher, St. Nicolas, St. Claude, St. Anthony Hermit, St. Anne, St. Mary Magdalene, St. Catherine, St. Margaret, St. Barbara, St. Apollonia.

ILLUSTRATION: Full-page miniatures are as follows: f. 13, Saint John on Patmos; f. 25, Annunciation, within architectural frame incorporating fictive sculptures showing scenes from the life of the Virgin; f. 44, Visitation; f. 56, Nativity; f. 60v, Annunciation to the Shepherds; f. 66, Adoration of the Magi; f. 70, Presentation in the Temple; f. 74v, Flight into Egypt; f. 82, Coronation of the Virgin; f. 98, Crucifixion; f. 128v, Job on the Dungheap. - Half-page miniature: f. 169v, Trinity. - Small miniatures; f. 15, St. Luke; f. 16v, St. Matthew; f. 18, St. Mark; f. 19, Virgin and Child; f. 22v, Pietà; f. 171v, God the Father; f. 172, Ecce Homo; f. 173, Pentecost; f. 173v, St. Veronica; f. 175, Crucifixion; f. 177, St. Michael Archangel; f. 177v, St. John the Baptist; f. 178v, St. John the Evangelist; f. 179, Sts. Peter and Paul; f. 179v, St. James the Greater; f. 181, St. Stephen; f. 181v, St. Laurence; f. 182v, St. Christopher; f. 184, St. Sebastian; f. 185, St. Nicolas; f. 185v, St. Claude of Besançon; f. 187, St. Anthony; f. 187v, St. Anne teaching the Virgin to read; f. 188v, St. Mary Magdalene; f. 189, St. Catherine; f. 189v, St. Margaret; f. 190v, St. Barbara; f. 191v, St. Apollonia.

OWNERSHIP: 1. The style of illumination securely places the origin of this Book of Hours in Lyons, where the illuminator, Guillaume II Le Roy or Guillaume Le Roy the Younger, was active from c. 1485 to 1528. The full Calendar is for widespread use, although of note is St Annemundus, bishop of Lyons (28 September). - 2. Jean-Baptiste Dessaignes: an inscription on the front endleaf, "Ex bibliotheca Ioan. Bapt. Dessaignes MDCLXI" and a note in the calendar on 29 October records the date of his birth, 1630. - 3. Sale, Paris,

Hôtel Drouot, Ader Picard Tajan, 21 June 1985, lot 10. - 4. Private North American Collection.

LITERATURE: Published in Avril, 1993, p. 363; Burin, 2001, cat. 95, pp. 212-213; on Guillaume II Le Roy, see also ibid, pp. 33-37. - Avril, F. and N. Reynaud. *Les manuscrits à peintures en France, 1480-1520*, Paris, 1993, pp. 357-63, citing the present manuscript. - Burin, E. *Manuscript Illumination in Lyons 1473-1530*, Turnhout, Brepols, 2001. - Joly, A. and H. "A la recherche de Guillaume Leroy 'le peintre'," *Gazette des Beaux-Arts*, 6e série, 61 (1963), pp. 279-292. - Martin, H.-J. (ed) et alia. *Mise en page et mise en texte du livre français. La naissance du livre moderne (XIVe-XVIIe siècles)*, Paris, 2000.

ONLINE RESOURCES:

For Lyons, BM MS 6881, Hours of Chalon-sur-Saône:
http://sged.bm-lyon.fr/

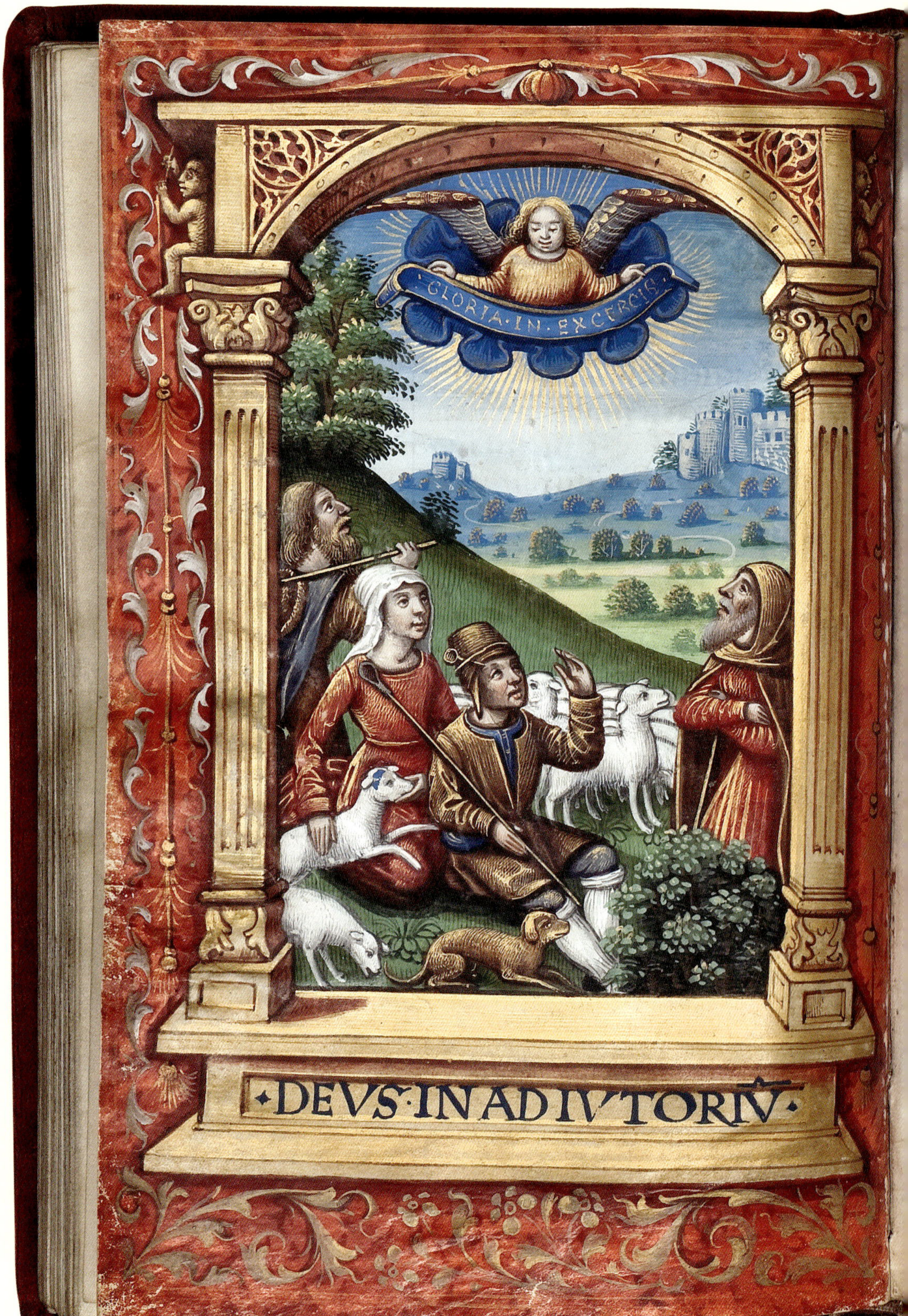

f. 60v, Annunciation to the Shepherds

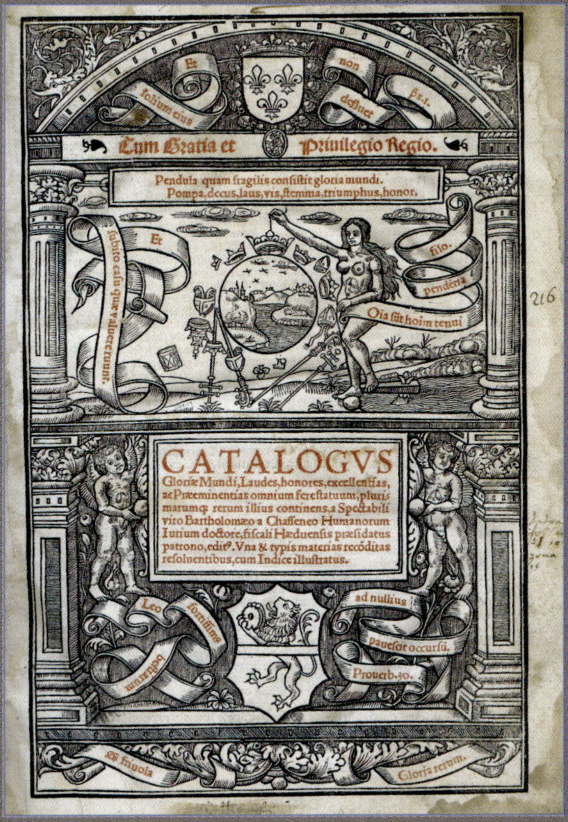

Private Collection, Barthélemy Chasseneux, *Catalogus gloriae mundi*, Lyons, S. Vincent, 1527, Title-page, Allegory of Fortuna, Arms of the City of Lyons, woodcuts attributed to the Master of the Nombril (Guillaume Le Roy).

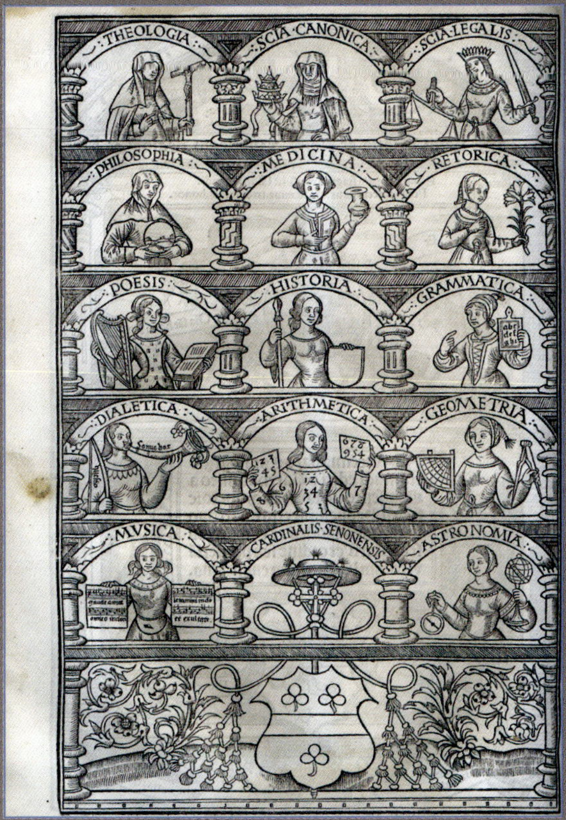

Private Collection, Barthélemy Chasseneux, *Catalogus gloriae mundi*, Lyons, S. Vincent, 1527, Pars X, f. 1v, Female Allegories of the Liberal Arts and other Categories of Knowledge, Arms of Antoine Duprat, Cardinal and Archbishop of Sens, woodcut attributed to the Master of the Nombril (Guillaume Le Roy).

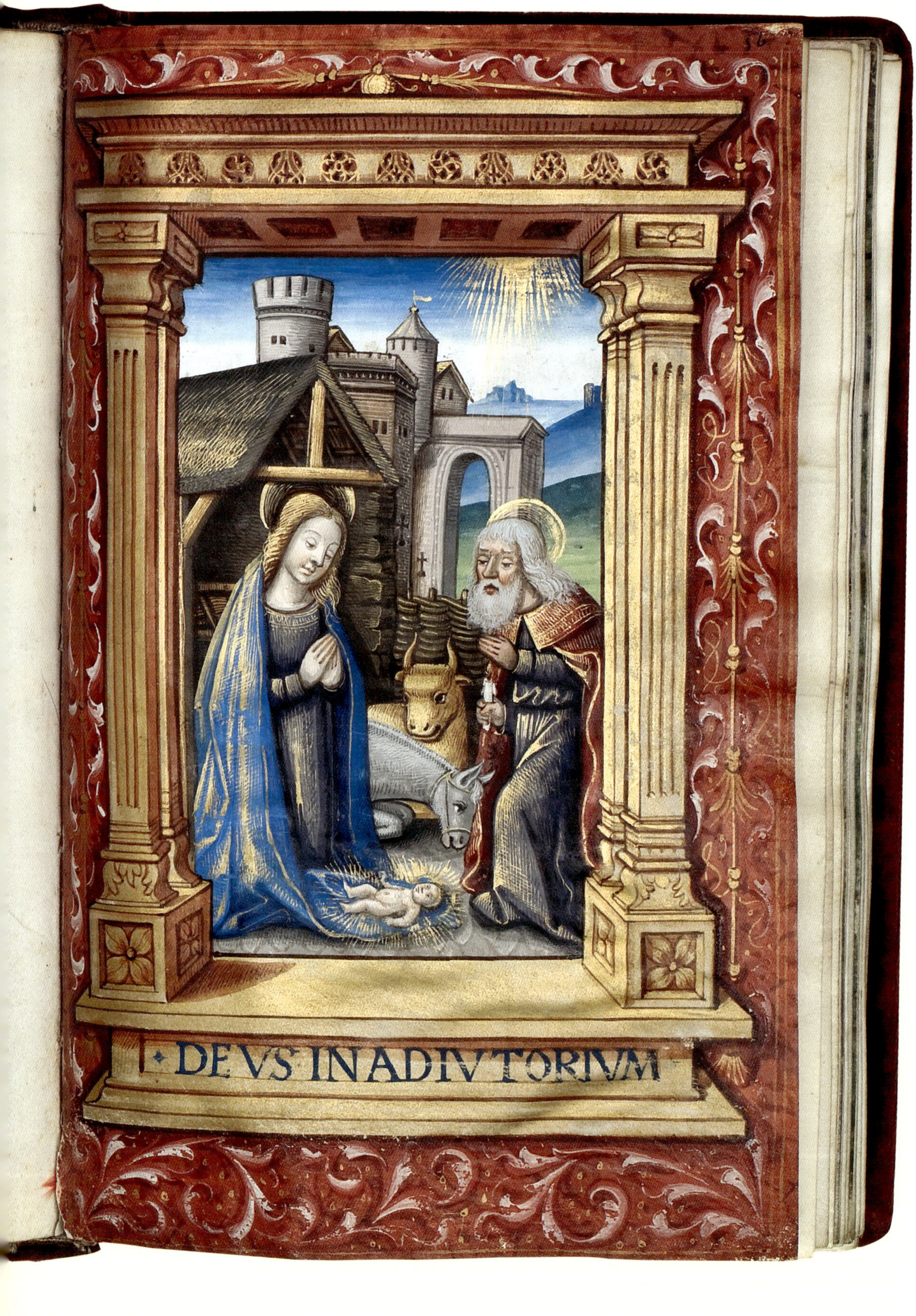

f. 56, Nativity

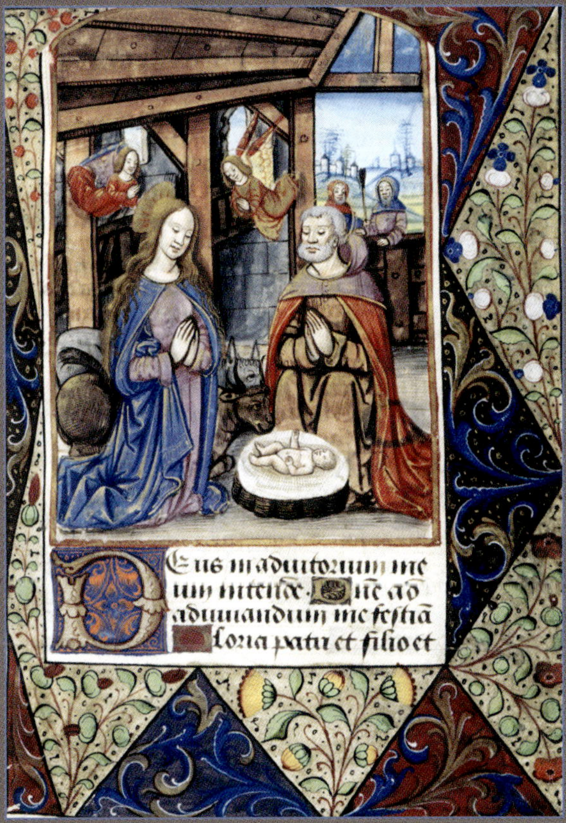

Lyons, Bibliothèque municipale, BM, MS 6881,
Book of Hours, f. 37, Nativity

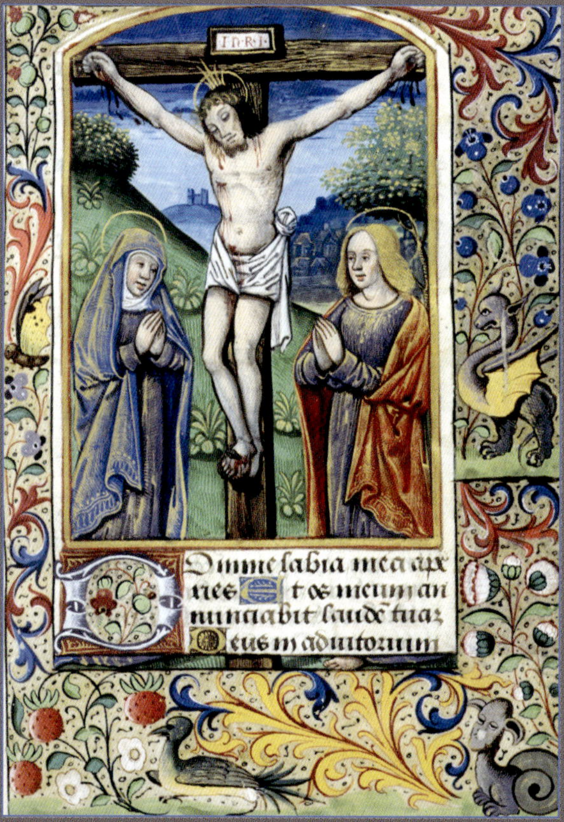

Lyons, Bibliothèque municipale, BM, MS 6881,
Book of Hours, f. 57, Crucifixion.

Facing page, f. 98, Crucifixion

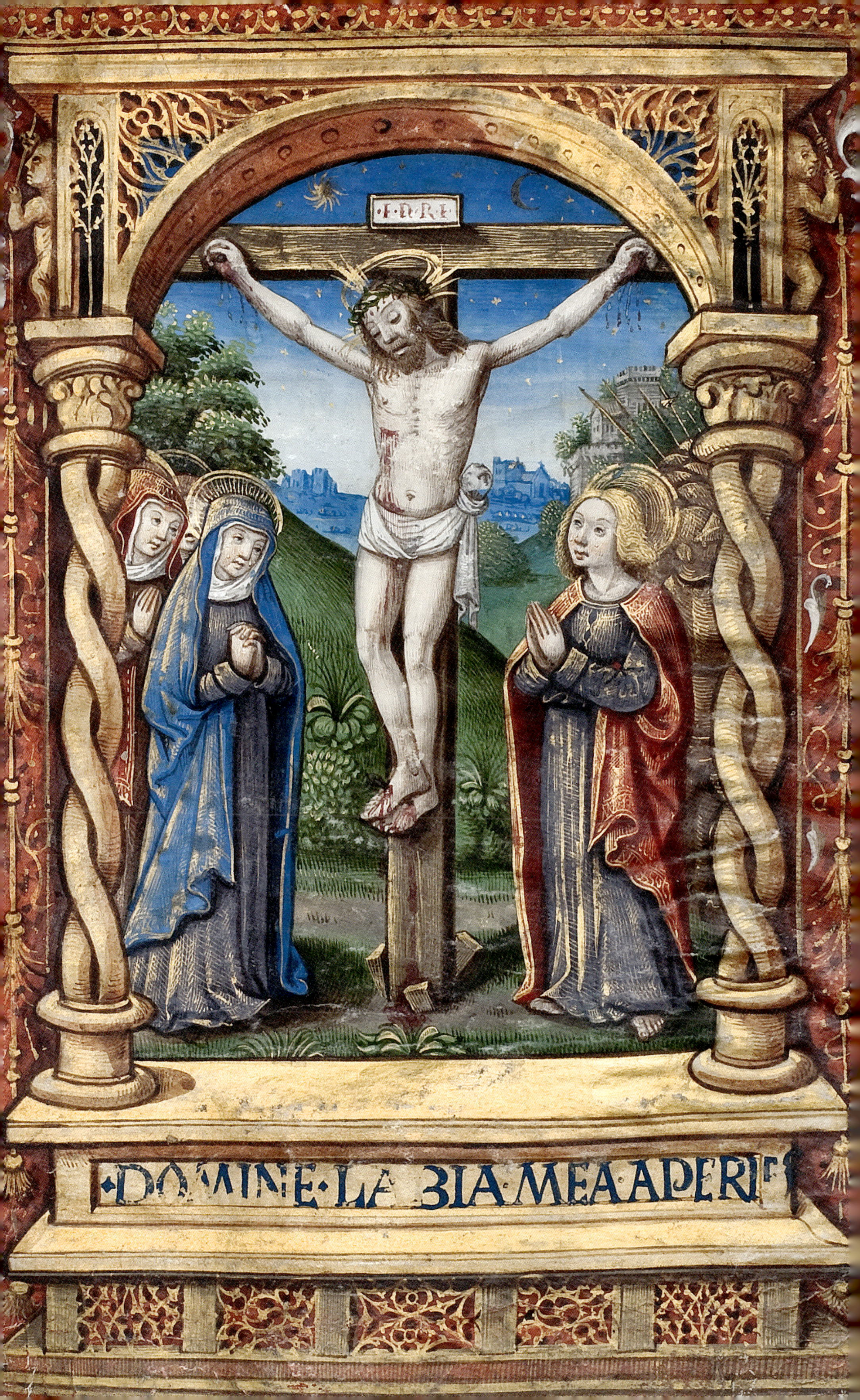
·DOMINE·LA BIA·MEA·APERI

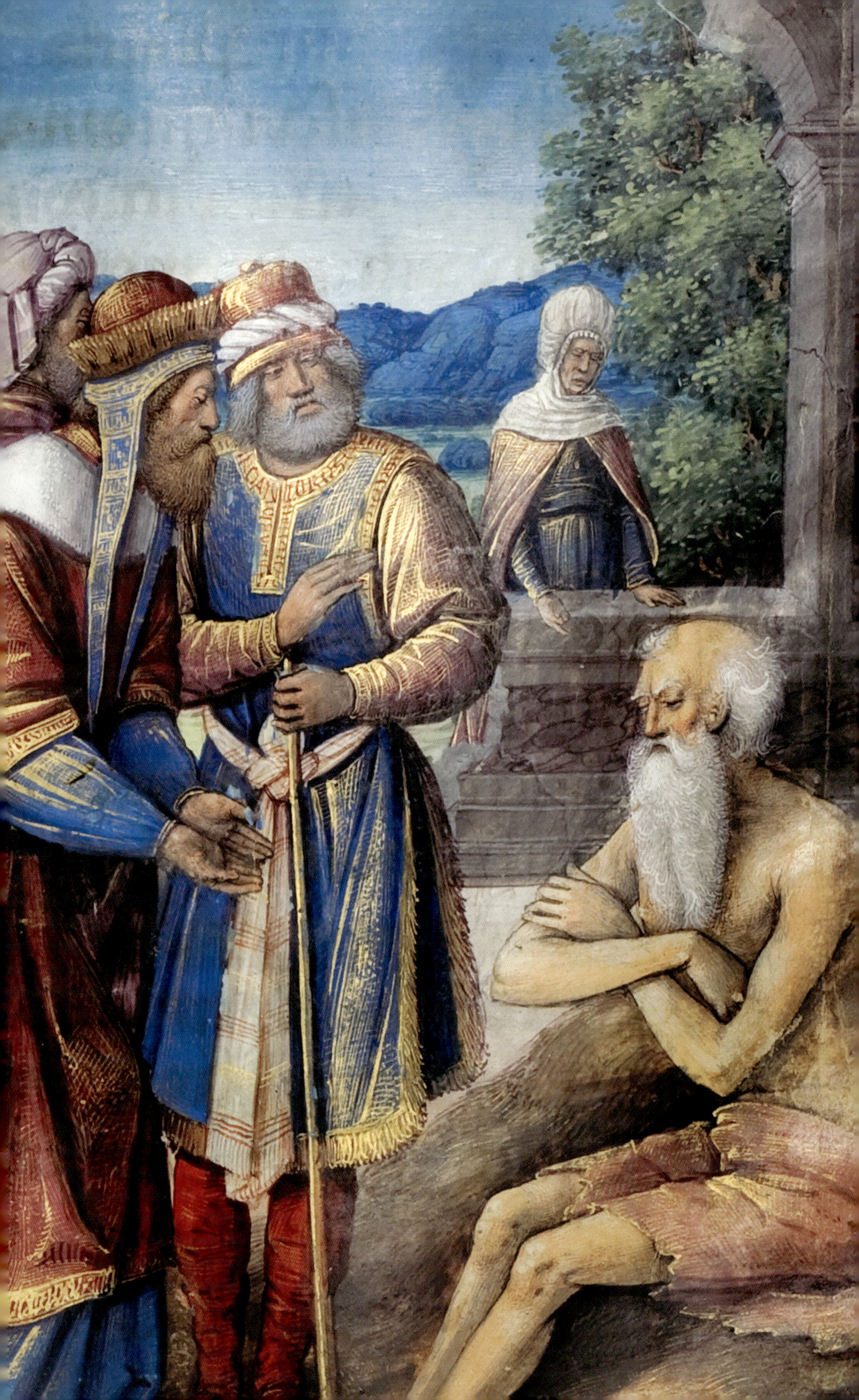

12

The "Signed Hours" (Use of Rome)

In Latin and French, illuminated manuscript on parchment
France, Tours, c. 1490-1500
5 large and 17 small miniatures by "Jean of Tours" of the Workshop of Jean Poyer and another illuminator

This is an undeniably pretty and important manuscript, produced at the height of the Renaissance in Tours, and associated with an artist allied with one of the greatest of the exponents of the Tours style, Jean Poyer. Thanks to enthusiastic royal patronage, the influence of Paris, and the presence of Italian artists, Tours enjoyed an incomparable success as a center of French Renaissance art around 1500. Long considered a follower of the mythic Jean Bourdichon of Tours, Poyer has been rehabilitated in the past several decades. His style, employing clearly articulated figures, a frequent use of chiaroscuro, and daring color juxtapositions, is at once more complex and more subtle than that of some of his famous contemporaries, such as Bourdichon. Of grand format and in beautiful fresh condition, the present manuscript survives as a fine example of his style and that of his workshop. With its five large miniatures, its numerous smaller miniatures, and its rich unusual border decoration on all pages, the manuscript presents a visual tour de force.

Early sixteenth-century literature on art in France praised Jean Poyer's name together with such illustrious artists like Jean Fouquet, Jan van Eyck, Simon Marmion, Albrecht Dürer and Michelangelo (on Jean Poyer see esp. F. Avril, 1993, pp. 306-318; R. Wieck, et al., 2002; and M. Hofmann, 2004). A few documents from 1465 to 1498 sketch Poyer's career. In 1497, for example, he received payment for a "petites heures" for Anne of Brittany, a fragment of which may survive in a tiny single leaf in Philadelphia (Free Library, Lewis M.11.15a). The real connection between Poyer's name and a consistent body of work depends on matching this oeuvre with the personality of the artist who emerges from the documents. Although Jean Bourdichon has been described as Fouquet's most important follower, Poyer, whose work was also greatly in vogue at court, was not only an exceptionally skilled painter but also, like Fouquet, an explorer of new artistic concepts. His style is marked by vibrant colours, increasingly dynamic figures, and amazing spatial effects that introduced Italian High Renaissance conceits to France at an early stage around

Facing page, f. 95, Job Seated on a Dungheap, with his Three Rich Friends

1500. A terminus ante quem for his death comes from Jean Lemaire de Belges's *Plainte du Désiré*, composed before Easter 1504, when he praises Poyer among other famous dead artists.

Most works that have survived in Poyer's style date from the last decade of the fifteenth century. Stylistic analysis reveals two main workshop-collaborators who understood the master's art to an exceptionally high degree. One of them was charged with decorating the present Book of Hours together with another otherwise unidentified painter. The central figure of the miniature with Job and his friends is dressed in a blue robe with a gold collar, decorated with red capitals. When the manuscript first became known in 1991, the script on the collar of this figure was deciphered as IOAN TURO[NEN]S[IS] standing for Johannes Turonensis or Jean of Tours. Basing himself on the inscription along with an analysis of the style, which shows undeniable "Poyetian" features, Eberhard König published the manuscript in 1993 as "the" autograph work by Jean Poyer. Apart from the fact that such inscriptions are difficult to decipher as they appear hidden among decorative fantasy letters, this manuscript cannot be linked to Poyer's core body of work for stylistic reasons. However, it may well include his collaborator's name: Jean was a common name in Tours.

This artist of the full-page miniatures has now been established as the Painter of the "Signed Hours," one of the major figures of Poyer's workshop (see M. Hofmann, 2004, esp. pp. 47-55). We identify him as Jean of Tours. Close to the master is the fine modelling of faces with overall tiny dense brush strokes including the use of light blue to animate grey zones. Also typical is the use of dense gold hatching for selected materials to enforce the strong effects of light and shadow. The occasional use of light pink in contrast to bright red and blue is a signature of Poyer's color scheme. On f. 26, the magnificent Annunciation is clearly based on the Poyer model from one of his most famous works, the masterful Briçonnet Hours (Haarlem, Teylers Museum, MS 78, f. 21). Although this master understands Poyer's language in detail, he sometimes lacks Poyer's anatomical fluency. Job, for example, is depicted in profile while his upper body is slightly turned towards us. This twist, however, does not succeed to convince us as the chest seems quite flat. This manuscript proves that Poyer's collaborators worked under strict control of the master following a high standard of quality. The borders too are unusually inventive: slim gold panels filled with flowers alternate with blue panels partly decorated with knotted rope, or tree branches with floral decoration; dynamic birds perch on the branches.

Hofmann has distinguished a second hand in the "Signed Hours," the hand responsible for many of the miniatures on the text folios, which she describes as "Bourdichonesque." This artist executed many of the miniatures in a manuscript so-called the "J. de M. Hours" in Geneva (Bibliothèque de Genève, Com. Lat. 124, ff. 126v, 133v, 174, and 211v), and his style is characterized by oval heads with high foreheads, the use of violet drawing for the faces with thin eyebrows, long noses, red cheeks and small heart-shaped mouths. The relationship between the Geneva manuscript, the "Signed Hours," and Poyer's masterpieces, including the Hours of Henry VIII in New York (Pierpont Morgan Library, MS H. 8), and the actual functioning of his workshop, still needs to be disentangled. A full study of the present "Signed Hours" will necessarily occupy a central place in such an investigation.

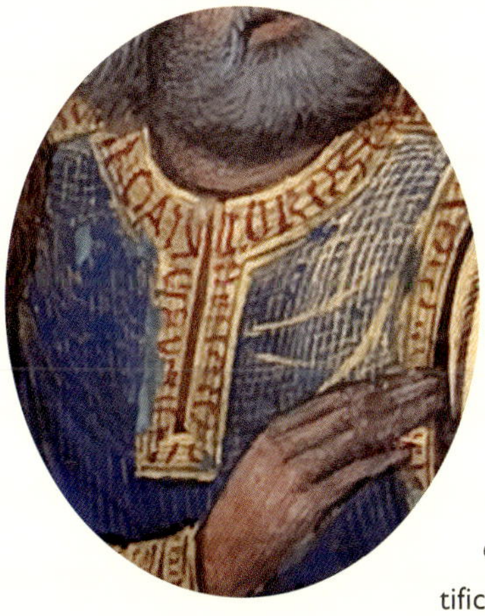

Detail above - Central figure in the miniature of Job, dressed in a blue robe with a gold collar, decorated with red capitals IOAN TURO[NEN]S[IS] standing for Johannes Turonensis or Jean of Tours

PHYSICAL DESCRIPTION: 184 ff. (including f.177a), preceded and followed by modern pastedowns and a single upper and lower flyleaf, lacking 1 miniature (Pentecost) at the beginning of the Hours of the Holy Spirit, today in Cleveland, Museum of Arts, inv. no. 24.426, also missing some text leaves (collation: i-ii^{6}, iii-xi^{8}, xii^{4}, xiii^{6} (8-2 [lacking miniature and a text leaf]), xiv-xvi^{8}, xvii^{5} [8-3, missing i, vii-viii, text leaves], xviii-xxiii^{8}, xxiv^{6}, xxv^{6+1} [lacking part of suffrages; added text leaf of suffrages]), first quire of Office of the Dead misbound as quire 14 (should follow after quire 17), a few catchwords, written in brown ink in a regular bâtarde script, on 16 lines (justification 108 x 70 mm), rubrics in red, 1- and 2-line high initials in grey and modelled in white on gold grounds infilled with colored flowers, line-fillers of tree branch work ("bois écotés") and flowers, a variety of outer borders on every page, mostly gold panels filled with colored flowers, blue panels decorated with knotted rope or tree branches, or tree branch work in gold or blue with floral decoration, similar three-quarter borders in calendar and surrounding small miniatures, 17 small and 5 full-page miniatures, two of them with overpaint (f. 61v and f. 89). Bound in modern blue velvet over wooden boards, back sewn on 4 raised bands, brass catches and clasps, gilt edges. Dimensions 177 x 125 mm.

TEXT: ff.1-12, Calendar, in red, blue and gold; ff. 13v-19, Gospel Sequences; ff. 19-22v, Obsecro te; ff. 23-25, O intemerata; ff. 26v-71v, Hours of the Virgin (Use of Rome), with Matins (f. 26v), Lauds (f. 36v), Prime (f. 48), Terce (f. 51v), Sext (f. 55), None (f. 58), Vespers (f. 61v), Compline (f. 68); ff. 72-80, Psalms for days of the week, rubric, *Tres psalmi sequentes dicuntur diebus martis et veneris*; ff. 80-88v, Short hours for Advent, rubric, *Per totum adventum dicitur hec antiphona*; ff. 89-91v, Hours of the Cross (lacking end); ff. 92-94, Hours of the Holy Spirit (lacking opening); ff. 95v-102v, Office of the

Dead (first quire misbound, the rest of the Office of the Dead found on ff. 124-147v); ff. 103v-123v, Penitential Psalms; ff. 124-147v, Office of the Dead (Use of Rome); ff. 148-170v, Prayers; ff. 170v-183, Suffrages (with last leaf added out of sequence).

ILLUSTRATION: There are 5 full-page miniatures: f. 13, St. John on Patmos, stony rocks rising from the blue sea, within narrow golden renaissance-style frame containing putti and dragons (outer margin of frame cropped and lightly rubbed); f. 26, Annunciation, within narrow gold Renaissance-style border, containing six angels playing musical instruments; f. 89, Crucifixion, with Mary Magdalene, her face hidden behind the Cross, her arms encircling the Cross, many soldiers at back, within architectural border (head of border cropped and outer margins rubbed; partly overpainted); f. 95, Job, seated on a dungheap, with his three rich friends standing, in a gold frame surround (very lightly rubbed, head of frame cropped); f. 103, Bathsheba bathing in a golden fountain, David and his companions gazing at her from the palace windows; within gold frame border (outer margin lightly rubbed). - There are 17 small miniatures: f. 15, St. Luke (45 x 43 mm); f. 16v, St. Matthew, with angel (52 x 48 mm); f. 18, St. Mark writing (52 x 45 mm); f. 19, Virgo Lactans, on gold ground (42 x 45 mm); f. 23, Virgin and John the Baptist at foot of the Cross (50 x 45 mm); f. 36v, Visitation, showing only half-length Virgin and head of Elizabeth, golden-green rocks behind (52 x 47 mm); f. 48, Nativity, Virgin and Child, Joseph's face at back (54 x 45 mm); f. 51v, Annunciation to the Shepherds, a group of Shepherds in brown robes holding staves (46 x 45 mm); f. 55, Adoration of the Magi, in the foreground the head of a white-haired bearded King, with Virgin and Child (53 x 45 mm); f. 58, Presentation in the Temple (53 x 45 mm); f. 61v, Massacre of the Innocents, a soldier tearing a child from the woman's arm (54 x 47 mm) (partly overpainted); f. 68, Coronation of the Virgin, two angels placing the crown (52 x 47 mm); f. 177, St. Anne teaching the Virgin to read (40 x 45 mm); f. 177a, Mary Magdalene. (45 x 45 mm); f. 177av, St. Catherine with crown and sword (48 x 45 mm); f. 178v, St. Margaret praying (50 x 45 mm); f. 179, St. Apollonia, holding a tooth with pincers (48 x 45 mm).

OWNERSHIP: 1. Copied and illuminated in Tours based on script and stylistic elements. The Calendar in French is very full but does not provide any particular localization. The liturgical of the Hours of the Virgin and the Office of the Dead is the universal use of Rome. - 2. Sold at Christie's, London, 26 June 1991, lot. 39. See also E. König, in Tenschert, *Leuchtendes Mittelalter* V, XXX (1993), no. 28, pp. 470-489. - 3. North American Private Collection.

LITERATURE: Published in Hofmann, 2004, p. 48, pl. 144-148. - Avril, F. and N. Reynaud. *Les manuscrits à peintures en France, 1440-1520*, Paris, 1993. [Exhibition]. *Tours 1500. Capitale des arts*, Paris, 2012.- Hofmann, Mara. Jean *Poyer: Das Gesamtwerk*, Turnhout, Brepols, 2004. - Wieck, R., W. Voelkle and M. Hearne. *The Hours of Henry VIII. A Renaissance Masterpiece by Jean Poyet*, New York, 2000.

ONLINE RESOURCES:

On Jean Poyer: http://fr.wikipedia.org/wiki/Jean_Poyer

Hours of Henry VIII at the Pierpont Morgan (New York)
http://www.themorgan.org/collections/

Leaf from the "Signed Hours," Pentecost in the Cleveland Museum of Art:
http://www.clevelandart.org/collections/

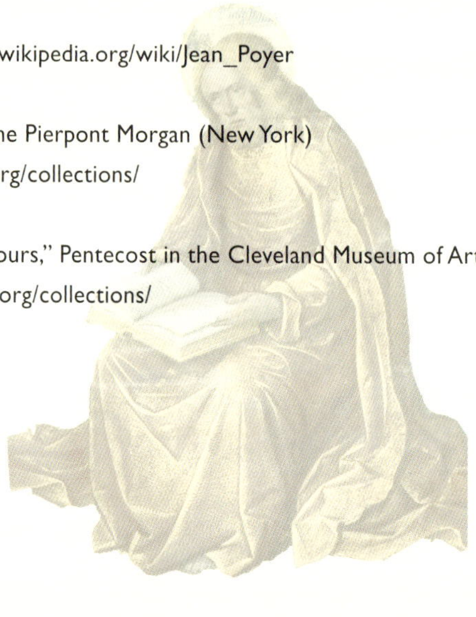

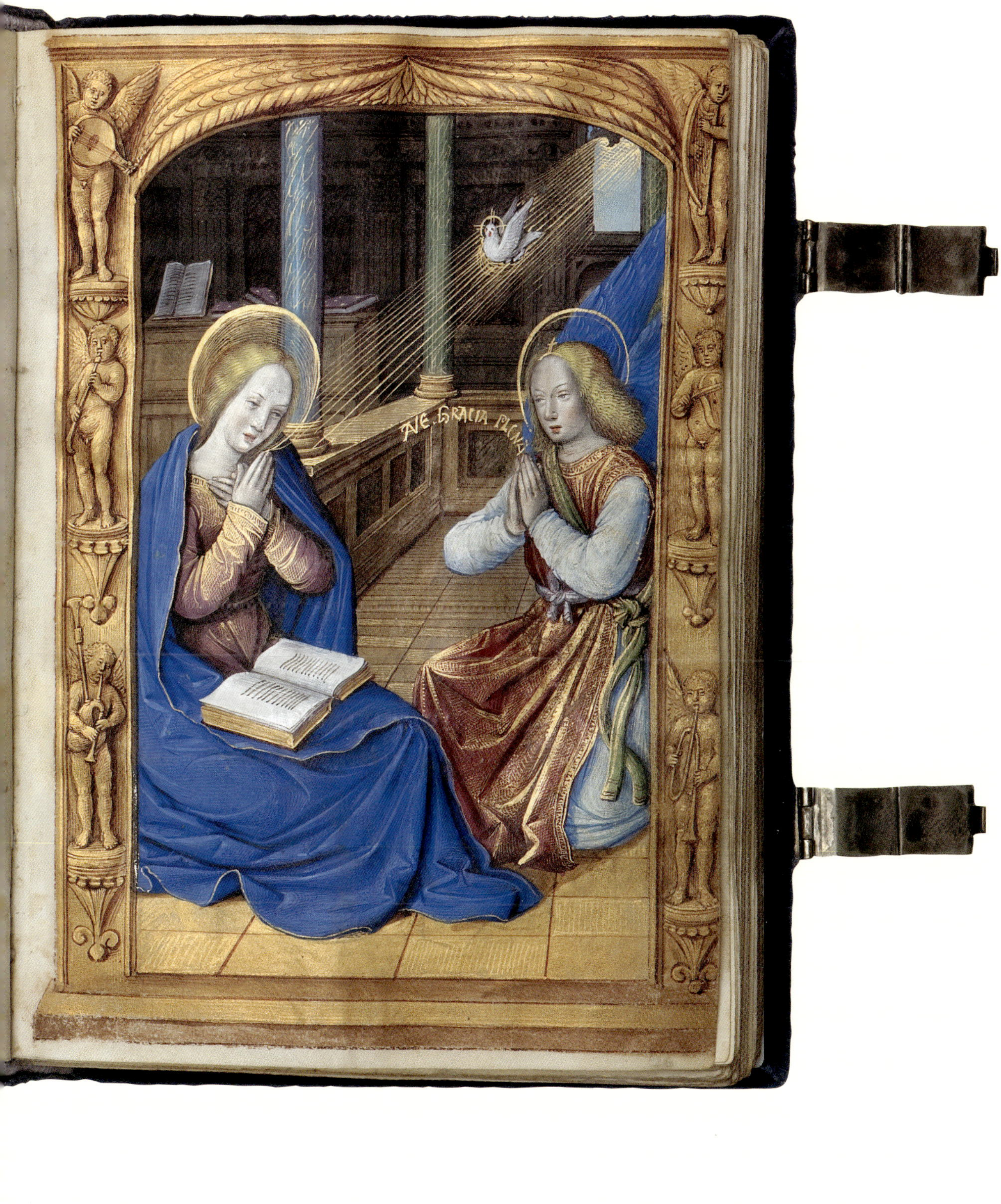

f. 26, Annunciation

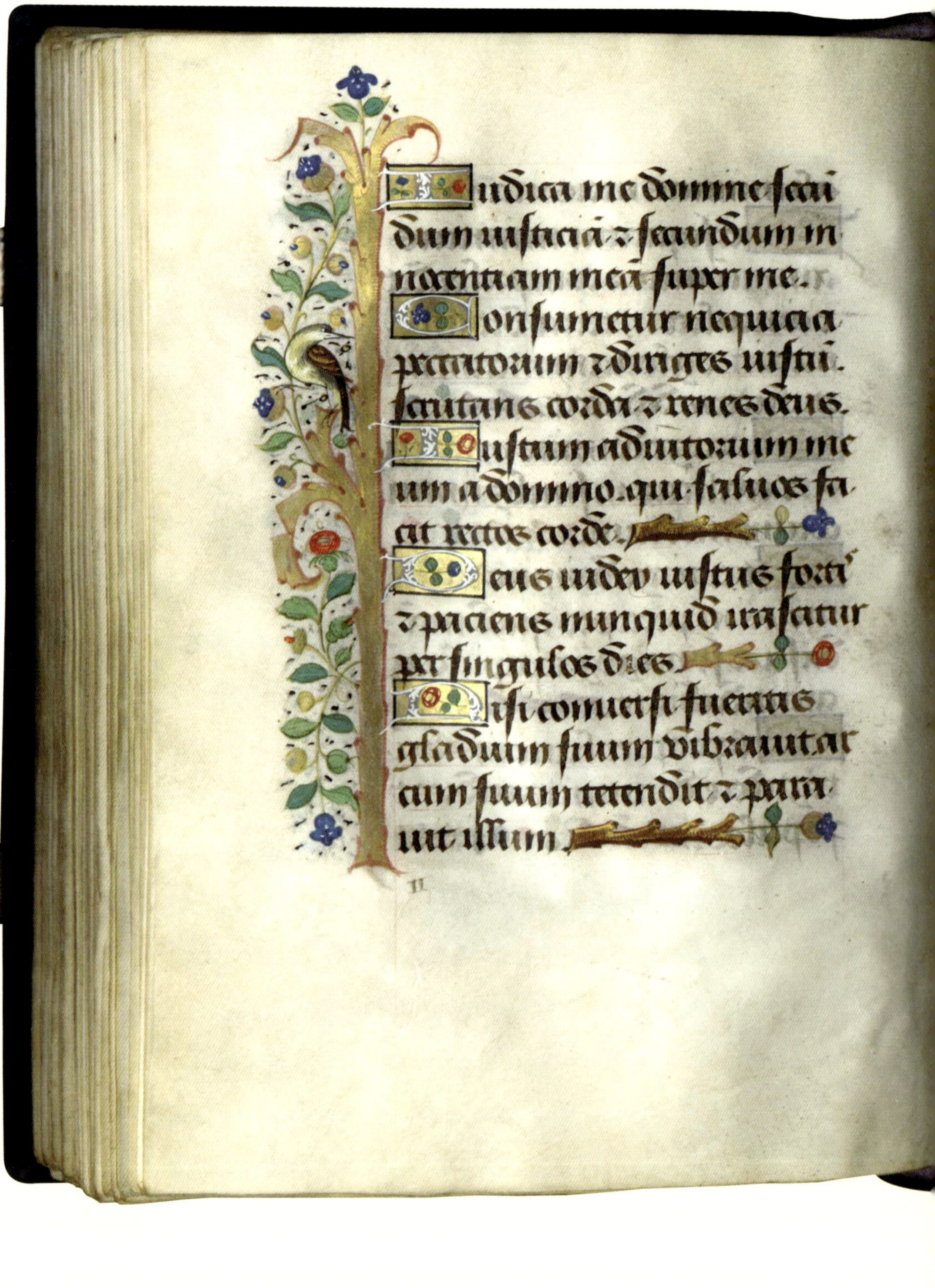
Iudica me domine secū
dum iusticiā ⁊ secundum in
nocentiam meā super me.
Consumetur nequicia
peccatorum ⁊ diriges iusti.
scrutans corda ⁊ renes deus.
Iustum adiutorium me
um a domino. qui saluos fa
cit rectos corde.
Deus iudex iustus forti'
⁊ paciens numquid irascatur
per singulos dies.
Nisi conuersi fueritis
gladium suum vibrauit ar
cum suum tetendit ⁊ para
uit illum

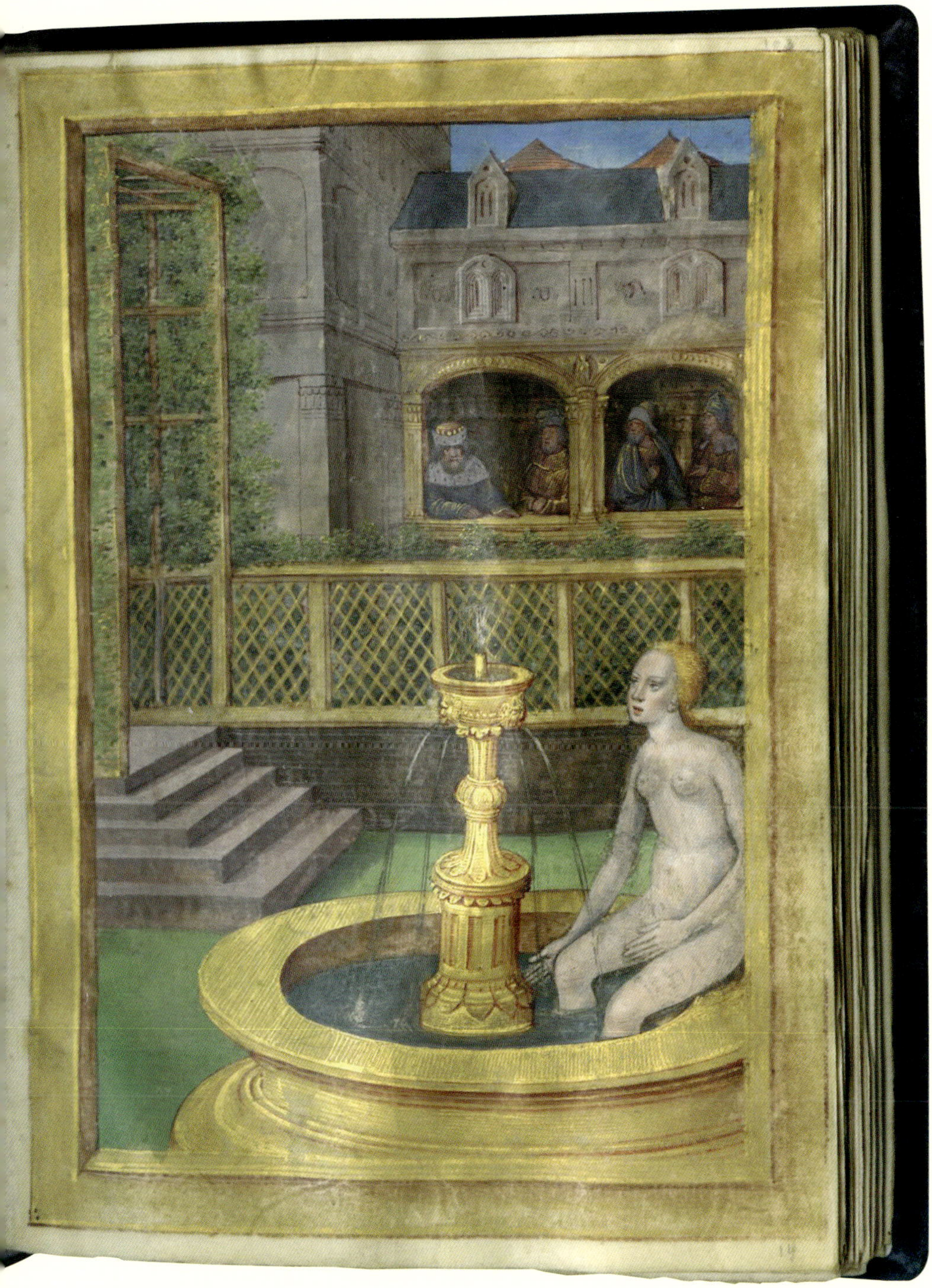

ff. 102v-103, Bathsheba Bathing in a Golden Fountain, David and his Companions

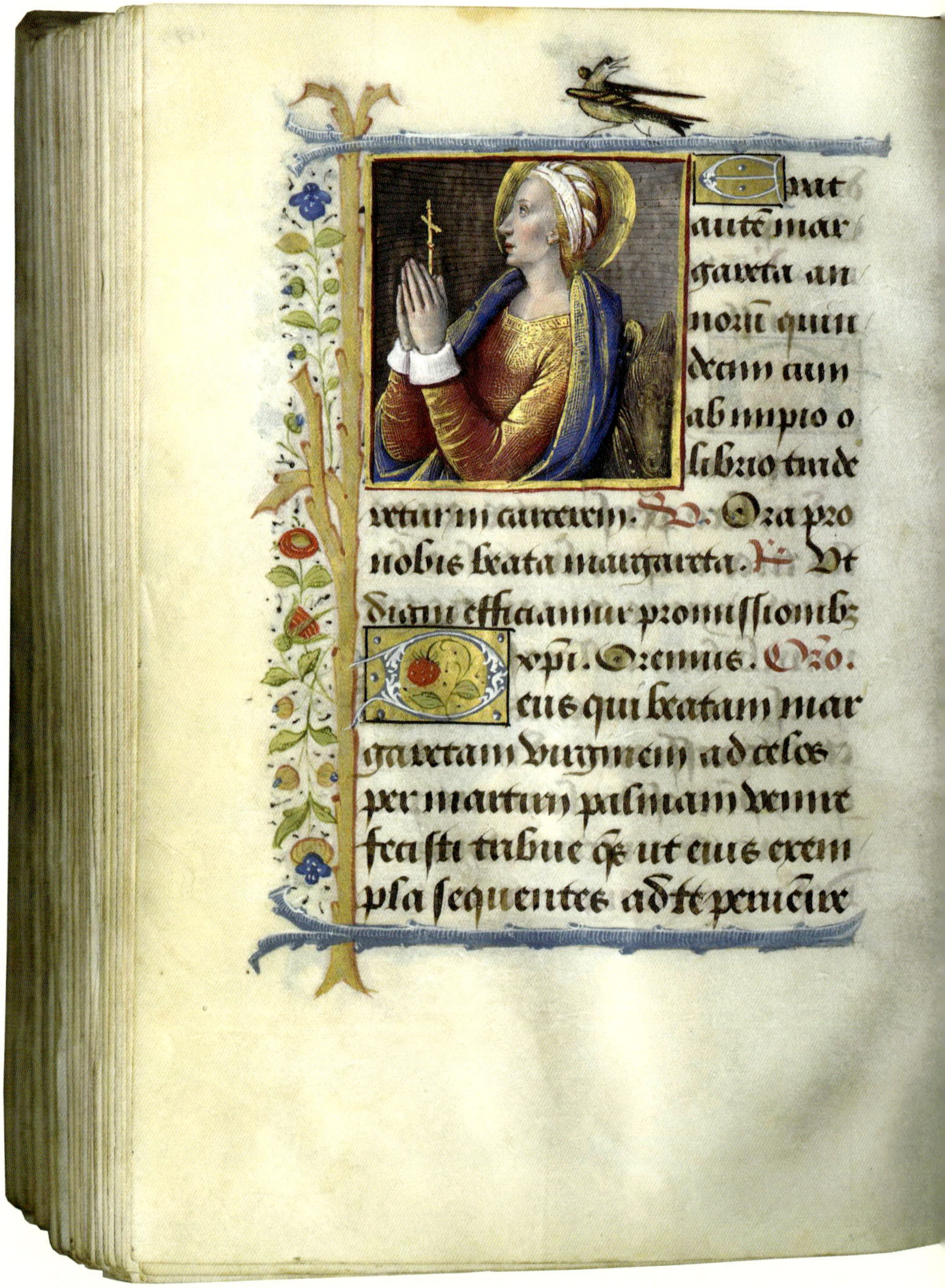

Erat
autē mar
garita an
norū quin
decim cum
ab impio o
librio trude
retur in carcerem. V. Ora pro
nobis beata margareta. R. Ut
digni efficiamur promissionibz
xpi. Oremus. Oro.
Deus qui beatam mar
garetam virginem ad celos
per martirii palmam venire
fecisti tribue qs ut eius exem
pla sequentes ad te pervenire

ff. 57v-58

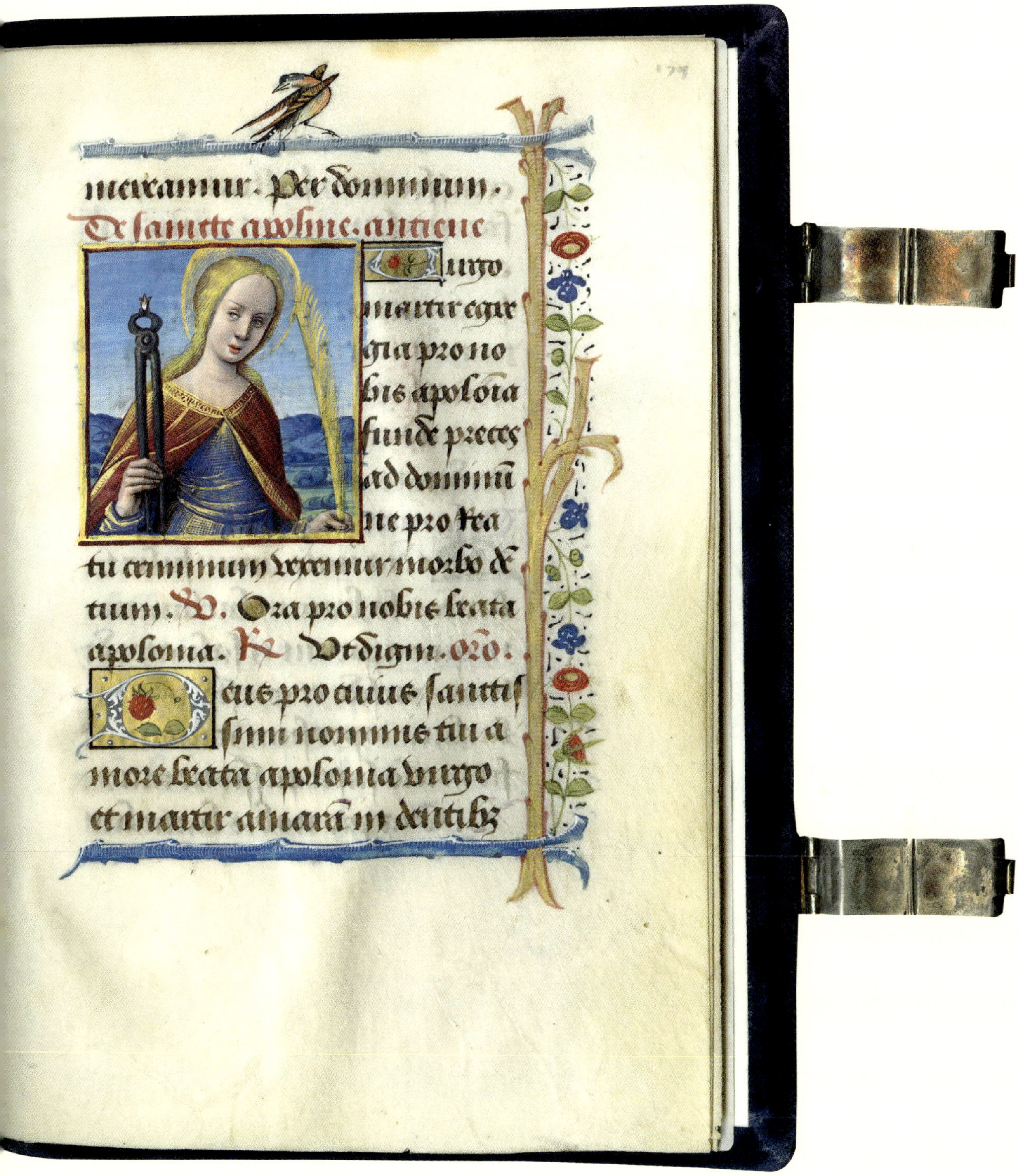

mereamur. Per dominum.
De sancte apoline. antiene
Virgo
martir egre
gia pro no
bis apolonia
funde preces
ad dominum
ne pro rea
tu criminum vexemur morbo de
tium. V. Ora pro nobis beata
apolonia. R. Ut digni. Oro.
Deus pro cuius sanctis
simi nominis tui a
more beata apolonia virgo
et martir amaram in dentibz

ff. 178v, St. Margaret Praying; St. Apollonia, Holding a Tooth with Pincers

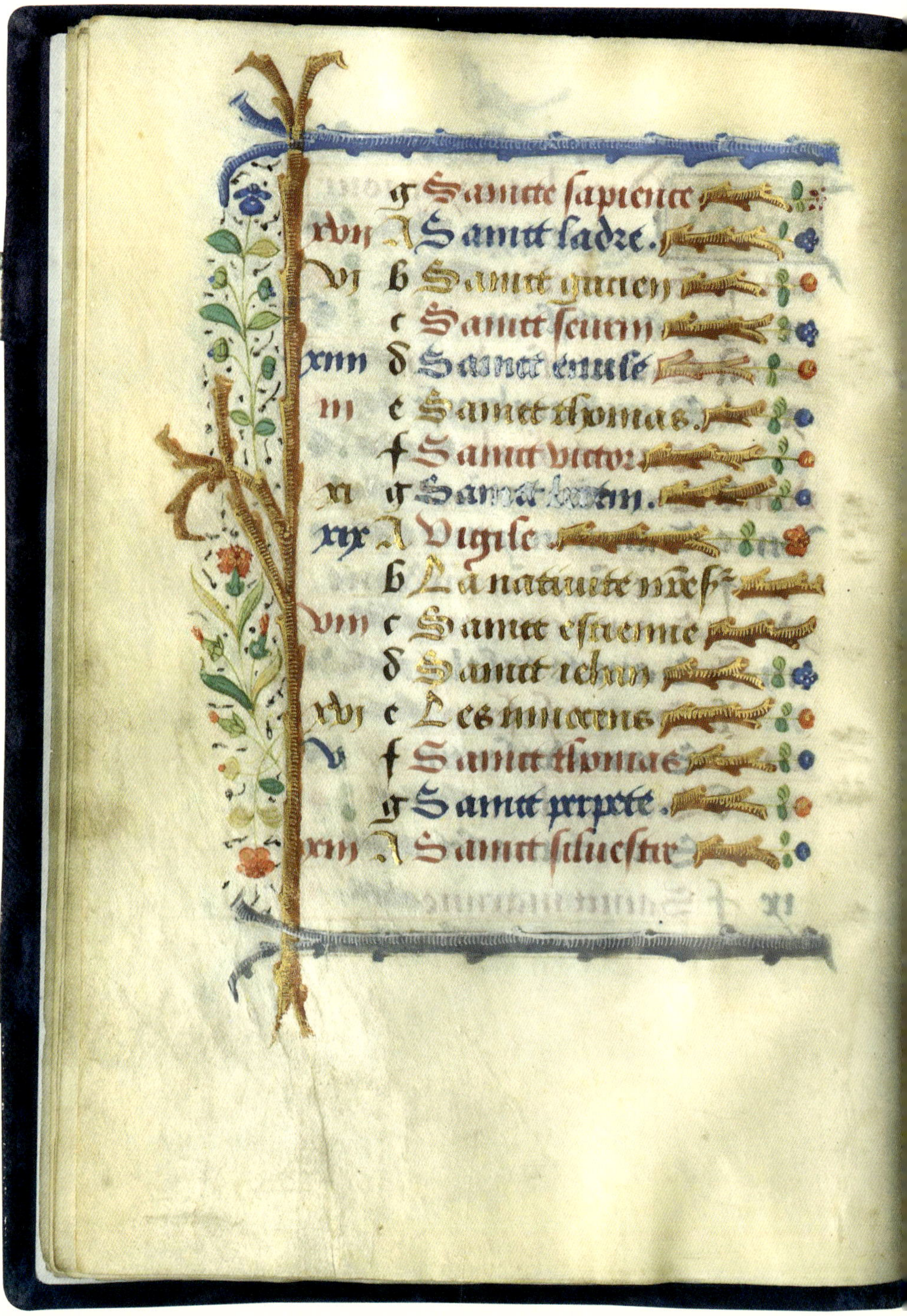

g Saincte sapience
xvii A Saint ladre.
vi b Saint gracien
c Saint seurin
xiiii d Saint eusebe
iii e Saint thomas.
f Saint victor
xi g Saint [illegible].
xix A Vigile.
b La natiuite n're s'
viii c Saint estienne
d Saint iehan
xvi e Les innocens
v f Saint thomas
g Saint perpete.
xiii A Saint siluestre

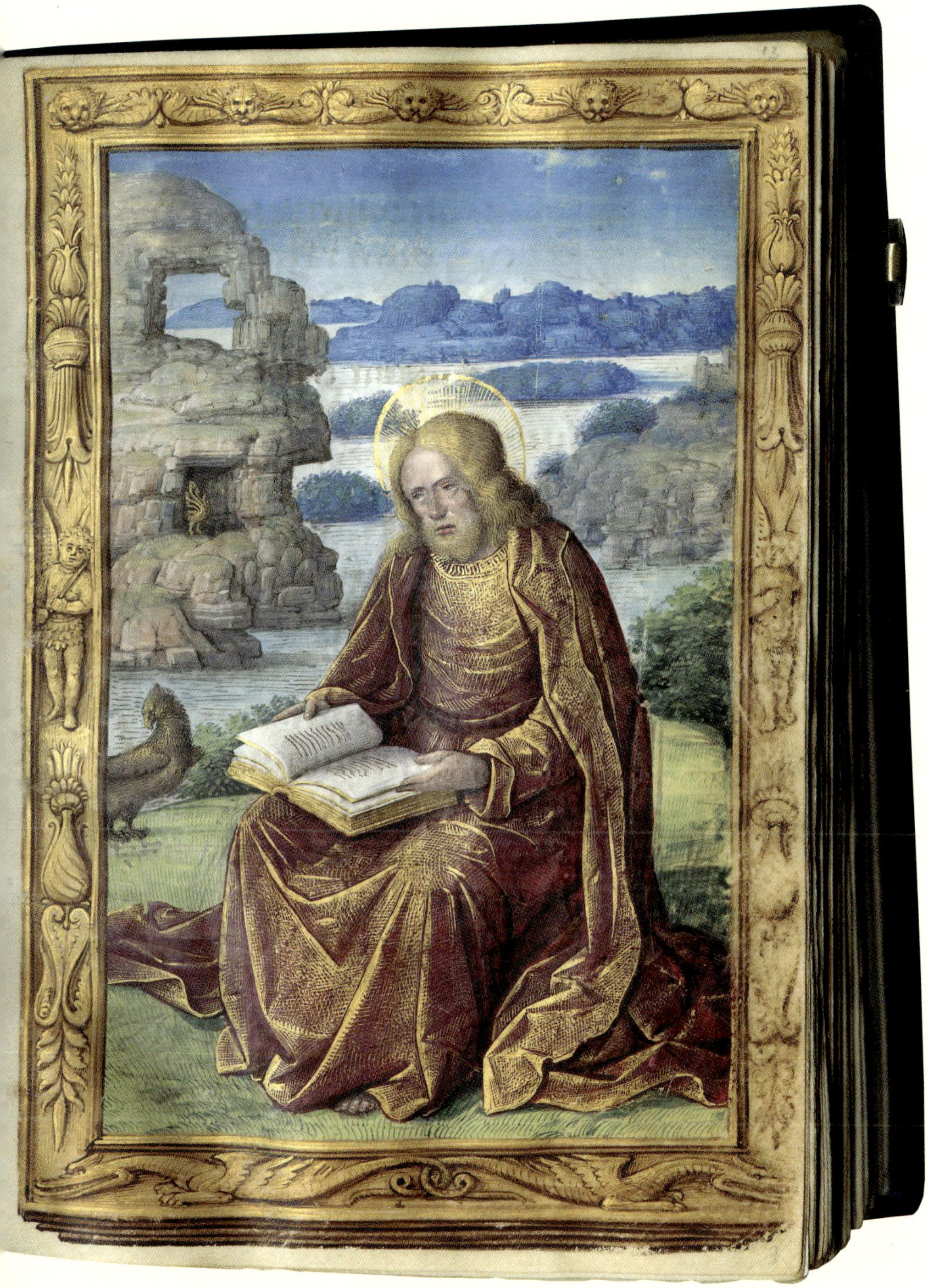

ff. 12v-13, Calendar Leaf (December); St. John on Patmos

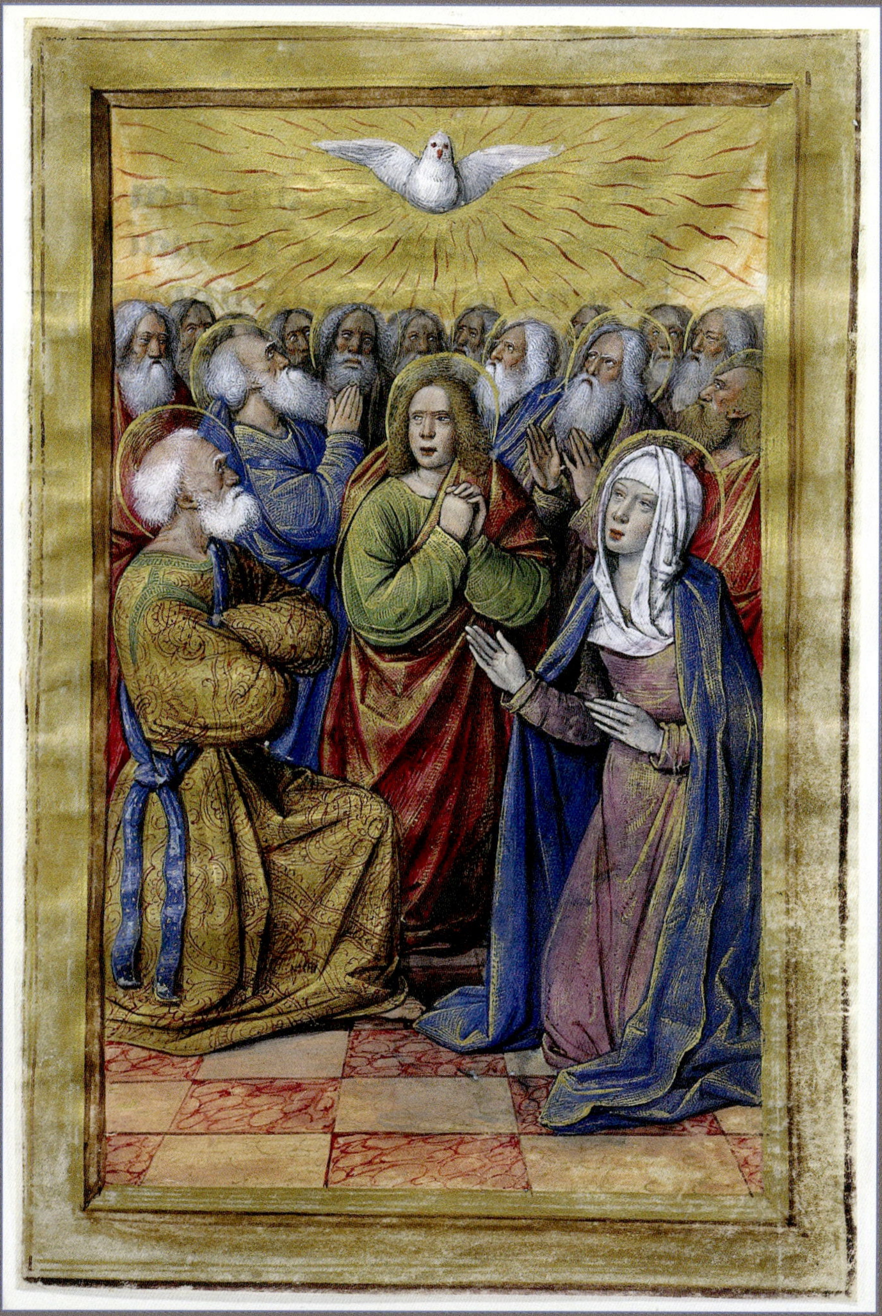

Cleveland Museum of Art, Gift J. H. Wade, 1924.426, Miniature from a Book of Hours, Pentecost

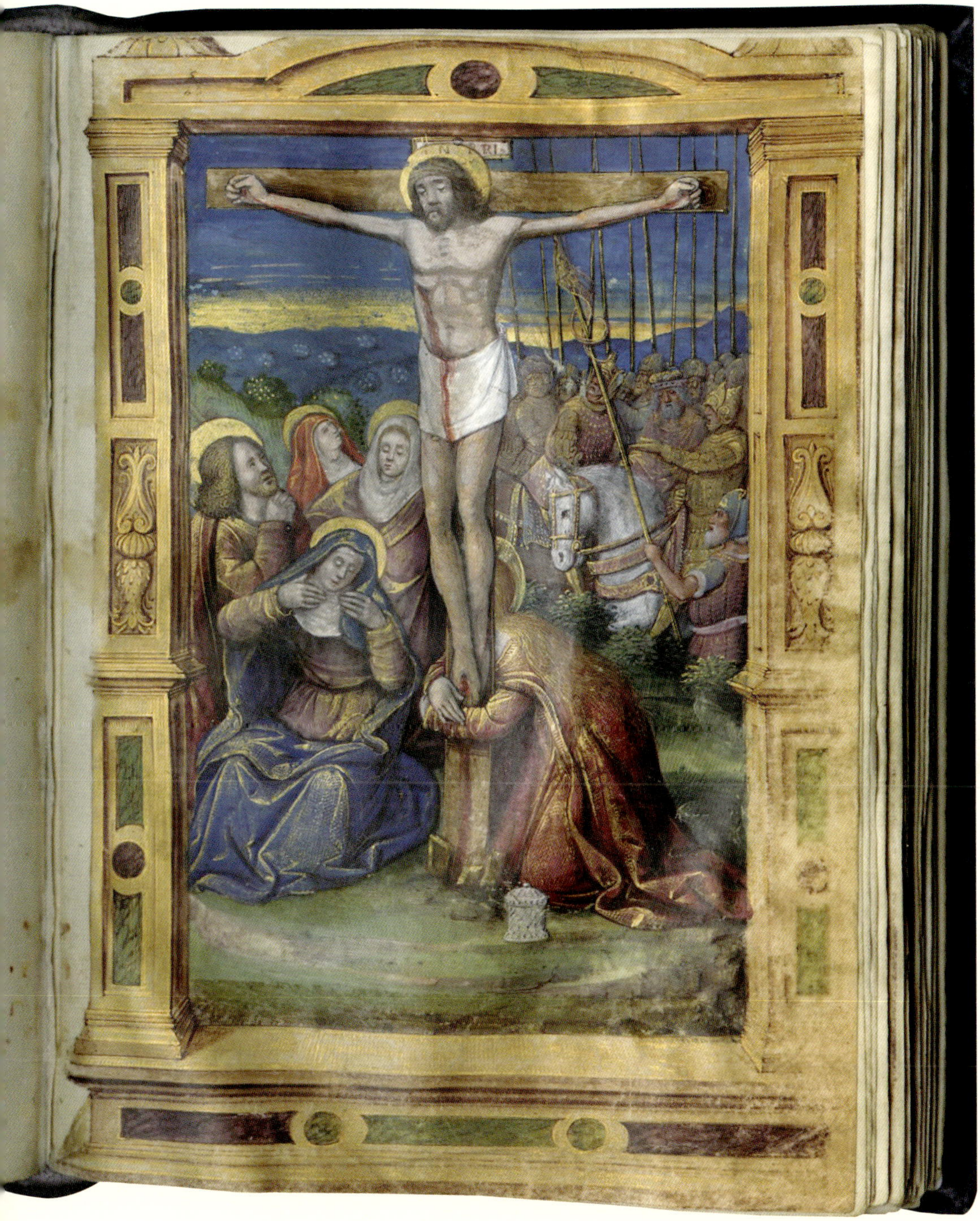

f. 89, Crucifixion, with Mary Magdalene, Her Face Hidden behind the Cross, Her Arms Encircling the Cross

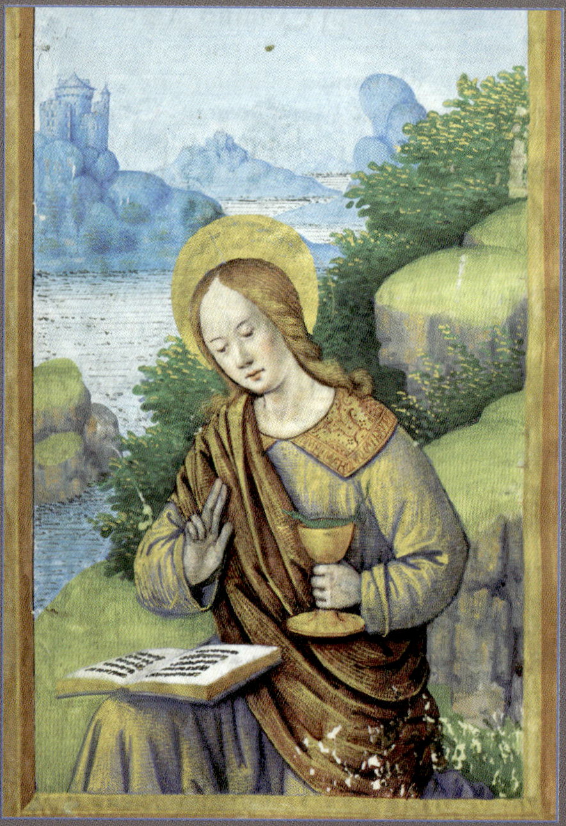

Bibliothèque de Genève, Comites Latentes 124,
Book of Hours, f. 133 v, St. John on Patmos

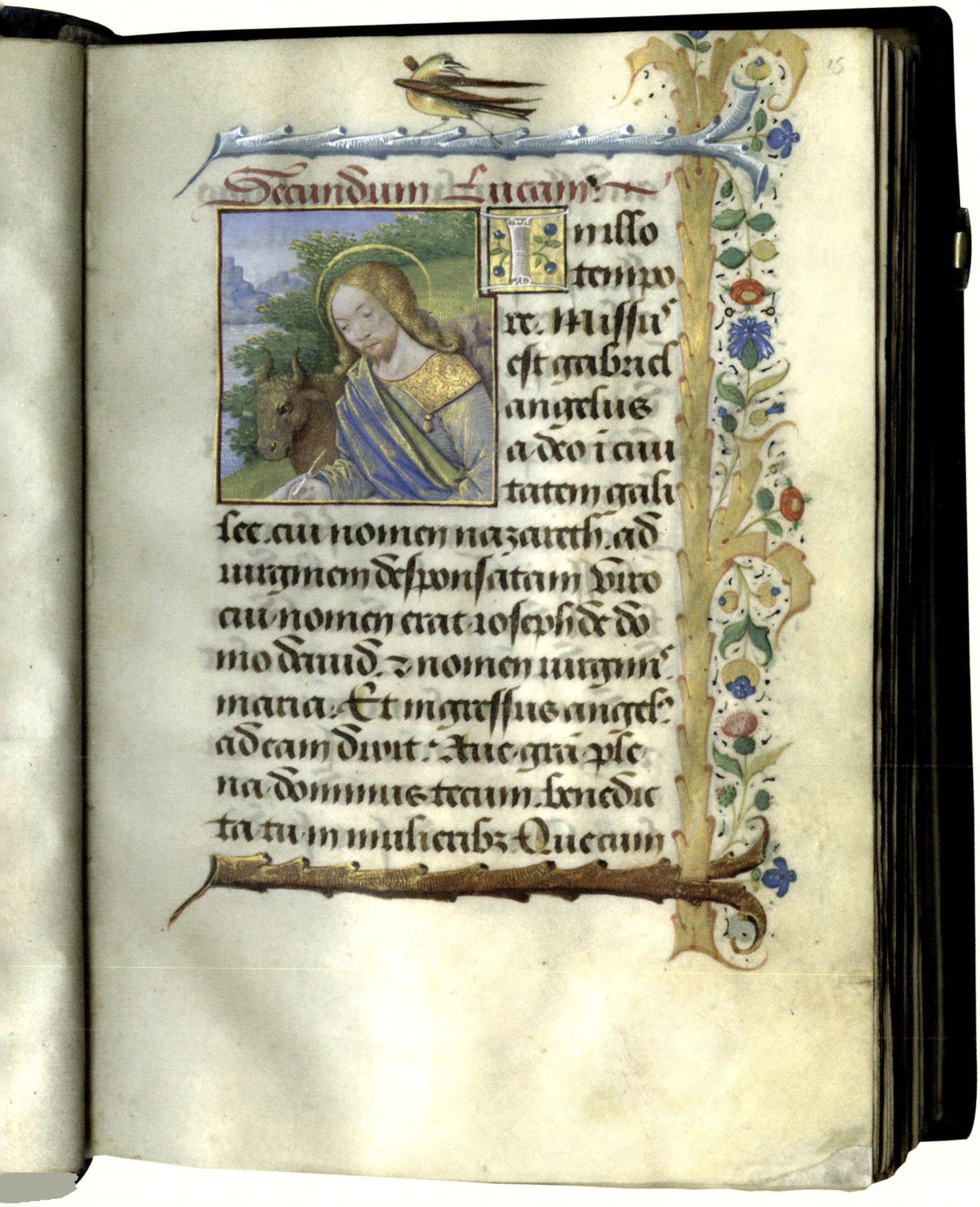

Secundum Lucam.
In illo
tempo
re. Missus
est gabriel
angelus
a deo i ciui
tatem gali
lee. cui nomen nazareth. ad
uirginem desponsatam viro
cui nomen erat ioseph de do
mo dauid. et nomen uirginis
maria. Et ingressus angelus
ad eam dixit. Aue gratia ple
na dominus tecum. benedic
ta tu in mulieribus. Que cum

f. 15, St. Luke

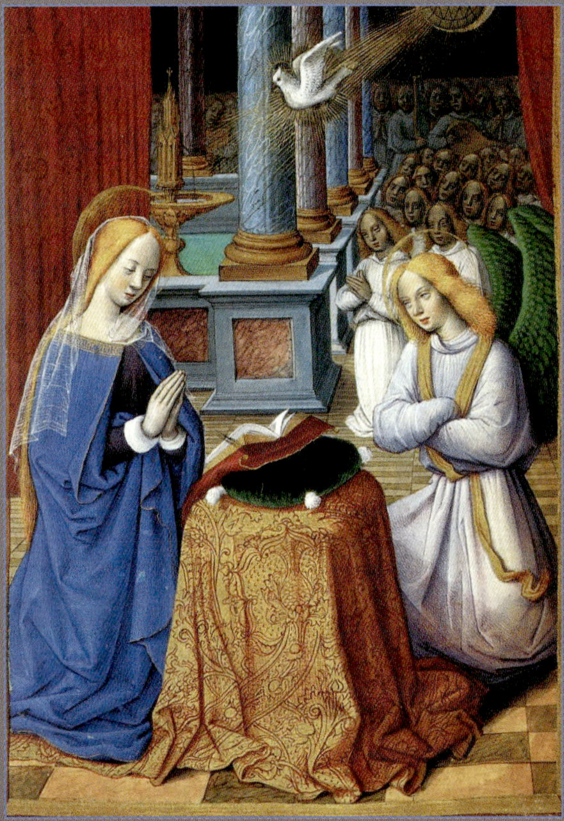

Haarlem, Teylers Museum, MS 78,
"Briconnet Hours," f. 21, Annunciation, attributed to Jean Poyer

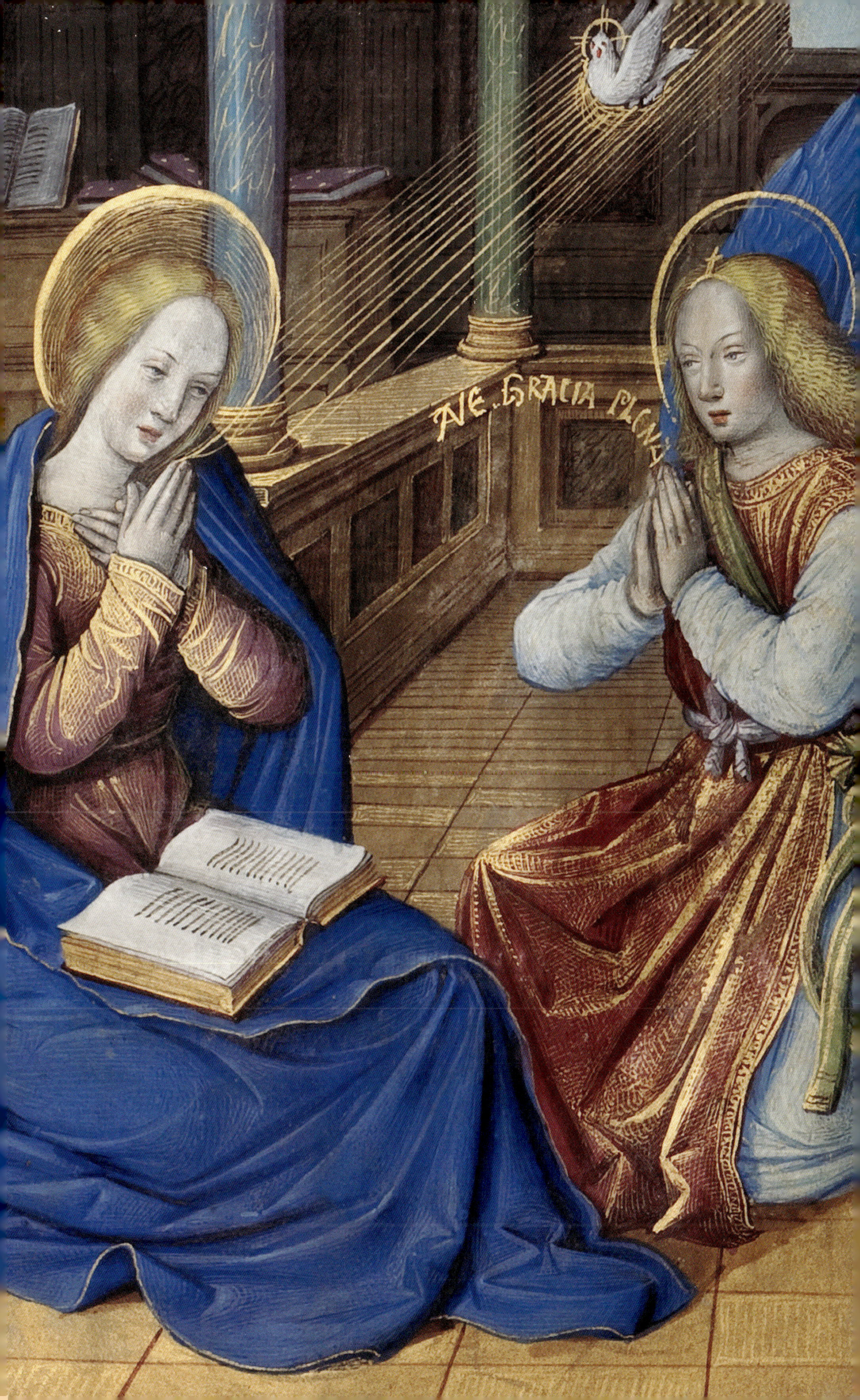
AVE GRACIA PLENA

Bibliography

ABU-LUGHOD, JANET L. *Before European Hegemony: The World System A.D. 1250-1350*, New York and Oxford, 1989.

ACHTEN, GERD. *Das christliche Gebetbuch im Mittelalter*, Berlin, 1980.

ANDREWS, CHRISTINE GEISLER. "The Boucicaut Master and the Commerce of Books of Hours in Early Fifteenth-Century Paris," Unpublished Doctoral Dissertation, Northwestern University, 2006.

AVRIL, FRANÇOIS AND NICOLE REYNAUD. *Les manuscrits à peintures en France, 1440-1520*, Paris, 1993.

BENNETT, ADELAIDE. "A Thirteenth-Century French Book of Hours for Marie," *Journal of the Walters Art Gallery [Essays in Honor of Lilian M. C. Randall]* 54 (1996), pp. 21-37.

BENNETT, ADELAIDE. "The Transformation of the Gothic Psalter in Thirteenth-Century France," in *The Illuminated Psalter: Studies in the Content, Purpose and Placement of its Images*, ed. F. O. Büttner, Turnhout, Brepols, 2004, pp. 211-221.

BENNETT, ADELAIDE. "Devotional Literacy of a Noblewoman in a Book of Hours of ca. 1300 in Cambrai," in *Manuscripts in Transition: Recycling Manuscripts, Text and Images* (Proceedings of the International Congress held in Brussels 5-9 November 2002), ed. Brigitte Dekeyzer and Jan Van der Stock, Louvain, 2005, pp. 149-205.

BOLLATI, MILVIA. *Il libro d'ore Visconti. Commentario al codice*, 2 vol., Modena, 2003.

BOLLATI, MILVIA, ED. *Dizionario biografico dei miniatori italiani. Secoli IX-XVI*, Milan, 2004.

BOUSMANNE, BERNARD. *"Item a Guillaume Wyeland aussi enlumineur" Willem Vrelant, Un aspect de l'enluminure dans les Pays-Bas meridionaux*, exh. cat., Brussels, Bibliothèque Royale, 1997.

BURIN, ELIZABETH. *Manuscript Illumination in Lyons 1473-1530*, Turnhout, Brepols, 2001.

CADEI, ANTONIO. *Belbello miniatore lombardo, artisti del libro alla corte dei Visconti*, Rome, 1976.

CARDON, BERT. "The Illustrations and the Gold Scrolls Group, Typologische Tafeleren uit het Leven van Jesus [Typological scenes from the Life of Christ]: A Manuscript from the Gold Scrolls Group (Bruges, c. 1440) in the Pierpont Morgan Library, New York, MS. Morgan 649," *Corpus of Illuminated Manuscripts from the Low Countries*, I, ed. M. Smeyers, Leuven, 1985, pp. 119-204.

CASTELFRANCHI VEGAS, LIANA. "La formazione e gli esordi di Michelino da Besozzo miniatore," in *Prospettiva* 83-84 (1996), pp. 116-127.

CHÂTELET, ALBERT. *L'âge d'or du manuscrit à peintures en France au temps de Charles VI*, Paris, 2000.

CHILDS, J. RIVES. *Casanoviana: An Annotated World Bibliography of Jacques Casanova de Seingalt and of Works Concerning Him*, Vienna, 1956.

CLANCHY, MICHAEL T. *From Memory to Written Record: England 1066-1307*, Oxford and Cambridge, 1993.

CLARK, GREGORY T. *The Hours of Isabel la Católica: The Facsimile Edition - Commentary*, Madrid, 1997.

DE HAMEL, CHRISTOPHER. *A History of Illuminated Manuscripts*, London, 1994.

DOGAER, GEORGES. *Flemish Miniature Painting in the 15th and 16th Centuries*, Amsterdam, 1987.

DEFOER, HENRY ET AL, EDS. *The Golden Age of Dutch Manuscript Illumination*, New York, 1990.

DONOVAN, CLAIRE. "The Mise-en-Page of Early Books of Hours in England," in *Medieval Book Production: Assessing the Evidence*, ed. L.L. Brownrigg, Los Altos Hills, 1990, pp. 147-161.

EUW, ANTON VON AND J. M. PLOTZEK. *Handschriften der Sammlung Ludwig*, 4 vols., Cologne, 1979-85.

[EXHIBITION]. Brussels, Bibliothèque Royale and Paris, Bibliothèque nationale de France, *Miniatures flamandes 1404-1482*, eds. Bernard Bousmanne and Thierry Delcourt, Brussels and Paris, 2011.

[EXHIBITION]. Chicago, Newberry Library, *French and Flemish Illuminated Manuscripts from Chicago Collections*, Chicago, 1969.

[EXHIBITION]. Paris, Grand Palais, *L'art au temps des rois maudits. Philippe le Bel et ses fils*, Paris, 1998.

[EXHIBITION]. Paris, Musée du Louvre, *Paris 1400: les arts sous Charles VI*, Paris, Fayard, 2004.

[EXHIBITION]. Tours, *Tours 1500. Capitale des arts*, ed. Béatrice de Chancel-Bardelot, Pascale Charron, Pierre-Gilles Girault, Jean-Marie Guillouët, Paris, 2012.

FARQUHAR, JAMES D. "The Vrelant Enigma: is the Style the Man?," *Quaerendo* 4 (1974), pp. 100-108.

FINKE, ULRICH, ED. *Katalog der mittelalterlichen Handschriften und Einzelblätter in der Kunstbibliothek*, Berlin, s.d. [c. 1967].

GRODECKI, C. "Le 'Maître Nicolas d'Amiens' et la mise au tombeau de Malesherbes. A propos d'un document inédit," *Bulletin monumental* 154 (1996), pp. 329-342.

HEID-GUILLAME, CAROLINE AND ANNE RITZ. *Manuscrits médiévaux de Chambéry*, Turnhout, Brepols, 1998 (on Chambéry, BM, MS 4, Bréviaire de Marie de Savoie, pp. 30-43).

HOFMANN, MARA. *Jean Poyer: Das Gesamtwerk*, Turnhout, Brepols, 2004.

HOLWECK, FREDERICUS G. *Calendarium liturgicum festorum Dei et Dei Matris Mariae, collectum et memoriis historicis...*, Philadelphia, 1925.

JOLY, A. AND H. "A la recherche de Guillaume Leroy 'le peintre'," *Gazette des Beaux-Arts*, 6e série, 61 (1963), pp. 279-292.

KIRSH, EDITH W. *Five Illuminated Manuscripts of Giangaleazzo Visconti*, University Park and London, 1991.

KÖNIG, EBERHARD. *Leuchtendes Mittelalter II* (Antiquariat Heribert Tenschert, Katalog 25), Rotthalmünster (D) & Ramsen (CH), 1990.

KÖNIG, EBERHARD. *Leuchtendes Mittelalter IV* (Antiquariat Heribert Tenschert, Katalog 29), Rotthalmünster (D) & Ramsen (CH), 1992.

KÖNIG, EBERHARD. *Devotion from Dawn to Dusk. The Office of the Virgin in Books of Hours of the Koninklijke Bibliotheek in The Hague*, Leiden, 2012.

KRAUSE, K AND ALISON STONES. *Gautier de Coinci: Miracles, Music, and Manuscripts*, Turnhout, Brepols, 2006.

LEROQUAIS, VICTOR. *Les livres d'heures manuscrits de la Bibliothèque nationale*, 3 vols., Mâcon, 1927.

MACDONALD, K. "Et verbum caro factum est: The Prayer-book of Michelino da Besozzo," in *Medieval Texts and Images. Studies of Manuscripts from the Middle Ages*, ed. M. M. Manion and B.J. Muir, Sydney, 1991, pp. 201-206.

MANZARI, FRANCESCA. "Italian Books of Hours and Prayer Books in the Fourteenth Century," in *A New Look at Books of Hours*, eds. Sandra Hindman and James Marrow, Turnhout, Brepols, 2012 (forthcoming).

MARTIN, HENRI-JEAN, ED., ET ALIA. *Mise en page et mise en texte du livre français. La naissance du livre moderne (XIVe-XVIIe siècles)*, Paris, 2000.

MEISS, MILLARD. "The Exhibition of French Manuscripts of the XIII-XVIth-centuries at the Bibliothèque Nationale," *Art Bulletin* 38 (1956), pp. 187-196.

MEISS, MILLARD. *French Painting in the Time of Jean de Berry: The Limbourgs and Their Contemporaries*, 2 vols., New York, Braziller, 1974, pp. 351-352, 393-397.

MEISS, MILLARD AND EDITH W. KIRSCH. *The Visconti Hours. National Library Florence*, New York, 1972.

MORGAN, NIGEL AND STELLA PANAYOTOVA, EDS. *Illuminated Manuscripts in Cambridge: A Catalogue of Western Book Illumination in the Fitzwilliam Museum and the Cambridge Colleges. Part 1, Volume 2: The Meuse Region [and the] Southern Netherlands*, London & Turnhout, 2009.

PELLEGRIN, ELISABETH. *La bibliothèque des Visconti et des Sforza, ducs de Milan, au XVe siècle*, Paris, 1955 (supplément, Florence and Paris, 1969).

PELLERIN, H. "Le culte de Saint Ursin à Lisieux," in *Bulletin de la Société des antiquaires de Normandie* 58 (1965-1966), pp. 175-212.

PELLERIN, ELIANE AND J. BERGERET. *La Cathédrale Saint-Pierre de Lisieux*, Lisieux, 1995.

PLUMMER, JOHN. *The Hours of Catherine of Cleves*, New York, 1966.

RABEL-JULIEN, CLAUDIA. *Les livres d'heures de Rouen peints par le Maître du trésor genevois et les enlumineurs influencé par lui, au 3e quart du 15e siècle: essai pour une étude stylistique, iconographique et historique*, Unpublished Dissertation, DEA, Paris, Université de Paris I, 1984.

RABEL, CLAUDIA. "Artiste et clientèle à la fin du Moyen Age: les manuscrits profanes du Maître de l'échevinage de Rouen," *Revue de l'art* 84 (1989), pp. 48-60.

RABEL, CLAUDIA. "Rouen. Maître de l'échevinage de Rouen," in *Enluminures du Louvre Moyen Age et Renaissance*, Paris, Musée du Louvre, 2011, especially pp. 208-211, no. 106.

RANDALL, LILIAN M.C. *Medieval and Renaissance Manuscripts in the Walters Art Gallery, Vol. 1, France, 875-1420*, Baltimore, 1989, cat. nos. 84-85, pp. 228-235.

RÉAU, LOUIS. *Iconographie de l'art chrétien. III, 1-3. Iconographie des saints*, Paris, 1958-1959.

RITZ-GUILBERT, ANNE. *Autour du Bréviaire de Marie de Savoie (Chambéry, Bibliothèque municipale, ms. 4): étude sur l'enluminure en Lombardie dans la première partie du XVe siècle* [Thesis], Lille, 2007.

ROGERS, NICHOLAS JOHN. "Books of Hours Produced in the Low Countries for the English Market," Unpublished M. Litt. Dissertation, University of Cambridge, 1982.

SAENGER, PAUL. *Catalogue of the Pre-1500 Western Manuscript Books at the Newberry Library*, Chicago, 1989.

SCHEIBER, EDUARD. *Niederländische Buchmalerei, die Miniaturen des Culenborch-Missales in Brixen*, Bozen, 1992.

SMEYERS, MAURITS. *Flemish Miniatures from the 8th to the mid-16th Century. The Medieval World in Parchment*, Leuven, 1999.

SOTHEBY'S. *A Selection of Illuminated Manuscripts from the 13th to the 16th centuries, The Property of Mr. J. R. Ritman, sold for the benefit of the Bibliotheca Philosophica Hermetica, Amsterdam*, London, 6 July 2000.

SOTHEBY'S. *A Second Selection of Illuminated Manuscripts from c. 1000 to c. 1522. The Property of Mr. J. R. Ritman, sold for the benefit of the Bibliotheca Philosophica Hermetica, Amsterdam*, London, 19 June 2001.

STONES, ALISON. "Les prières de Gautier de Coinci, leur distribution et leur réception d'après la tradition manuscrite," in *Le recueil au Moyen âge: le Moyen âge central*, Yasmina Foehr-Janssens and Olivier Collet (dir.), Turnhout, Brepols, 2010, pp. 237-268.

STONES, ALISON. *Illuminated Manuscripts Made in France, Gothic Manuscripts 1260-1320*, A Survey of Manuscripts Illuminated in France, eds. J.J.G. Alexander and F. Avril, London, 2012 (forthcoming).

SUTTON, KAY. "Codici di lusso a Milano: gli esordi," in *Il Millennio Ambrosiano, ed. C. Bertelli, III. La nuova città, dal Commune alla Signoria*, Milan, 1989, pp. 110-139.

SUTTON, KAY. "Giangaleazzo Visconti as Patron. A Prayer Book illuminated by Pietro da Pavia," *Apollo* 137 (1993), pp. 89-96.

THOSS, DAGMAR. *Flämische Buchmalerei*, exh. cat., Vienna, Österreichische Nationalbibliothek, 1987.

VAN BUREN, ANN. "Willem Vrelant. Questions and Issues," *Revue belge d'archeologie et d'histoire de l'art. Belgisch tijdschrift voor oudheidkuunde en kunstgeschiedenis* 68 (1999), pp. 3-30.

WATSON, ROWAN. *The Playfair Hours. A Late Fifteenth Century Illuminated Manuscript from Rouen (V & A, L. 475-1918)*, London, 1984.

WATSON, ROWAN. *Victoria and Albert Museum. Western Illuminated Manuscripts. A Catalogue of Works in the National Art Library from the Eleventh to the Early Twentieth Century, with a complete account of the George Reid Collection*, 3 vols., London, V & A Publishing, 2011.

WIECK, ROGER, WILLIAM VOELKLE, AND MICHELLE HEARNE. *The Hours of Henry VIII. A Renaissance Masterpiece by Jean Poyet*, New York, 2000.

WILMART, A. *Auteurs spirituels et textes dévôts du Moyen Age*, Paris, 1932.

WINKLER, FRIEDRICH. *Die flämische Buchmalerei des XV. und XVI. Jahrhunderts*, Leipzig, 1925 (repr. Amsterdam, 1978).

ZAMBRELLI, CATIA. "Balzerrino Pusterla, Beatrice Visconti e il Libro d'ore di Modena," *Quaderni Utinensi* VII, 13/14, pp. 51-56.

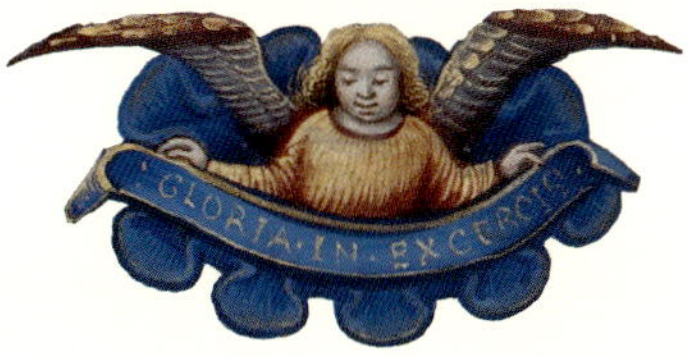

Acknowledgments

We gratefully acknowledge the help of the following individuals for the text of the catalogue: Adelaide Bennett (no. 1), Margaret Bloem (no. 5), Gregory Clark (nos. 6, 7, 8), Christopher De Hamel (Introduction), Isabelle Delaunay (no. 10), Nicholas Herman (no. 4), Mara Hofmann (no. 12), Francesca Manzari (no. 3), James Marrow (no. 5), Alison Stones (no. 2), Kay Sutton (no. 3).

FOR ALL OTHER ADVICE AND HELP OBTAINING REPRODUCTIONS, WE THANK: François Avril, Bruce Barker-Benfield, David-Jonathan Benrubi, Isabelle de Conihout, Charlotte Denoël, Gaudenz Freuler, Pierre Guinard, Gilles Kagan, Martin Kauffman, Eberhard König, Anne Korteweg, Hanna Nelson, Nathalie Picque, Claudia Rabel, Barbara Roth, Paul Saenger, Yann Sordet, Dominique Stutzmann, Dominique Vanwijnsberghe, Christophe Vellet, William Voelkle, Roger Wieck, Rowan Watson.

THE TEAM AT LES ENLUMINURES PITCHED IN IN DIVERSE WAYS: Fabio Epifani, Miriam Ex, Keegan Goepfert, Karen Gennaro, Kendra Grimmett, Gaia Grizzi, Perrine Humeau, Karolina Kubik.

PHOTOGRAPHIC CREDITS:

Baltimore, Walters Art Museum, p. 78

Berlin, Kunstbibliothe, p. 112

Cambrai, Médiathèque municipale, pp. 47-48

Cambridge, Fitzwilliam Museum, p. 124

Chambéry, Bibliothèque municipale, p. 67

Chicago, Newberry Library, p. 134

Cleveland, Cleveland Museum of Art, p. 198

Florence, Biblioteca Nazionale, p. 67

Geneva, Bibliothèque de Genève, Comites Latentes, p. 200

Haarlem, Teylers Museum, p. 202

London, British Library, p. 32

London, Victoria & Albert Museum, National Art Library, p. 152

Lyon, Bibliothèque Municipale, pp. 183-184

New York, Metropolitan Museum of Art, p. 32

New York, Morgan Library and Museum, pp. 68-124-134

Oxford, Bodleian Library, p. 47

Paris, Bibliothèque Nationale de France, pp. 167-168

Paris, Bibliothèque Mazarine, p. 80

The Hague, Koninklijke Bibliotheek, p. 92

DESIGNED: Virginie Enl'art

PHOTOGRAPHY: Tom Van Eynde

PRODUCTION MANAGER: Guido Zanella

PRINTED IN ITALY: San Martino B.A. Verona, Società Editoriale Grafiche AZ S.R.L.